THE ARCHITECTURE OF THE IMAGINATION

The Architecture of the Imagination

New Essays on Pretence, Possibility, and Fiction

Edited by
SHAUN NICHOLS

CLARENDON PRESS · OXFORD

OXFORD

UNIVERSITY PRESS

Great Clarendon Street, Oxford OX2 6DP

Oxford University Press is a department of the University of Oxford.
It furthers the University's objective of excellence in research, scholarship,
and education by publishing worldwide in

Oxford New York

Auckland Cape Town Dar es Salaam Hong Kong Karachi
Kuala Lumpur Madrid Melbourne Mexico City Nairobi
New Delhi Shanghai Taipei Toronto

With offices in

Argentina Austria Brazil Chile Czech Republic France Greece
Guatemala Hungary Italy Japan Poland Portugal Singapore
South Korea Switzerland Thailand Turkey Ukraine Vietnam

Oxford is a registered trademark of Oxford University Press
in the UK and in certain other countries

Published in the United States
by Oxford University Press Inc., New York

British Library Cataloguing in Publication Data

Data available

Library of Congress Cataloging in Publication Data

Data available

Typeset by Laserwords Private Limited, Chennai, India
Printed in Great Britain
on acid-free paper by
Biddles Ltd., King's Lynn, Norfolk

ISBN 0–19–927572–6   978–0–19–927572–4
ISBN 0–19–927573–4 (Pbk.)   978–0–19–927573–1 (Pbk.)

1 3 5 7 9 10 8 6 4 2

For Sarah and Julia, more dear to me than I ever could have anticipated.

Acknowledgements

This volume would not exist had it not been for Peter Momtchiloff of Oxford University Press. Peter suggested the volume to me, and he provided characteristically astute advice throughout the entire process. I'm most grateful for his help.

Contents

IV. IMAGINATION AND POSSIBILITY

Contributors

Paul Bloom (Yale University)

Peter Carruthers (University of Maryland)

Gregory Currie (University of Nottingham)

Tamar Szabó Gendler (Cornell University)

Alvin Goldman (Rutgers University)

Christopher S. Hill (Brown University)

Carl Matheson (University of Manitoba)

Aaron Meskin (Leeds University)

Adam Morton (University of Alberta)

Shaun Nichols (University of Arizona)

Timothy Schroeder (University of Manitoba)

Deena Skolnick (Yale University)

Roy Sorensen (Dartmouth College)

Kendall Walton (University of Michigan)

Jonathan M. Weinberg (Indiana University)

1

Introduction

Shaun Nichols

Thought experiments, modal judgment, counterfactual reasoning. All of these activities, so central to philosophical inquiry, involve the 'propositional imagination', the capacity we exploit when we imagine that there is an evil genius, that everyone is color-blind, or that Holmes had a bad habit. Philosophy would be unrecognizable if we extracted all the parts that depend on the imagination. So too, everyday life would be unrecognizable if we excised imaginative activities. The imagination undoubtedly played an essential role in the growth of civilization, since the imagination is involved in hypothetical reasoning and planning. It's likely that small-group social life depends heavily on the imagination as well. For our capacity to understand others relies on our ability to deploy the propositional imagination. Indeed, the propositional imagination is implicated in such a vast and fundamental set of practical and philosophical endeavors that it's a wonder that the topic lay dormant for most of the twentieth century. Before the 1980s, there seems to have been no systematic tradition of work on cognitive accounts of the propositional imagination.

Over the last two decades, there has finally been a concerted research effort to develop a cognitive account of the propositional imagination (e.g. Carruthers 2002; Currie 1995, 1998; Currie and Ravenscroft 2002; Goldman 1989, 1992; Gordon and Barker 1994; Harris 2000; Harris and Kavanaugh 1993; Jarrold et al. 1994; Leslie 1987, 1994; Lillard 1994; Nichols 2004*a*, forthcoming; Nichols and Stich 2000; Perner 1991; Perner et al. 1994).[1] This volume capitalizes on this new work by extending the theoretical picture of the propositional imagination and exploring the implications of cognitive accounts of the imagination. The volume also investigates broader philosophical issues surrounding the propositional imagination. In this Introduction, I will provide a general overview

I'd like to thank Greg Currie, Aaron Meskin, and Kendall Walton for helpful comments on an earlier version of this introduction.

[1] Much of this work is expressly aimed at explaining *pretend play*. But in most cases, the accounts of pretense include a cognitive account of the propositional imagination. This is no surprise, of course, since most theorists in this area maintain that in pretend play, the child carries out scenarios that are developed in her imagination.

of the central issues in recent discussions of the propositional imagination, followed by brief summaries of the chapters in the volume.

1. PROPOSITIONAL IMAGINATION IN PHILOSOPHY

Philosophy and the propositional imagination are intimately connected. But as an explicit *topic* in philosophy, there are three especially prominent discussions of the propositional imagination in contemporary work.

1.1. Imagination and modality

It's an old idea in philosophy that the imagination reveals possibilities. By the time of his *Treatise on Human Nature* (1739), Hume tells us that it is an 'establish'd maxim' that '*whatever the mind clearly conceives, includes the idea of possible existence,* or in other words, *nothing we imagine is absolutely impossible*' (1. 2. 2. 8). The idea is old, but it continues to ring through the corridors of philosophy departments. In his influential discussion of this maxim, Stephen Yablo maintains that philosophers have not found any 'seriously alternative basis for possibility theses' (1993: 2). If the imagination doesn't tell us what things are possible, then it's not clear what else would.

Because he was an empiricist, Hume's notion of 'imagination' is naturally interpreted as *imagistic,* since on his view all ideas are copied from the impressions. Some philosophers might thus maintain that since imagining is imagistic, it is an entirely distinct faculty of *conceiving* that informs us about possibility. However, from the perspective of recent discussions of propositional imagination, this seems largely a terminological dispute. For contemporary accounts of the propositional imagination are (or can be) neutral on the vehicle of the imagination. As we'll see below, contemporary cognitive accounts of the imagination tend *not* to treat the imagination as imagistic. And indeed, on Yablo's notion of imagination, sensory-like images are not required (1993: 27 n. 55). In fact, Yablo explicitly characterizes conceiving in terms of propositional imagining (1993: 29; see also Chalmers 2002).

Philosophers also maintain that imaginative activities provide the basis for *impossibility* theses. For instance, some philosophers suggest that we cannot imagine that $2 + 3 = 7$, and that this provides a basis for expressing the view that it is impossible that $2 + 3 = 7$ (e.g. Blackburn 1993; Craig 1975). More generally, philosophers working on modality often invoke the imagination as a crucial tool for modal argumentation (Lewis 1986; Rosen 1990; Sidelle 2002).

Philosophers have, of course, challenged the use of the imagination to establish modal theses. For example, Christopher Hill criticizes philosophical arguments that move from facts about what we can imagine or conceive to conclusions about the possibility that there could be zombies who are physically identical to us (Hill 1997). And Wright questions how we can be warranted in drawing conclusions about impossibility on the basis of our own imaginative limitations, since it seems a 'tendentious step to inflate our imaginative limitations into a metaphysical discovery' (Wright 1980: 90). These issues about the relation between imagination and modality continue to occupy a central place in philosophical debates (e.g. Gendler and Hawthorne 2002).

1.2. Imaginative resistance

The next issue also traces a history to Hume. 'On the Standard of Taste' concludes with a series of philosophically dense paragraphs in which Hume raises problems in the space now known as 'imaginative resistance'. In a key passage, Hume writes: 'where vicious manners are described, without being marked with the proper characters of blame and disapprobation; this must be allowed to disfigure the poem, and to be a real deformity. I cannot, nor is it proper I should, enter into such sentiments' (paragraph 32). The idea seems to be that when I read a poem that makes pronouncements that run deeply against my own moral values, I can't bring myself to share the reactions; moreover, I shouldn't try to do so.

Richard Moran (1994) and Kendall Walton (1990, 1994) resurrected Hume's issues in the context of the aesthetics of fiction. In his illuminating discussion of the issue, Moran sets the problem as follows:

If the story tells us that Duncan was *not* in fact murdered on Macbeth's orders, then *that* is what we accept and imagine as fictionally true. . . . However, suppose the facts of the murder remain as they are in fact presented in the play, but it is prescribed in this alternate fiction that this was unfortunate only for having interfered with Macbeth's sleep that night. (Moran 1994: 95)

In the former case, in which the story says that Duncan wasn't murdered, we happily go along; but in the latter case, Moran suggests, we would not accept it as true in the fictional world that murdering one's guest is morally okay. In most cases, it seems, we imagine whatever the fiction directs us to imagine, and we also accept it as fictionally true. But in cases of moral depravity, we often refuse to let our imaginations and judgments of fictional truth follow. Thus, the problem of imaginative resistance (see also Gendler 2000: 55).

Fictional truths, according to Walton's prominent account, are defined by prescriptions to imagine (Walton 1990). So, it is fictionally true that Othello is jealous just because the play prescribes that we imagine this. If we adopt this view of fiction, it's clear that there are importantly different issues implicated in discussions of imaginative resistance (see e.g. Walton 1994; Weatherson 2004). One question concerns why we refuse to accept some things as fictionally true. That is, we seem to reject the idea that we *ought* to imagine that murdering Duncan was okay (even if the play said so). A different question concerns why we in fact seem to find ourselves unable to imagine that Duncan's murder was okay. The first puzzle, about the fiction, and the second puzzle, about the psychology, are at least partly independent. But both involve considerations about the propositional imagination.

The issue of imaginative resistance has sparked much debate, especially since Tamar Gendler's 'The Puzzle of Imaginative Resistance' (Gendler 2000).[2] Although the discussion of imaginative resistance arose in the context of the aesthetics of fiction, once the puzzles about fiction and psychology are distinguished, it becomes clear that the psychological puzzle exceeds the boundaries of fiction. The fact that we seem to resist imagining certain contents applies even when we aren't consuming fiction. It is a more general, striking, fact about our minds that the imagination rebels against certain contents.

1.3. Imagination and emotion

As with imaginative resistance, philosophical discussion about imagination and emotions arose in the context of the aesthetics of fiction (Radford 1975; Walton 1978). Discussions have largely focused on the 'paradox of fiction', which is generated by a triad of prima facie plausible claims:

a. We often feel emotions for fictional characters (e.g. I pity Anna Karenina).
b. To feel emotions for something, you have to believe it exists.
c. We don't believe in the existence of characters that we know are fictional (e.g. I don't believe Anna Karenina exists).

In the enormous literature on the topic, philosophers have denied each of these claims. While some treatments of the paradox do not invoke considerations about the imagination, the imagination has been a persistent player in these discussions.

The central questions are the following:

(i) Are the affective responses to fiction caused by imaginative activities, and if so, how does the imagination generate these effects? (See e.g. Carroll 1990, 1998; Copland 2004; Currie 1995; Feagin 1996; Meskin and Weinberg 2003; Walton 1997).

(ii) Under what conditions (if any) is it rational to have affective responses to imaginative activities concerning fictions? (Cf. Livingstone and Mele 1997; Radford 1975; Walton 1990).

(iii) Do the affective responses to fiction count as instances of genuine emotions like pity and indignation, or are we imagining that we have those emotions, as part of a broader game of make-believe? For example, do we literally feel pity when reading *Anna Karenina*, or do we imagine, as part of a broader game of make-believe, that we feel pity? (e.g. Carroll 1990; Currie

---

[2] Recent discussions include the following: Currie and Ravenscroft 2002; Matravers 2003; Nichols 2004*a*; Weatherson 2004; Yablo 2002.

1997; Friend 2003; Lamarque 1981; Moran 1994; Neill 1991; Walton 1978, 1990).

Although the philosophical issues about imagination and the emotions took soil in the aesthetics of fiction, as with imaginative resistance, the psychological phenomena exceed the boundaries of aesthetics. For the imagination seems to drive affective responses even when there is no associated fiction. Many of the same questions arise when we detach from fiction: How does the imagination cause affective responses in everyday life? Under what conditions is it rational to have those affective responses from the imagination? And are the affective responses we have to imagination (outside the context of fiction) instances of genuine emotions?

2. PRECURSORS TO A COGNITIVE ACCOUNT OF THE PROPOSITIONAL IMAGINATION

To evaluate how the propositional imagination does and should function in philosophy, it would obviously be beneficial to draw on cognitive characterizations of the capacity. But until recently, there was little to draw from. Why did it take so long for philosophers and psychologists to devote themselves to a cognitive account of the imagination? A large part of the explanation is the massive influence of behaviorism in psychology and philosophy of mind throughout the twentieth century. Indeed, in the analytic philosophical tradition, perhaps the best-known discussion of the imagination is in Ryle's manifesto of logical behaviorism, *The Concept of Mind*. Not surprisingly, Ryle doesn't give a cognitively rich accounting. Rather, he chides, 'If we are asked whether imagining is a cognitive or a noncognitive activity, our proper policy is to ignore the question. "Cognitive" belongs to the vocabulary of examination papers' (Ryle 1949: 258).

The reemergence of the representational theory of mind (e.g. Fodor 1975) provided the intellectual backdrop for cognitivist accounts of imagination. According to the representational theory of mind, beliefs (among other mental states) are internal representations. To believe that p is to have a representation token with the content p stored in some functionally appropriate way in the mind. This broad view of cognition underpinned the early cognitivist accounts of the imagination. Indeed in these early accounts authors often adverted explicitly to prior research that defends a representationalist approach to the mind (see e.g. Leslie 1987: 414, 424; Morton 1980: 64–5).

A second important background assumption is that beliefs and desires are distinct kinds of mental states, and what distinguishes them is not the *content* of the mental state, but rather the *functional role* the two states play. That is, beliefs and desires have different causal interactions with stimuli, behavior, and other mental states. So, if we allow that the desire that p is a representation stored in the mind, this representation exhibits a significantly different functional profile from the belief that p, despite the fact that they both represent the same content. These differences in functional role are what make *belief* and *desire* different kinds of mental state.

3. CENTRAL FACTS ABOUT THE PROPOSITIONAL IMAGINATION

The background assumptions about representations and functional roles set the stage for the development of cognitive accounts of the imagination. In addition to these high-level theoretical assumptions, there are several central facts about the propositional imagination that have shaped nearly all of the theorizing in the recent literature. Here is a brief overview.

3.1. Early emergence of the imagination

Before their second birthday, most children engage in pretend play. Consider, for instance, the common childhood activity of pretending to talk on a phone using a banana as a prop (Leslie 1987). In these instances, children seem to distinguish what's imagined from what's real; even when they are pretending that the banana is a telephone, they don't seem to think that the banana really *is* a telephone (Leslie 1987). Two-year-old children certainly don't seem to confuse bananas with telephones, and a bit later, when it's easier to test them, it becomes quite clear that children do indeed distinguish what is imagined from what is real. For instance, in one experiment, children were told about two individuals, one of whom has a cookie and one of whom pretends to have a cookie. Even three-year-olds were more likely to say that the person who was merely pretending to have a cookie couldn't see it or touch it (Wellman and Estes 1986). In a different paradigm, researchers found that children distinguished between what the experimenter was pretending an object to be (e.g. a telephone) and what it really was (a pen) (Flavell et al. 1987; see also Harris et al. 1994).

3.2. It's possible to imagine that p and believe that p simultaneously

Typically we regard imagination as departing from belief. We imagine things that we don't believe. One might thus be tempted to assume that it's impossible for a person to imagine and believe the same thing at the same time. In contemporary work on the imagination, this assumption is largely rejected, by both the philosophers and the psychologists. For instance, Walton writes: 'imagining something is entirely compatible with knowing it to be true' (Walton 1990: 13). In psychology, a nice example of this comes from an experiment of Alan Leslie's (1994). An experimenter plays a tea-party game with young children. The experimenter pretends to fill a cup with tea, then proceeds deliberately to overturn the cup. The children now imagine that the cup is empty, and they also, of course, believe that the cup is empty.

3.3. Imagination and belief generate different action tendencies

When children engage in pretend play, they carry out behavioral sequences that conform in important ways to the actions they would perform if they really had the beliefs. For example, if the child believed Grandma was on the phone, she really would talk to her. Nonetheless, there are important behavioral discontinuities. When pretending that mud globs are delicious pies, even hungry children don't eat the 'pies'. Moreover, as adults, when we consume fiction, daydream, or fantasize, we don't typically produce actions that would be produced if we believed what we are imagining.

3.4. Intentions direct the imagination

Just as imagination and belief produce different kinds of outputs, so too are they generated by different kinds of inputs. Belief is not at the whim of our intentions, but imagination is. We typically decide when to engage in an imaginative episode, and in many ways we can also control the particular contents that we imagine. As a result, we can fill out an imaginative episode in all kinds of surprising ways.

3.5. Imagination exhibits inferential orderliness

Although the imagination is flexible in some ways, it's fairly rigid and predictable in other ways. In particular, when people engage in imaginative activities, they often follow orderly inference chains. When I read that Wilbur is a pig, I infer (in imagination) that Wilbur is a mammal. When I hear that Hamlet is a prince, I infer (in imagination) that he is not a member of the hoi polloi. These inferences track the kinds of inferences that I would have if I really believed that Wilbur was a pig and Hamlet was a prince.[3] Such orderly inferences emerge on the scene very early in childhood. In one study, the experimenter introduces two-year-old children to several toy animals including 'Larry Lamb', and tells them that the animals are going outside to play. The experimenter designates part of the table top as 'outside', points to a smaller part of this area, and says, 'Look, there's a muddy puddle here.' Then the experimenter takes Larry Lamb and makes him roll over and over in this area. The children are asked, 'What has happened? What has happened to Larry?' Nearly all of the children indicated that Larry got muddy. Here then, they are apparently drawing inferences over the contents of what they are pretending, and the inferences parallel the inferences that the

---

[3] Of course, there are many exceptions to this, some of which are to be explained by the fact (noted in 3.4) that intentions can direct (and redirect) the contents of our imaginings.

children would draw if they had the corresponding beliefs (Leslie 1994; see also Harris et al. 1994).

3.6. The imagination activates affective systems

It is common wisdom in psychology that imagining scenarios can have significant affective consequences, and different affective consequences follow from imagining different scenarios. Indeed, one traditional experimental technique for inducing affect is precisely to have subjects imagine scenarios that are expected to produce particular kinds of affective responses (Izard 1991: 172). Furthermore, the research suggests that the affective response to imagining a scenario closely tracks the affective response that would occur if the subject came to believe that the scenario was real (for reviews see e.g. Harris 2000; Lang 1984).

4. CONVERGENCES

Among cognitive scientists and philosophers of psychology, there is a growing consensus about a basic account of the imagination that answers to the central facts above. There are, of course, important disagreements (see Section 5), but most people working in this area agree on several substantive claims about the nature of the imagination (Carruthers 2002; Currie and Ravenscroft 2002; Goldman 1989; Gordon and Barker 1994; Harris 2000; Morton 1980; Nichols and Stich 2003).[4]

First, recent cognitive accounts of the propositional imagination adopt a representational approach. To believe that *p* is to have a 'belief' representation with the content *p*. Analogously, to imagine that Macbeth is ambitious is to have an 'imaginational' representation with the content *Macbeth is ambitious*.

Imaginational states are contentful representations, but they are not distinguished from beliefs by their contents. Rather, and this is the second point of agreement, imaginational representations are distinguished from belief representations by their *functional roles*. Just as desires are distinguished from beliefs by their pattern of causal interaction, so too imaginings are distinguished from beliefs by their pattern of causal interaction. The appeal to a distinction at the level of function rather than content can accommodate the fact that it's possible to believe and imagine the same thing (as noted in 3.2). Further, the central facts reviewed in Section 3 provide us with some of the critical functional differences between believing and imagining. The inputs to the imagination are at the whim

---

[4] One major theorist who doesn't fit quite so well is Alan Leslie. Leslie was a pioneer in the subject, and several of the key ideas in the consensus view were promoted by him (Leslie 1987, 1994). However, he maintains that all imaginings are really beliefs in which the concept *pretend* is implicated. Thus, his theory bears a complicated relationship to the consensus view (see e.g. Nichols and Stich 2000).

of intention, but this is not the case for belief, and the imagination and belief make different causal contributions to action tendencies (3.3 and 3.4). These are major differences in the causal roles of imaginational representations and belief representations. In addition, though this is somewhat less explicit, most theorists assume that the capacity for propositional imagination is a basic part of human psychology. This makes sense of the early emergence of pretend play and the early ability to distinguish fantasy and reality (3.1). It also accommodates the presumption that imagining cannot be reduced to other mental states like believing or desiring.

The third important point of agreement is that imaginational representations interact with some of the same mental mechanisms that belief representations interact with, and these shared mechanisms treat imaginational representations and belief representations in much the same ways. That is, imagining and believing have shared pathways in the mind, and those pathways process imaginational input and belief input in similar ways. For instance, most theorists maintain that our inferential mechanisms process input both from beliefs and from the imagination. Further, most theorists maintain that some affective systems can be activated both by beliefs and by imaginational representations. The consensus view holds that the shared mechanisms will treat the imaginational representation *p* and the belief representation *p* in much the same way. This then makes sense of the fact that we see inferential orderliness in imagination (3.5) and that we see similar affective responses to believing that *p* and imagining that *p* (3.6).

5. DIVERGENCES

The areas of agreement listed above suggest an impressive degree of convergence in theorizing about the imagination. Of course, there are also important areas of disagreement. Perhaps the most important fault line is the dispute over the existence of 'pretend desires'.

For those familiar with the debates over 'simulation theory' (e.g. Davies and Stone 1995*a,b*), it will be evident that the above celebration of unity tells no more than half of the story. According to one influential version of simulation theory (Goldman 1989; Gordon 1986), when I predict another's behavior, I don't exploit a specialized body of knowledge about psychology; rather, I insert 'pretend' versions of the target's beliefs and desires into my practical reasoning mechanism, which then generates a 'pretend' decision which I use to predict the decision of the target. Thus, for this version of simulation theory, one important notion is 'pretend belief' (e.g. Goldman 1989; Gordon 1986) or 'belief-like imaginings' (Currie and Ravenscroft 2002), and something like the notion of 'pretend belief' fits fairly well into most contemporary cognitive accounts of the imagination. However, many simulation theorists also defend the existence of pretend *desires* or desire-like imaginings—imaginational states that are related to real desires in much the way that pretend beliefs are related to real beliefs (Currie 1995; Currie and Ravenscroft 2002; Goldman 1989; Gordon 1986; Gordon and Barker 1994). On that topic, there is serious disagreement.

If there are pretend desires, this counts as a profound addition to the architecture of the imagination as set out in Section 4. It also greatly expands the available resources for explaining the phenomena surrounding the imagination. So the stakes in this debate are very high. Advocates of pretend desires invoke them to explain pretend play behavior (Gordon and Barker 1994), emotional responses to fiction (Currie and Ravenscroft 2002), and imaginative resistance (Currie and Ravenscroft 2002). Most centrally, however, advocates of pretend desires maintain that such states play a crucial role in the prediction and explanation of others' behavior (Currie and Ravenscroft 2002; Goldman 1989; Gordon 1986). When we try to predict or explain the behavior of a target, we must accommodate her differing mental states in some way. Our predictions will often go wrong if we are insensitive to the different beliefs and desires of the target. It is widely agreed that one often accommodates the target's discrepant belief that p by imagining that p. However, how do we accommodate the target's discrepant desire that q? According to many simulation theorists, we do this by taking on the pretend desire that q. In parallel with the case of pretend belief, the pretend desires get processed much like real desires. This explains how we succeed at predicting and explaining the behavior of those with discrepant desires.

On the other side of the theoretical divide, skeptics about pretend desires maintain that pretend desires play no role in predicting behavior (or anything else) (e.g. Carruthers 2003; Nichols 2004*b*; Nichols and Stich 2003; Weinberg and Meskin 2005). These theorists maintain that there are several ways in which a predictor can accommodate another's discrepant desire. For instance, I can believe that the person has a certain desire, I can imagine that the person has the desire, I can imagine that *I* have the desire. But none of this requires having pretend desires.

Each side in this debate holds a well-entrenched position, and the issue continues to be an important rift among prevailing theories of the propositional imagination. Nonetheless, it shouldn't obscure the widespread agreement that has been reached about the architecture of the imagination.

6. A GUIDE TO THE VOLUME

6.1. The nature of the imagination

The essays in Part I focus on basic questions about the nature of the propositional imagination.

The central concern of the chapter by Timothy Schroeder and Carl Matheson (Chapter 2) is to explain how imaginative episodes (including experiences of fiction) generate such strong responses. They begin by noting that most philosophers working on the imagination maintain that imagining is what Schroeder and Matheson call a Distinct Cognitive Attitude (DCA), which is similar to belief in some respects but not others. Schroeder and Matheson agree with this consensus, and more specifically with the view that the DCA produces the striking emotional responses that the imagination engenders. However, they maintain that the consensus view lacks a key line of support—theorists have not provided evidence of a causal pathway from the stimulus to the DCA of imagining to the felt response. Schroeder and Matheson argue that this pathway can be shown by looking to neuroscience. Neuroscientific work indicates that imaginary stimuli lead to emotional effects via the same kinds of causal pathways that generate emotion from 'real' stimuli.

Alvin Goldman (Chapter 3) also considers how imagination generates emotion. He distinguishes 'supposition-imagination' (S-imagination) from 'enactment-imagination' (E-imagination). The former kind of imagination involves entertaining or supposing various hypothetical scenarios. With E-imagination, on the other hand, one tries to create a kind of facsimile of a mental state. Thus, one might try to create a perception-like state as in visual imagination or motoric imagination. Goldman argues that this much richer form of imagination generates typical emotional reactions to fiction. Indeed, Goldman maintains that emotional reactions to fiction are generated in several different ways, including a process in which we E-imagine being a hypothetical reader or observer of fact.

In his chapter, Adam Morton (Chapter 4) takes up the surprisingly delicate question of imaginative accuracy. In particular, he tries to determine the ways in which we can make mistakes when using the imagination to capture another person's mental states. One might err by failing to represent the things or propositions that the other person is actually thinking about. But one might err in a different way by failing to imagine appropriately the other person's *perspective*. For instance, one's imaginative activity might fail to adjust for the way the other person mentally locates herself in space or time. Morton argues that when we engage in the complex activity of embedded imaginations, as when we imagine another person imagining something, we are actually less likely to make mistakes. For in these cases, Morton maintains, there is less chance of making an error with respect to the other's perspective.

A great deal of work in developmental psychology shows that even young children understand the difference between the real world and the merely imaginary. In their contribution, Deena Skolnick and Paul Bloom (Chapter 5) argue that children don't merely lump all imaginary contents into a single fictional world. Rather, children, like adults, apparently distinguish the world of SpongeBob from the world of Batman. Children also think that within a fictional world, the characters believe that the other characters are real. As Skolnick and Bloom point out, this raises a number of interesting and unexplored questions about the intuitive relationships among fictional worlds and between those worlds and the real world.

6.2. Pretence

In Part II, the chapters address pretence in children and adults. Peter Carruthers (Chapter 6) explores the motivation for pretend play. It's well known that children engage in imaginative activities and pretend play from a young age. But why do they carry out behavior corresponding to what transpires in their imagination? Carruthers distinguishes two somewhat different phenomena that need explaining. First, children carry out only some of the things they imagine. Second, Carruthers maintains that childhood pretend play exhibits a salient patterning: viz. children tend to pretend to be or do things that they find valuable or admirable in real life. Carruthers argues that when we imagine an action, the contents of this imagining will be processed by mechanisms that generate desires and emotions, and this will affect one's motivations about the execution of the action. The child will be most strongly motivated to carry out the actions associated with *positive* emotional reactions. This would explain why children carry out only some of the scenarios they imagine and also why children's pretend behaviors pattern as they do. For children will be most inclined to carry out the behaviors that would (in reality) generate positive reactions in them.

Pretence clearly plays an important role in the lives of children. In his contribution, Gregory Currie (Chapter 7) maintains that pretence also plays an important role in adult communication. In particular, irony implicates pretence. In some cases of irony, for instance, the ironist is pretending to state something, and she means to draw attention to her reservations about the statement. Currie defends the pretence theory of irony against a range of objections, and goes on to argue that even the most prominent rival to pretence theory, the 'echoic theory' of irony, is defective unless it makes recourse to pretence.

6.3. Imaginative resistance

As noted above, the problem of 'imaginative resistance' has enjoyed considerable attention in recent years. If a story says that mice are super-intelligent, then this is what we imagine and accept as fictionally true; however, if a story says that female infanticide is morally right, we would likely resist imagining and accepting this as fictionally true. The essays in Part III treat a cluster of issues surrounding the problem of imaginative resistance.

Kendall Walton (Chapter 8) argues that it's vital to keep distinct several different issues that get lumped together in discussions of imaginative resistance. In particular, Walton argues that it's easy to confuse the 'imaginative puzzle' with the 'fictionality puzzle'. The fictionality puzzle, which Walton regards as the deepest and most difficult problem here, concerns why it is (apparently) not fictional that female infanticide is morally right, even when the author says so. The imaginative puzzle concerns why we are reluctant or unable to imagine certain things, and Walton argues that this differs from the fictionality puzzle, since whether something is fictional depends on whether we *ought* to imagine it, not whether we *do* imagine it.

Tamar Szabó Gendler's contribution (Chapter 9) focuses on the imaginative puzzle as inherited from Hume's 'On the Standard of Taste'. Gendler distinguishes between 'can't' and 'won't' solutions to the imaginative puzzle. *Can't* solutions claim that the resistance emerges because there is some barrier to imagining the content; *won't* solutions claim that the resistance emerges because we don't want to imagine the content. Gendler's suggestion is that in the classic cases of resistance (e.g. those discussed by Hume), both kinds of resistance are present. So, for example, if the author asks us to imagine that it's morally permissible to beat one's slaves to death, we won't and can't do it. Gendler goes on to maintain that these cases of imaginative resistance flow from a more general phenomenon of refusing to accept the author's authority. According to Gendler, such breakdowns in authorial authority are typically accompanied by 'pop-out' effects, in which the reader interprets the author as asking her to believe something about the actual world.

Jonathan Weinberg and Aaron Meskin (Chapter 10) explore several different philosophical issues surrounding the imagination: fictionally directed emotions, imaginative resistance, and the supposition/imagination distinction. They defend a shift in methodology for addressing these issues. Rather than relying exclusively on folk psychological and philosophical analysis, Weinberg and Meskin exploit an empirically oriented approach that draws on cognitive accounts of the imagination. Using this method, they argue, leads to novel solutions to the philosophical puzzles about the imagination.

6.4. Imagination and possibility

In Part IV, the essays all explore the relation between imagination and modality. A number of philosophers have maintained that the conceivability of a scenario provides grounds for believing the scenario possible. In his chapter, Christopher Hill (Chapter 11) distinguishes between conceptual possibility and metaphysical possibility. He argues that if we can conceive (in an appropriately coherent way) of its being the case that p, this is a good basis for drawing the conclusion that it's *conceptually* possible that p, but it is not a good basis for drawing the conclusion that it's *metaphysically* possible that p. As a result, Hill maintains, it is a mistake to infer metaphysical conclusions (e.g. property dualism) from facts about what we can conceive. Hill also offers a positive proposal about the proper understanding of metaphysical necessity and possibility. On his account, metaphysical necessities can be reduced to subjunctive conditionals.

In Chapter 12, I attempt to give a naturalistic account of the psychology of modal judgment. Drawing on the use of modals in children, I maintain that a primary function of modal judgment is to represent risks and opportunities. This would obviously be a useful function, and the imagination, I suggest, plays an important role in generating such modal judgments. Philosophers are interested in more basic modal judgments about 'absolute impossibility', which are plausibly delivered by the imagination as well. I argue that contemporary accounts of the imagination can explain why we have the kinds of imaginative failures that underwrite judgments of absolute impossibility.

Roy Sorensen (Chapter 13) explores a more complex form of imagination—meta-conceiving—in which one imagines someone imagining something. Sorensen maintains that meta-conceptions have played an important role in numerous philosophical arguments. He also argues that we can exploit meta-conceiving to undermine the *entailment thesis* that conceivability entails possibility. For the entailment thesis leads, according to Sorensen, to the *meta-entailment* thesis that conceivability of conceivability entails possibility. And it is easy to generate counterexamples to this thesis. This should lead us to be skeptical of the entailment thesis itself.

REFERENCES

BLACKBURN, S. (1993) 'Morals and Modals', in his *Essays in Quasi-Realism* (Oxford: Oxford University Press), 52–74.

CARROLL, N. (1990) *The Philosophy of Horror; or, Paradoxes of the Heart* (New York: Routledge).

——(1998) 'Simulation, Emotions, and Morality', in his *Beyond Aesthetics* (Oxford: Oxford University Press), 306–16.

CARRUTHERS, P. (2002) 'Human Creativity: Its Evolution, Its Cognitive basis, and Its Connections with Childhood Pretence', *British Journal for the Philosophy of Science*, 53, 1–25.

——(2003) 'Review of Currie and Ravenscroft, Recreative Minds', *Notre Dame Philosophical Reviews*, 11(12), <http://ndpr.icaap.org>.

CHALMERS, D. (2002) 'Does Conceivability Entail Possibility?', in Gendler and Hawthorne 2002, 145–200.

COPLAND, A. (2004) 'Empathic Engagement with Narrative Fictions', *Journal of Aesthetics and Art Criticism*, 62, 141–52.

CRAIG, E. (1975) 'The Problem of Necessary Truth', in S. Blackburn (ed.), *Meaning, Reference, and Necessity* (Cambridge: Cambridge University Press), 1–31.

CURRIE, G. (1995) 'Imagination and Simulation: Aesthetics Meets Cognitive Science', in Davies and Stone 1995*b*, 151–69.

——(1997) 'The Paradox of Caring', in M. Hjort and S. Laver (eds.), *Emotion and the Arts* (New York: Oxford University Press), 63–77.

——(1998) 'Pretence, Pretending and Metarepresenting', *Mind & Language*, 13, 35–55.

——and RAVENSCROFT, I. (2002) *Recreative Imagination* (Oxford: Oxford University Press).

DAVIES, M., and STONE, T. (1995*a*) *Folk Psychology: The Theory of Mind Debate* (Oxford: Blackwell).

—— and ——(1995*b*) *Mental Simulation: Evaluations and Applications* (Oxford: Blackwell).

FEAGIN, S. (1996) *Reading with Feeling* (Ithaca, NY: Cornell University Press).

FLAVELL, J. H., FLAVELL, E. R., and GREEN, F. L. (1987) 'Young Children's Knowledge about the Apparent–Real and Pretend–Real distinctions', *Developmental Psychology*, 23, 816–22.

FODOR, J. (1975) *Language of Thought* (Cambridge, Mass.: Harvard University Press).

FRIEND, S. (2003) 'How I Really Feel about JFK', in M. Kieran and D. Lopes (eds.), *Imagination, Philosophy, and the Arts* (London: Routledge), 35–53.

GENDLER, T. (2000) 'The Puzzle of Imaginative Resistance', *Journal of Philosophy*, 97, 55–81.

____ and HAWTHORNE, J. (eds.) (2002) *Conceivability and Possibility* (Oxford: Oxford University Press).

GOLDMAN, A. (1989) 'Interpretation Psychologized', *Mind & Language*, 4, 161–85.

____ (1992) 'In Defense of the Simulation Theory', *Mind & Language*, 7, 104–19.

GORDON, R. (1986) 'Folk Psychology as Simulation', *Mind & Language*, 1, 158–70.

____ and BARKER, J. (1994) 'Autism and the "Theory of Mind" debate', in G. Graham and G. L. Stephens (eds.), *Philosophical Psychopathology: A Book of Readings* (Cambridge, Mass.: MIT Press), 163–81.

HARRIS, P. (2000) *The Work of the Imagination* (Oxford: Blackwell).

____ and KAVANAUGH, R. D. (1993). *Young Children's Understanding of Pretense, Monographs of the Society for Research in Child Development*, 58, 1.

____ and MEREDITH, M. C. (1994) 'Young Children's Comprehension of Pretend Episodes: The Integration of Successive Actions', *Child Development*, 65, 16–30.

HILL, C. (1997) 'Imaginability, Conceivability, Possibility, and the Mind–Body Problem', *Philosophical Studies*, 84, 61–85.

HUME, D. (1739/1964) *A Treatise of Human Nature* (Oxford: Clarendon Press).

IZARD, C. (1991) *Psychology of Emotion* (New York: Plenum Press).

JARROLD, C., CARRUTHERS, P., SMITH, P., and BOUCHER, J. (1994) 'Pretend Play: Is it Metarepresentational?', *Mind & Language*, 9, 445–68.

LAMARQUE, P. (1981) 'How Can We Fear and Pity Fictions?', *British Journal of Aesthetics*, 21(4), 291–304.

LANG, P. (1984) 'Cognition and Emotion: Concept and Action', in C. Izard, J. Kagan, and R. Zajoncs (eds.), *Emotions, Cognition and Behavior* (Cambridge: Cambridge University Press), 192–226.

LESLIE, A. (1987) 'Pretense and Representation: The Origins of "theory of mind"', *Psychological Review*, 94, 412–26.

____ (1994) 'Pretending and Believing: Issues in the Theory of ToMM', *Cognition*, 50, 211–38.

LEWIS, D. (1986) *On the Plurality of Worlds* (Oxford: Basil Blackwell).

LILLARD, A. (1994) 'Making Sense of Pretense', in C. Lewis and P. Mitchell (eds.), *Children's Early Understanding of Mind: Origins and Development* (Hillsdale, NJ: Lawrence Erlbaum Associates), 211–34.

LIVINGSTONE, P., and MELE, A. (1997) 'Evaluating Emotional Responses to Fiction', in M. Hjort and S. Laver (eds.), *Emotion and the Arts* (New York: Oxford University Press), 157–76.

MATRAVERS, D. (2003) 'Fictional Assent and the (So-called) "Puzzle of Imaginative Resistance"', in M. Kieran and D. Lopes (eds.), *Imagination, Philosophy, and the Arts* (London: Routledge), 91–106.

MESKIN, A. and WEINBERG, J. (2003) 'Emotions, Fiction, and Cognitive Architecture', *British Journal of Aesthetics*, 43, 18–34.

MORAN, R. (1994) 'The Expression of Feeling in the Imagination', *Philosophical Review*, 103, 75–106.

MORTON, A. (1980) *Frames of Mind* (Oxford: Oxford University Press).

NEILL, A. (1991) 'Fear, Fiction and Make-Believe', *Journal of Aesthetics and Art Criticism*, 49, 47–56.

NICHOLS, S. (2004*a*) 'Imagining and Believing: The Promise of a Single Code', *Journal of Aesthetics and Art Criticism*, 62, 129–39.

_____ (2004*b*) Review of G. Currie and I. Ravenscroft's *Recreative Minds: Imagination in Philosophy and Psychology, Mind*, 113, 329–34.

_____ (forthcoming) 'Just the Imagination: Why Imagining Doesn't Behave Like Believing', *Mind & Language*.

_____ and STICH, S. (2000) 'A Cognitive Theory of Pretense', *Cognition*, 74, 115–47.

_____ and _____ (2003) *Mindreading* (Oxford: Oxford University Press).

PERNER, J. (1991) *Understanding the Representational Mind* (Cambridge, Mass.: MIT Press).

_____ BARKER, S., and HUTTON, D. (1994) '*Prelief*: The Conceptual Origins of Belief and Pretense', in C. Lewis and P. Mitchell (eds.), *Children's Early Understanding of Mind: Origins and Development* (Hillsdale, NJ: Lawrence Erlbaum Associates), 261–86.

RADFORD, C. (1975) 'How Can We Be Moved by the Fate of Anna Karenina?', *Proceedings of the Aristotelian Society*, suppl. vol. 49, 67–80.

ROSEN, G. (1990) 'Modal Fictionalism', *Mind*, 99, 327–54.

RYLE, G. (1949) *The Concept of Mind* (London: Hutchinson).

SIDELLE, A. (2002) 'On the Metaphysical Contingency of Laws of Nature', in Gendler and Hawthorne 2002, 309–36.

WALTON, K. (1978) 'Feaning Fictions', *Journal of Philosophy*, 75, 5–27.

_____ (1990) *Mimesis as Make-believe: On the Foundations of the Representational Arts* (Cambridge, Mass.: Harvard University Press).

_____ (1994) 'Morals in Fiction and Fictional Morality', *Proceedings of the Aristotelian Society*, suppl. vol. 68, 27–50.

_____ (1997) 'Spelunking, Simulation and Slime: On Being Moved by Fiction', in M. Hjort and S. Laver (eds.), *Emotion and the Arts* (New York: Oxford University Press), 37–49.

WEATHERSON, B. (2004) 'Morality, Fiction, and Possibility', *Philosophers' Imprint*, 4, <http://www.philosophers.imprint.org/>.

WEINBERG, J. and MESKIN, A. (2005) 'Imagine That!', in M. Kieran (ed.), *Contemporary Debates in Aesthetics and the Philosophy of Art* (Oxford: Blackwell), 222–35.

WELLMAN, H. M., and ESTES, D. (1986) 'Early Understanding of Mental Entities: A Reexamination of Childhood Realism', *Child Development*, 57, 910–23.

WRIGHT, C. (1980) *Wittgenstein on the Foundations of Mathematics* (London: Duckworth).

YABLO, S. (1993) 'Is Conceivability a Guide to Possibility?', *Philosophy and Phenomenological Research*, 53, 1–42.

_____ (2002) 'Coulda, Woulda, Shoulda', in Gendler and Hawthorne 2002, 441–92.

PART I
THE NATURE OF THE IMAGINATION

2

Imagination and Emotion

Timothy Schroeder and Carl Matheson

In philosophy, more than in most disciplines, it is generally premature to announce consensus. Nonetheless, in this chapter we sketch out a convergence of opinion that appears, as much as anything ever does, to approach consensus in the current philosophical community, and defend that convergence with a new and, we think, decisive line of evidence. The particular topic is the power of imaginative acts to move us emotionally. How imaginative acts have this power has been an ongoing topic of discussion within the philosophy of art under the heading 'the paradox of fiction', and has also been taken up by recent work on the imagination more broadly. Over time, the view has emerged that these acts have their power to move us through their activation of special cognitive attitudes, akin to beliefs in structure and in some of their effects, but distinguished from beliefs in others. This view, positing what we will call a 'distinct cognitive attitude', or 'DCA', is ultimately an empirical thesis in certain important respects, defended by empirical evidence available from the armchair and from cognitive science. We aim to add the blessings of neuroscience to the view, and thereby to put a final seal of approval on it.

1. FICTION

That fiction produces strong feelings in most of us is an undeniable truth. Take Little Nell, the heroine of Charles Dickens's *The Old Curiosity Shop*. In 1841, much of Great Britain blurrily read through its tears as Little Nell slowly died via weekly installments of *Master Humphrey's Clock*. In New York, crowds of people greeted incoming British ships with cries of 'Is Little Nell dead?' Upon learning of her death, an Irish MP exclaimed, 'He should not have killed her,' and threw his copy of the novel out of the window of his railway carriage. More recent objects of grief have run the gamut from adolescent vampire slayers (Buffy Summers) to animated deer (Bambi's mother).

However undeniable these feelings may be, their existence has been thought to pose a philosophical problem. How can one have such strong feelings about situations that one knows not to be real?

Philosophers have interpreted the question of our reactions to fictions in at least three ways. First is the Classificatory Question: can our feelings towards fictional characters be properly classified as emotions? That is, can we literally grieve for Little Nell or fear Dracula?[1] This question is especially motivated for those who adopt a view of emotions according to which emotions require beliefs, perhaps in addition to subjective feelings or somatic indicators. For such philosophers, in order to experience the emotion of fear, I would have to believe that I am—or the person or thing for which I fear is—in danger. Given this requirement, emotional reaction to fiction might seem impossible, because I simply do not believe that anyone is really in danger when I experience fiction.

The natural next question is that of whether our response to fiction relies on some sort of mistake. In other words, in order to be affected by fictions, must one hold a false belief, or be deluded or irrational in some way? Call this question the Flaw Question. Radford (1975) asserts that our reactions to fiction are essentially irrational, where most others take our reactions to be free of flaws.

Finally there is the Explanatory Question. For the moment, ignore the matter of whether the feelings inspired by fictions are emotions, irrational or otherwise. Instead, concentrate on the unassailable datum that most of us have such feelings. Why and how is it that our experiences of fiction produce such strong reactions in us? The question of primary interest to us here is this Explanatory Question, and we mention the other two questions principally to make it clear that they are indeed distinct questions.

From Kendall Walton's (1978) 'Fearing Fictions', philosophers have been increasingly concerned to address the Explanatory Question. In these early days, a thousand flowers bloomed. According to Walton, the reader does not fear Dracula or feel fear on Mina's behalf; rather, she makes believe that she is fearing Dracula or fearing for Mina. Gregory Currie held a related view, that the reader 'plays a game of make-believe, adopting the attitude of make-believe to the propositions of the story. He makes believe that he is reading a true account of events.' The interaction of his make-beliefs with his make-desires[2] causes 'feelings of certain kinds. And, typically these causal processes mirror the causal processes that would take place if his attitude was not make-belief but straightforwardly belief' (Currie 1990: 197).

Like Currie and Walton, Peter Lamarque (1981) claimed that our felt responses to fictions arise from a cognitive attitude taken toward them, but, unlike Currie and Walton, Lamarque denied that this attitude is one of make-believe. In this paper Lamarque held the theoretically central attitude to be conscious mental representation or, less technically, thought. It is the thought

---

[1] Assuming one can have an attitude toward a non-existent entity at all.

[2] Currie originally formulates his position in terms of the interaction between make-beliefs and desires. Currie's move to make-desires is mainly motivated by his conviction that one can't have real desires about fictional characters without having the relevant real beliefs about them (1990: 205).

of Little Nell's dying that moves us to sadness, the thought of Dracula drinking Mina's blood that inspires horror, and so on. Because thoughts are not beliefs, the thought of Little Nell's death does not require us to believe that there is someone out there dying; nonetheless, because the thought itself is a real thing, it has the causal force to generate strong reactions in us.

Robert Yanal had a rather different, and to us somewhat puzzling, view that our emotional responses to fictions merely parallel our emotional responses to distant people:

Knowing about someone only through reputation and letters is a lot like knowing about fictional characters; and it is quite odd to know someone only in this way. . . . The emotions we have towards fictional characters are the emotions we have to personages, who while we may know details about their inner lives that are astonishingly secret, are known to us without the emotional marks of prior acquaintance or the consideration of future relationships. Were we to have the same relation with real people that we have with fictions we would have the same emotions towards those people as we have to fictions. We just rarely are in the same relation. (Yanal 1994: 73)

A number of other theories also flourished. There were, for instance, theories that our responses are based on our belief that it is fictionally the case that such-and-such an event is occurring (Neill 1993), and theories that our responses occur once we play the counterfactual game of thinking what it would be like if the relevant fictional events were actually happening. Eddy Zemach (1996) defended the view that in responding emotionally to fictions, we are responding emotionally to merely possible individuals with true beliefs about them. Although Anna Karenina is not real, she 'occurs' at the possible world described by Dostoyevsky, and so 'the statement "Anna threw herself under the train" is true at that world. A world that does not exist may yet be imagined or envisaged, and through envisaging such worlds, we may be moved by events that occur in them' (Zemach 1996: 43) simply because we form true beliefs about what occurs in them. William Charlton (1986) held the view that fictions covertly remind us of real people we have encountered, and stir our emotions through thoughts of them. And so on.

Over the years, there has slowly come to be a convergence, and a certain amount of agreement upon the existence of such a convergence.[3] A number of philosophers interested in art and the emotions now hold that there is a DCA activated by fictions—not belief, but not entirely unlike belief—and it is the presence of this attitude in people appreciating fictions that causes many of the felt responses that fictions cause (though not all of them). Works in the philosophy of art defending some form of DCA as the answer to the Explanatory Question include Carroll 1990; Currie 1990; Currie and Ravenscroft 2002; Feagin 1996, 1997; McCormick 1985; Meskin and Weinberg

---

[3] For dissent, see e.g. Levinson 1997.

2003; Scruton 1974; Walton 1978, 1990; and Yanal 1999. Worth (2000) goes so far as to attribute to Aristotle the view that tragedy relies on a DCA to elicit fear and pity, and Yanal (1999: 90–1) finds a form of the view in the letters of Coleridge. In addition, a number of philosophers writing principally on the emotions have also held that there must be a DCA responsible for the emotional effects of fictions, including DeLancey (2002: ch. 6) and Green (1992: 35–7).

2. THE IMAGINATION

That the imagination produces strong feelings in most of us is just as evident as that fictions do. Imagining the deliberations that might have led the CIA to orchestrate the overthrow of Allende's government in Chile is the sort of thing that can make one feel angry, while imagining what it will be like to be reunited with an absent loved one can make one feel contented, and so on. Empirical investigations of the phenomenon have turned up just the findings one might expect. In just one experiment among many, for instance, Lang and colleagues monitored the visceral bodily responses of socially anxious people and people with snake phobias as they were exposed to both snakes and public speaking, and naturally found that people were moved more by their own fear objects than by the fear objects of the other group. The experimenters then found similar if attenuated patterns of response when subjects (trained to imagine vividly) were asked to imagine these same stimuli: people with snake phobias were very moved by imagining snakes but hardly moved by imagining public speaking, and vice versa (Lang et al. 1983). We take it that the power of the imagination to produce these strong feelings raises the same Classificatory, Flaw, and Explanatory Questions as does the power of fictions to do so. Further, we take it that since it is imaginative engagement with a fiction that allows fiction to move us, the power of fictions to move us, and so to raise our three sorts of questions, is simply a special case of the power of the imagination to do so.

While the emotional power of fictions has been a special topic of study in the philosophy of art, the emotional power of the imagination more generally has not received the same scrutiny from the philosophy of psychology.[4] Nonetheless, it appears that philosophers of psychology are converging on the view that the imagination requires a distinct cognitive attitude, in perfect parallel to their colleagues in the philosophy of art. According to Shaun Nichols and Stephen Stich, for instance, our imaginative capacities stem from a distinctive attitude 'found' (if that metaphor can be used) in a 'possible world box'. 'Like the Belief Box and the Desire Box, the Possible World Box contains representation tokens. However, the functional role of these tokens—their pattern of interaction with other

---

[4] Though psychologist Paul Harris (2000) dedicates a chapter of his book-length treatment of the imagination to the subject.

components of the mind—is quite different from the functional role of either beliefs or desires' (Nichols and Stich 2003: 28).

Nichols (2004) goes on to claim that something similar can be found across a broad spectrum of research on the imagination from a cognitive science perspective. Certainly, there are a number of examples where this does seem to be the case. For example, Gregory Currie and Ian Ravenscroft hold that the imagination (at least, the sort of imagination that might move us emotionally, 'recreative imagination') involves 'the having of states that are not beliefs, desires, or perceptions but are like them in various ways' (2002: 2): DCAs, in short, and perhaps further distinctive attitudes besides.

Goldman (1989, 1992), Gordon (1986), and Gordon and Barker (1994) defend what are often called 'simulation theories' about our knowledge of the minds of others, holding that one's power to imagine what another will think, feel, or do comes particularly from one's capacity to simulate another's mental states. In this simulative activity, one imagines the experiences, thoughts, and so on of the other, and then allows one's own mental processes to operate on these imagined mental states. The resulting products are also imagined, and this gives rise to relevant non-imaginary beliefs about what the imagined person would feel, think, or do. Nichols (2004) argues that, insofar as simulation theorists envision the imagination containing contents akin to the contents of perception or belief, but distinct in their functional effects, they too are committed to the existence of a DCA to explain the operation of the imagination, and we agree: simulation theorists of this sort are also DCA theorists of the imagination, and thereby also a part of the trend we see in the literature. It is thus no surprise that Walton (1997), Currie (1997), and Feagin (1997) underpin their accounts of feeling for fictions with simulation theories of this sort.

Finally, it is worth mentioning that psychologist Paul Harris, though less clear about the matter, seems to share a similar view, distinguishing between children's pretences and their beliefs while holding that pretences have their impact on the emotions because fictional material is processed in a 'default mode' that is indifferent to whether one is pretending or actually believing (Harris 2000: 82; see also Nichols and Stich 2003: 45–6). Not every important theorist of the imagination has been willing to agree that the imagination requires a DCA (see especially Leslie 1987), but the view seems at least widespread.

3. MAKING PROGRESS

What, exactly, do we have in mind in talking of a DCA? Our commitments are minimal. For our purposes, a DCA is a kind of content-bearing state, tokens of which play a functional role distinct from that of the most familiar propositional attitudes (beliefs, desires, intentions, etc.) and distinct also from perception and hallucination. We break with (most notably) each of Currie (1990), Lamarque

(1981), and Walton (1990) at a number of points here, since our interest is in the broad convergence, and not in settling the particular details. Although a DCA must bear content, we have no special commitments to the vehicle of content being sentence-like or picture-like, and no special commitments to the content itself being conceptual or non-conceptual, Fregean or Russellian. Perhaps DCAs are sometimes (always?) conscious, perhaps sometimes (always?) unconscious. We will accept all sorts. And although DCA tokens must play a distinct functional role, we do not insist that the only possible functional role for a DCA is one like that played by acts of imagination. There may be a whole raft of DCAs not typically explored by philosophers. Our only thought is that there is a growing trend toward positing that there exists one such DCA, tokens of which play the role played by imaginative thoughts and mental images.

Evidence that a DCA mediates between the imagination and our feelings needs to show three things: (1) that imagining that p characteristically involves or provokes the forming of a content-bearing mental state with the content p;[5] (2) that these mental states are strongly differentiated from beliefs and perceptions (etc.) in their functional roles, thus counting as distinct attitudes; and (3) that these mental states produce the feelings we associate with emotionally laden imaginative acts.

So far, the evidence for these claims provided by philosophers and scientists has been substantial. While we will not review it all here, we will recall to the reader's mind a few of the most salient points.

Regarding (1), it has seemed to many that the experience of engaging a fictional work involves entertaining the ideas presented as part of the fiction. Reading of the death of Little Nell, one has the thought that Little Nell is dead. One does not, typically, explicitly think that Dickens has arranged that the character of Little Nell dies; nor does one think that there is a possible world in which a Little Nell dies. And if one has the thought that there have been many deaths like that fictionalized through the character of Little Nell, this thought is only a supplementary thought to the primary one likely to invoke sadness (or, at least in the case of Oscar Wilde, mirth: 'One must have a heart of stone to read the death of Little Nell without laughing'). In the same way, when one imagines what it would be like to be alone on a desert island, one might conjure up a visual image of oneself alone on a desert island, but one typically does not conjure up a visual image of it being possible that one be alone on a desert island, or a visual image of a fictional presentation of the possibility, or the like. All this suggests that the content of one's most central mental state in imagining that p carries the content that p. One could also point to the fact that children

---

[5] This is meant to include forming a visual image that p, or an auditory image, and so on. There are philosophers who are skeptical about the power of content attributions to fully characterize the nature of a visual image, auditory image, or other state of consciousness, but we leave this thorny issue to one side for the sake of expository clarity.

engage in playing 'make-believe' at an age (generally around two years (Harris 2000)), so young that it would seem incredible to attribute to them thought contents involving possible worlds, fictional characters, represented types of events, or even false beliefs on the part of themselves and their playmates. For this reason, too, it has seemed best to attribute an attitude with the content p on occasions of imagining that p.

Regarding (2), it is trivial that if imagining that p involves having some attitude with the content p, then that attitude must be distinct from belief, perception, or other standard attitudes, as Nichols and Stich (2003) emphasize. After all, attitudes are, at least standardly, characterized by their functional roles. Beliefs that p are distinguished from desires that p, in that beliefs play one functional role, while desires play another. But clearly, imagining that p involves having a mental state that plays a role very different from that played by belief, desire, perception, or any other familiar attitude. In particular, imagining that p is most obviously distinguished from believing that p, in that imagining that p does not lead one to automatically store in one's memory that p, and it does not lead one automatically to act in a way that would be desire satisfying if p; it is most obviously distinguished from perceiving that p in just the same ways. So if imagining that p involves having an attitude with the content p, that attitude must be a distinct one.

Regarding (3), the case is straightforward, but not quite as secure. (3) is the claim that the DCA we are pressed to believe in because of (1) and (2) actually gives rise to the emotional effects caused by acts of imagination. Certainly it is undeniable that there is a correlation: the onset and end of imaginative acts often correlate well with the onset and end of strong feelings, and the feelings are sensitive to the content of the imaginative acts in much the way that feelings are sensitive to the content of beliefs (Lang et al. 1983 is one empirical result among many providing empirical confirmation, insofar as that is needed). But (3) is not completely supported unless one is able to trace a clear causal pathway from stimulus to DCA to feeling. Without this evidence, there remains the possibility that the DCA exists, but is epiphenomenal to the feelings that are produced by the imagination. Perhaps the imagination produces a DCA, but also produces a distinct covert belief—an irrational one, in the style of Radford (1975), or a belief in what is fictional, in the style of Neill (1993), or a belief in possibilities, in the style of Zemach (1996)—and it is the covert belief that causes the emotional effects. Or perhaps, impressive as the evidence is, there is some hidden flaw overlooked in the many arguments that have been made for thesis (1) or thesis (2). So the defender of the growing consensus on the emotional power of the imagination should wish to trace the causal pathway directly. But the tracing of such causal pathways is not within the competence of armchair philosophy; nor is it within the competence of cognitive psychology. It is really a job for cognitive and affective neuroscience: for the disciplines that study the implementation of the attitudes and feelings posited by philosophers and cognitive psychologists.

4. A NEUROSCIENTIFIC APPROACH TO THE EXPLANATORY QUESTION

The time has come to sketch out the relevant facts, as they are known, at the neuroscientific level. In the next section, we interpret these facts in terms of the DCA hypothesis, but in this section we restrict ourselves to the perspectives of cognitive and affective neuroscience, so as to present the evidence without begging questions.

The neuroscientific approach to the Explanatory Question begins with the senses, and the production of sensory and quasi-sensory representations. Stimulation of the sense organs produces neural signals, which in turn create patterns of activity in the brain. These patterns of activity are initially segregated by sense modality, and they produce what neuroscientists call 'unimodal sensory representations' (e.g. Kandel, Schwartz, and Jessell 2000: ch. 18).[6] Unimodal representations are said by scientists to represent things such as light/dark boundaries, edges, surfaces, and distances (in the visual system), pitches, loudness, chords, and word boundaries (in the auditory system), and the like.[7]

From unimodal representations the brain is thought to create multimodal representations, representations which can be evoked through multiple sensory channels (Kandel, Schwartz, and Jessell 2000: ch. 18). At least some of these multimodal representations are representations of things as forks, as flowers, as anything one can readily experience a thing as being through the use of more than one sense. Dispositions to token such representations seem to underlie what is often called 'semantic memory' or 'semantic knowledge' (Kandel, Schwartz, and Jessell 2000: ch. 62), i.e. one's general beliefs. Others of these multimodal representations appear to be motor-oriented representations (see e.g. Jeannerod 1997); they will not be our focus. From now on, our talk of multimodal representations will be intended to refer only to those that are used to represent things (objects, properties, relations) in the world, rather than those used to instruct the body to make movements. Multimodal representations are activated by sensory stimulation just as unimodal representations are, and generally cease activation when sensory stimulation is no longer causing one to experience something as a fork, flower, etc. in just the same manner as unimodal representations (Kandel, Schwartz, and Jessell 2000: ch. 62).[8]

The structures producing these representations send their signals to a number of other targets in the brain, including the orbitofrontal cortex (Rolls 2000),

---

[6] A standard graduate-level text, Kandel, Schwartz, and Jessell (2000) will be our default reference for familiar facts of neuroscience.

[7] Visual and auditory representations making a difference to consciousness appear to be localized to the occipital and temporal lobe (Kandel, Schwartz, and Jessell 2000: ch. 19).

[8] These representations seem to be especially clearly found in the temporal lobe (Kandel, Schwartz, and Jessell 2000: ch. 19).

the affective division of the striatum (Mello and Villares 1997), and the amygdala (LeDoux 1996). A few words about each are in order.

The primary role of the orbitofrontal cortex appears to be the discrimination of rewarding and punishing stimuli, in order to influence feelings, visceral responses, and decision-making (Rolls 2000; Schultz et al. 2000; Damasio 1994). Damage to the orbitofrontal cortex is associated with inappropriate euphoria, lack of affect, irresponsibility, decreased visceral responses to emotional stimuli, and impoverished sensitivity to the goodness or badness of future outcomes (Bechara et al. 1994; Damasio 1994; Elliott et al. 2000; Kandel, Schwartz, and Jessell 2000: ch. 50). The affective division of the striatum, on the other hand, appears involved in producing a reward signal (Schultz et al. 2000), with obvious implications for feelings (see e.g. Kandel, Schwartz and Jessell 2000: ch. 51). In one case study, for instance, electrical stimulation of the affective striatum was found to induce episodes of mania in a person (Miyawaki et al. 2000). As for the amygdala, it is best known as the neural underpinning of Pavlovian fear conditioning, but it is involved in other forms of emotionality as well, and directly exerts powerful influence upon centers in the brain controlling heart rate, sweating, blood pressure, rate of breathing, startle tendencies, facial expressions, urination, digestion, and other functions whose modification one associates with powerful emotions (Kandel, Schwartz, and Jessell 2000: ch. 50; LeDoux 1996). To get a hint of the importance of the amygdala to the emotional life, consider the fact that damage to the amygdala in one fascinating case resulted in a man who, though not indifferent to his own life or to the harms others might do him, was all but incapable of feeling fear or anger (Sprengelmeyer et al. 1999).

Now that each stage in the neural production of felt responses has been described separately, the whole process can be described as a unit. In the simplest case, a life event causes sensory stimulation, which in turn causes a mass of unimodal and multimodal representations to be formed, representing the event as involving a shadow here, a cry of 'Help!', danger, and the like. These representations send signals to the orbitofrontal cortex, affective striatum, and amygdala, and these structures in turn cause feelings of pleasure or displeasure, racing hearts, churning stomachs, and so on. This is the main set of pathways for felt responses to life.

A few wrinkles remains to be explored, for not all powerful feelings are triggered through neuroscientists' unimodal and multimodal representations. For instance, Panksepp (1997) reviews the evidence that panic, as opposed to fear, is mediated by an importantly distinct system that is typically triggered more primitively. It should also be noted that there is a pathway from the senses directly to the amygdala, without intermediate unimodal or multimodal representations (see e.g. LeDoux 1996, 2000). This pathway appears to allow for certain powerful feelings to be produced by stimuli even before they have been fully processed by the brain's unimodal and multimodal representational systems. For a possible example, pictures of the objects of one's phobias have the power to cause strong feelings of fear even when one is very briefly exposed to the pictures—so briefly, even, that one cannot consciously identify what one saw (Lang, Davis, and Öhman 2000). The activation of strong feelings under such circumstances may well make use of the primitive, pre-conscious pathways to the amygdala. Scientists remain uncertain of the details, but, given the neural connections, it appears plausible that some powerful feelings can be triggered without intermediate representation. Still, these are peripheral sorts of cases. In the main, the production of strong feelings by everyday stimuli goes through the pathways described.

What about the pathway from imaginative acts to feelings? Perhaps surprisingly, this turns out to be a very similar overall pathway. There is no distinct anatomical region of the brain used for representing the merely imaginary; nor is there a distinct set of nerve fibers carrying information exclusively about the merely imaginary; nor does there seem to be a special affective or, for that matter, motor region designated for receiving input about the merely imaginary. Imaginatively engaging, say, a film causes the activation of unimodal and multimodal representations. Some of these representations are of real things, such as the softness of the cinema seat, but many are of misleading appearances (Hollywood's 'illusions'). Films of fictions contain simulated assaults, simulated emotions, and so on. In spite of the fact that these are all known simulacra, they are represented much as real things would be, by the same unimodal and multimodal representational structures. Once formed, these unimodal and multimodal representations have some of their characteristic effects, including sending impulses to emotional centers like the orbitofrontal cortex, affective striatum, and amygdala. These emotional centers, once activated in turn, go on to cause their characteristic effects: the feelings and physical responses one associates with emotions.

That known fictional stimuli entrain neural consequences similar to nonfictional stimuli is absolutely central to our explanatory strategy here. Fortunately for us, the phenomenon has been documented in detail, with Kosslyn et al. (1993) documenting the parallels being seeing and imagining, and Cabeza and Nyberg (2000) providing a more recent review of work on perception and imagery. Some concrete examples will help to make clear how broad the evidence is. It has been found that the same cells in the monkey representational system representing faces will respond powerfully to realistic puppet faces, and even to extremely schematic two-dots-over-a-line-type 'faces' which would never be mistaken for real faces (Kandel, Schwartz, and Jessell 2000: 566). Real and known artificial faces thus activate the same sensory representation. In a study of audition, Zatorre et al. (1996) found that hearing a song activated very similar regions of auditory cortex as compared to imagining the same song. And for an example involving a truly abstract concept, consider that pretend money has been found to activate the orbitofrontal cortex of human experimental volunteers (O'Doherty et al. 2001) just as real money does (Thut et al. 1997). And on we could go, were it necessary: the commonalities between the neural effects of fictional and non-fictional stimuli are known to be so great in the brain's representational and emotional systems that scientists experiment upon human subjects using fictions to elicit feelings (e.g. Teasdale et al. 1999) just as they experiment using non-fictions to elicit them (e.g. Dougherty et al. 1999).

What about the unassisted exercise of the imagination? It turns out that it makes no difference to the common core of real/imaginary activation whether the brain is activated by a representation of a thing or merely by voluntarily imagining that thing. Findings from brain imaging indicate that the same regions of the brain are used in very similar patterns, whether one visually experiences a given object or one imagines such an object (Kandel, Schwartz, and Jessell 2000: ch. 20; Kosslyn 1994).[9] There are also findings from patients with neurological injuries that confirm this. For instance, in a well-known experiment subjects with injuries to the right parietal lobe (a region often associated with failing to be aware of the left side of one's world) were asked to imagine standing in a square and to report the buildings 'visible' in the mind's eye. Subjects reported the buildings that would have been visible on their right, but not on their left. When subjects were then asked to imagine standing at the other end of the square, subjects again could report the buildings that would have been visible on the right (those previously not reported), but could no longer report the buildings that would now have been on the left (those just previously reported). Injury to the imagination thus appeared to match perfectly injury to vision (Kandel, Schwartz, and Jessell 2000: ch. 20).

Although fictional and otherwise imaginary stimuli have many of the same effects as 'real' stimuli do, they obviously do not have all the same effects, or else people would leap onto stages in order to prevent murders, and so on. But it appears that fictional and imaginary stimuli have their emotional effects via the same types of causal pathways as 'real' stimuli. This causal pathway is one that begins with the brain's capacity to represent states of affairs, both real and imaginary, and continues on to connect these representations to the orbitofrontal cortex, affective division of the striatum, and amygdala, which in turn produce the strong feelings sometimes aroused in us. Insofar as fictional and imaginary stimuli have a smaller or different impact from what they would have if thought to be real, this difference must come from a difference in the representations evoked, or not evoked, or in the downstream causal effects of these representations, or background knowledge and dispositions. Generally, there will be a

---

[9] Our neuroscientific story is clear about how more passive imaginative engagement might work, but we say nothing about how more active imagination is actually initiated, only what follows from it. Strictly speaking, this is beyond our purview, but we can reasonably speculate that the 'articulatory loop' and 'visuospatial sketch pad', connections between prefrontal cortex and the corresponding sensory regions, are likely involved. The connections are identified as central to rehearsing silently a phone number one needs to dial and other tasks for working memory, but it is not unreasonable to think that the same connections can be deployed to rehearse silently conversations that are purely invented, to visualize things one has never seen, and so on. See Kandel, Schwartz, and Jessell 2000: ch. 62.

plethora of such differences, and so many possible explanations of why a particular work of fiction produces feelings different from some non-fiction. Yet what
is important for our purposes is that insofar as the imagination causes the same
feelings as the real, it does so by using the same structures in the brain as those
used by the real world.

5. ANSWERING THE EXPLANATORY QUESTION

Even if scientists can explain what happens in our brains when imagined states
of affairs and events move us, neuroscience alone cannot answer the Explanatory Question. A proper answer to the Explanatory Question must be given in
mental terms, not neuroscientific ones, for the original question was why we have
certain mental responses, not certain biological responses, to what we imagine
(through fictions or otherwise). Neuroscience has described its unimodal and
multimodal representations. Are these best interpreted as the DCAs posited by
the growing swell of philosophers? Our judgment is that these neuroscientific
entities are indeed the hypothesized DCAs. It turns out, then, that the majority
has by and large grasped the correct mental kind for an answer to the Explanatory Question—or so we claim. But we will now proceed to do what those in
the growing consensus have not been able to do: justify this answer on combined
philosophical and neuroscientific grounds, replacing 'how possibly' with 'how
actually'.

Our outline of an answer to the Explanatory Question, then, is this. When
we engage our imaginations through the experience of fictions, through play, or
otherwise, our engagement causes in us simple sensory representations, which, in
their turn, cause more complex representations. The contents of some of these
various representations include the contents that would be true in the imagined
scenario: these content-bearing representations are the DCAs so widely posited.
En masse, these representations, together with all other representations occurrent in us at that time, have their characteristic effects. These effects include the
activation of centers in the brain producing the feelings and physical responses
characteristic of emotions.

Why interpret unimodal and multimodal representations as content-bearers?[10]
We will consider each in turn. One might doubt that unimodal representations
truly bear contents on the grounds that mental content is a property only of
beliefs and the like, and these neural structures realize sensations, not beliefs.
However, there is widespread agreement in the philosophy of mind that at least
the vast majority of sensations have attendant representational or informational content. Philosophers of mind distinguish, at least for purposes of discussion,

---

[10] Note that by 'representation' we do not mean to commit ourselves to a mental state made up
of concepts. If the reader prefers the terms 'information-bearer' or 'mental content-bearer', we will
not object.

between the felt quality of sensations (the qualia, the 'what-it-is-like' feature) and their contents, but they go on to add that for every phenomenal quality there is also a content (e.g. Byrne 2001; Dretske 1995; Lycan 1987; McDowell 1994; Searle 1992; Tye 1995), or that for almost every phenomenal quality there is also a content, the exceptions being things such as the phenomenal quality of pain or of orgasm (e.g. Block 1995; Peacocke 1983). The position that experiences do not have any proprietary content associated with them is not unknown in present work on consciousness (e.g. Akins 1996), but it is very much a minority position. We propose to accept the near-consensus position on sensation and content on the strength of work done elsewhere, and so conclude that since so-called unimodal representations make a difference to consciousness, they must also have contents. Our conclusion can be made conditional upon the correctness of at least some of this work.[11]

One might doubt that multimodal representations truly bear contents, but this is also unpromising. (Nearly) everyone agrees that beliefs have contents, and we take this much for granted. But multimodal representations are by far the best, and also the only, candidates for the neural realizers of belief (more carefully: tokenings of such representations, plus appropriate functional dispositions, are the best candidates for the neural realizers of occurrent beliefs). Hence multimodal representations bear contents, at least when playing the belief role. One might doubt that multimodal representations bear contents when not playing the functional role of belief, but to us this move seems ad hoc. Since it is clear that one and the same structures (playing different functional roles, true, but the same structures nonetheless) are used whether one occurrently judges that *p* or whether one occurrently imagines that *p* for some cognitively sophisticated state of affairs *p*, there is no clear motivation for holding that these structures bear their contents only when deployed as beliefs, and not when deployed in acts of imagination. On many theories of mind (Fodor's being most prominent; see e.g. Fodor 1998: ch. 1), representational resources have their contents independently of the functional roles these contents play, supporting the idea that the neural structures identified as multimodal representations would have their contents whether used in thinking or in imagining. And even on quite different theories of mind, such as Davidson's (see Davidson 1980), if our best interpretative practice interprets

---

[11] Perhaps the simplest and most obvious argument for consciousness having contents comes from the cognitive impenetrability of illusion. When one looks at an optical illusion, it looks as though, e.g., one line is longer than another. It appears, in a clear sense, that the lines differ in length. But one is perfectly well aware that the lines do not differ in length. One's experience reports one thing, one's beliefs another. Hence experiences make reports (bear content), and are not identical to beliefs. One could try holding that one has inconsistent beliefs in such circumstances, but this seems forced. We are all familiar with inconsistent beliefs in ourselves and in others, and with the standard phenomenology of such beliefs. Generally, one avoids the inconsistency; if brought to one's attention, one denies the inconsistency, or is puzzled, etc. This is not the nature of looking at an optical illusion. For detailed (and very different) defenses of the claim, see McDowell 1994; Tye 1995.

people's imaginative acts in part through ascribing content to them, then this interpretation is correct, and we may at least token-identify imagining that p with tokening a particular multimodal representation that p. It seems, then, that there is broadly ecumenical reason to interpret multimodal representations as bearing their contents whatever role they may be playing on a given occasion.

So the representations of neuroscience are genuine content-bearers. Can we say that these content-bearers actually play the causal role they are thought to play, producing emotional-type responses to their contents when these contents are deployed in imagination? Yes. These structures activate the orbitofrontal cortex, the affective division of the striatum, and the amygdala through direct, long-lasting, stable connections subject (for the most part) only to very local causal influence. Thus, when the neurons making up the capacity to represent that p (whether in sensory or more cognitive mode) fire, tokening a representation, they also send neural signals down to the brain's 'emotional centers', causing responses that are ultimately experienced as the strong feelings that ideas can evoke in us, whether believed or imagined. This part of the story is documented fairly uncontroversially by neuroscience, and so we will not belabor the point here.

So far, we have focused on the more belief-like DCAs generated by the imagination, but many philosophers have been keen to emphasize that desires must play a role in the generation of feelings by fictions or the imagination, or at least that 'make-desires' parallel to make-beliefs must exist to generate feelings. We have nothing to contribute to this specific debate, but agree that something should be said. It is quite reasonable to speculate that real desires or make-desires (or both: we take no stand here) influence our felt responses to imagined scenarios. Is there room in the neuroscientific account for these further real or make-believe attitudes? The answer is straightforward: insofar as desires have some influence upon feelings and actions, and insofar as the postulated make-desires are to have their influence upon feelings, they are best thought of as realized in the structures already described by affective neuroscience as playing such roles: the orbitofrontal cortex, the affective division of the striatum, and the amygdala. Unfortunately, there is no well-established neuroscientific work on the localization of desire as such. However, among philosophers who have given some consideration to the localization of desire in the human brain, Morillo (1990) has emphasized the affective division of the striatum and its connections to dopamine, and Schroeder (2004) has emphasized connections between representational capacities, the orbitofrontal cortex, and the affective division of the striatum. Hence, while it is yet early to make firm commitments, it seems likely that desires will turn out to have a role to play in the causation of feelings by the imagination, just as one would have thought. What, then, of make-desires? Here there is less evidence: no demonstration of the voluntary creation of short-lived dispositions in the orbitofrontal cortex, striatum, or amygdala is known to us. But it is certainly not out of the question, and the neural regions to be investigated, at least, are well defined.

This ends our basic argument. Belief- and perception-like DCAs exist, and they are realized in unimodal and multimodal representations that we somehow learn (by about the age of two) to utilize in the special functional role distinctive of imaginative engagement with ideas. These unimodal and multimodal representations are the same basic resources used to form occurrent sensations and beliefs. They cause in us the feelings caused by the literal world and also by fictions and other spurs to the imagination, doing so by direct neural connections to the centers in the brain that produce such feelings: centers that realize desires or desire-like DCAs, and centers causally downstream from such realizers.

At this point, a number of explanatory questions remain unanswered, and three in particular stand out:

(1) Why are the behavioral effects of imagined scenarios so unlike the behavioral effects of the non-imaginary world?

(2) Why are felt responses to the imagination not identical to felt responses to the non-imaginary?

(3) Does our account work as well for imaginative acts inspired by written works of fiction as it does for other imaginative acts?

While answering these questions is not the central focus of our work, and while a number of philosophers have contributed insightful answers to them, we think this chapter will not quite stand on its own without a brief discussion of them.

The puzzle presented by the first question is especially pressing for us because, as we read the neuroscientific evidence, the causal pathways leading away from representing that p in the case of belief are just the same as the causal pathways leading away from representing that p in the case of imagining it. But, given that it is the very same representational capacity used in both cases, having its causal effects through the same long-standing causal connections to other parts of the brain, how possibly can it be that tokening p in one attitude leads to action, while tokening p in the other attitude does not? The beginning of an answer to this first question is that actions are influenced more by belief than by mere representation in general, while feelings tend to be much more powerfully influenced by representation without regard to belief, regardless of whether the imagination is involved or not. Tim is quite certain that he can stand safely upon the transparent floor of the CN Tower and gaze the hundreds of meters down to the ground, but this belief has a very modest impact upon the feelings he experiences looking down. On the other hand, this belief in his safety has a much greater impact upon his willingness to act. So long as he does not look downwards, he does not find it hard to step out onto the transparent floor, and even looking downwards he can, with an effort of will, walk about on the floor. But no matter how well he knows his own safety, his fear and nausea are only a little less than they would be if his life were in fact in his hands. In the same way, one's belief that certain events are only being played by actors has a very modest impact upon one's feelings, but this belief is quite enough to keep one seated during a convincingly depicted murder. So the phenomenon is not peculiar to the imagination as such.

This is not much of a causal explanation, however, and in this chapter we would certainly prefer a causal explanation if one is available. Unfortunately, we know of no hard empirical evidence that can help us at the neural level; plausible speculations will have to serve. To begin: even though the representations conjured by the imagination are sending signals to the brain's decision and action centers, other representations are sending competing messages to those centers. Imagining being a pirate does not prevent one from seeing that the 'ship' is a sofa, contra what one imagines to be the case. This much, at least, is uncontroversial. By the age of two, when we begin pretend play (Harris 2000), our brains have somehow begun to learn how to assess these conflicting pieces of information, and the result, somehow, is the familiar functional difference. Perhaps the causal explanation for this is as simple as the term 'learning' suggests. Our brains go through a lifelong process of learning what actions to produce in response to currently tokened representations, and this learning relies heavily on changes in long-term connections deep in unconscious action-selection systems (see e.g. Schroeder 2004: chs. 2, 4). This learning shapes our dispositions to respond to current representations, whatever their source. Perhaps, then, coming to have an imaginative faculty as a distinct DCA comes down to learning to treat representations that one creates oneself, or representations created by what one grasps to be fictions, or the like, as not warranting the sorts of behavioral responses that they would were the representations created externally by non-imaginary events and objects: learning, that is, to give such representations a distinct functional role. Unfortunately, there has been no detailed study of how the brain uses the differences between, say, fiction and non-fiction to govern action, and so our answer must remain schematic. But in essence, this question is no longer philosophical, but straightforwardly empirical.

The emotional, as opposed to behavioral, differences between the imaginary and the non-imaginary are even more interesting. Here one can mention a number of points. One is the point just made about action: that the imagination generally activates different sensory representations from those activated by what is not imaginary. These different representations have, one might reasonably speculate, come to be associated with distinct feelings. One reads of the death of Little Nell in what looks like a novel; one reads about the death of a real person in what looks like a newspaper, or one hears about it from a newscaster. One sees Dracula attack Mina in a movie theater, surrounded by the smell of popcorn; one sees a mugger attack a pedestrian on the street by the park. And so on. Of course, these differences are not invariable. There are novels written in the style of works of non-fiction, television programs which include simulated news broadcasts as components, and so on. But even in these cases, one is generally conscious that these events are fictional—i.e. one represents them as fictional—and this makes all the difference to one's emotional life. If, somehow, one ceases occurrently to represent the fictional nature of one's source, one will naturally be expected to feel more as one would feel were the source factual.

Another, related point is that our sensory representations of real events are internally consistent in a way that our sensory representations of fictions and other imaginative scenarios are often not. One's eyes can be telling one that everything is on fire, but if one's nose is saying that there is margarine-lathered popcorn nearby, and one's skin is saying that there are no nearby heat sources, one's emotional response will be one thing; if one uses a full virtual reality system to engage one's other senses, so that one also smells an apparent fire and feels the heat of it, one's emotion-like response will, *ceteris paribus*, be that much stronger—even though one knows that it is just an illusion one experiences.

Then there are the emotions brought on by imaginative engagement with the unreal as, say, artworks or creative products: the pleasure in seeing a well-executed depiction of grinding poverty, for example. One could also describe the disappointment one feels in seeing a less-exciting-than-expected thriller, the illicit thrill of identifying with a wicked character, and so on. These extra layers are important to understanding the felt impact of fiction, but they are not particularly our concern here, precisely because one need not appeal to any DCA to describe their appreciation.

As for the third question, whether what has been said about fiction in general will carry over into written fiction in particular, the worry is reasonable, but misplaced. Most readers (in our experience, at any rate) use unimodal mental imagery while reading. They visualize scenes, 'hear' dialogue in different voices, imagine well-evoked smells, and so on. Because unimodal mental imagery uses the unimodal representational capacities, books have an obvious route to DCAs, and so to emotion-like responses, for these readers. Reading evokes unimodal conscious representations, which in turn evoke multimodal conscious representations as well. The only readers for whom the account so far raises worries are those not making use of unimodal representations. Yet such readers tell us that reading nonetheless does make a difference to their conscious lives: it is simply not a difference made up of unimodal imagery. Their reading utilizes conscious representations of a higher-order, multimodal nature. Empirical research agrees: in addition to activating regions specialized purely for linguistic purposes, reading also activates known multimodal regions of cortex (see e.g. Price and Friston 1997; Scott et al. 2000).

6. CONCLUSION

Our aim here has been on a target identified from high altitude. Stepping back from the many individual disagreements, the literature appears to show a growing consensus on how it is that fictions produce strong feelings in us, and a structurally identical convergence of opinion regarding how the imagination operates. Both lines of research seem to be leading to the view that a DCA is created when one imaginatively engages fictions, play scenarios, daydreams realms, or the like, and that this DCA is responsible for the emotional effects of the imagination.

Although the arguments for such a DCA are impressive, the literature was lacking a positive tracing of the causal pathway from the world to DCA to felt response. This we have provided. With this final bit of *terra incognita* mapped, we think that the arguments for the role of a DCA in the imaginative effects of the emotions have become as complete as they can reasonably be expected to be, and as impressive as any philosophical view ever is.

REFERENCES

AKINS, KATHLEEN (1996) 'Of Sensory Systems and the "Aboutness" of Mental States', *Journal of Philosophy*, 93, 337–72.

BECHARA, A., DAMASIO, A., DAMASIO, H., and ANDERSON, S. (1994) 'Insensitivity to Future Consequences following Damage to Human Prefrontal Cortex', *Cognition*, 50, 7–15.

BLOCK, NED (1995) 'On a Confusion about a Function of Consciousness', *Behavioral and Brain Sciences*, 18, 227–87.

BYRNE, ALEX (2001) 'Intentionalism Defended', *Philosophical Review*, 110, 199–240.

CABEZA, R., and NYBERG, L. (2000) 'Imaging Cognition II: An Empirical Review of 275 PET and fMRI Studies', *Journal of Cognitive Neuroscience*, 12, 1–47.

CARROLL, NOEL (1990) *The Philosophy of Horror or Paradoxes of the Heart* (New York: Routledge).

CHARLTON, WILLIAM (1986) 'Radford and Allen on Being Moved by Fiction: A Rejoinder', *British Journal of Aesthetics*, 26, 391–4.

CURRIE, GREGORY (1990) *The Nature of Fiction* (Cambridge: Cambridge University Press).

_____ (1997) 'The Paradox of Caring: Fiction and the Philosophy of Mind', in M. Hjort and S. Laver (eds.), *Emotion and the Arts* (Oxford: Oxford University Press), 63–77.

_____ and RAVENSCROFT, I. (2002) *Recreative Imagination* (Oxford: Oxford University Press).

DAMASIO, ANTONIO (1994) *Descartes' Error: Emotion, Reason and the Human Brain* (New York: G. P. Putnam).

DAVIDSON, DONALD (1980) *Essays on Actions and Events* (Oxford: Oxford University Press).

DELANCEY, CRAIG (2002) *Passionate Engines: What Emotions Reveal about Mind and Artificial Intelligence* (New York: Oxford University Press).

DRETSKE, FRED (1995) *Naturalizing the Mind* (Cambridge, Mass.: MIT Press).

DOUGHERTY, D., SHIN, L., ALPERT, N., PITMAN, R., ORR, S., LASKO, M., MACKLIN, M., FISCHMAN, A., and RAUCH, S. (1999) 'Anger in Healthy Men: A PET Study Using Script-Driven Imagery', *Biological Psychiatry*, 46, 466–72.

ELLIOTT, R., DOLAN, R., and FRITH, E. (2000) 'Dissociable Functions in the Medial and Lateral Orbitofrontal Cortex: Evidence from Human Neuroimaging Studies', *Cerebral Cortex*, 10, 308–17.

FEAGIN, S. (1996) *Reading with Feeling* (Ithaca, NY: Cornell University Press).

—— (1997) 'Imagining Emotions and Appreciating Fiction', in M. Hjort and S. Laver (eds.), *Emotion and the Arts* (Oxford: Oxford University Press), 50–62.

FODOR, JERRY (1998) *Concepts: Where Cognitive Science Went Wrong* (New York: Oxford University Press).

GOLDMAN, ALVIN (1989) 'Interpretation Psychologized', *Mind & Language*, 4, 161–85.

—— (1992) 'In Defense of the Simulation Theory', *Mind & Language*, 7, 104–19.

GORDON, ROBERT (1986) 'Folk Psychology as Simulation', *Mind & Language*, 1, 158–71.

—— and BARKER, J. (1994) 'Autism and the "Theory of Mind" debate', in G. Graham and G. L. Stephens (eds.), *Philosophical Psychopathology: A Book of Readings* (Cambridge, Mass.: MIT Press), 163–81.

GREEN, O. (1992) *The Emotions: A Philosophical Theory* (Dordrecht: Kluwer).

HARRIS, PAUL (2000) *The Work of the Imagination* (Oxford: Blackwell).

JEANNEROD, MARC (1997) *The Cognitive Neuroscience of Action* (Cambridge, Mass.: Blackwell).

KANDEL, ERIC, SCHWARTZ, JAMES, and JESSELL, THOMAS (2000) *Principles of Neural Science*, 4th edn. (New York: McGraw-Hill).

KOSSLYN, STEPHEN (1994) *Image and Brain: The Resolution of the Imagery Debate* (Cambridge, Mass.: MIT Press).

——ALPERT, N., THOMPSON, W., MALJOKOVIC, V., WEISE, S., CHABRIS, C., HAMILTON, S., RAUCH, S., and BUONNANO, E. (1993) 'Visual Mental Imagery Activates Topographically Organized Visual Cortex: PET Investigations', *Journal of Cognitive Neuroscience*, 5, 263–87.

LAMARQUE, PETER (1981) 'How Can We Fear and Pity Fictions?', *British Journal of Aesthetics*, 21, 291–304.

LANG, PETER, DAVIS, MICHAEL, and ÖHMAN, ARNE (2000) 'Fear and Anxiety: Animal Models and Human Cognitive Psychophysiology', *Journal of Affective Disorders*, 61, 137–59.

—— LEVIN, DANIEL, MILLER, GREGORY, and KOZAK, MICHAEL (1983) 'Fear Behavior, Fear Imagery, and the Psychophysiology of Emotion: The Problem of Affective Response Integration', *Journal of Abnormal Psychology*, 92, 276–306.

LEDOUX, JOSEPH (1996) *The Emotional Brain: The Mysterious Underpinnings of Emotional Life* (New York: Simon and Schuster).

—— (2000) 'Emotion Circuits in the Brain', *Annual Review of Neuroscience*, 23, 155–84.

LESLIE, ALAN (1987) 'Pretence and Representation: The Origins of "theory of mind"', *Psychological Review*, 94, 412–26.

LEVINSON, JERROLD (1997) 'Emotion in Response to Art', in M. Hjort and S. Laver (eds.), *Emotion and the Arts* (New York: Oxford University Press), 20–34.

LYCAN, WILLIAM (1987) *Consciousness* (Cambridge, Mass.: MIT Press).

MCCORMICK, PETER (1985) 'Feelings and Fictions', *Journal of Aesthetics and Art Criticism*, 43, 375–83.

MCDOWELL, JOHN (1994) *Mind and World* (Cambridge, Mass.: Harvard University Press).

MELLO, LUIZ, and VILLARES, JOÃO (1997) 'Neuroanatomy of the Basal Ganglia', *Psychiatric Clinics of North America*, 20, 691–704.

MESKIN, A., and WEINBERG, J. (2003) 'Emotions, Fiction, and Cognitive Architecture', *British Journal of Aesthetics*, 43, 18–34.

MIYAWAKI, E., PERLMUTTER, J., TROSTER, A., VIDEEN, T., and KOLLER, W. (2000) 'The Behavioral Complications of Pallidal Stimulation: A Case Report', *Brain and Cognition*, 42, 417–34.

MORILLO, C. (1990) 'The Reward Event and Motivation', *Journal of Philosophy*, 87, 169–86.

NEILL, ALEX (1993) 'Fiction and the Emotions', *American Philosophical Quarterly*, 30, 1–13.

NICHOLS, SHAUN (2004) 'Imagining and Believing: The Promise of a Single Code', *Journal of Aesthetics and Art Criticism*, 62, 129–39.

—— and STICH, S. (2003) *Mindreading* (Oxford: Oxford University Press).

O'DOHERTY, J., KRINGELBACH, M., ROLLS, E., HORNAK, J., and ANDREWS, C. (2001) 'Abstract Reward and Punishment Representations in the Human Orbitofrontal Cortex', *Nature Reviews Neuroscience*, 4, 95–102.

PANKSEPP, JAAK (1997) *Affective Neuroscience: The Foundations of Human and Animal Emotions* (New York: Oxford University Press).

PEACOCKE, CHRISTOPHER (1983) *Sense and Content: Experience, Thought and their Relations* (New York: Oxford University Press).

PRICE, C. J., and FRISTON, K. J. (1997) 'The Temporal Dynamics of Reading: A PET Study', *Proceedings of the Royal Society of London, Series B: Biological Sciences*, 264, 1785–91.

RADFORD, COLIN (1975) 'How Can We Be Moved by the Fate of Anna Karenina?', *Proceedings of the Aristotelian Society*, suppl. vol. 49, 67–80.

ROLLS, E. (2000) 'Orbitofrontal Cortex and Reward', *Cerebral Cortex*, 10, 284–94.

SCHROEDER, T. (2004) *Three Faces of Desire* (New York: Oxford University Press).

SCHULTZ, W., TREMBLAY, L., and HOLLERMAN, J. (2000) 'Reward Processing in Primale Orbitofrontal Cortex and Basal Ganglia', *Cerebral Cortex*, 10, 272–83.

SCOTT, S., BLANK, C., ROSEN, S., and WISE, R. (2000) 'Identification of a Pathway for Intelligible Speech in the Left Temporal Lobe', *Brain*, 123, 2400–6.

SCRUTON, ROGER (1974) *Art and Imagination: A Study in the Philosophy of Mind* (New York: Barnes and Noble).

SEARLE, JOHN (1992) *The Rediscovery of the Mind* (Cambridge, Mass.: MIT Press).

SPRENGELMEYER, R., YOUNG, A., SCHROEDER, U., GROSSENBACHER, P., FEDERLEIN, J., BUTTNER, T., and PRZUNTEK, H. (1999) 'Knowing No Fear', *Proceedings of the Royal Society of London, Series B: Biological Sciences*, 266, 2451–6.

TEASDALE, J., HOWARD, R., COX, S., HA, Y., BRAMMER, M., WILLIAMS, S., and CHECKLEY, S. (1999) 'Functional MRI Study of the Cognitive Generation of Affect', *American Journal of Psychiatry*, 156, 209–15.

THUT, G., SCHULTZ, W., ROELCKE, U., NIENHUSMEIER, M., MISSIMIES, J., MAGUIRE, R., and LEENDERS, K. (1997) 'Activation of the Human Brain by Monetary Reward', *Neuroreport*, 8, 1225–8.

TYE, MICHAEL (1995) *Ten Problems of Consciousness* (Cambridge, Mass.: MIT Press).

WALTON, KENDALL (1978) 'Fearing Fictions', *Journal of Philosophy*, 75, 5–27.

___ (1990) *Mimesis as Make Believe* (Cambridge, Mass.: Harvard University Press).

___ (1997) 'Spelunking, Simulation, and Slime: On Being Moved by Fiction', in M. Hjort and S. Laver (eds.), *Emotion and the Arts* (New York: Oxford University Press), 37–49.

WORTH, SARAH (2000) 'Aristotle, Thought, and Mimesis: Our Responses to Fiction', *Journal of Aesthetics and Art Criticism*, 58, 333–9.

YANAL, ROBERT J. (1994) 'The Paradox of Emotion and Fiction', *Pacific Philosophical Quarterly*, 75, 54–75.

___ (1999) *Paradoxes of Emotion and Fiction* (University Park: Pennsylvania State University Press).

ZATORRE, R., HALPERN, A., PERRY, D., MEYER, E., and EVANS, A. (1996) 'Hearing in the Mind's Ear: A PET Investigation of Musical Imagery and Perception', *Journal of Cognitive Neuroscience*, 8, 29–46.

ZEMACH, EDDY (1996) 'Emotion and Fictional Beings', *Journal of Aesthetics and Art Criticism*, 54, 41–8.

3

Imagination and Simulation in Audience Responses to Fiction

Alvin Goldman

A central problem in contemporary aesthetic theory is the psychology of consumers of fiction. What cognitive processes or mechanisms are activated or engaged when people read novels or observe films, television, and theatrical productions? One question here is how to make sense of the fact that consumers of fiction get emotionally involved in, or have affective reactions to, fictional works. This is puzzling, because consumers know that the described or depicted scenarios are not actual; they are merely fiction. So why do the works engage their emotions? Can we make sense of the empathy they ostensibly display vis-à-vis characters in these works? Fiction focuses heavily on the mental states of the characters it portrays, their aspirations, motivations, feelings, and the like. So it wouldn't be surprising if the cognitive mechanisms utilized by consumers of fiction overlap with those used in detecting and responding to the mental states of real people (mindreading). Exactly how extensive this overlap is, however, and what it implies about engagements with fiction, remains to be explored.

1. SUPPOSITIONAL AND ENACTMENT IMAGINATION

Mental engagement with fiction involves the imagination, at least to a minimal extent. The reader or observer must imagine that certain states of affairs or scenarios *p*, *q*, and *r*—scenarios depicted in the narrative work—are happening or have happened. This is not 'pure' imagination, perhaps, because the reader/observer's mental representation of the scenario is partly guided by actions and scenes actually perceived (on stage or screen) or verbally described by someone else (the author). Still, we may presume that every consumer of a fictional work recognizes that what is shown or related is intended to depict a fictional series of events. The consumer is invited to *suppose* that such-and-such occurs, in the absence of evidence that it actually does occur and despite disbelieving (in the typical case) that it actually occurs. This mental act of supposition is what I mean by the 'minimal' sense in which consuming fiction involves imagination. Let us call this type of imagination *supposition-imagination*

(S-imagination). S-imagination is typically formulated with a 'that'-clause, 'X imagines that p', where p can refer, unrestrictedly, to any sort of state-of-affairs. To S-imagine that p is to entertain the hypothesis that p, to posit that p, to assume that p. Unlike some forms of imagination, S-imagination has no sensory aspect; it is purely conceptual.

By contrast with the notion of S-imagination, I want to introduce the concept of *enactment-imagination* (E-imagination). Elsewhere I introduce this notion in connection with mindreading, and specifically, the simulation approach to mindreading (Goldman 2006; cf. Currie and Ravenscroft 2002). But it isn't inherently related to mindreading. Enactment-imagination is a matter of creating or trying to create in one's own mind a selected mental state, or at least a rough facsimile of such a state, through the faculty of imagination. Prime examples of E-imagination include sensory forms of imagination, where one creates, through imagination, perception-like states. Acts of visual and auditory imagination, which involve the production of vision-like or hearing-like states, are familiar types of E-imagination. Another type of E-imagination is motor imagination, where one produces action-directed representational states, without intending to execute the selected action. The term 'imagery' is commonly applied to these cases; there is visual imagery, auditory imagery, and motor imagery. (Motor imagery is less familiar introspectively, because it is only minimally conscious.) Not all modes of E-imagination, however, involve imagery.

Is it true that episodes of visual, auditory, and motor imagery are facsimiles of seeing, hearing, and issuing motor commands respectively? Do these imagination-generated states really *resemble,* to any appreciable degree, the percepts produced by genuine perception or the representations involved in genuine motor execution? Both behavioral studies and cognitive neuroscience provide extensive evidence of such similarities. Let me give some sample pieces of such evidence (for more extensive presentation of the evidence, see Goldman 2006: ch. 7).

It may seem unlikely that visualizing a scene corresponds at all closely to seeing that scene, because seeing usually involves saccadic eye movements whereby the objects are scanned. Where there is no scene to be scanned, isn't this important part of seeing omitted? No. Michael Spivey et al. (2000) had subjects listen to spoken scene descriptions while their eye movements were tracked by a hidden camera. Their eyes tended to move in directions that accorded with the directionality of the scene described. A downward story, for example, was a vignette in which someone is described as standing at the top of a canyon watching people rappel down to the canyon floor. In four critical stories, the average proportion of eye movements in a preferred direction was significantly greater than the average proportion of eye movements in the unpreferred directions. Thus, subjects apparently *enacted* seeing so robustly that their enactment was not confined to pure imagination, but extended to oculomotor activity as well.

Turning to cognitive neuroscience, it is established that a region of the brain called the fusiform gyrus is distinctively activated when we see faces. The same region is also activated when we imagine faces (Kanwisher et al. 1997; O'Craven and Kanwisher 2000). Lesions to the fusiform face area impair both face recognition ability and the ability to imagine faces (Damasio et al. 1990; Young et al. 1994). Stephen Kosslyn has been the leading researcher defending the neural overlap between vision and visual imagery. Kosslyn concedes that only some processes used in vision are also used in visual imagery (Kosslyn 1994: 329–34; Kosslyn et al. 1997). This is not surprising, given that imagery relies on previously organized and stored information, whereas perception requires performance of all aspects of figure–ground segregation, recognition, and identification. In particular, we should not expect imagery to share low-level processes involved in organizing sensory input. Kosslyn et al. (1997) identified subsystems that perform high-level visual processing tasks in the analysis of perceptual or imagistic materials, and found that two-thirds of the activated areas were activated in common. I would consider this to be substantial similarity between the neural substrates of vision and visual imagery, respectively.

The evidence for similarities between motor execution and motor imagination are, if anything, more striking. In ordinary manipulation of objects, each hand is controlled by its opposite (contralateral) cerebral hemisphere. Parsons et al. (1998) showed that imaginative processes for the two hands are similarly controlled by their opposite hemispheres. Imagining a movement for a given hand appears to be executed by the same cerebral mechanism that executes ordinary movements of that hand. Sirigu et al. (1995) tested a subject who had motor cortex damage related to finger movements on one of her hands. One test involved a finger movement task to keep up with a metronome. In her actual performance, the subject's maximum speeds were 90 beats with the impaired hand and 170 beats with the intact hand. Doing the tasks in imagination, her maximum speeds were 95 beats with the impaired hand and 160 beats with the intact hand—remarkably similar. This suggests the use of the same mechanisms and processes for both execution and imagination.

A rather different example involves enhancement in athletic performance from mere motor imagination. Yue and Cole (1992) had subjects generate motor imagery of training, and compared their increases in muscular strength from such imagery with the increase in subjects who actually trained. Actual training produced a 30 percent increase in maximal force; motor imagery produced a 22 percent increase. This effect is solely the result of cortical activity, not covert muscular activity, because subjects did not make covert muscular contractions during motor imagery.

Thus, imagination uses very similar processes and/or produces very similar outputs across an interesting pair of domains. Analogous processes and outputs engaged by imagination have been less intensively studied in other domains. But it certainly appears that E-imagination, as we have defined it, is a robust phenomenon. E-imaginative events have substantial similarities—including functional similarities—to their actual counterparts across an interesting array of domains.

Let us now return to S-imagination. How is it related to E-imagination? One possible approach holds that there are two distinct kinds of imagination, with no essential connection to one another. S-imagination is *sui generis*, a type of imagination different from, and irreducible to, E-imagination. A second possible approach holds that E-imagination is the fundamental kind of imagination, and that S-imagination is simply one species of it. Which species? It is the species in which the mental state enacted is belief. Supposing that p is E-imagining believing that p. Of course, this implies that some species of E-imagination involve no imagery. But that seems fully acceptable; there is no reason to tie E-imagination to the having of imagery. We should leave room for such states as E-imagining hoping that p, E-imagining intending to A, etc., all of which states are also devoid of imagery. I shall not make a firm choice between these alternative construals of S-imagination. In either case, there is a substantial difference between the view that S-imagination covers all important uses of imagination in the consumption of fiction and the view that E-imagination (even in its non-suppositional variants) is essential to the consumption and appreciation of fiction.

2. COMPETING EXPLANATIONS OF IMAGINATION-INDUCED AFFECT

Which approach to the imagination's role in the cognizing of fiction is most promising: one that centers entirely on S-imagination, or one that emphasizes the role of E-imagination in its non-suppositional variants? Let's examine a specific proposal that develops the S-imagination approach, a proposal of Shaun Nichols (2004).

Nichols adopts a cognitive architecture developed elsewhere with Stephen Stich (Nichols and Stich 2003) and applies it to the role of imagination in fiction. Their architecture countenances supposition but not E-imagination. The architecture is presented in boxological terms, where each box depicts a cognitive system or kind of state. For present purposes we can focus on three boxes: the belief box, the desire box, and the possible world box, later called by Nichols the pretend box. Each box is understood to specify a distinct functional role. The boxes can contain representation tokens. In the case of the pretend box, the job of the tokens is not to represent the world as it is, but to represent what the world would be like given some set of 'assumptions' (Nichols and Stich 2003: 28). Nichols and Stich speak of the pretend box as containing pretense 'premises' (2003: 29). The language of 'assumptions' and 'premises' clearly intimates supposition rather than E-imagination more generally. Moreover, they elsewhere express skepticism about the existence of pretend desire (Nichols and

Stich 2000), which again suggests a restriction of pretense to pretend belief, i.e. supposition. Although I have allowed the possibility that supposition might be a species of E-imagination, I don't think that Nichols and Stich share my conception of E-imagination. So Nichols's approach to imagination and fiction seems quite different from the one I contemplate (and will elaborate upon below).

The first question, then, is whether Nichols's 'thin' conception of imagination, viz. supposition, accounts adequately for imagination's role in the experience of fiction. Returning to his boxological approach, what is the difference between belief representations (i.e. representations in the belief box) and pretense representations (i.e. representations in the pretense box)? Not the *content* of the representations, says Nichols, because pretense representations and beliefs can have exactly the same content. The natural cognitivist proposal, he says, is that pretend representations differ from belief representations by their *function* (Nichols 2004: 130). Just as desires are distinguished from beliefs by their characteristic functional roles, so pretenses are distinguished from beliefs by their functional roles. One thing they have in common, though, is that both kinds of representations use the 'same code'. This is a crucial theme in his paper entitled 'Imagining and Believing: The Promise of a Single Code'. Here is why sameness of code is important, says Nichols:

If pretense representations and beliefs are in the same code, then mechanisms that take input from the pretense box and from the belief box will treat parallel representations much the same way. For instance, if a mechanism takes pretense representations as input, the single-code hypothesis maintains that if that mechanism is *activated* by the occurrent belief that p, it will also be activated by the occurrent pretense representation that p. More generally, for any mechanism that takes input from both the pretense box and the belief box, the pretense representation p will be processed much the same way as the belief representation p. I will count any theory that makes this claim as a 'single-code' theory. (2004: 131)

Nichols applies the single-code theory to his explanatory project in the theory of fiction. He wants to explain why pretense representations used by consumers of fiction have comparable affective consequences to belief representations. His answer is to invoke the single-code hypothesis:

According to the single-code hypothesis ... the emotional systems will respond to pretense representations much as they do to parallel beliefs. That is, if the pretense representation that p gets processed by an affective mechanism, the affective outputs should parallel those of the belief that p. (2004: 131)

So, Nichols proposes to explain the fact that pretense representations are processed by affective systems in 'much the same way' as beliefs by appeal to the fact that the two types of representations use the same code.

This purported explanation is unconvincing. It's in the nature of an explanation, I'll assume, that the explaining facts (the *explanans*) should imply, or at least make probable, the fact to be explained (the *explanandum*). How does this apply here? It would have to be the case that if two tokens of the same representation, in one and the same code, are housed or contained in two different states (or boxes), then it's either guaranteed or quite probable that these representations will be processed equivalently by cognitive mechanisms. Is this plausible?

I think not. As we've seen, talk of cognitive 'boxes' is talk of functional roles. Different boxes have different functional roles associated with them, and this applies to the pretense and belief boxes. Now, functional roles are specified largely by dispositions to interact with other states and mechanisms in the larger cognitive system. Since pretense differs from belief in functional role, why should it be true that 'for any mechanism that takes input from both the pretense box and the belief box, the pretense representation p will be processed much the same way as the belief representation p'? It could happen, of course, that some selected mechanism would process a pretense representation p and a belief representation p equivalently. But why is this implied, predicted, or made probable, for a random mechanism? Having a representation in a given code is only one component of the complex state of affairs (the propositional attitude token). Another component is the box that contains the representation, i.e. the attitude type. Why is sameness of code *sufficient* to guarantee, or even make probable, the equivalence of treatment by processing mechanisms? On the contrary, one would think that the distinctive functional role associated with each box or attitude type would also be relevant. And it would tilt in the general direction of difference in treatment. So why does sameness of code imply, or make probable, sameness of treatment?

Let's reflect more on Nichols's proposal. Consider the case of desire and belief. Desire representations and belief representations should also share the same code. Otherwise, how could desires and beliefs 'talk' to one another, which they have to do when a person executes practical reasoning? Despite a shared code, desires and beliefs with the same content (believing that p and desiring that p) are certainly not processed in an equivalent way. By parity of thinking, why should pretenses and beliefs be processed in an equivalent way? Or take a second example. Agnosticism is a distinct attitude type from belief. In the Nichols–Stich approach to cognitive architecture, there should therefore be a belief box and an agnosticism box, and their respective representations would surely use the same code. But this hardly makes it reasonable to expect content-equivalent inputs from these two boxes to generate equivalent outputs.

Now let us consider the E-imagination approach. Fundamental to the E-imagination approach is that pretense, or imagination, isn't yet another mental state category, analogous to belief, desire, fear, and so forth. Rather, E-imagination is a method or faculty that causes mental states of the various categories. Instead of causing them in a 'primary' way (each mental state type has its own distinctive cluster of primary causes), E-imagination is a 'secondary' way of causing tokens of the same (or a very similar) type. A familiar kind of

E-imaginative causation is causation by the *will*. Somehow (and the details are murky) one can successfully will to have a visual experience as of seeing the surf at the beach, despite having no current perceptual access to any beach. Admittedly, a good image of the surf requires more than the will alone. One also needs information stored in visual memory about what the surf looks like. If one has never seen the surf, either directly or in pictures, one's willed image probably won't approximate a percept of the surf.

E-imagination isn't always triggered by the will; that may not even be the most common mode of triggering. An avid surfer who hears someone else utter the word 'surf' might have an involuntary image of the surf spring to mind. This is still the product of E-imagination. Whichever way visual E-imagination is triggered, it can generate a state that resembles a counterpart perceptual state. Importantly, the imagined state resembles its perceptual counterpart not only in their shared *code* and *content*, but in a shared kind of *state*, in this instance a *visual* kind of state. State resemblance is what Nichols's approach neglects. Sharing a kind of state (which frequently reflects a sharing of neural substrate) normally implies *some* downstream causal similarities. Among the downstream causal similarities in the surf case is probably the activation of action propensities that would prepare the agent for interacting with the represented scene in appropriate ways. For an avid surfer, this would mean mental preparations for maneuvering a surfboard in specific ways. Of course, merely having a visual image of the surf doesn't lead to actual surfing behavior. But this might equally be true of seeing the surf. Perhaps no surfboard is available; perhaps one sees the surf on television; or perhaps one's leg is in a cast that makes surfing impossible. Still, similar modes of mental action preparation would flow both from seeing the surf and from having a visual image of the surf. Once we recognize this general characteristic of states generated by E-imagination, we can approach the effects of imagination in the consumption of fiction more fruitfully.

To illustrate the idea, let's borrow a familiar example from the aesthetics literature, Kendall Walton's (1997) spelunking example. Walton writes as follows:

Imagine going on a spelunking expedition. You lower yourself into a hole in the ground and enter a dank, winding passageway. After a couple of bends there is absolute pitch darkness. You light the carbide lamp on your helmet and continue. The passage narrows. You squeeze between the walls. After a while you have to stoop, and then crawl on your hands and knees. On and on, for hours, twisting and turning and descending. Your companion, following behind you, began the trip with enthusiasm and confidence; in fact she talked you into it. But you notice an increasingly nervous edge in her voice. Eventually, the ceiling gets too low even for crawling; you wriggle on your belly. Even so, there isn't room for the pack on your back. You slip it off, reach back, and tie it to your foot; then continue, dragging the pack behind you. The passage bends sharply to the left, as it descends further. You contort your body, adjusting the angles of your shoulders and pelvis, and squeeze around and down. Now your companion is really panicked. Your lamp flickers a few times, then goes out. Absolute pitch darkness. You fumble with the mechanism . . . . (1997: 39)

As Walton remarks, this experiment demonstrates the power of the imagination. When composing the paragraph, he says, he found his imaginative experience genuinely distressing; it gave him the shivers. What accounts for this?

Walton's explanation is that his imagining the spelunking expedition tapped into his actual personality and character, and that's why it affected him as it did. Imagining the expedition released psychological mechanisms he really possesses, and brought on genuine distress. I don't disagree with this explanation, as far as it goes, but it doesn't plumb deeply enough. It doesn't explain why merely imagining the spelunking episode triggered the same psychological mechanisms that actually experiencing the described episode would have triggered. The further explanation is straightforward, and fits precisely with what I have been arguing; but it needs to be added to complete the explanation. The reason why imagining the episode and really experiencing the episode trigger the same psychological mechanisms (which in turn yield the affective responses) is that the real experience and the E-imagining of it (when accurate) are intrinsically pretty similar. With their neural similarities, the imagining state is wired into many of the same neural circuits as the state that would occur if the episode were real. So it is understandable that they should produce some of the same downstream consequences. The whole idea of E-imagination is that it is capable of producing (when guided by suitable information) states with these sorts of similarities to states produced in 'primary' ways. Imagination simulates, or replicates, in many important respects, the hypothetical situation as it would transpire.

Am I ascribing excessive powers to E-imagination? Colin McGinn would probably say so. Although McGinn (2004: ch. 1) credits the imagination with a great deal of power and importance, he views the outputs of imagination (images) as quite different from the outputs of perception (percepts). First, images, unlike percepts, are subject to the will, and hence are mental *actions*, which percepts aren't. Second, percepts are informative about the world, whereas images aren't, because the latter contain only what their subject intentionally bestows upon them. Third, there are a variety of phenomenological differences between images and percepts. McGinn sums this up by saying that images differ 'dramatically' from percepts (2004: 41). This is why I think he would object to my characterization.

But McGinn's characterization, examined more carefully, does not warrant the conclusion that images differ dramatically from percepts, especially not in *intrinsic* terms. McGinn agrees that being the product of the will versus the environment is only an extrinsic difference, not an intrinsic difference, between images and percepts. Moreover, as he acknowledges, images aren't always caused by the will. So, the difference between being caused by the will and being caused otherwise is a difference that distinguishes among visual state *tokens*, not visual state *types* (at least not intrinsic types), as McGinn seems to think. Second, the different epistemological status of images and percepts is a direct result of their extrinsic differences, not of any intrinsic differences. It's because they are (often) the product of the will that images aren't informative about the world. With respect to the phenomenological differences that McGinn presents, some of them I find questionable (though there isn't room to pursue this in detail), and others simply flow from the different psychological and neurological characteristics we conceded earlier. Despite these differences, there are many significant similarities, which are more fully documented in the scientific literature (see Kosslyn 1994; Palmer 1999: 607–13; Goldman 2006: sect. 7.3).

3. INTERPERSONAL SIMULATION IN FICTION

I have been arguing that E-imagination, rather than merely S-imagination, is an important component in the cognitive processes associated with the consumption of fiction. As I have defined E-imagination, however, it has no essential connection to interpersonal mental simulation, i.e. to the activity of putting yourself in the mental shoes of *others*, or 'identifying' with them. Yet this is a very tempting story to tell about how readers or spectators get involved in works of fiction. They put themselves into the characters' shoes, and try to 're-live' their lives. There has been no shortage of theorists who have advanced this idea. Gregory Currie has held that simulation is central both to working out what is fictionally the case, primarily with respect to a character's experience, and to how and why we care about and affectively respond to fictional characters (Currie 1995: 153–4). Similarly, Susan Feagin (1996) argues that although there are important differences between empathizing with real people and empathizing with fictional characters, simulation underlies both types of empathy.

Noel Carroll, by contrast, rejects the view that our engagement with fiction typically involves taking up characters' points of view or simulating characters' psychological states (Carroll 1990, 1998, 2001). He writes:

We do not typically emote with respect to fictions by simulating a character's mental state; rather . . . we respond emotionally to fiction from the outside. Our point of view is that of an observer of a situation and not . . . that of the participant in the situation. When a character is about to be ambushed, we feel fear for her; we do not imagine ourselves to be her and then experience 'her' fear. (2001: 311–12)

Carroll offers several arguments in support of this position (instructively summarized in Coplan 2004). First, readers' emotions have different objects from those of the characters. We feel *for* the character, which isn't the same as simulating her fear. Second, readers often have different (usually, more) information than the characters do, which commonly generates different emotions. In the opening sequence of *Jaws*, viewers who know that a killer shark is nearby have different emotions than the character swimming in the water, who is happy and carefree in her ignorance. Third, readers often experience desires and preferences with regard to narrative outcomes that differ from the desires and preferences of the characters. Even when we care about the characters, we do not necessarily want them to get what they want.

These are good reasons to challenge the notion that the reader or observer of a fictional narrative usually adopts the perspective or position of a character or protagonist. But characters aren't the only candidates for the 'targets' of simulation by consumers of fiction. Currie (1997) has advanced a different, and to my mind more plausible, account: viz. that one usually adopts the position of a hypothetical 'reader of fact' (or observer of fact). This is a hypothetical person who observes or learns of the events portrayed in the narrative as if these events were facts (unlike a real reader or filmgoer who encounters the events as segments of a work of fiction). A fictional work, like a novel or a film, is presented at the entry level as an account of a series of events as if they were happening or did happen. This is not to suggest that an optimal aesthetic appreciation of the work accrues from adopting this simple perspective on the narrative to the exclusion of any other. Still, it is hard to follow a narrative at all, to imbibe what it is intended to convey, without using this perspective as a *baseline* for all further responses to the work. A typical narrative text or film is a *prop* that induces one to adopt the factual reader or factual observer perspective. Films make it highly compelling—at least in a prereflective, precritical stance—that one is seeing an unfolding scenario from the camera's perspective. It takes no creativity to E-imagine being such a hypothetical observer; the filmic medium makes it difficult to avoid being such, which helps account for its power. In Walton's (1990) terminology, it is difficult to avoid 'making believe' as a simulative response. Again, I do not suggest that taking the perspective of a hypothetical reader or observer of fact exhausts the stance of an actual reader or viewer, especially a sensitive one; but it's an important part of an actual consumer's stance.

The hypothetical-observer-of-fact theory readily accommodates Carroll's points. A hypothetical observer commonly has different information about the goings-on than do characters, and this breeds different emotions or emotional objects. A hypothetical observer of the *Jaws* scenario knows that a shark is around, and therefore feels fear *for* the swimmer; he doesn't feel *her* fear, because she doesn't have any. At the same time, the actual observer (who is simulating the hypothetical observer) feels fear, at least simulated fear, because E-imagined or make-believe knowledge that a shark is around produces (when fed into suitable emotion-generating equipment) fear or fear-like output. Cognitive mechanisms that operate on E-imagined input states produce roughly the same sorts of outputs as their genuine, non-imagined counterpart inputs produce.

None of this precludes the idea that there is also perspective taking of characters. Either the reader or observer 'directly' simulates a character, or she simulates a hypothetical-observer-of-fact simulating a character. The latter, indirect possibility is a bit more baroque, though by no means impossible, so

I shall focus on the former possibility. There is empirical research, summarized by Harris (2000) and by Coplan (2004), that people who read narratives track the perspective of one or more protagonists. This research supports the idea that character simulation is a common form of mental engagement with fiction.

Rinck and Bower (1995) had subjects memorize the diagram of a building and objects located within it. Then they had their subjects read narratives describing characters' movements and activities within the building. While reading, they were probed with sentences referring to memorized objects in the building's rooms. The consistent finding was that readers processed more quickly sentences describing objects close to the current location of the protagonist. The interpretation was that readers were experiencing the narrative from the spatiotemporal standpoint of the protagonist, and were moving through the building 'with' the protagonist. Other studies by Black et al. (1979), Bryant et al. (1992), and Rall and Harris (2000) lend further support to this idea. Finally, Gernsbacher, Goldsmith, and Robertson (1992) did a series of experiments indicating that readers often process the emotional implications of narrative events from the standpoint of one of the protagonists. Subjects read narratives in which a central character was likely to feel a particular emotion. They were then probed with target sentences, which included emotion terms that either matched the emotional state of the character or did not match it. They hypothesized that if readers appraise narrative events from the character's perspective, then target sentences matching the character's emotions should be processed more quickly than sentences not matching it. This is exactly what they found. A study by Harris and Martin (unpublished) provides additional support for the simulation, or empathizing, account (see Harris 2000: 70).

Matthew Kieran has offered a number of objections to the simulation theory of fictional engagement as *he* construes it (a construal responsive to earlier claims by simulationists like Currie and Feagin). Kieran considers the following two-part claim:

(1) When I want to really understand the nature of a character's experience and their attitude toward their own experience (what their character is really like), then I need to simulate. A deep understanding of fictional characters requires simulation, though a shallow understanding of them need not.

(2) In order to capture the full nature of our affective responses to a narrative, we must understand the simulation process that we go through as readers—because that simulation process is central to our acquiring an understanding of characters.

(Kieran 2003: 69–70)

Kieran denies that an understanding of characters requires me, as reader, to imagine myself in their shoes. It doesn't even require me to simulate the narrator or other hypothetical observer of the scene. To support these claims, Kieran presents the opening of Dickens's *Hard Times*, which portrays Gradgrind delivering some emphatic statements about his teaching philosophy. Gradgrind's appearance and speaking mannerisms are described in vivid detail. Kieran claims that our understanding of, and affective response to, Gradgrind do not require simulation.

A wise simulationist should first respond by objecting to Kieran's formulations of the 'simulation thesis' as unnecessarily strong in certain respects. They are phrased in terms of simulation being 'needed' or 'required' for understanding. A simulationist might respond that simulation is something readers naturally *do*, even if it isn't something they are required to do to achieve understanding. She might add that when Kieran concludes that we acquire a deep and sophisticated understanding of Gradgrind just by making inferences (not Kieran's exact wording) from Dickens's description of him, how does Kieran purport to know this? The question of simulation versus inference is the nub of the simulation theory/theory-theory dispute, a matter not readily settled in the armchair. So Kieran is not entitled to conclude that simulation by the reader isn't needed, or isn't used. Finally, turning to the second part of Kieran's formulation of the simulation thesis, concerning affective responses, the *Hard Times* passage is a weak example for Kieran's purposes. Dickens's description of Gradgrind portrays his appearance as square-legged, square-shouldered, and hard set, his carriage as obstinate, and his voice as inflexible, dry, and dictatorial. Introspectively, my affective reaction to these descriptions seems to arise from the visual and auditory imagery I create in my mind of Gradgrind's appearance and speech. In other words, I imagine myself being present in the schoolroom and witnessing the scene described by Dickens. Whether or not I *need* to imagine this to elicit these affective reactions, it seems to me that I actually do it, contrary to what Kieran implies.

4. AUTOMATIC RESONANCE RESPONSES TO DRAMATIZED WORKS

I have been arguing that immersion in a work of fiction typically involves a certain type of cognitive activity: viz. E-imagining in its interpersonal variant. One's imaginative powers are enlisted to create a series of states in the self that are intended to correspond to a series of states of some person or persons associated with a fictional work. (Of course, neither the persons in question nor the series of states in question are actual, in the typical case, so the correspondence relation is merely an intentional one. But that's OK.) Another class of cognitive activities is also important in our responses to fiction, but probably restricted to dramatized works that are viewed on stage or screen, or audio productions that are heard. This class of cognitive activities may also be considered 'simulational', though they don't involve the faculty of imagination (Goldman 2006).

The cognitive activities in question are examples of 'mirroring' or 'resonance' mechanisms. The discovery of these types of mechanisms is due to a group of Italian neuroscientists led by Giacomo Rizzolatti. Mirror systems were initially discovered in the motor domain. In the premotor cortex of the monkey's brain, individual neurons are specially dedicated to the planning or preparation of specific types of movement: e.g. grasping, holding, or tearing. When one individual observes a second individual execute one of those actions, e.g. grasping, a particular subset of the observer's grasp-related neurons also fire (but don't usually produce imitative behavior). Those neurons that display this observation–execution matching property were dubbed 'mirror neurons' (Rizzolatti et al. 1996; Gallese et al. 1996). Similar systems in humans were also identified, using more inferential techniques, rather than single-cell recordings. A much wider range of mirroring systems have now been discovered, in which neural substrates associated with certain mental states and behavioral manifestations thereof prompt an observer's system to 'resonate' with activation of matching substrates in her own brain. For example, part of the somatosensory cortex of the brain that is activated when one's own body is touched is also activated when one merely observes another individual being touched (Keysers et al. 2004). Similarly, when one person's facial expression manifesting a certain emotion, such as fear or disgust, is observed by a second person, the second person automatically undergoes an experience of the matching emotion (Wicker et al. 2003). The observer's emotion usually occurs at a sub-threshold level; that is, it is quite attenuated, so it doesn't reach, or barely reaches, the level of consciousness. I call this interpersonal mental matching 'low-level' simulation (Goldman 2006: ch. 6). It contrasts with 'high-level' simulation, which I associate with the process of interpersonal E-imagination, as discussed earlier. Whereas E-imagination is often guided by the will, simulation of the mirroring, or resonance, variety is entirely involuntary. It is also confined (so far as is known) to observational modalities, i.e. sight and audition (see Kohler et al. 2002, for the auditory modality).

It is a further question whether mirroring, or resonance, simulation is used in mindreading. I think the answer to this question is affirmative. The category for which the evidence is strongest is the reading of other people's emotional states from their observed facial expressions (Goldman and Sripada 2005; Goldman 2006: ch. 6). The evidence that supports this mindreading conclusion is intricate, however, and I won't review it here. But it does support the notion that one strand of our understanding of others' mental states is based on automatic resonance, which might also be called 'empathy' (Gallese 2001; Gallese et al. 2004).

If all of the foregoing is correct, it seems likely that works of the performing arts in which expressions of feelings and emotions are seen or heard will produce a distinctive impact on viewers or listeners. Audience members will experience the same sorts of feelings and emotions as the characters (or the actors that portray them), though at an attenuated or minimally conscious level. In other words, in one sense of the term 'empathy', they undergo empathy with the characters seen or heard. In different terminology, the actors' feelings and emotions have contagious effects on the audience. This is not an unprecedented insight. The novelty is that now there is a better scientific understanding of the phenomenon, which makes it harder to mount skeptical assaults on its reality and robustness. This enlarges our picture of how simulational mechanisms, of one kind or another, play important roles in audience reactions to works of fiction, especially when these are dramatized in a perceptually accessible medium.

REFERENCES

BLACK, J. B., TURNER, T. J., and BOWER, G. H. (1979) 'Point of View in Narrative Comprehension, Memory, and Production', *Journal of Verbal Learning and Behavior*, 18, 187–98.

BRYANT, D. J., TVERSKY, B., and FRANKLIN, N. (1992) 'Internal and External Spatial Frameworks for Representing Described Scenes', *Journal of Memory and Language*, 31, 74–98.

CARROLL, NOEL (1990) *The Philosophy of Horror, or Paradoxes of the Heart* (London: Routledge).

——— (1998) *A Philosophy of Mass Art* (New York: Oxford University Press).

——— (2001) *Beyond Aesthetics: Philosophical Essays* (Cambridge: Cambridge University Press).

COPLAN, A. (2004) 'Empathic Engagement with Narrative Fictions', *Journal of Aesthetics and Art Criticism*, 62, 141–52.

CURRIE, GREGORY (1995) *Image and Mind: Film, Philosophy and Cognitive Science* (Cambridge: Cambridge University Press).

——— (1997) 'The Paradox of Caring: Fiction and the Philosophy of Mind', in M. Hjort and S. Laver (eds.), *Emotion and the Arts* (New York: Oxford University Press), 63–77.

——— and RAVENSCROFT, IAN (2002) *Recreative Minds* (Oxford: Oxford University Press).

DAMASIO, A. R., TRANEL, D., and DAMASIO, H. (1990) 'Face Agnosia and the Neural Substrates of Memory', *Annual Review of Neuroscience*, 13, 89–109.

FEAGIN, SUSAN (1996) *Reading with Feeling: The Aesthetics of Appreciation* (Ithaca, NY: Cornell University Press).

GALLESE, V. (2001) 'The "Shared Manifold" Hypothesis: From Mirror Neurons to Empathy', *Journal of Consciousness Studies*, 8 (5–7), 33–50.

——— FADIGA, L., FOGASSI, L., and RIZZOLATTI, G. (1996) 'Action Recognition in the Premotor Cortex', *Brain*, 119, 593–609.

——— KEYSERS, C., and RIZZOLATTI, G. (2004) 'A Unifying View of the Basis of Social Cognition', *Trends in Cognitive Sciences*, 8, 396–403.

GERNSBACHER, M. A., GOLDSMITH, H. H., and ROBERTSON, R. R. W. (1992) 'Do Readers Mentally Represent Characters' Emotional States?', *Cognition and Emotion*, 6, 89–111.

GOLDMAN, ALVIN (2006) *Simulating Minds: The Philosophy, Psychology, and Neuroscience of Mindreading* (New York: Oxford University Press).

——— and SRIPADA, C. (2005) 'Simulationist Models of Face-based Emotion Recognition', *Cognition*, 94, 193–213.

HARRIS, PAUL L. (2000) *The Work of the Imagination* (Malden, Mass.: Blackwell).

———and MARTIN, L. (unpublished) 'From Little Red Riding Hood to Othello: Empathizing with a Naïve Protagonist'.

KANWISHER, N., McDERMOTT, J., and CHUN, M. M. (1997) 'The Fusiform Face Area: A Module in Human Extrastriate Cortex Specialized for Face Perception', *Journal of Neuroscience*, 17, 4302–11.

KEYSERS, C., WICKER, B., GAZZOLA, V., ANTON, J.-L., FOGASSI, L., and GALLESE, V. (2004) 'A Touching Sight: SII/PV Activation during the Observation of Touch', *Neuron*, 42, 335–46.

KIERAN, M. (2003) 'In Search of a Narrative', in M. Kieran and D. M. Lopes (eds.), *Imagination, Philosophy, and the Arts* (London: Routledge), 69–87.

KOHLER, E., KEYSERS, C., UMILTA, M. A., FOGASSI, L., GALLESE, V., and RIZZOLATTI, G. (2002) 'Hearing Sounds, Understanding Actions: Action Representation in Mirror Neurons', *Science*, 297, 846–8.

KOSSLYN, S. M. (1994) *Image and Brain: The Resolution of the Imagery Debate* (Cambridge, Mass.: MIT Press).

———et al. (1997) 'Neural Systems Shared by Visual Imagery and Visual Perception: A Positron Emission Tomography Study', *Neuro-Image*, 6, 320–34.

McGINN, COLIN (2004) *Mindsight: Image, Dream, Meaning* (Cambridge, Mass.: Harvard University Press).

NICHOLS, SHAUN (2004) 'Imagining and Believing: The Promise of a Single Code', *Journal of Aesthetics and Art Criticism*, 62, 129–39.

———and STICH, STEPHEN (2000) 'A Cognitive Theory of Pretense', *Cognition*, 74, 115–47.

———(2003) *Mindreading: An Integrated Account of Pretence, Self-Awareness, and Understanding of Other Minds* (Oxford: Oxford University Press).

O'CRAVEN, K. M., and KANWISHER, N. (2000) 'Mental Imagery of Faces and Places Activates Corresponding Stimulus-specific Brain Regions', *Journal of Cognitive Neuroscience*, 12, 1013–23.

PALMER, STEPHEN (1999) *Vision Science: From Photons to Phenomenology* (Cambridge, Mass.: MIT Press).

PARSONS, L., GABRIELI, J., PHELPS, E., and GAZZANIGA, M. (1998) 'Cerebrally Lateralized Mental Representations of Hand Shape and Movement', *Journal of Neuroscience*, 18, 6539–48.

RALL, J., and HARRIS, P. L. (2000) 'In Cinderella's Slippers: Story Comprehension from the Protagonist's Point of View', *Developmental Psychology*, 36, 202–8.

RINCK, M., and BOWER, G. H. (1995) 'Anaphora Resolution and the Focus of Attention in Situation Models', *Journal of Memory and Language*, 34, 110–31.

RIZZOLATTI, G., FADIGA, L., GALLESE, V., and FOGGASI, L. (1996) 'Premotor Cortex and the Recognition of Motor Actions', *Cognitive Brain Research*, 3, 131–41.

SIRIGU, A., DUHAMEL, J., PILLON, B., COHEN, L., DUBOIS, B., AGID, Y., and PIERROT-DESEILLIGNY, C. (1995) 'Congruent Unilateral Impairments for Real and Imagined Hand Movements', *NeuroReport*, 6, 997–1001.

SPIVEY, M., TYLER, M., RICHARDSON, D., and YOUNG, E. (2000) 'Eye Movements during Comprehension of Spoken Scene Descriptions', in *Proceedings of the 22nd Annual Conference of the Cognitive Science Society* (Mahwah, NJ: Erlbaum), 487–92.

WALTON, KENDALL (1990) *Mimesis as Make-Believe: On the Foundations of the Representational Arts* (Cambridge, Mass.: Harvard University Press).

—— (1997) 'Spelunking, Simulation and Slime: On Being Moved by Fiction', in M. Hjort and S. Laver (eds.), *Emotion and the Arts* (New York: Oxford University Press), 37–49.

WICKER, B., KEYSERS, C., PLAILLY, J., ROYET, J-P., GALLESE, V., and RIZZOLATTI, G. (2003) 'Both of us Disgusted in *my* Insula: The Common Neural Basis of Seeing and Feeling Disgust', *Neuron*, 40, 655–64.

YOUNG, A. W., HUMPHREYS, G. W., RIDDOCH, M. J., HELLAWELL, D. J, et al. (1994) 'Recognition Impairments and Face Imagery', *Neuropsychologia*, 32, 693–702.

YUE, G., and COLE, K. (1992) 'Strength Increases from the Motor Program: Comparison of Training with Maximal Voluntary and Imagined Muscle Contractions', *Journal of Neurophysiology*, 67, 1114–23.

4

Imagination and Misimagination

Adam Morton

IMAGINING MINDS

Suppose that you see someone about to get on a bus, then pause, step back to the street, and look around on the ground. You may wonder why this person is acting this way, and you are likely to run little scenarios through your mind. Perhaps she noticed that she did not have her hat, sunglasses, or purse. Perhaps she had seen some money—or a diamond necklace—on the ground and went back to check if it was worth picking up. You may not have enough confidence in any of these scenarios to believe that these were her thoughts and motives, or to attribute them to her, or to use them to explain her actions. You may even be sure that no such story is the case, so that the scenario is just a fantasy to amuse yourself. Whatever your attitude, you are imagining the person's state of mind.

We imagine other people's minds all the time. It is central to the texture of human social life. We frequently imagine our own minds: when you responded to the instruction 'Suppose that you see someone about to get on a bus . . .', you imagined yourself wondering about the person's motives and coming up with various scenarios. So you imagined yourself imagining. We frequently imagine other people imagining us, as when, for example, we go out of our way to prevent someone even supposing that our motives might be exploitative or seductive. We do a lot of very complicated imagining of one another's minds, quite routinely, without remarking on it. And very often the imagining is extremely vivid. It seems very real to us. Suppose, for example, that you are comforting a friend who has recently been bereaved and is extremely upset. His feelings, as you imagine them, are for you just a definite fact about the situation. They are among the things you have to take account of in deciding what you should do.

The first draft of this chapter was presented to a symposium on imagination organized by Jonathan Adler for the Association for the Philosophy of Education at the Eastern Division of the American Philosophical Association in December 2004. Later versions were read at the University of Sussex and King's College London. I am grateful for advice from Peter Goldie, Michael Martin, Véronique Munoz-Dardé, Shaun Nichols, Elisabeth Schellekens, Kathleen Stock, and participants on all these occasions whose names I did not note.

In describing this example, I said 'his feelings, as you imagine them'. You are doing a lot more than simply imagining his feelings. You believe that he is upset; you attribute feelings of despair to him. These beliefs and attributions draw on a background of imagination, though. Your belief that he is in despair is richer than an application of the predicate 'is in despair' to him, since you also have a sense of what kind of despair he is in, what it is like for him, a sense that you can only partially express in words. You think 'he feels like *this*', where the demonstrative points to the emotions you imagine him to have. (It is somewhat like what happens when you imagine the exact colour you want to paint a wall, and then in the paint store you think that a sample is like that, the imagined colour.) I shall in fact take this as a defining characteristic of imagining minds, in the relevant sense, in which imagination is different from belief, and imagining someone's mind is more than entertaining the thought that a person is in a given state of mind. To imagine that a particular person is in a particular state of mind is to be oneself in a state such that one is thinking of the person as being in a state like that state. (See McGinn 2004: ch. 1 and Currie and Ravenscroft 2002: ch. 1 for the differences between imagination and belief. See Tappolet 2000 and Deonna forthcoming, for the immediacy of other's emotions. And see Harris 2000 on imagination in children and human life generally.)

There is an ambiguity in what I have just said, that will be important later. The simple way to think of someone as being in a state like your state is to think of her as being in a state that has the same objects. If you are thinking of the Eiffel Tower, then you think of her as thinking of the Eiffel Tower. You get a more intimate imagination by thinking of her as being in a state that has the same objects presented in the same way. You think of her as looking at the Eiffel Tower from the western edge of the Place du Trocadéro. You get a yet more intimate imagination by thinking of her as being in a state that has other characteristics in common with yours. You think of her as seeing the Eiffel Tower looming in the east as a symbol of hope. There is a progression of kinds of imagination here, from those that we can call *transparent*, because all that is important is the particular objects of the imagined state (the imagination goes right through the state to its objects), to those that we can call *intimate*, because the detailed psychological workings of the state are also relevant.

MISIMAGINATION

Imagination may be more central to our interactions with other human beings than to any other part of our life. But its very centrality and vividness give us a tendency to take our imagination of others as reality, to assume that people are as we imagine them to be. There is also a subtler form of the danger: not only do we tend to assume that most of the time we get it right when we imagine a person's mind, we almost never reflect on what the difference between getting it right and getting it wrong is. This chapter, being a philosophy paper, is mainly about that subtler issue: what is it to imagine someone correctly? One often meets claims that we can understand other people by imagining their states of mind. And philosophers often praise the role of fiction in expanding our capacities for imaginative understanding. But these claims are hollow if understanding a person does not mean getting something right about her. Otherwise, anything we imagine can count as understanding. Or, to put the point differently, it has to be possible to *mis*-imagine, and consequently misunderstand, why someone acted or what their experience was like.

It is not easy to say what it is to misimagine another person. It is easier to give a useful description of some other kinds of misimagination. If I am asked to imagine my aunt's face and I imagine instead my grandmother's face, I have misimagined. In general, if the aim is to imagine a particular object or event, or a particular proposition's being true, then you misimagine if you imagine something different. Of course, this is only as clear as the idea of imagining something in the first place, in particular the idea of imagining that *p*, for some definite proposition *p*. But at any rate, we can say that the idea of imagining in these cases carries with it a description of what it is to misimagine. It is either not to imagine at all or to imagine the wrong thing. A more subtle case is that of generic imagining, as when you imagine a green cube rotating about a line between two opposite vertices while slowly turning red. If you were asked to do this, you might get it wrong by imagining something other than a cube, or a cube rotating about a different axis, or changing colour quickly rather than slowly. It seems that we can take the object of imagination to be a proposition here too, but a rather indefinite one: that there is a cube, and it is rotating in this way while changing colour in this way. (For the philosophy of the psychology of images, see Tye 1991.)

Some kinds of correctness do not come down to the truth of an imagined proposition. Suppose that I am imagining walking through a revolving door carrying a parcel. I might imagine this in order to tell whether I could get through the door without crushing the parcel. Suppose that I imagine this by visualizing the door directly in front of me and then visualizing the scene looking straight ahead as my body and the parcel fit in and emerge. My imagination might then be accurate in that I represent the parcel emerging unscathed, but inaccurate in that I represent the event with a straight-ahead perspective while in fact, when I later experience it, I turn with the door and look at the exit out of the corner of my right eye instead of straight ahead. It is as if the individual items of information were the same, but organized differently. So after I have later actually gone through the door with the parcel, I might say, 'It wasn't the way I imagined it.' This aspect of correctness, correctness of point of view, will be very important later when we discuss one person's imagination of another person's motivation or experience.

Just as one can imagine facts correctly, but misimagine their presentation, so one can imagine facts correctly but misimagine their causal connections. If the aim is to imagine why the dam burst, then you have to imagine the dam bursting and some antecedent condition or situation, and you have to imagine this situation causing the dam to burst. You are imagining correctly if you are imagining the actual bursting of the dam, imagining some actual antecedent events or situation, and imagining these latter causing the bursting, where they are in fact causes of the dam's bursting. These are quite demanding, and slightly mysterious, but it is not a real mystery what it is to satisfy them. It is not obvious what it is to imagine one event causing another (one can imagine a ball hitting a window and the window just shattering, coincidentally, and then one can use the same visual content to imagine the impact causing the shattering). And it is not obvious how significant the cause one imagines has to be in the real production of the event; this is presumably a fairly context-dependent business. But still, though we have to do some work to see the line between correct imagination and misimagination of why a physical event occurred, it is not in doubt that there is such a line.

On the other hand, it is not obvious that there is an objective difference between accurate imagination and misimagination when one person imagines the mind of another. I think there is a difference: in this chapter I am defending the imagination/misimagination contrast as applied to our imagination of one another. But it is important to see that this is something that needs defence. When we imagine what it is to be a particular person at a particular moment, why a person did some particular action, or why a person's life takes the direction it does, we are doing something very different from imagining that some proposition is true. We are experiencing and thinking, in a way that is aimed at another person's experiencing and thinking, and aims somehow to fit it. How?

Suppose you imagine being a refugee, for example, forced to live somewhere where people speak a language you have never learned, where the social rules are mysterious to you, and where the preparations you have made for earning your living are useless. In trying to imagine this, you imagine a situation and imagine features of it causing you to experience various emotions, adopt various strategies, or form various beliefs. So you imagine emotions, strategies, and beliefs, and you imagine why the person might have them. You will inevitably get it wrong, in part. (Even if you have been a refugee yourself, your capacity to imagine the connections between the parts of your experience is likely to be inaccurate, infiltrated by your image of yourself and by theories of human nature, so that you will not represent to yourself completely reliably even the subjective quality of what has happened to you, let alone its causal structure.) But if you want to have some sort of understanding of a refugee's life, you have no choice but to undertake some such imaginative exercise, knowing that larger or smaller parts of it will be wrong. You know this, but it is not easy to say what it is you know.

This was a very complex case, in that it is a case of someone trying to imagine something large-scale about another person's life. Sometimes what we do is much easier. But the problems in knowing what we do, and what it is to do it right, remain the same. The problems are easiest to see if we consider what correct imagination of a person does *not* consist in. If inside every person's head there was a clockwork mechanism, whose motions were that person's thoughts and produced that person's actions, and if when we imagine that person, we imagine this mechanism and its operations, then accuracy would be a simple matter. You would imagine someone right if your imagination was of the clockwork motions that were actually responsible for that person's thoughts and actions. But it's not like that. A person's thoughts and actions are the result of processes in her brain, and broad general patterns of these processes are represented with varying degrees of inaccuracy by psychological theories and by the ideas of folk psychology. When you imagine what is going on in a person, you rarely imagine the direct physical causes involved. What you do is to undergo states and experiences with some reference to the person, and somehow represent them as being why the person is as she is. So what can be right and wrong about this?

Correctly imagining a person would also be less problematic if when we imagined a person we imagined only the things that she is aware of. But, as the revolving door example above shows, we also have to present the things the person is aware of *as* she is aware of them. At the very least, this involves presenting them with the same perspective and focus as she is aware of them: the things that are firmly in the middle of her awareness have to be imagined as such, and the things that are more peripheral as such. But imagining situations and events as experienced by someone else involves a lot more than this, as we can see when we try to imagine events as experienced by a colour-blind person or a paranoid person.

It is beginning almost to seem as if correct imagination of another person requires the impossible: that one become the other person. It is not just that the task seems daunting; it is not clear what would count as succeeding. There are several ways in which the task could be so ill-defined that the contrast between success and failure becomes meaningless. This is the topic of the next section.

SCEPTICAL POSSIBILITIES

It is not obvious that we ever imagine another person accurately. There is a crude and a subtle way in which our attempts could be less successful than we think.

The whole business might be an illusion; there might be nothing to imagine. That is the most extreme possibility. Our vivid impressions of what it is like to be someone we know well, or that we can intuit their reasons for acting, might be baseless, because what we imagine has nothing to do with the causes of actions. It might even be that our conviction that others do have experiences such as those we imagine them to have is an illusion. The illusion might be based in part on an illusion about ourselves: we imagine our own experience, or imagine others imagining it, and persuade ourselves that we have a direct awareness of something that we can describe accurately.

This possibility may seem incredible. But it can come with an explanation of why it seems incredible, of how the imagination illusion seems so vivid. The explanation is based on the fact that we do imagine, whether or not what we imagine is real. So when you think of someone's imagining your thoughts or experiences, you imagine your own mind and then imagine someone imagining that. So of course the other person's imagination has an object, which it might or might not fit: namely, your mind as you imagine it. (The explanation will work just as well for imagining someone imagining the mind of someone other than you.) So the reason for the illusion that there is something to imagine, a defender of this radical sceptical position can say, is imagination itself. We see that one imagination can match another, and then forget that the whole mental exercise is within the scope of 'imagines', so that we end up thinking that imagination can match reality. Again a colour analogy may help. There is a respectable metaphysical position which claims that colours are not objective properties of physical objects. Before we appreciate the arguments for this position, we find it hardly credible. And why? Because when we think of objects, we think of them as coloured. (The extreme sceptical view might be the classic position of Churchland 1978, or more subtly that of Dennett 1991. I have used an appeal to something like the imagination illusion in exploration II of Morton 2002 as part of an argument *for* the reality of subjective experience.)

Subtler possibilities involve systematic error in processes that can also give true verdicts. We can produce evidence relevant to these possibilities. Social psychology in the last thirty years has produced ample evidence that our introspective sense of ourselves leads us to systematically false views about the causes of our own behaviour. Even when we are right about what we are doing and what we are thinking, we are often wrong about why. So—projecting speculatively but not unreasonably from this—when we put ourselves imaginatively in the position of another person, we are likely to take as the causes of their actions what we would in the imagined situation take as the causes of our own. And these causes are likely to be systematically mistaken. (The classic empirical work is summarized in Ross and Nisbett 1991. For an application of it to issues similar to those discussed here, see Stich and Nichols 1996.)

I will not go into detail about these possible failings. I mention them only to warn us against thinking complacently that imaginative understanding must be a real source of knowledge, the only philosophical problem being what kind of knowledge it is. If we are aware that this vivid and persuasive aspect of our experience may be deceptive, we may be more wary of others. One closely related topic is the presentation of character in fiction. When we read fiction, or watch a play or a film, we imagine what the characters are going through and why they are doing what they are represented as doing. In fact, in plays and films, and much prose fiction, there is very little explanation of why characters act as they do. In telling the story to a small child, we count on her imagining that the wolf disguises himself as Grandma in order to deceive Little Red Riding Hood, and that her father kills the wolf in order to save his daughter. We don't state these things explicitly, because we don't need to. The occasions where we are left temporarily or permanently in doubt about the reasons for characters' actions, their general state of mind, and the kind of people they are, stand out as exceptional, and it takes a good deal of authorial skill to work them in, in a way that the reader or spectator will accept.

Imagined fictional personalities cannot be an illusion in the sense of failing to match the real truth about the characters.[1] But they can be an invitation to illusion. This is because when we respond to fiction, we react to the characters in many of the ways we do to real people, and so if a way of reacting makes sense with respect to a fiction, we tend to think that it makes sense with respect to real people. This can have two bad consequences. It can give us the impression that a certain kind of personality is possible, when in fact people cannot be that way. Or, alternatively, it can give us an impression that some kind of action is often caused by some particular kind of motive, or that some motive is a plausible cause of some particular kind of action, when in fact this is psychologically wrong. Such people never or rarely exist, and such motivational processes are never or rarely behind the actions in question. I am sure that both illusions are quite common, and should make us wary of claims that fiction educates us about human nature. It is, after all, hardly a startling suggestion that *Crime and Punishment* is a misleading picture of a deranged murderer, just as *Lolita* is a misleading picture of a paedophile, and *The Silence of the Lambs* a very misleading picture of two serial killers. Perhaps more surprising is the suggestion that many, perhaps most, fictional characters do not qualify for immigration to the actual world. (Everyone in Dickens! Or so I would argue. And this is not a criticism of Dickens, but one of his glories. Wonderfully believable impossible people: to real personalities as bel canto is to the sounds of speech.)

In theory one could resist these effects, and keep one's reactions to fiction and one's reactions to human beings in separate compartments. To keep the two completely separated would require superhuman control, though, and might make it impossible to enjoy fiction. One reason why it is hard to separate the two is that we tend to think of real people as if they were fictional characters. This is a consequence of the famous fundamental attribution error of social psychology. This is our well-documented tendency to suppose that people's behaviour is more constant than it is, that liars always lie and benevolent people always help. This is our natural mode, to populate our social environment with characters with easily grasped profiles of action from which they rarely depart. As a result, if a work of fiction is to appeal to our natural capacities to imagine the personalities of other

---

[1] If there is a real truth about the characters in a fiction, then one can misimagine it. On Kendall Walton's (1990) account, e.g., what is true in a fiction is determined by the reactions an ideal reader would have to it. So by reacting as an un-ideal reader, one can imagine e.g. that Othello was moved by racial hatred rather than jealous rage, and be objectively wrong about a fictional mind. (Thanks to Shaun Nichols on this point.)

people, it can most easily do this by encouraging us to think of them as more constant and definite than people actually are. So even when the personalities we imagine are like the personalities we take real people to have, there is an element of illusion. Moreover, the demands of a plot will often require an imagined personality that fits smoothly into the array of personalities we attribute to our real acquaintances, but which wouldn't result from any combination of actual human psychological attributes.

(This raises a delicate issue in describing the realism of works of fiction. Is a fiction that encourages an imagination of a social situation that is similar to the misleading imagination we might have of an actual situation thereby realistic, since it encourages reactions we could actually have; or not, since it encourages a mischaracterization of social reality? The question is like that raised by a picture, say, of a confusing scene of mirrors and puzzling perspectives, which accurately captures the mistakes in understanding the scene that a person would naturally make, but represents the actual structure of the scene less well than a picture that represents the same scene in a more precise but less visually natural way.)

In a way, then, our social lives are works of fiction, which we live through a constant imaginative process which bears a very subtle relation to the psychological facts. Or so one can argue with some plausibility. The possibility should make us take seriously scepticism about the imagination of other people, which suggests a degree of inaccuracy that raises hard questions as to whether there is a robust contrast between accurate imagining and misimagining of another person. (See Doris 2002 and Goldie 2004 for discussions of the fragility of attributions of personality that connects with issues about literature. See also Nehamas 2000.)

THE LINK WITH MINDREADING

I hope to have aroused in my readers a sceptical attitude towards imagination of mind. You should by now see the point of thinking carefully what the difference is between simply imagining someone's mind and imagining it correctly or accurately. In the rest of this chapter I shall make the beginning of a principled distinction between accurate imagination and misimagination.

Three points from earlier in this chapter give us the basic ideas we need. We saw a difference between imagination and belief. One can imagine a state of mind in a way that requires an essential demonstrative element to one of one's own states: one imagines the person to be in a state like this state one is in at the moment. We also saw how imagination of states of mind can be framed by a perspective. One thinks of certain information from the perspective of the person one is imagining. And, thirdly, we saw how readily we do what one might think was a very demanding task, to embed one imagining in another, so that we imagine one person imagining another person's imagining. Given these three ideas, a partial solution to the problem can be found.

My assumption is that we do imagine people's states of mind. I take this as simply a given of human life. I shall also assume that the capacity to imagine minds is closely linked to what philosophers and psychologists refer to as variously 'folk psychology', 'theory of mind', or 'mindreading'. This is the basic human capacity to attribute to one another states of mind that can be used to predict and explain behaviour. (For a summary of recent work see Nichols and Stich 2003 and Morton forthcoming. In my writings on the topic I have stressed uses of folk psychology *other* than prediction and explanation: see Morton 2002: chs. 1 and 5.) There are a number of competing accounts of how we do this, not all of which are necessarily rivals. In all of these accounts, attributing a state of mind to a person on the basis of their behaviour requires some thought. On some accounts—what Stich and Nichols (1996) call 'information-rich' accounts—one combines information about behaviour in a particular situation with more general information about the reasons for human behaviour in general to produce an explanation of how the person has acted. On other, 'information-poor' accounts, one mimics the other person's thinking with one's own, and then somehow records some result of one's own thinking as an attribution to the other person. (The standard versions of information-rich accounts are often called the theory-theory of mindreading, and standard versions of information-poor accounts are often called simulation theories.) On either kind of account, there is something for imagination to latch on to. The connection is more natural, perhaps, with information-poor accounts. If such an account is right, one can imagine someone's state by activating a process in oneself that might mimic the other person's thinking—though one is not required to attribute the result of this process to the other person—and then taking some part of this thinking as the imagined state of the other. (This would give a theory-based simulation of simulation!) According to a very information-rich account, one might activate some part of one's general account of human thinking and apply it to the person in question to get a conclusion and then, suspending any definite attribution to the other, take this conclusion as the content of the state one imagines the other to be in.

So, when one imagines a person's state of mind, one is following part of one strategy for getting an explanation of their action. The imagination has the content 'she is in *that* state', referring to some state that could play a role in an explanation or prediction of that person.

GETTING IT RIGHT

With this as a rough characterization of what it is to imagine a person's state of mind, the aim is to distinguish accurate imagination from misimagination. Now the second basic idea comes into play: perspective. Remember the examples of imagining someone going through a revolving door with a parcel, or imagining someone seeing the Eiffel Tower from the west. In such cases one organizes the information that one is in imagination relating the person to, in a way that is intended to match her organization of it. In particular, one has to match the way in which the person organizes information with a view to planning sequences of actions. When a person plans an action, she has to anticipate possible ways the action might develop. To do this, she has to have at hand a lot of relevant information, much of which will not be used, and to anticipate how she may assimilate and react to information that might come in. One way, a typical and central human way, of managing this is to prepare a framework into which present and anticipated information can be fitted, and from which it can be quickly retrieved and related to other relevant information. A simple example is seeing space in terms of directions and distances to one's own location, even as one moves, providing a quick guide to bodily actions, reactions to things coming towards one, and paths of approach and escape. The result is like a coordinate system in geometry, with oneself at the origin, the central point. Another example is understanding past and future in terms of stages in the lives of a few particular people, oneself in particular. These two data-organizing templates, spatial perspective and narrative structure, are often combined, to give the typical human perspective on the world: a fabric of interweaving person strands, each strand at each moment being the origin of a self-centred coordinate system. One strand in each person's perspective, her own life, glows with a special significance, providing each moment with an especially significant set of spatial relations.

There's a clear connection with imagination. When a person plans an action in terms of an information-organizing framework with an origin and coordinates, she is in effect centering her imagining of her performance on this origin. So if someone else is to imagine performing that action the way the first person did, he has to imagine an action with the same origin; he has to use the same information-organizing framework that she did. That framework *centers* the second person's imagination of the first person, to use Peter Goldie's terminology, in terms of the first person's perspective. (See Goldie 2000 for perspective in imagination. For narrative structure in fiction and its connection with imaginative perspective, see Currie 1995: part 2; Stock forthcoming.)

Most of our imagination of people is centered, though the perspective can vary, depending on the states being imagined and the imagining person's take on the imagined. They do not vary too much, though. For the variety of perspectives we have on our actions is limited. Self-centered spatial representation and agent-centered narration are rarely absent. And the structures we use to organize our thinking even about very abstract matters have to respect the fixed limits of short-term memory, of speed of recall, and of ability to handle complex information. In fact, the main point of these structures is to allow us to manage these limitations. As a result, when one person imagines another, they usually attribute to that other person a perspective not too unlike the one the other is actually using.

Still, it is possible to get it wrong. A person could plan an action in terms of spatial relations that do not connect with her own body's position, and someone else could mistakenly imagine her actions through a conventional own-body-centered perspective. For example, I could be in a burning building and planning an escape route in terms of distances from the room in which my child is sleeping, because for me the sleeping child is the center of the situation, while you, imagining my plight, think of it in terms of my actual location and the directions to the child and the exit from there. In this case the imagination would have gone wrong. It would have missed an important part of the imagined person's actual thinking. So we can define a clear and significant aspect of accurate imagination as follows: one person's imagination of another's mind is *perspectivally accurate* to the extent that it represents the thinking of the other person in terms of a perspective like that which the other person is in fact using. To capture a point from earlier in the chapter, we can define an imagination as *target-accurate* when it represents the thinking of the other person as directed at the things or propositions that it is in fact directed at. So when one person imagines another in a way that has both perspectival and target accuracy, he has in a pretty substantial way imagined her correctly. It is, to use the terms I used earlier, both transparent and intimate.

Perspectival accuracy is one way in which the imagination/misimagination distinction can be clearly drawn. It can be extended to areas which are less clear than cases in which one person is imagining an action which another is doing or has done. When one person is imagining another doing or thinking something completely imaginary, the imagining is still perspectivally accurate to the extent that it represents the person as using a framework that she might or would have used. Extreme misimagination is still possible, and it is still an objective matter that it is in this respect misimagination. But the case that is easiest to analyse is that in which one person does some definite thing for some definite purpose, and another person imagines the first person's thinking and motivation. When the second person does this accurately, the two people use similarly centered information structures, but in the solution of different problems. The imagined person uses hers to solve some first-order practical problem, and the imaginer uses his to solve the problem of anticipating the solution to that first-order problem. The imaginer will usually do this by embedding the information structure he is using to imitate that of the imagined person in a larger structure, typically one more centered in his self and his purposes, appropriate to the larger task of which imagining the other person is a part. It is this difference in the problems to be solved, and this embedding of one structure in another, that makes the act of imagining someone different from simply employing a similar way of thinking.

This does not mean that imagining is always an explicit, deliberate, or conscious business. Consider dances and conversations. When one person dances with another, they try to stay mentally half a step ahead of the other by imagining the other's dance planning from the other's point of view, an imagining that forms part of their own dance planning. This happens without much deliberation; indeed, more than minimal deliberation would upset it. Similarly, when one person talks to another, she imagines the conversational direction of the other and the reactions the other will have to what she says. As with dancing, this happens more by learned instinct than by explicit planning. And as with dancing, the imagination is mutual: each is imagining the other and to some extent imagining the other's imagining of them. Human social life is a fabric of such shared imaginative projects, projects which could not even get off the ground were our imaginations of one another not by and large reasonably accurate.

IMAGINING IMAGINING

In perspectival accuracy we have a reasonably clear description of one way in which one kind of imagination can represent or fail to represent its target. Moreover, it describes a dimension of accuracy that is essential to the kind of imagination that underlies shared cooperative activities. That ought to be enough to make it worth paying attention to. I would like to push the ideas just a little further, though, to address the question not of what constitutes accuracy in imagination but of how much of our imagining of other people is accurate. I will do this by discussing iterated imagination, imagining imagining.

There is a thin line between the information structures of imagining and action planning. When you plan or rehearse an action, you are almost imagining doing it. You may have the same reference points and basic relations (the same origin and coordinates) in both cases, though in imagining the action these are usually embedded in a larger project, which may involve considering your projected action without actually doing it. And when two people coordinate their actions by mutual imagination—dancing, conversing—their action planning and their imagining of each other's planning are almost inseparable.

If planning is almost imagining, then imagining planning is almost imagining imagining. Consider a situation in which two people have to take account of one another's possible actions. They are at opposite ends of a crowded hall, full of people, tables, and pillars, and they aim at an embrace somewhere in the middle. Each person could simply plot a route into the hall, dodging the obstacles until they might be within kissing distance of the other. Even if this worked, at this point they would both have to take account of the other person's probable route. More likely, from the very beginning each will take account of the obstacles facing the other in order to imagine the route the other will take. In fact, they will imagine each other's imagining of themselves, in order to anticipate the choices that each will make as a result of imagining the possibilities open to the other. So in planning a coordinated action, each person is imagining the other person's imagining their planning.

Much imagining of imagining is like this, when the imaginings are clearly centred and the perspectives of the outer and the inner imaginings are related in some simple way. In effect, one constructs a single, slightly more complex and flexible information structure and uses it to manage the information processed in both the outer and the inner thinking. The effect will often be of a shifting point of view, as the cognition taking place is, just as it would be were it governed by one or another simpler perspectival information structure. But these shifts of apparent point of view can happen smoothly as effects of a simple underlying pattern of thought.

I believe that these rich, diffuse information structures with their shifting subsidiary origins are crucial in human life. I believe that they make sense of the intuitive but thoughtful way with which we enter into shared cooperative activities, and I conjecture that they are at the root of our capacity to attribute felt experience to ourselves and others. I have argued elsewhere (Morton 2002; 2004: ch. 4) for these things, in a way that would have been clearer had I been able to use the concepts of perspectival accuracy and embedded centered imagination, but which I am not going to repeat here. Instead, I shall argue that a very natural assumption about human psychology suggests that embedded imaginations have a good chance of accurately representing the thinking of the person imagined.

The assumption is that our choice of ways to graft one information structure on to another to get a usable complex structure is rather limited. This is meant as a crude empirical generalization from a mental survey of cases. One can start with one person's spatial perspective and attach to a point in that perspective another person's perspective, as children readily learn to do in learning to share visual attention. (See the essays in Eilan et al. 2005.) One can start with a problem of finding a means satisfying certain definite constraints to achieve a specific end, and attach to some intermediate goal the problem of finding means to it satisfying those or other criteria, as people learn to do when learning to fit in with one another's plans. One can start with a strategic situation, a problem that might be characterized in terms of game theory, and take one agent's set of possible moves and the consequences of them to her, and attach to it another competing agent's outlook on each stage of the game, as people learn to do when learning to think out which of their possible moves opponents are likely to have anticipated. And, simplest of all, one can start with a problem to be solved, and embed it in the problem of predicting what solution another will find to it. Intuitively, there are not very many more ways of constructing an information structure that will contain within it the crucial information for one person's action as a subset of the crucial information for that of another.

Assume this is right. Suppose that A has managed to imagine B's imagining of C, in the sense that A has constructed a shifting information structure which allows her to predict successfully what C will do as a consequence of her prediction of C. (C may be A, as in many of the examples above.) And suppose that A can do this for many of B's predictions of others. Given that there are not many ways in which B can imagine C, the chance is pretty small that A has found a wrong one, which still works in that it could be used by B to imagine C and for A to imagine B's imagining C, and still come up with the right predictions of B's actions.

So when we imagine imagining and the effort is successful on the predictive level, we can have some confidence that it is also right in terms of the processes underlying the other person's actions. That is, it is likely to work in terms of an information structure that does have as a substructure the one the other person is using for their imagining. This provides no guarantee that the rest of the processes working in the imaginer's attempts to anticipate the other do in fact resemble those operating in the other. But first, as we saw above, it is not at all clear which of these processes are relevant to accurate imagination in any case, or even what accuracy means when applied to them. And second, even though there are a limited number of ways in which we can structure centered imagination of others, the process is still demanding, and a person imagining someone else will have invested a lot of their mental capital in the imagining alone, so that there is a limit to the complexity of the thinking that can serve it.

It may help to state a very simple special case. Suppose a person, B, imagines another person, C, and B's imagination of C is inaccurate because of the fundamental attribution error. That is, B imagines that C's personality is more constant in the actions it leads to than it really is. Now suppose that a third person, A, imagines B imagining C, and suppose that A's thinking is also subject to the attribution error. But A's tendency to the error will not interfere with the accuracy of her imagining of B. For if she imposes her way of thinking on the imagined B, she will be imposing something that is already present. This is a very general pattern: factors that make simple imagination inaccurate can be neutral or even increase the accuracy of imagination of imagination.

This point becomes even more significant when the embedding of imagination is deeper, as when one person imagines another person's imagining of a third person's imagining of the first person's state. (Which, complicated as the description may be, is a typical human accomplishment.) Then the mental space left over for the processes that serve the information structure is decidedly constrained. So, for both these reasons, we can have some faith that predictively successful embedded imaginings are fairly often accurate. More accurate embedding means less room for misimagination.[2]

---

[2] Multiply embedded points of view are common in literature. My argument suggests that the capacity of literature to mislead us about human possibilities is less when the reader is asked to test her imagination against her capacity to embed one point of view in another. The suggestion is only that, though, and needs a lot more thought.

REFERENCES

CHURCHLAND, PAUL (1978) *Scientific Realism and the Plasticity of Mind* (Cambridge: Cambridge University Press).

CURRIE, GREGORY (1995) *Image and Mind* (Cambridge: Cambridge University Press).

—— and RAVENSCROFT, IAN (2002) *Recreative Minds* (Oxford: Oxford University Press).

DENNETT, DANIEL C. (1991) *Consciousness Explained* (Boston: Rowan, Brown).

DEONNA, JULIEN A. (forthcoming) 'The Structure of Empathy', *Journal of Moral Philosophy*.

DORIS, JOHN (2002) *Lack of Character* (Cambridge: Cambridge University Press).

EILAN, NAOMI, HOERL, CHRISTOPH, McCORMACK, TERESA, and ROESSLER, JOHANNES (eds.) (2005) *Joint Attention: Communication and Other Minds: Issues in Philosophy and Psychology* (Oxford: Oxford University Press).

GOLDIE, PETER (2000) *The Emotions: A Philosophical Exploration* (Oxford: Oxford University Press).

—— (2004) *On Personality* (London: Routledge).

HARRIS, PAUL (2000) *The Work of the Imagination* (Oxford: Blackwell).

McGINN, COLIN (2004) *Mindsight* (Cambridge, Mass.: Harvard University Press).

MORTON, ADAM (2002) *The Importance of Being Understood: Folk Psychology as Ethics* (London: Routledge).

—— (2004) *On Evil* (London: Routledge).

—— (forthcoming) 'Folk Psychology', in Brian McLaughlin (ed.), *The Oxford Companion to the Philosophy of Mind* (Oxford: Oxford University Press).

NEHAMAS, ALEXANDER (2000) 'An Essay on Beauty and Judgement', *Threepenny Review* (winter).

NICHOLS, SHAUN, and STICH, STEPHEN (2003) *Mindreading* (Oxford: Oxford University Press).

ROSS, L., and NISBETT, R. (1991) *The Person and the Situation* (Philadelphia: Temple University Press).

STICH, STEPHEN, and NICHOLS, SHAUN (1996) 'How Do Minds Understand Minds? Mental Simulation versus Tacit Theory', in Stephen Stich, *Deconstructing the Mind* (Oxford: Oxford University Press), 136–67.

STOCK, KATHLEEN (forthcoming) 'Fiction and Psychological Insight', in Matthew Kieran and Dominic Lopes (eds.), *Knowing Art* (Dordrecht: Kluwer).

TAPPOLET, CHRISTINE (2000) *Emotions et valeurs* (Paris: Presses Universitaires de France).

TYE, MICHAEL (1991) *The Imagery Debate* (Cambridge, Mass.: MIT Press).

WALTON, K. (1990) *Mimesis as Make-believe: On the Foundations of the Representational Arts* (Cambridge, Mass.: Harvard University Press).

5

The Intuitive Cosmology of Fictional Worlds

Deena Skolnick and Paul Bloom

Children spend much of their lives immersed in fiction as they engage with stories in fairy tales, books, movies, and television shows. Because of this immersion, developmental psychologists have long been interested in how children make sense of fictional characters such as Batman and SpongeBob SquarePants. For an adult, there is a sharp division between what is real and what is not, but this might not be the case for children. One traditional view of development, defended most notably by Piaget (1962), is that young children are prone to magical thinking—they lack the capacity to distinguish the real from the make-believe.

There is now abundant evidence that this view is mistaken. When explicitly asked, even three-year-olds understand that ghosts, monsters, and witches are 'make-believe' and dogs, houses, and bears are 'real-life' (e.g. Morison and Gardner 1978; Wellman and Estes 1986; DiLalla and Watson 1988; Harris et al. 1991; Samuels and Taylor 1994; Golomb and Galasso 1995). They also do not confuse imagination with reality—a child who imagines that a pencil is in a box will not mistakenly direct someone asking for a pencil to the box (Woolley and Phelps 1994; see also Leslie 1994). And, contrary to popular belief, those children who create imaginary friends are aware of their friends' status as imaginary (Taylor 1999). The consensus from this work, then, is that an understanding of the distinction between what is real and what is make-believe is present by the age of three, if not earlier.

In our own research and in this chapter, we will accept the general conclusion that children can distinguish reality from fantasy, and we will present our own evidence that supports this claim. But our main purpose here is to argue that this body of previous research has not yet asked the right questions. Adults' and children's intuitive understanding of fiction[1] is considerably more nuanced than developmental psychologists have assumed.

We thank Tamar Gendler, Shaun Nichols, and Geoff Pynn for helpful comments on earlier drafts of this chapter.

[1] We use the terms 'fiction', 'fantasy', and 'make-believe' interchangeably in our discussions.

REALITY AND FICTION

Imagine someone who could make only a reality/fantasy distinction. Someone with this binary categorization scheme would correctly separate fictional characters from real people. All real people belong in the same (real) world, and all of these people could potentially meet and interact in this world. This world is separate from anything fictional, so all real people are unable to meet or interact with fictional characters. This separation is what has been explored in all of the developmental research to date.

Despite having complete success with the reality/fantasy distinction, our binary categorizer would miss an important fact about the nature of fiction. She would create a single fictional world, separate from the real world, and she would populate it with all of the fictional characters. All of the characters in this single fictional world could potentially meet and interact, just as all real people can potentially meet and interact. Batman and SpongeBob could potentially sit down in Gotham City together for a chat; James Bond might meet Alexander Portnoy; Superman could rescue Anna Karenina.

Something seems flawed about this aspect of the categorization scheme, so much so that the idea of these crossovers can be funny, as in the *New Yorker* cartoon in Fig. 5.1.

We want to separate Batman from SpongeBob, eliminating the possibility of contact between these characters. Batman and SpongeBob belong to different

"It's a very sweet note from Batman and Robin."

Figure 5.1 When fictional worlds meet

fictional worlds, and Batman's world is just as disconnected from SpongeBob's world as it is from the real world.

At least, this is our intuition. But do 'normal' adults (without any philosophical or psychological axes to grind) feel the same way? What about young children? We explored this by asking adults and five-year-old children questions such as the following:

Do you think Batman is real or make-believe?
Do you think your friend is real or make-believe?
Does Batman think Robin is real or make-believe?
Does Batman think SpongeBob is real or make-believe?

This method might need some justification, as one might object that there should be no constraints on a fictional character's beliefs, or that it is nonsensical to attribute any beliefs to characters. But we claim that, in order to make sense of fiction at all, we must attribute mental states to fictional characters, including beliefs about what is real and what is make-believe. For instance, consider that Batman will travel across Gotham City, risking life and limb to rescue Robin from the clutches of the Joker. This would make no sense at all if Batman thought that Robin did not really exist. Additionally, Batman's beliefs are constrained in certain ways. While we as readers are aware that Batman is stuck in a fantasy, Batman does not share this awareness; he believes that he is real. Indeed, many fictions draw heavily on a character's struggle to tell fantasy from reality, including *Hamlet* and *Spellbound*. These stories work precisely because we can attribute beliefs to the characters in them and evaluate those beliefs as being true or false in the world of the story.

In support of this analysis, our subjects provided consistent and clear answers to our questions. Not surprisingly, adults and children both reported that Batman is make-believe and that their friends are real, correctly separating reality from fiction. This is a replication of previous work. More interesting, however, are their responses about Batman's beliefs.

First, adults report that Batman believes Robin is real. Five-year-olds tended to have the same intuition, although they sometimes misinterpreted the questions about Batman's beliefs in terms of their own beliefs, and hence said that Batman believes that Robin is make-believe. Second, adults report that Batman believes SpongeBob is make-believe. So do five-year-olds. Because of children's occasional egotistical reinterpretations, we conducted a second study that asked children to judge which actions were possible between two characters, rather than asking them to judge the real or make-believe connection directly. Using this method, we obtained the same results: characters in different worlds cannot act on each other, while characters in the same world can (see Skolnick and Bloom forthcoming, for discussion).

Children and adults thus seem to assume that fictional characters do not all belong to the same world. We have yet to test younger children, but our results so far strongly suggest that the hypothetical binary categorizer may not actually exist.

THE RELATIONSHIPS AMONG FICTIONAL WORLDS

In our discussions we characterize our patterns of intuition in terms of worlds (see Currie 1990; Eco 1990; Lewis 2000). There is a single real world, which contains everything in our universe: people, planets, laws of physics, and so on. When we categorize something or someone as real, we judge that that object or person belongs in this real world. When we categorize something or someone as fictional, we judge that that object or person does not belong in our world; it belongs in the realm of fantasy. As our study shows, there are many fictional worlds in this realm: one for Batman and Robin, another for SpongeBob and Patrick, another for James Bond and Dr No, and so on.

These results suggest two general principles: (1) Within a world, characters are connected by an 'is-real-to' relationship, and (2) across worlds, characters are connected by an 'is-fictional-to' relationship. As a direct consequence of these principles, we can infer characters' beliefs about each other. Two characters in the same world should believe each other to be real; two characters in different worlds should believe each other to be fictional. The results from our study could be taken to support these principles as adequately describing our commonsense cosmology of fictional worlds.

We believe that claim (1) is mostly correct, with the qualification that the appropriate knowledge connection must exist in order for characters to make the 'is-real-to' judgment correctly. After all, you are in the same world as many people you don't believe to be real—not because they aren't, but because you have never heard of them. There are certainly fictional worlds in which characters might not know of each other, as in mystery stories where a detective is unaware of the identity of a criminal. There are also cases in which characters are confused or mistaken about another character's status, as when some of the characters in *The Usual Suspects* start the movie believing that Keysar Soze does not exist. We will simply conclude that all characters within a world could *potentially* know each other, and hence are all potentially real to each other.

But claim (2), which describes the nature of across-world relationships, is mistaken. It is not necessarily true that characters in any one world are fictional to characters in every other world. For one thing, there are asymmetrical relationships. You might think that Batman is fictional, but Batman shouldn't think that *you* are fictional. Batman presumably thinks that he is in the real world, and should have no thoughts about our (actually real) world. If Batman did know about the real world, it would be possible for him to know about his creators at DC Comics, and thereby to know that he is actually a fictional character. This might be acceptable for experimental fiction, but not for a garden-variety superhero.

There exist asymmetrical relationships within the realm of fiction as well. A realistic fictional character, such as the mobster Tony Soprano, has presumably heard of Batman and could judge Batman to be fictional. But has Batman heard of Tony Soprano? Maybe, but probably not. Tony Soprano has heard of Cinderella; has Cinderella heard of Tony Soprano? Certainly not.

It is thus clear that our second claim needs modification. Every fictional character does *not* believe that every fictional character in a different world is fictional. In fact, our study might have over-estimated the extent to which people believe that SpongeBob is fictional to Batman. This is because we used a forced-choice method, asking our subjects to answer only 'real' or 'make-believe'. Suppose our subjects had a firm intuition that 'real' was the wrong answer. This might lead to a response of 'make-believe', even if they weren't sure that this option was correct. If we had included a 'neither of the above' or a 'never heard of him' alternative, our subjects' responses might have been different. We are currently in the process of running a study that addresses these issues.

This new study will reveal the intuitions that people have about the knowledge connections between characters. But how are they able to make these judgments? How can they tell when it is appropriate for one character to have beliefs about another? We believe that these intuitions are the direct result of how we create fictional worlds.

THE CREATION OF FICTIONAL WORLDS

Every time we encounter a new fictional story, we create a new world. The default assumption is that this world contains everything that the real world contains. We then modify this representation based on several constraints: what the story tells us explicitly, what we can directly deduce from specific conventions of the fictional genre, and, most importantly, how similar to the real world the fictional world is described as being (for discussions of similar world-creation theories, see Walton 1990; Ryan 1991; Gerrig 1993; for an alternate perspective, see Thomasson 1998).

For example, when we read a story about Batman, we begin by creating a representation of the real world. We know explicitly from the story that Batman's world must contain Batman himself, Robin, and a host of other characters that do not exist in the real world. So we modify our representation of the world by adding these characters to it. The story also tells us implicitly that other modifications need to be made in order to turn our world representation into Batman's world. For instance, although the denizens of Batman's world are fairly intelligent, they somehow lack the resources or inclination to figure out that Bruce Wayne and Batman are the same person—despite the fact that he's an obvious candidate to be a caped vigilante, and, really, a cowl is a poor disguise. (Superman is a worse offender here, since one must assume that the people of that world are unable to recognize that Superman + glasses = Clark Kent.) So our world-creation process modifies the intelligence level of the average Batman-world person with respect to these particular facts.

One subtle change we must make to any fictional world is to remove any fictional representation of the characters. That is, Batman's world cannot contain any of the Batman movies or comic books; that would require the same character to be both real and fictional within Batman's world. Changes in the same vein must be made to the worlds of movies and plays and other media that rely on actors. The realistic movie *Million Dollar Baby*, for instance, stars Clint Eastwood as the boxing instructor Frankie Dunn. For this to make sense, someone watching the movie has to tacitly assume that world of the movie differs from ours in that it lacks the actor Clint Eastwood. (Consider that if Clint Eastwood did exist in the world of the movie, people would gawk at Frankie Dunn on the street, because he looks exactly like the famous actor.) This requirement can lead to some clever playing with these conventions. In the movie *Oceans 12*, the actress Julia Roberts plays the character of Tess, who is enlisted as part of a plan to steal a valuable work of art. Tess's friends decide that the best way for her to do so is by impersonating a famous person, and they decide to have her impersonate an actress whom Tess somewhat resembles: Julia Roberts. Even this playful case requires some adjustments to reality. For instance, one has to accept that Tess bears only a vague resemblance to Julia Roberts, not obvious to a casual onlooker.

These adjustments to the real world are made on the basis of what is explicitly stipulated in the story, or what is implicit in the genre. But most things in fictional worlds stay the same. People in Batman's world have kidneys, when water gets cold it turns into ice, bacon is made from pigs, 14 comes after 13, the word 'hello' is a greeting, and so on. There are countless default assumptions that are extended, unconsciously, from the real world to the fictional world (see Gendler 2000).

We believe that this theory of world creation explains our intuitions about fictional characters' beliefs about other characters. Importantly, our intuitions about this relationship are *not* a direct property of the similarity between the fictional worlds themselves. Rather, these intuitions are established via the real world. For instance, when we ask what James Bond thinks of Cinderella, we don't compute the relationship between Bond's world and Cinderella's world directly. Rather, we ask whether Bond's world is similar enough to our own to reasonably export the fact 'Cinderella is fictional' from our world to his—just as we exported facts about ice and bacon to Batman's world in virtue of its similarity to our own world. This indirect method of setting up the relationships between fictional worlds explains the occasional asymmetries mentioned earlier. James Bond can think that Cinderella is fictional, but Cinderella should have no intuitions about James Bond; her world is too different from our own for us to credit her with the same beliefs about James Bond that we have.

Two examples can help to illustrate this point. First, consider Ian McEwan's novel *Saturday*, which takes place in London, on February 15, 2003. It is realistic in tone, and we assume that the story's world is the same as our world, except for the specific story characters and events. So it is perfectly consistent that the main character coincidentally bumps into Prime Minister Tony Blair. Blair is part of our real world and has been imported into this fictional world as part of its creation. It is also perfectly consistent when the main character complains that *Madame Bovary* is a boring work of fiction. *Madame Bovary* is fictional to us; since the character is realistic, it is fictional to him as well. If we were to wonder what the character thought of Batman, we would assume that, as a normal adult, he would have heard of Batman and would believe that he is fictional. In fact, we would make the same inferences about his mental states as we would about those of a real adult living in London in 2003.

Second, consider SpongeBob SquarePants. SpongeBob is an animated, talking, pants-wearing sponge. He lives in a pineapple under the sea in a land called Bikini Bottom. His best friend, Patrick, is a talking starfish. His world has bizarre principles of physics and biology and few constraints on internal logic. For instance, a boring character might start to speak, and a title card will appear saying 'Fifty years later'. The character will still be speaking, with his audience now fifty years older. But in the next scene, all the characters will return to their usual age. Although radical changes must be made to our representation of the real world in order to turn it into SpongeBob's world, it is not anarchy in Bikini Bottom. There are countless real-world facts that are imported in to this world, such as the meanings of English words, the proper interpretation of facial expressions, properties of artifacts (i.e. chairs are still solid objects), and so on. Furthermore, someone watching this show can infer that the usual 'is-real-to' relationship holds among the characters belonging to this world; SpongeBob correctly believes that Patrick is real, and vice versa.

On the other hand, this world is so different from our own that specific geographical or historical facts might not be imported. It's hardly obvious that his world contains Tony Blair. Furthermore, because the inhabitants of Bikini Bottom are sufficiently different from us, it is not clear that just because something is fictional to us, it will be fictional to them.

CHALLENGES AND EXTENSIONS

The intuition driving much of our discussion is that Batman, SpongeBob, and characters from all other stories belong to separate worlds. Our research suggests that this way of structuring the fictional realm is intuitive even for young children. We contend that different stories belong in separate worlds because of how they are created. Whenever we encounter a new story, we start with a new representation of our own world and modify it accordingly, populating the universe of fantasy with multiple worlds. Starting with our own world as the basis of all fictional worlds ensures that each fictional world has enough detail to fill in unspecified or underspecified elements. It also ensures that the multiple fictional worlds share the correct relationship to each other. Batman is a fictional character for us in the real world; so, when we make modifications to our world in order to create Tony Soprano's world, Batman is exported as a fictional character during the creation process. Thus, Tony Soprano believes that Batman is fictional.

So our theory goes. But there are many objections that one could raise to this theory of the fictional cosmology and certain subtleties that our discussions so far glossed over.

Crossovers

Crossovers are cases in which characters from different worlds actually do meet, contrary to our multiple-worlds picture. (More generally, the problem also extends to events and entities, but we'll restrict ourselves here to characters.) One example is the *New Yorker* cartoon reproduced in Fig. 5.1. Other examples include the movie *Who Framed Roger Rabbit*, some episodes of *The Simpsons*, cartoons where Spider-Man and Batman team up, and so on. How can these situations fit with our theory of the commonsense ontology of fiction?

One possible solution, proposed by Walton (1990), is that these creative innovations involve the creation of a novel world. A crossover story in which Batman meets Spider-Man involves three separate worlds: one for Batman, one for Spider-Man, and one in which they interact. The easiest way to create this third world is to import all of the distinctive facts about each of the other two worlds. The catch is that, for this three-world solution to be coherent, the characters involved must be similar enough to each other to interact effectively in a single world. There can be a crossover between the television programs *CSI* and *Crossing Jordan*, for instance, because their worlds are roughly our world, and so the creation of this third world poses no special problems. The worlds of Batman and Spider-Man both depart from reality in similar ways (e.g. the existence of super-villains) and so can also coalesce well enough. Consider, in contrast, a fiction that brought together a realistic drama such as *Law and Order* with the world of SpongeBob SquarePants. It is not clear that this is even possible, given that the two worlds conflict in so many ways.

A different possibility for crossovers is to continue with the story in an already established world. This works best when the world in question has been designed to be open to importing characters and events from other worlds. The world of the *Shrek* movies, for instance, by design contains all of the fairy-tale characters. Perhaps Batman could show up in this world as well without creating too much of a stir.

The likelihood of a crossover reflects the organization of our fictional-world cosmology. Stories that describe highly realistic worlds are close to each other and to the real world in fictional space, and relatively far from worlds that are highly unrealistic, like those in sword-and-sorcery type stories. Fictions that share certain attributes tend to cluster together, like all superhero stories.

Putting characters in the right world

How do we determine whether someone or something is real or fictional? In many cases, the information about reality status is explicit, as when we pick up a novel, or watch a televised drama, or when we are told that such-and-so is real or make-believe. But such explicit information may be lacking in many cases, so even children must develop a sensitivity to other cues.

In general, children can gain a good idea of what kinds of things belong in the real world and what kinds of things don't, through their own experiences. When confronted with a representation of a new character or creature, they can do a quick perceptual comparison: Is this new thing similar enough to objects in the real world to count as real? Conversely, is it similar enough to other fictional objects to be counted as fictional? Most of the characters that children know are highly unrealistic: superheroes, cartoon characters, talking animals, and the like. These are so different from the objects that make up their everyday experience that it should be easy for children to separate them into a different category using just perceptual properties. Children know, for example, that they don't see cartoon characters walking among us. This makes it easy for them to judge that a cartoon character is fictional. This inference might lead them astray in rare instances, as when they see Stephen Hawking on *The Simpsons*, but it is usually accurate in its division of real from fictional. Additionally, if children use similarity as their main cue in making reality/fantasy distinctions, they should have more difficulty understanding that a realistic character is fictional, an issue that warrants further research.

Once reality has been accurately separated from fiction, there remains the issue of putting fictional characters into the right worlds. Our theory states that we create a new world every time we encounter a new story. But this is a little misleading, since it hinges on how we define 'story'. Surely it is not the case that every novel or movie is its own story, since that would involve creating new worlds for sequels. The Sherlock Holmes stories by Arthur Conan Doyle all clearly belong to the same world; we should not create a new world for each Holmes novel. A story must thus be broader than a single work of fiction.

So what is a single story? What is contained in a single world? One promising direction to look for a definition has to do with characters. A single story could be one that involves the same character or set of characters. This takes care of the Holmes case and all other cases involving serial books or movies. As long as Sherlock Holmes is there, the new book belongs in the same, already created Holmes world. Note that sameness of character not a necessary condition for a single world, since there are cases in which one identifies two fictions as corresponding to the same world, even if none of the characters overlap. For example, various television shows have taken place in the world of *Star Trek*, including the original 1960s series, *The Next Generation, Deep Space 9*, and *Enterprise*.

Even after accounting for cases where multiple character sets occupy the same world, determining which characters belong in which worlds is still not entirely straightforward. James Bond, for example, first appeared in Ian Fleming's novel *Casino Royale* in 1953. There is much debate about Bond's exact birth date, but in order for him to have been a spy by 1953, he must have been born around 1920. Since the novel is realistic enough to assume that time passes normally, he should be long retired by now. But we know from modern James Bond movies like *Die Another Day* that he's not—he's still middle-aged. So is the world of *Casino Royale* just a different world from that of *Die Another Day*? It's possible that a new Bond world is created every time a new actor plays the role, eliminating the problem of Bond's failure to age and change in appearance over time. But this solution creates new problems. We now have multiple Bonds, each of which has no shared history with the others, which fails to acknowledge that we're still dealing with the same character in all cases.

One promising solution to this problem of multiple Bonds relies on the distinction between essential and accidental properties (similar to ideas proposed in Kripke 1980). It is likely that some properties of a character are essential to that character, while others are not. As discussed above, Bond's birth date is intuitively irrelevant, for instance. So are his precise appearance and certain personal habits, such as whether or not he is a smoker. But other properties are essential to making James Bond *James Bond*, particularly the fact that he is a British spy.

Our solution thus involves creating a single Bond world that includes all of Bond's essential properties while leaving Bond's accidental properties underspecified (see Lewis 1978). This solution allows us to say that all of the Bonds in the various novels and movies are the same character, while still accounting for the differences in details among the various novels and movies. One advantage to this solution is that it allows us to account for cases where a work of fiction plainly would *not* correspond to the same Bond world. If there was a movie about a character named James Bond who was a depressed stockbroker who decides to quit his job and become a dancer, plainly this wouldn't be a Bond movie at all, merely a movie with a character with the same name. This movie thus requires its own fictional world, separate from the Bond world.

We are still left with marginal cases, illustrated by speculations before Pierce Brosnan was cast that a future Bond might be black (played by Wesley Snipes), female ('Jane Bond', played by Sharon Stone), or gay (played by Rupert Everett). It is unclear whether these Bond movies would belong in the same Bond world as the previous movies and novels. Although determining the classification of these characters is still difficult, we can now highlight the source of the difficulty: Is Bond's race, gender, or sexual orientation an essential or an accidental property of the character? Our answer to this question will indicate whether any new Bond belongs in the same fictional world or a different one.

Errors versus alterations

We have described the creation of fictional worlds as a straightforward exportation and modification of the real world. But there are occasions in which things don't go quite this smoothly. Consider the case of Robert Parker's detective novels that take place in Boston. Being realistic in tone, these novels involve very little modification of the real world. But in one of his novels, Parker writes that his detective drove the wrong way down a one-way Boston street, leading to letters from angry Bostonians. What's going on here? Common sense tells us that Parker got it wrong. It is not as if he has created a fictional world where Boston has a subtly different driving pattern; he just messed up. The readers were complaining, justifiably, that he did an inadequate job in creating his fictional world. In contrast, it would be ridiculous for someone to complain about how unrealistic it is for the denizens of Bikini Bottom to be cooking at the campfire even though they are underwater—this is an intentional modification of the real world and should be understood as such.

Such cases are easy to identify as errors, but things are often not so easy. Consider again McEwan's novel *Saturday*. Near the end of the novel, a violent criminal named Baxter is pacified by a young woman reciting a poem. As part of a critical review, Banville (2005) complains that this is 'a remarkable response from the kind of thug [Baxter] is portrayed as being'. Is Baxter's response really a mistake on McEwan's part? Yes, if McEwan really is trying to depict a perfectly realistic world. No, if McEwan should instead be read as having purposefully created a world where such things can happen. Of course, one might argue that McEwan's creation of such a world is artistically flawed, that his world is uninteresting, unimaginative, and morally suspect—and Banville argues all of these things. But this is different from accusing McEwan of ignorance or carelessness. The crucial issue here is our ability to tell the difference between a mistake, like Parker's wrong-way street, and a purposeful depiction.

Another illustration of this boundary between mistakes and deliberate violations comes from a *Far Side* cartoon by Gary Larson. The cartoon depicts a male mosquito coming home after a long day's work, hanging up his hat in the entryway, and complaining to his mosquito wife that he's had an exhausting day spreading malaria to thousands of people. Larson reports getting mail from concerned readers about this cartoon, informing him that it is the female mosquito, not the male, who does the biting (Larson 1989: 124). His response is that none of his readers had a problem with the fact that his cartoon mosquitoes lived in houses, wore clothes, or spoke English, so why should they care about the mosquitoes' gender roles? But in this case, Larson is wrong, and the readers are right.

Larson's cartoon changed the rules in such a way that allowed the mosquitoes to behave like humans, but it did not switch the roles of male and female mosquitoes. It is tempting to argue that all bets are off in cases that are as far from reality as *Far Side* cartoons, but the letters from readers indicate otherwise. They clearly expected certain laws of reality to be violated and certain ones to be upheld.

Porous boundaries

Much research has shown that both adults and children separate reality from fiction. Despite this fundamental separation, this boundary can occasionally be *porous*; there are cases in which we treat fictional events as if they were real. This is particularly so when it comes to our emotional reactions. One long-standing puzzle in philosophy arises from the fact that we are moved by the fate of fictional characters in much the same way as we are moved by real events (e.g. Radford 1975; Walton 1990; Clark and Van Der Wege 2003; Gendler and Kovakovich 2005). This is puzzling because of the apparent conflict between feeling bad about the death of Anna Karenina, say, and knowing full well that no such person exists.

Facts, not only emotions, can pass through the reality/fiction boundary; we can use fiction to form beliefs about the real world (see Gendler, Ch. 9). It is no secret that people often seek out certain types of fiction (historical novels, for example) because they want a painless way of learning about the real world. Much of the appeal of Arthur Golden's novel *Memoirs of a Geisha* is that it accurately depicts what it is like to be a real geisha. The publication of *The DaVinci Code* led to a booming tourist industry in Scotland. The novel claimed that the Holy Grail was buried under a certain church in Scotland, so people visited the church to look for it, despite their awareness that the book is a work of fiction. In general, much of what we believe to be true—about police procedure, for instance, or life aboard a submarine—is, for many of us, acquired through fiction.

These porous boundaries can sometimes cause confusion. Robert Young, who played the title role in the television show *Marcus Welby, M.D.,* reported getting thousands of letters each week asking for medical advice (Real 1977: 121). The actor later exploited this confusion by appearing in commercials as an authority on the health benefits of Sanka decaffeinated coffee. Presumably people sending the letters and watching the ads were fully aware that *Marcus Welby, M.D.* was not a documentary and that Robert Young was not really a doctor. But for some reason, they could not resist the inference that Young would know a lot about medicine because the character did. In general, it seems to be particularly difficult for people to avoid drawing conclusions about actors based on the roles that they play.

These confusions illustrate the importance of similarities between the real world and fictional worlds. Often these similarities lead people to make correct inferences about the real world based on a fictional one, as when we read historical fiction. But similarities can also fool people with cases like *Marcus*

Welby, M.D., where exportation of information from the fictional world to the real world looks like it should be licensed, but isn't.

The issues we have discussed in this section present genuine challenges to our theory of how fictional worlds are created. Problems with crossovers, issues of character identity, the differences between mistakes and deliberate violations, and the nature of the boundary between reality and fiction are not easily solved. But there is a sense in which our theory predicts that they shouldn't be. Our goal in this chapter has been to create a theory that captures our commonsense understanding of fiction, and, in many cases, common sense does not give us clear intuitions about the issues raised here. It is genuinely confusing for people to determine which characters could meet in a crossover, or which properties of a new James Bond or Batman should be imported from previous versions of the character. In future research, we hope to determine more precisely how people think about these difficult issues and to refine our theory of world creation based on these intuitions.

BEYOND FICTION

The focus of this chapter has been fictional worlds, but we should conclude by noting that that there are other non-real worlds that children and adults deal with. These include the worlds that we invoke when planning the future, the worlds that we create when we daydream, the worlds that scientists use when constructing models or thought experiments, and the worlds created by young children when they pretend. Indeed, the fact that young children are adroit at keeping their pretend worlds separate (see Harris 2000) raises the possibility that the creation of multiple worlds might be a unlearned default for how imagination works.

An investigation of the nature of the relationship between planning and fiction, particularly in children, could prove fruitful in discovering not only *how*, but also *why*, we create fictional worlds. We hope that gaining a greater understanding of the issues raised in this chapter can help us to understand this (uniquely human?) ability to think far beyond our current surroundings.

REFERENCES

BANVILLE, J. (2005) 'A Day in the Life' [Review of the book *Saturday*], *New York Review of Books*, 26 May, 52.

CLARK, H. H., and VAN DER WEGE, M. M. (2003) 'Imagination in Discourse', in D. Schiffrin, D. Tannen, and H. E. Hamilton (eds.), *The Handbook of Discourse Analysis* (Oxford: Blackwell), 776–86.

CURRIE, G. (1990) *The Nature of Fiction* (Cambridge: Cambridge University Press).

DiLALLA, L. F., and WATSON, M. W. (1988) 'Differentiation of Fantasy and Reality: Preschoolers' Reactions to Interruptions in their Play', *Developmental Psychology*, 24, 286–91.

Eco, U. (1990) 'Small Worlds', in *The Limits of Interpretation* (Indianapolis: Indiana University Press), 64–82.

Gendler, T. S. (2000) 'The Puzzle of Imaginative Resistance', *Journal of Philosophy*, 97, 55–81.

——— and Kovakovich, K. (2005) 'Genuine Rational Fictional Emotions', in M. Kieran (ed.), *Contemporary Debates in Aesthetics and the Philosophy of Art* (Oxford: Blackwell), 241–53.

Gerrig, R. J. (1993) *Experiencing Narrative Worlds* (New Haven, Conn.: Yale University Press).

Golomb, C., and Galasso, L. (1995) 'Make Believe and Reality: Explorations of the Imaginary Realm', *Developmental Psychology*, 31, 800–10.

Harris, P. L. (2000) *The Work of the Imagination* (Oxford: Blackwell).

——— Brown, E., Marriot, C., Whittal, S., and Harmer, S. (1991) 'Monsters, Ghosts, and Witches: Testing the Limits of the Fantasy–Reality Distinction in Young Children', *British Journal of Developmental Psychology*, 9, 105–23.

Kripke, S. A. (1980) *Naming and Necessity* (Cambridge, Mass.: Harvard University Press).

Larson, G. (1989) *The Prehistory of* The Far Side (Kansas City, Mo.: Andrews McMeel).

Leslie, A. M. (1994) 'Pretending and Believing: Issues in the Theory of ToMM', *Cognition*, 50, 193–200.

Lewis, D. (1983) 'Truth in Fiction', *American Philosophical Quarterly*, 15, 37–46.

——— (2000) *On the Plurality of Worlds* (Oxford: Oxford University Press).

Morison, P., and Gardner, H. (1978) 'Dragons and Dinosaurs: The Child's Capacity to Differentiate Fantasy from Reality', *Child Development*, 49, 642–8.

Piaget, J. (1962) *Play, Dreams, and Imitation in Childhood* (New York: Norton).

Radford, C. (1975) 'How Can We Be Moved by the Fate of Anna Karenina?', *Proceedings of the Aristotelian Society*, 49 (suppl. 1), 67–80.

Real, M. R. (1977) *Mass-mediated Culture* (Englewood Cliffs, NJ: Prentice Hall).

Ryan, M.-L. (1991) *Possible Worlds, Artificial Intelligence, and Narrative Theory* (Bloomington: Indiana University Press).

Samuels, A., and Taylor, M. (1994) 'Children's Ability to Distinguish Fantasy Events from Real-life Events', *British Journal of Developmental Psychology*, 12, 417–27.

Skolnick, D., and Bloom, P. (forthcoming) 'What Does Batman Think about Sponge-Bob? Children's Understanding of the Fantasy/Fantasy Distinction', *Cognition*.

Taylor, M. (1999) *Imaginary Companions and the Children who Create them* (New York: Oxford University Press).

Thomasson, A. L. (1998) *Fiction and Metaphysics* (Cambridge: Cambridge University Press).

Walton, K. L. (1990) *Mimesis as Make-believe* (Cambridge, Mass.: Harvard University Press).

Wellman, H. M., and Estes, D. (1986) 'Early Understanding of Mental Entities: A Reexamination of Childhood Realism', *Child Development*, 57, 910–23.

Woolley, J. D., and Phelps, K. E. (1994) 'Young Children's Practical Reasoning about Imagination', *British Journal of Developmental Psychology*, 12, 53–67.

PART II
PRETENCE

6

Why Pretend?

Peter Carruthers

In this chapter I shall take up the question of children's motivations to engage in pretence.[1] I shall use the account provided by Nichols and Stich (2003) as a stalking horse: arguing that they are correct about much of the basic cognitive architecture necessary to explain pretence, but wrong on the question of motivation. Following a discussion of the views of Currie and Ravenscroft (2002) on this issue, I shall draw on Damasio's (1994) description of the way in which emotions enter into practical reasoning involving mental rehearsal. This will enable me to defend a novel explanation of the motivations underlying pretence.

1. NICHOLS AND STICH ON THE COGNITIVE ARCHITECTURE OF PRETENCE

Nichols and Stich (hereafter N&S) (2003) argue that a number of additions need to be made to the standard cognitive architecture of belief, desire, and practical reason, in order to explain the phenomenon of pretence. Most importantly, they argue that we need to recognize the existence of a distinct type of attitude, alongside belief and desire—namely, the attitude of *supposing*. When children pretend, they are *supposing* that something is the case (e.g. that the banana is a telephone, that they have an invisible friend called 'Wendy', etc.), and they act out their pretence within the scope of that supposition. Moreover, *supposing* can't be reduced to believing, or to desiring, or to any combination thereof (nor can it be reduced to any sort of planning or intending). It therefore needs to be assigned its own 'box' within a functional boxology of the human mind.

N&S (2003) suggest, in fact, that *two* new boxes need to be added to the standard architecture (see Fig. 6.1). One is a mechanism for generating novel

Thanks to Shaun Nichols for his comments on an earlier draft.

[1] The question that forms my title is ambiguous: it can be taken in either a proximate or a distal sense. When we ask why children engage in pretence, this can be taken as a question about children's desires and motivations (proximate), or it can be taken as a question about the evolution and adaptive function of pretence (distal). Both questions are interesting and important. But I focus almost entirely on the former (proximate) question here. For discussion of the evolutionary function of pretence, see Carruthers 2002 and 2006.

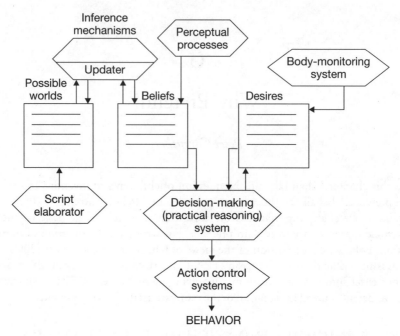

Figure 6.1 Nichols and Stich's account of pretence

suppositions. The other is a working-memory system within which those suppos-itions get elaborated. (These elaborations take place partly by inference, partly by drawing on those of the subject's beliefs that aren't inconsistent with the initial suppositions.) They label the former the 'script elaborator'. But this is mislead-ing, since the mechanism they envisage doesn't just add suppositions to an ongo-ing supposed scenario; it is also meant to *initiate* episodes of supposing. I shall therefore refer to this mechanism in my own discussion as the 'supposition gen-erator'. The working memory system they label the 'possible worlds box', since what it does is contain a partial representation of the possible world in which the initial suppositions are true (as elaborated by inference and by drawing on the subject's existing beliefs).

The possible worlds box, in N&S's (2003) model, interacts with a set of infer-ential mechanisms. These are the very same mechanisms that interact with exist-ing beliefs to generate novel beliefs. Amongst these mechanisms is what N&S call the 'updater'. This is normally employed to update our beliefs as our cir-cumstances change, and as we acquire novel beliefs, so far as possible eradicating inconsistencies that may have been introduced by the adoption of new beliefs. But the updater is also employed to 'screen out' beliefs that are inconsistent with the current contents of the possible worlds box, preventing them from being added to it.

N&S's (2003) account of what happens cognitively during an episode of pretence, then, is this. An initial supposition is placed in the possible worlds box by the supposition generator. That supposition is then worked on by the subject's inferential mechanisms, drawing on the subject's existing beliefs to elaborate and extend the initial supposition. But at the same time the updater screens out any of the subject's existing beliefs, or their consequences, that are inconsistent with the initial supposition, in such a way that the possible world representation being elaborated in the possible worlds box remains internally consistent. At any time, moreover, yet further suppositions can be added to the possible worlds box by the supposition generator, resulting in a further round of inference and elaboration.

All of this is very plausible, and I propose to accept it for the purposes of the discussion that follows. (For a discussion of some different ways in which N&S's architecture might be implemented, see Carruthers 2006.) I shall be focusing on, and criticizing, what N&S (2003) have to say about the way in which the possible worlds system interacts with the desires box. And in the present context, that means focusing on N&S's account of the motivations that underlie pretend play.

2. NICHOLS AND STICH (2003) ON THE MOTIVATION TO PRETEND

N&S's idea is this: what the pretender wants is to behave in the way in which some person or thing represented in their possible worlds box would behave. Put differently, someone who pretends that P does so because he wants to behave more or less as he would (or might) behave if P were the case. And N&S postulate that such desires are both *basic* (that is, intrinsic, or non-instrumental) and *innate*, in much the same way that desires for food or sex are basic and innate.[2]

These claims have a certain initial plausibility. For it seems quite natural to say of the child pretending that the banana is a telephone that she is acting as she does because she wants to behave in the way that she *would* behave if the banana *were* a telephone (e.g. by making a telephone call to Grandma). And likewise it isn't implausible to say that the child who is pretending to be a steam train is acting as he does because he wants to behave in the way that he *would* behave if he *were* a steam train (e.g. moving his arms in circles and going 'Chuff, chuff, choo, choo').

---

[2] Nichols (in correspondence) distinguishes between the *general* motivational question ('What motivates people to engage in pretence at all?') and the *specific* motivational question ('What motivates someone to engage in some particular pretend behavior?'), and claims that the N&S account is intended to address only the former. On this reading, the discussion that follows in this section is about the different ways in which the N&S account might be extended to answer the specific motivational question. My own view, in contrast (to be elaborated in Section 5), is that it isn't anything motivational that is innate (as N&S claim), but rather a species-specific disposition mentally to rehearse supposed actions. These rehearsals then interact with our motivational systems, giving rise to new desires in the way that mental rehearsals normally do.

Moreover, episodes of pretence are characteristically engaged in for their own sake—or 'for fun'—and pretend play is a universal species-specific behavior. So the desires that serve to motivate pretence must normally be intrinsic, rather than instrumental, even if they aren't outright innate.[3]

In light of the above, it is plain that N&S need to add a further arrow to their box-and-arrow diagram of the mechanisms involved in pretence. Either they need an arrow from the 'script elaborator'/'supposition generator' to the desires box; or they need an arrow from the possible worlds box to the desires box. And the former of these suggestions seems to be the more plausible. For otherwise they would need to provide some account of *which* representations in the possible worlds box are used to generate a corresponding desire. On this interpretation, then, the idea is that whenever a novel supposition is generated—that the banana is a telephone, that I am a steam train, that I have an invisible friend called 'Wendy', and so on—this causes a novel desire to come into existence: the desire, namely, to behave as one would behave if the supposition were true. This would happen at the outset of an episode of pretence, and would also occur whenever supplementary suppositions are added during the course of the pretence. Each such supposition would give rise to a novel desire: the desire to behave as one would behave if that supposition were true.

2.1. Why don't all suppositions give rise to desire?

But now we (or rather, N&S) have a problem. For as they themselves acknowledge, the supposition generator and possible worlds box are *also* employed for purposes of hypothetical and counterfactual reasoning quite generally, and not just for purposes of pretence. And it just isn't the case—obviously—that I have a desire to behave in the way that I would if my supposition were true *whenever* I make a novel supposition. In the course of a discussion of the abortion issue with students, for example, I might say, 'Suppose that Roe versus Wade were overturned.' This surely doesn't cause in me any desire to behave as I would behave if Roe versus Wade were overturned (e.g. carrying a placard in front of the Capitol). Likewise, when considering potential house repairs, I might think, 'Suppose we had the roof redone this year, and then had the outside painted next year.' But this surely doesn't cause in me any desire to behave as I would behave if we did have the roof renewed this year (e.g. visiting the bank for a loan).

The obvious suggestion to make on N&S's behalf is that the arrow that we have said needs to be added between the supposition generator and the desires box is there to represent a *channel* for information, which can either be open or closed. When it is open, each novel supposition gives rise to a corresponding

---

[3] But those desires need not *always* be intrinsic, of course. A child taking part in a psychological experiment might pretend to be a steam train, not for its own sake, but in order to comply with a request from the experimenter. And likewise a child might engage in a novel pretence (like pretending to be a dead cat), not for its own sake, but in order to make his parents laugh.

desire; but when it is closed, no new desires get created. And the proposal could be that episodes of pretending occur whenever a novel supposition is made while the channel between the supposition generator and desires box is open, whereas in all other forms of suppositional thinking and reasoning, that channel is closed. The problem now, however, is to give some non-arbitrary account of what might cause the opening or closing of the postulated channel.

One proposal might be that the status of the channel (as open or closed, that is) is age-specific. Perhaps it is open in childhood and closed in adulthood. But this is highly implausible. Children are perfectly well capable of entertaining novel suppositions when engaging in hypothetical or counterfactual reasoning (Harris 2000), without thereby being motivated to engage in some sort of pretence. And likewise, adults are perfectly well capable of pretending—and not just on instrumental grounds, either, but for its own sake. (Think here of a mother playing at dolls with her daughter.)

Another proposal might be that the channel between the supposition generator and the desires box only gets opened by specific types of behavioral cue, such as someone expressing the supposition in question with a characteristic 'let's pretend' voice intonation. For there does at least seem to *be* a characteristic tone of voice that is used to initiate games of pretence (Harris 2000), somewhat as the play-bows of dogs and wolves are used to initiate games of chase (Bekoff and Allen 1998). And it might be suggested that we are hard-wired to respond to such a tone of voice by creating an appropriate motivation. Moreover (and in response to the obvious objection that people frequently engage in solitary forms of pretence), it might be suggested that imagined utterances in 'inner speech' with the same sort of (imagined) voice intonation can *also* serve to open the channel between the supposition generator and the desires box.

This proposal isn't very plausible either, however. One problem is that infants begin to engage in pretend play while still quite young—around the age of eighteen months—at which age many of them are barely talking, and almost certainly aren't yet mentally rehearsing episodes of *inner* speech. Another problem is that, even with somewhat older children (who are certainly *capable* of inner speech), it seems highly implausible that every episode of solitary pretence should begin with some sort of speech act (whether overt or mentally rehearsed) using an appropriate voice intonation. Consider the child pretending that the banana is a telephone: might not the episode begin when the child is *reminded* of a telephone by its similarity in shape to the banana that he sees? And this surely needn't require that the child should articulate to himself in English, 'That is a telephone', or anything similar. Or the episode might begin when the child visualizes himself lifting the banana, making dialing movements, and placing it to his ear. Surely no forms of verbalization (inner or outer) need be required.

The most plausible suggestion that I can make on N&S's behalf is that the channel between the supposition generator and the desires box is opened by a pre-existing desire to pretend *something*. When one is in the mood for pretence, as it were, then novel suppositions will automatically give rise to desires to behave as one would behave if those suppositions were true. *One* way of getting into the right mood might be by hearing (or mentally rehearsing) utterances made with a 'let's pretend' voice intonation. But perhaps boredom, or other sorts of stimuli or background circumstance, can give rise to a generalized desire to pretend, as well.

It seems to me doubtful, however, whether every episode of pretence first requires the activation of some sort of generalized desire to pretend, before it can begin. Granted, it is sometimes the case that one first wants something to pretend, and then casts around for some suitable supposition to make. But I doubt whether this has to be so. Mightn't the child have had *no* pre-existing desire to pretend anything when he spotted the resemblance between the banana and a telephone handset, for example? And yet we can't say that *spotting resemblances* is one of the cues that causes a generalized desire to pretend, either, since we are perfectly well capable of seeing a resemblance without being motivated to engage in pretence.

2.2. How to explain the patterning of pretence?

I have been arguing that it is difficult for N&S to explain why only *some* suppositions should give rise to the desire to behave as one would if those suppositions were true. But there is a further (if not unrelated) problem with their account. This is to explain the distinctive *patterning* that we see in forms of pretence.

For the most part, people pretend to be, or to do, things that they find in some way admirable or valuable. Children who admire farmers and farm machinery pretend to drive tractors and harvesters; children who don't, don't. Likewise, children who admire soldiers, and who take an interest in weapons and warfare, pretend to fight battles and shoot one another; whereas children who admire homemaker roles pretend to bathe babies and make mud pies. These facts are puzzling if (as N&S seem bound to maintain) any sort of supposition that gets made (in the right kind of pretend mode) gives rise to a desire to behave as one would behave if that supposition were true.

Of course, children *can* (and sometimes do) pretend to be or do almost anything, whether admirable or not. They can pretend to be lying in hospital badly injured and in pain; they can pretend to be eating their most hated kind of food; or they can (in N&S's memorable example) pretend to be a dead cat. But the fact is that children don't *often* engage in these forms of pretence. And when they do, their pretence can plausibly be explained as being instrumentally, rather than intrinsically, motivated. Children engaged in forms of cooperative role-play (such as doctors and patients) may have to take their turn at playing the less desirable role, for example. And children can engage in strange and unexpected forms of play in order to make other people laugh.[4]

---

[4] It is noteworthy that the child who pretended to be a dead cat began by drawing the attention of an audience, saying, 'Hey, look at me: I'm a dead cat', before lying down to enact the role (N&S 2003: 20).

I think that the only real option for N&S at this point is to claim that background concerns and interests tend to influence the sorts of suppositions that get entertained in the first place. While any supposition, once made (and made in the presence of a generalized desire to pretend, perhaps), will give rise to a desire to act as if that supposition were true, perhaps only those suppositions that are in some way interesting to the subject will tend to get entertained at all. Hence the patterning that we see in children's pretence can be explained: it is because the child is interested in guns and warfare that he entertains the supposition, *I am creeping with my* [toy] *gun behind enemy lines*; and it is because the child is admiring of home-making roles that she entertains the supposition, *This* [doll] *is my baby and it is time for the baby's bath.*

Although at one level this account can work, at another level it just introduces a new set of mysteries. For *how* do background interests and values make it the case that some suppositions, but not others, are entertained? For suppositions aren't *actions* that might be chosen in the light of one's desires or interests. So how are background interests supposed to influence them?—And not just *influence* them, but bring it about that suppositions that are incongruent with one's interests and values are hardly ever entertained. (For if they *were* entertained, then they would automatically give rise to a desire to act as if that supposition were true, on the account that we are considering—in which case we would expect to see a great deal more value-incongruent pretence than we actually do.)

N&S might reply, with some justice, that it is mysterious where novel thoughts appear from in any case. So it is nothing really to be wondered at if it should remain mysterious how subjects' interests might channel the suppositions that they entertain. Now, I think this would be a fair point if there were no *other* account of the motivations involved in pretence that can do better on this score. But as we shall see shortly, there is.

Notice, too, that the account sketched above has some implausible consequences. If the influence of background interests and values occurs only at the point of supposition generation, then we should predict that any child who can be induced to entertain another's supposition should feel motivated to pretend accordingly. So if a little girl who cares nothing for fighting can be induced to *suppose* that she is creeping behind enemy lines with a gun in her hand, she should *want* to behave as she would if that supposition were true. And if a little boy who hates even to be in the house during the daytime can be induced to *suppose* that his sister's doll is his baby, then he should likewise *want* to behave as if that supposition were true. To me these predictions don't carry the ring of truth.[5]

---

[5] Sometimes, of course, children have social desires that might lead them to want to play *at something* with another child. In order to fulfill this desire, they might have to engage in forms of pretence that wouldn't otherwise interest them.

2.3. How to explain the connections with other uses of imagination

I have argued that N&S have difficulty in explaining why it isn't the case that *every* supposition gives rise to a desire to behave as if that supposition were true. And I have argued that N&S have difficulty in explaining the ways in which pretence tends to be *patterned* in accordance with the agent's interests and values. But this is by no means the end of their problems. For their account can't easily be extended to account for the ways in which motivations are involved in other uses of imagination, either. And yet it seems plausible that the phenomena in question should admit of a common explanation.

N&S claim that the *cognitive* components in their account of pretence (roughly, everything on the left-hand side of Fig. 6.1) can be regarded as a good account of imagination in general. (What is distinctive about pretence, in their view, is just that it is a kind of imagination that is paired with desires of the sort that issue in pretend behavior: desires, namely, to act as if the imagined states of affairs were the case.) Hence their claim is that the very same apparatus of supposition generator, possible worlds box interacting with inferential systems, and so forth, is also involved in fantasy, in novel-writing and novel-reading, in suppositional reasoning about possible courses of action, and so on. And in the abstract, this claim seems right. It is highly plausible that the very same capacities to generate and to reason with novel suppositions lies at the core of each of these activities.

As is familiar to everyone, however, fantasy, novel-reading, and mental rehearsal of action can all of them engage with our motivational systems, giving rise to emotions. Thus imagined sex can make you sexually aroused, imagined insults and slights can make you angry, imagined dangers can make you afraid, and so on. Similarly, people experience a whole range of emotions when reading carefully crafted novels, and often have desires regarding the fates of the characters therein. And likewise, when I mentally rehearse what might happen when I go to see my boss to demand a raise, the results can bring me out in a cold sweat. All of this suggests very strongly that there ought to be an arrow direct from the possible worlds box to the systems that generate desires and emotions.[6] (Only 'body-monitoring systems' get marked on N&S's diagram, in this regard, but plainly there must in any case be others. Not all desires result from changed states of the body.) It looks as if the contents of the possible worlds box can be received as input by the systems that are responsible for generating emotions and desires, and that the latter are thereby keyed into action very much as if those contents were the contents of current perception or current belief.

---

[6] Note that it is an arrow from the possible worlds box that is needed here, and not just from the supposition generator. For it isn't the supposition that I visit my boss to ask for a raise itself that brings me out in a sweat, but rather the further predictions generated by my inferential systems operating on the initial supposition once it is placed in the possible worlds box.

All of this is missing from N&S's account, however.[7] And this is a significant problem. For, as I remarked above, it seems very plausible that the same sorts of mechanisms should underlie pretence as underlie both fantasy and the mental rehearsal of action. For all are instances of a kind of *supposing*. And as we shall see in Section 5 below, once it is recognized that the contents of the possible worlds box will routinely be received by the emotion-generating systems, then we will have to hand a very different and more plausible explanation of the motivations that underlie pretence behavior. But before I develop my own approach to this question, I shall discuss the account given by Currie and Ravenscroft (hereafter, C&R) (2002). For they are quite explicit in proposing a theory that will explain all of the many uses of the imagination, and not just pretence.

3. CURRIE AND RAVENSCROFT ON DESIRE-LIKE IMAGINING

C&R (2002) argue that propositional (as opposed to perceptual/sensory) forms of imagination come in two different varieties: belief-like and desire-like. When we entertain *suppositions*, we enter into states that are significantly belief-like: these states guide our reasoning, and to some extent our acting (in pretence), in ways that are similar to the influence of belief. *Supposing* that the banana is a telephone, and drawing the conclusion that it can be used to call Grandma, is not very different from *believing* that I am confronted with a telephone and drawing the very same conclusion. And likewise *acting* on the supposition that the banana is a telephone is not so very different from acting on the belief that there is a telephone on the hall table in front of me. So, while the suppositions that are involved in pretence *aren't* beliefs, they are belief-*like*—they have an inference-guiding and action-guiding role similar to that of belief.

C&R (2002) argue that there is, in addition, a variety of imagination that is *desire*-like. It consists of states that, while they *aren't* desires, can motivate both practical reasoning and action in a manner that is similar to that of desire. Thus the child who is pretending that the banana is a telephone may form a desire-like state to call his grandma. It is this state that motivates the subsequent sequence of pretend actions (making dialing movements while holding the banana, putting the banana to her ear, and then talking as if Grandma had answered).[8] But it is only desire-*like*—it isn't a full-blown desire to call Grandma, according to C&R.

[7] In fact N&S do briefly mention that the contents of the possible worlds box might be received as input by the emotion systems (2003: 33); but they do nothing further with this suggestion. In later work Nichols (2004, forthcoming) develops this idea much more fully, but doesn't turn it in the direction of explaining the motivations for pretence.

[8] While C&R do commit themselves to the existence of desire-like imaginings, they don't fully commit themselves to this account of the motivations underlying pretend actions. (See C&R 2002: 130–1.) For present purposes, and to simplify my discussion, I shall treat them as if they did.

For that would send the child heading to the hall where the real telephone is, or send her looking for her mother to seek her permission to place a call. Note that the content of the state, however (just like the content of a real desire to call Grandma), is: *that I call Grandma*. The content isn't this: *that I* want *to call grandma*. To have a pretend desire, on C&R's account, isn't to pretend *that I have a certain desire*. Hence pretend desires don't generally have contents that are higher-order in character. To have a pretend desire is, rather, to enter into a state with a first-order world-directed content (e.g. *calling Grandma*) whose causal role is significantly *like* (while also being partly *unlike*) the causal role of desire.

In terms of this account it is now easy to explain why it isn't the case that *all* episodes of supposing or imagining lead to action, in the way that pretending does. For only those belief-like imaginings that are accompanied by a suitably related desire-like imagining will lead to pretend actions. So this is why *supposing* that Roe versus Wade is overturned doesn't lead to *pretending* (acting as if) Roe versus Wade is overturned—it is because this belief-like imagining occurs in the absence of any suitably related desire-like imagining, such as a desire-like state to make a protest at the change. What is distinctive of pretence, according to C&R, is that belief-like imaginings are paired with desire-like imaginings in just the right sort of way to cause (pretend) actions.

Such an account can also be put to work to explain the commonalities between the ways in which desire-like states figure in pretence and the ways that they figure in other uses of the imagination, such as our responses to fiction. In all of the various domains of imagination (fantasy, fiction, pretence, and so on) desire-like states are implicated, according to C&R. While watching a perform-ance of *Othello*, for example, I might *want* Desdemona to survive. While this state is desire-*like*—perhaps causing me to cry when she doesn't—it isn't a real desire. For at the same time I want the play to be performed as it was writ-ten, and take delight in the tragedy of it; and this means wanting that Desde-mona should *not* survive. And neither, of course, do I leap up onto the stage to help her.

What of the patterning that we see in children's pretence, however? Can C&R's (2002) account explain that? This is much more problematic. For what needs to be explained is why children's *real* desires, values, and interests should constrain their adoption of states that are desire-*like*. Why is it that, for the most part, children only pretend (for its own sake) to be or to do what they admire, value, or want? For there are no similar constraints on the adoption of belief-like states. Children routinely suppose things, in their pretending, that conflict with what they actually believe. Thus the child has no difficulty in supposing that the banana is a telephone, although she really knows, of course, that it is just a banana. Indeed, children have no difficulty entertaining suppositions that are actually impossible, such as the supposition that they can fly faster than a bullet (like Superman), or the supposition that they are steam trains or airplanes.

C&R (2002) notice this phenomenon, and stress that it figures importantly in our responses to fiction, too. (They term it 'imaginative resistance', following Moran 1994.) They point out that we are often highly resistant to adopting an imaginative perspective that involves desires or moral values that are alien to our own. It is hard for us to identify with a character in a novel whose main desire is to kill and cook little children. And novelists will have to devote considerable effort and skill if they are to induce us to take a story seriously that requires the adoption of an alien moral system as one of its central background assumptions. In contrast, it is easy for us to adopt alien beliefs while imagining. (Consider how easy it is for us to become immersed in a work of science fiction, in which people can transform their bodily size and shape as they wish—e.g. turning into an insect—or can travel faster than the speed of light.) C&R acknowledge these points, but make no real attempt to explain them. Their problem, in short, is to explain why we can't, in our imaginings, adopt contrary-to-desire suppositional desire-like states at will, in the way that we *can* adopt contrary-to-belief suppositional belief-like states at will.

Now notice, as is quite familiar, that imagination can certainly evoke real *emotions*. Imagined insults can make you angry; imagined danger can make you afraid; the death of a character in a novel or film can make you cry; and so forth. So why shouldn't we also accept that imagination can evoke real *desires*? And indeed, imagined delicacies can make you hungry (wanting food), just as imagined sex can make you sexy (wanting sexual relief). Our account can then be that suppositions (belief-like imaginings) aren't just taken as input by a suite of inferential mechanisms that would otherwise be employed in generating new beliefs from old, or in practical reasoning, as C&R claim, but that they are also taken as input by a variety of desire-generating and emotion-creating mechanisms. Hence we can claim that the desire-like states that occur in imagination are actually *real* desires, produced by the normal operations of such mechanisms, but in this case responding to suppositional input. And we can claim that this is the *only* way in which such states can be generated—passively, in response to belief-like and perception-like imaginings.

But how can these be real desires if they don't lead to real actions? (Although frightened by the film, I don't run out of the theatre; and although saddened by a character's death, I don't write a condolence note.) The answer to this is easy. It is that real desires will normally lead to real actions only *when interacting with real beliefs*. (I shall return to consider the case of pretend action in Section 5.) We are allowing that suppositions and belief-like imaginings *aren't* real beliefs. They differ from real beliefs in crucial aspects of their functional role. For example, the deduced consequences of suppositions are themselves merely suppositions, and aren't stored in memory and reactivated in the manner of beliefs; and the practical reasoning that takes place within the scope of belief-like imaginings doesn't normally give rise to action, or directly to intentions to act. So it is easy to allow that the desire-like states that occur during episodes of imagining are genuine desires, while explaining why they don't have all of the usual functional consequences of desires. This is because those desires aren't, during the episode of imagining, interacting with real beliefs.[9]

This account can readily explain why it is so difficult for us to adopt alien desires or values in imagination. This is because there isn't any desiderative equivalent of *supposing*, or because there is no such thing as desire-like imagining. What a novelist or playwright has to do, in order to evoke in us a motivational response that we wouldn't normally have, is to manipulate our belief-like imaginings in such a way that a response of that kind might naturally be created. We are induced to suppose that Othello and Desdemona are real people and (later) to suppose that Desdemona, although innocent of any wrongdoing, has just died because of Iago's deceit. This latter supposition is received as input by our emotion-generating systems and processed in the usual way, creating real sadness (and perhaps real anger). Hence, although *we* aren't fooled into thinking that anyone has really died, our emotion systems *are* so fooled.

And I suspect, too, that what an author has to do, in order to bring us to full imaginative acceptance of an alien moral system, is to encourage us to take on in imagination a rich network of normative *beliefs* ('It is good for the weak to suffer', 'The strong ought to express their dominance over the weak', or whatever). The author then relies on the fact that such attitudes are designed to straddle the belief/desire divide in order to produce in us at least some echo of the corresponding emotions and motivations. (In general, when I come to *believe* that I ought to do something, I also have some corresponding motivation to do that thing. See Carruthers 2004; Sripada and Stich 2006.)

But *why* should there be this sort of difference between beliefs and desires in respect of their suppositional counterparts? Arguably, the explanation derives from the role of supposition in the mental rehearsal of action, and in reflective practical reasoning more generally, as we will see in the next section. If we assume that mental rehearsal of action is what the human suppositional capacity was originally *for* (in evolutionary terms), then it is easy to understand why the *inputs* to supposition-based processes should all of them derive from the factive (belief-like or perception-like) side of the mind. For it is by supposing that I do something, or by imagining myself doing something, that such rehearsals get started; and it is important to the success of such rehearsals that my motivational reactions should be reliably similar to the ways in which I *would* really respond if the envisaged events were to occur.

---

[9] Notice, however, that once you *finish* fantasizing about the meal that you might order during your next visit to Paris—in the course of which you haven't *really* tried to call a waiter, of course—the real hunger that you have generated may send you heading to the kitchen for a snack. And children who play at making telephone calls will often say things like 'Now let's *really* call Grandma', after the episode of pretence has finished.

4. DAMASIO ON MENTAL REHEARSAL AND SOMATIC MONITORING

Damasio (1994, 2003) develops an account of human practical reasoning and decision-making that is both body-centered and feeling-involving.[10] The idea is that when reasoning about what to do, we envisage performing the various actions available to us, together with their likely outcomes. These suppositions are received as input by the various emotion-generating and desire-generating systems, which respond as appropriate, and which set in train the suite of neural and chemical changes distinctive of the emotion that gets created. Thus if the option under consideration is processed as fearful, a partial fear response is initiated: muscles tighten, heart rate and breathing rate increase, adrenaline is released into the bloodstream, and so on. These changes are monitored by our somasensory systems, and our motivation to perform the action in question is adjusted accordingly. That action gets *marked* as being desirable or undesirable.[11]

According to Damasio (1994), the somatic marking system is inoperative in patients who have undergone damage to certain parts of their frontal lobes. Such people are capable of *reasoning* very sensibly about practical matters. Moreover, they still respond emotionally to stimuli whose emotional salience is unlearned (like sudden loud noises) or that give rise to real beliefs whose emotional significance has been learned prior to their brain damage (as when they are attacked by a bear or a mugger). But they no longer respond emotionally when they *imagine* acting one way rather than another. And they are incapable of learning to respond emotionally to new stimuli (as when they experience repeated losses from a particular deck of cards in a gambling game). As a result, their lives as practical agents are a terrible mess. Few of them can hold down a job or maintain their social

[10] A related but somewhat different account is presented by Schroeder (2004). (See also Rolls 1999.) According to Schroeder, what we monitor isn't our *somatic* responses to our emotional and motivational states, but rather the pleasure and/or displeasure that is occasioned by such states. He argues that the basic determinants of desire satisfaction and desire frustration (which he identifies with the traditional psychological properties of *reward* and *punishment* respectively) are unconscious, and realized in activity deep amongst the more ancient parts of the brain. But these states are *represented* in the frontal cortex, in an area that appears to be the neural seat of pleasure and displeasure. And it is these hedonic states that we monitor when making decisions. For my purposes it doesn't matter much which of these two accounts is endorsed. Whether what are monitored are hedonic states of pleasure and displeasure, representing states of desire satisfaction and frustration, or rather a wider set of bodily responses to satisfaction and frustration (or both), essentially the same sort of self-monitoring decision-making architecture would seem to be involved. In what follows I shall make use of Damasio's framework for convenience.

[11] Damasio (1994) envisages that for much of the time we actually make use of a faster 'as if' neural circuit, which simulates and anticipates our bodily responses without really needing to create them. I shall, for the most part, ignore this complication in what follows.

relationships for very long. And while they can plan sensibly for the future, maintaining and acting on those plans proves beyond them.

Here is how the somatic marker account can be mapped onto a development of N&S's (2003) architecture. When we are reasoning about what to do, the various actions open to us are entertained as suppositions and entered into the possible worlds box. There they are elaborated using a battery of different inferential systems, and some likely consequences are predicted. All of these contents (the initial supposed actions, together with their predicted consequences) are made available as inputs to the desire-generating and emotion-generating mechanisms. The latter set to work processing that input and produce a suite of emotional/bodily reactions. These are monitored, and our motivations towards executing the envisaged actions are adjusted up or down as a result, depending upon the valence (positive or negative) of the emotions in question.

The emotions generated by this process are real ones, not just emotion-*like*. But they are directed towards one or more of the suppositions contained in the possible worlds box, not towards some real (believed-in) state of affairs. Hence, of course, they don't normally issue in the actions that might be appropriate for those emotions, since there aren't the appropriate beliefs to guide them. For example, the fear that I feel when I mentally rehearse walking into my boss's office to ask for a raise is real enough — my heart beats faster, my mouth goes dry, and my hands start to sweat. But it doesn't (of course) lead me to stop and retreat, since I don't believe that I am *actually* walking into my boss's office to confront him. Rather, the awareness of fear makes me less inclined to do so, perhaps to the point that I abandon the idea altogether.

Once a mechanism of this sort has evolved, it is easy for it to become parasitized in fantasy and in literature. I can entertain the supposition that I walk into a Paris bistro and order my favorite French dish, not as part of an episode of practical reasoning, but for its own sake. For that supposition, together with a number of further elaborations and consequences (e.g. carried forward to the point where I am imagining that the dish in question has just been placed on the table before me), will be received as input by my various emotion-generating and desire-generating systems — in this case producing some of the emotional satisfaction that would attend actually *smelling* the distinctive garlic and wine sauce, for example, as well as producing real (albeit faint) hunger.

Likewise, when I enter the theatre to watch a performance of *Othello*, I entertain the supposition that these are real people, really saying and doing the things that are acted out on the stage. Those suppositions are received as input by my emotional and desire-generating systems, which set to work to produce many of the same feelings that they would create if the events being witnessed were real. Some of these feelings are directly pleasurable (as when Iago gets what he deserves). But even where the feelings caused would otherwise be aversive (such as sadness at the death of Desdemona), I retain an important element of control over them. For at any moment, by reminding myself that this is only a play, and that no one has really died, I can close down the pretend inputs to my emotion-generating systems, hence shutting down or modulating their response. And this might (in a different way) be pleasurable.[12]

N&S's possible worlds box architecture, then, when combined with the somasensory-monitoring architecture proposed by Damasio (1994), has the capacity to explain many of the commonalities between pretence, fantasy, literature, and mental rehearsal of action for purposes of practical reasoning. In each case the initial suppositions and their consequences are received as input by the agent's motivational systems, and real desires or emotions are produced as a result. At the same time we can explain the phenomenon of emotional resistance. The reason why we cannot take on alien desires or values at will is because there is no such thing as a desire-supposer, distinct from the belief-like supposition generator. On the contrary, the only way that desires and emotions can enter into imaginative episodes is by being produced 'passively' by the motivational systems operating on belief-like suppositional input.[13]

5. EXPLAINING PRETENCE

This sort of account can explain how emotions are caused *during* episodes of pretence, plainly—as when a little boy playing war games becomes frightened at the thought that his hiding place is about to be discovered. So our account of why people are motivated to engage in *some* forms of pretence can parallel an account of why people should watch tragedies and attend horror movies. In both sorts of case the attraction will be a combination of aversive emotional reactions with the element of control that comes with the knowledge that nothing of the sort pretended or envisaged is really taking place (and/or with admiration at ourselves for responding in the ways that we do). But while this kind of account might explain why children engage in games of hide-and-seek, or play war games, it can't fit many other cases, or explain the simple forms of pretence in which infants engage.

So can the hybrid N&S–Damasio account suggested above be extended to explain why children should engage in simple forms of pretence at all? What sort of desire is it that explains the child's pretence, if not the desire to act in the way

---

[12] There is a long-standing puzzle about how it is possible for us to take pleasure in negative emotional responses to theatre, literature, or music, of course (Levinson 1997). And while some writers do seek to explain this pleasure in terms of *control*, in something like the manner sketched in the text (Eaton 1982; Morreall 1985), this is only one possibility amongst others. Another idea consistent with those being developed in the present chapter would be that the pleasure I take in negative emotional responses to tragedy results from thinking myself to be in various ways *admirable* for being susceptible to those emotions (Levinson 1982; Feagin 1983).

[13] Of course I can always imagine *that I desire something*. But this is a (belief-like) supposition that takes a desire as its *content*, rather than a desire-like supposition of the sort that C&R (2002) envisage.

that they would act if their suppositions were true (as N&S suppose)? And can the account explain, moreover, the sorts of *patterning* that we see in children's pretence? I shall address the former pair of questions first.

5.1. Why pretend?

Let us suppose that infants are capable of non-verbal mental rehearsal. Then consider the child who is prompted to entertain the supposition, *That* [banana] *is a telephone*, perhaps caused by the similarity in shape between the banana in question and a telephone handset. This supposition is placed in the child's possible worlds box, and taken as input by a variety of inferential systems, one of which delivers the thought, *That* [banana] *can be used to call Grandma*. The child then mentally rehearses the action of using *that* [banana] to call Grandma, and this supposition together with its further likely consequences (e.g. talking with Grandma) are received as input by the child's motivational systems. Since she loves her grandma, and also loves talking with her grandma, she experiences some positive emotions as a result. These are noted by the somasensory monitoring system, and used to index the envisaged action as desirable. Since the child now *wants* to use *that* [banana] to call Grandma, she goes ahead and executes the envisaged action schemata (making dialing movements, placing the banana to her ear, beginning to talk). It is a real desire (to call Grandma on *that*) combined with a supposition (that *that* is a telephone) that explains the child's actions.[14]

What is it that is innate and/or species-specific, on this account, sufficient to explain the species-specific character of pretend play? I am confident that in other animal species, too, worldly similarities of various sorts can lead to partial activation of concepts, together with some of the resulting inferences. Thus although no animal is likely to possess the concept *telephone*, a chimpanzee perceiving a ball might have her concept *coconut* partially activated as a result. And I am myself confident that some other animals engage in mental rehearsal of action (Carruthers 2006). What is distinctive of human children may be just that they are disposed to use the former partial activations as a basis for activating and mentally rehearsing some of the related action schemata.

But why does the child actually *do* anything? Why doesn't she stick to fantasy? For the rewarding emotions involved in talking with Grandma will *already* have been experienced, resulting from her mental rehearsal of the action. After all, adults are perfectly capable of mentally rehearsing an action (such as entering a Paris restaurant and eating dinner) and enjoying the emotions involved, without thereby starting to do anything. So why should the child be any different? A

---

[14] The description provided in this paragraph has been modified slightly—away from what I actually think takes place—to make it fit more naturally within N&S's (2003) framework. But these modifications aren't relevant to the main themes and arguments of this chapter. For a fuller account, see Carruthers 2006.

number of distinct (but mutually consistent) answers to these questions can be given.

One answer is that the use of mental rehearsal to initiate action may be the default mode of its operation. That is to say, a mentally rehearsed action that leads to positive emotional rewards will automatically lead to the execution of (or intention to execute) that action unless something intervenes to prevent it.[15] And then the difference between the child and the adult may just be that the adult has learned to use his knowledge that he is not really in Paris and so forth to pre-empt the action that would otherwise be initiated (e.g. calling the restaurant to make a reservation).

Another answer is that the child's imaginative capacities may be insufficient for her to derive significant pleasure from the act of *imagining* talking to Grandma alone. As we all know, fantasy can be hard work. Attention has to be carefully focused, and the various imaginary scenarios have to be envisaged in significant detail and with considerable vividness. So it may be that young children are incapable of holding their imagined actions *steady* and/or *vividly* enough in mind to reap significant emotional rewards from them.[16] It may then be that *acting out* the pretence is necessary for the child to get a vivid enough representation of herself talking with her grandma for her to experience much real emotion.

Relatedly (and even if the initial mental rehearsal of the action *does* yield significant enjoyment), it is likely that acting out the pretence will reinforce, enhance, and extend that enjoyment. For the child's physical movements will be performed under the (supposed) description, *talking to Grandma*. (Remember, the action schema being executed is: *using that* [banana] *to call and talk to Grandma*.) There will therefore be vivid perceptual representations of various sorts that get subsumed under that description, and that get made available as input to the child's desiderative and emotional systems. So when she hears herself chatting into the 'telephone', this will be conceptualized in a manner coherent with her initial suppositions (that the banana is a telephone, and that she is now talking to Grandma). So those experiences will be received as input by her emotional systems with the content, *I am talking to Grandma* attached, and a much more intense and temporally extended sequence of rewarding emotion is likely to result.

Our N&S–Damasio hybrid can explain why the child engages in pretence, then. But what does it tell us about the *goal* of her action? What is she aiming at when she begins the sequence of movements in question? Is she aiming, in

---

[15] Where the emotional rewards of a mentally rehearsed action are sufficiently negative, the result will be that the action is *not* performed. The imaginative episode will lead to action only if it is extended to initiate the rehearsal of some *other* action, which does issue in positive rewards.

[16] What the child does may nevertheless be enough for the action in question to be indexed as desirable. For as Damasio (1994) emphasizes, the operations of somasensory monitoring can be both extremely swift and operate below the level of consciousness, while still having its effects on our goals and choices. Indeed, it can also operate in a purely simulatory 'as if' manner, on his account, in which case no real emotions will be experienced (whether conscious or unconscious).

particular, to undergo a rewarding emotional experience? This might be one
natural way of interpreting the import of Damasio's (1994) account, issuing in
a kind of *hedonism*. The child mentally rehearses talking to Grandma on *that*
[banana] and experiences a rewarding emotion. So she then executes the mentally
rehearsed action in order to undergo that experience again, or more vividly. So
the goal of her action is to experience a rewarding emotion.

Although this sort of hedonistic reading of Damasio (1994) might be tempting, I believe it is wrong. For he talks of the emotions that result from mental
rehearsal as *indexing* the actions rehearsed (as desirable or undesirable), not as
themselves becoming the *objects* of desire. And this is all to the good, since there
are well-known difficulties with hedonistic accounts of agency (Feinberg 1985).
Rather, the account is this: the child mentally rehearses the action schema, experiences a positive emotion, and thereby comes to desire the execution of that action
schema. So her goal, when she acts, is *to talk to Grandma on that* [banana]. This is
a goal that both exists within, and only makes sense within, the scope of the initial
supposition, that *that* [banana] *is a telephone*, of course. (This is why the child
isn't disappointed when her grandma doesn't answer; for she retains the knowledge that you can't really talk to Grandma on a banana.)

5.2. The limits of pretence

But how are we to explain the limits that children place on the acting-out of their
pretence? Why don't they 'go all the way'? For example, consider a child who is
playing at domestic roles, and who acts out the action schema *cooking* [mud] *pies
to eat for dinner*. If her goal is *to cook and eat* [mud] *pies*, why doesn't she follow
through and *really* eat the mud? A pair of related, and mutually consistent, replies
can be given to this question.

One is that the action schema that the child rehearses is unlikely to include
all of the elements involved in the corresponding real (non-pretend) action.
Although at the most abstract level the schema rehearsed is *cooking pies and eating
them*, the more detailed implementation of that schema that gets rehearsed in
the child's imagination is unlikely to include actual chewing and swallowing. For
of course the child retains the knowledge that the 'pies' are made of mud, and
that mud doesn't taste good; and this knowledge is likely to guide the child's
construction of a detailed action schema.

The second answer (and an answer that might provide us with one explanation
of how the first can be true) is that the child might rehearse a number of more
or less complete action schemata, one of which *does* involve putting the 'pies'
into her mouth, chewing, and swallowing them. When this schema is mentally
rehearsed in combination with the knowledge that the pies in question are made
of mud, the sensations and tastes that get predicted are likely to produce a strong
negative emotional reaction. This tags that action schema as undesirable. We
can therefore suppose that the action schema on which the child acts is a sort of

compromise between an attractive abstract description ('cooking and eating pies for dinner') and an aversive detailed implementation of that description ('putting those mud objects in my mouth, chewing, and swallowing'). The aversiveness of the latter will shape just how far the child will go in acting out the former.

5.3. The patterning of pretence

Besides its other advantages, the hybrid N&S–Damasio account sketched above provides an elegant explanation of the patterning of pretence. The reason why, in general, children pretend to do or to be only things that they find in some way valuable or admirable, is that only in these cases will the mental rehearsal of the pretend actions give rise to the sorts of positive emotional reactions that index them as desirable. Let me work through a couple of our earlier examples to illustrate the point.

When the boy who finds guns and warfare exciting and admirable supposes that he is a US marine, and mentally rehearses the action schema *creeping along with my* [toy] *gun behind enemy lines*, he experiences emotions of excitement, which tag the action as desirable. And when he then acts out the pretence, and creeps along behind the living-room sofa while representing what he is doing under that description, he not only experiences some of that same excitement, but throughout the episode he will be representing himself *as* something that he finds admirable: namely, a US marine.

Likewise, when a boy who finds steam trains to be admirable entertains and acts on the supposition *I am a steam train*, he will be representing himself *as* something that he admires. So the perceptions of his current actions will be made available to his motivational and emotional systems tagged with the content *I am a steam train going 'chuff, chuff, choo, choo'*, and so forth. Since he admires steam trains, and is representing himself to *be* a steam train, the episode is likely to be emotionally rewarding.[17] (We all like to think that we are admirable, or to be reminded of admirable features of ourselves, of course!)

In contrast, when a boy entertains and acts on the supposition *I am a dead cat*, he is unlikely the find the episode intrinsically rewarding. For he is unlikely to find dead cats to be especially admirable. We can thus explain why children often pretend to be steam trains (and the like) while rarely pretending to be dead cats (and the like). The kinds of pretence in which children engage will be a direct reflection of their interests and values. So the patterning of children's pretence is satisfyingly explained.[18]

---

[17] This sort of episode might also—or instead—be rewarding for other reasons, of course.

[18] Of course it isn't a problem for this account that a child might *sometimes* pretend to be a dead cat while finding nothing intrinsically admirable about dead cats. For acts of pretence, like any other types of action that are normally intrinsically motivated (like eating or sex), can sometimes be performed for instrumental motives. In this case I hypothesize that the child's goal was to do something funny.

6. CONCLUSION

In this chapter I have used the views of N&S and C&R to triangulate my own position. From the former I have taken the basic architecture of supposition-generator and possible worlds box. From the latter I have taken the idea that the motivations involved in pretence should somehow be of a piece with those involved in fantasy, in literature and theatre, and in the mental rehearsal of action. I have suggested that we can meet all of the main desiderata for a theory of pretence by combining N&S's architecture with Damasio's (1994) account of mental rehearsal, and his account of somasensory monitoring of emotional reactions to those rehearsals. In short, children pretend because they find both the mental rehearsal and the performance of the pretend actions (under suppositional descriptions) to be emotionally rewarding, reflecting their standing desires, values, and interests.

REFERENCES

BEKOFF, M., and ALLEN, C. (1998) 'Intentional Communication and Social Play: How and Why Animals Negotiate and Agree to Play', in M. Bekoff and J. Byers, *Animal Play* (Cambridge: Cambridge University Press).

CARRUTHERS, P. (2002) 'Human Creativity: Its Evolution, its Cognitive Basis, and its Connections with Childhood Pretence', *British Journal for the Philosophy of Science*, 53, 1–25.

—— (2004) 'Practical Reasoning in a Modular Mind', *Mind & Language*, 19, 259–78.

—— (2006) *The Architecture of the Mind: Massive Modularity and the Flexibility of Thought* (Oxford: Oxford University Press).

CURRIE, G., and RAVENSCROFT, I. (2002) *Recreative Minds: Imagination in Philosophy and Psychology* (Oxford: Oxford University Press).

DAMASIO, A. (1994) *Descartes' Error: Emotion, Reason, and the Human Brain* (London: Papermac).

—— (2003) *Looking for Spinoza: Joy, Sorrow, and the Feeling Brain* (New York: Harcourt).

EATON, M. (1982) 'A Strange Kind of Sadness', *Journal of Aesthetics and Art Criticism*, 41, 51–63.

FEAGIN, S. (1983) 'The Pleasures of Tragedy', *American Philosophical Quarterly*, 20, 95–104.

FEINBERG, J. (1985) 'Psychological Egoism', in his *Reasons and Responsibility* (New York: Wadsworth).

HARRIS, P. (2000) *The Work of the Imagination* (Oxford: Blackwell).

LEVINSON, J. (1982) 'Music and Negative Emotion', *Pacific Philosophical Quarterly*, 63, 327–46.

—— (1997) 'Emotion in Response to Art: A Survey of the Terrain', in M. Hjort and S. Laver (eds.), *Emotion and the Arts* (New York: Oxford University Press).

MORAN, R. (1994) 'The Expression of Feeling in the Imagination', *Philosophical Review*, 103, 75–106.

MORREALL, J. (1985) 'Enjoying Negative Emotions in Fiction', *Philosophy and Literature*, 9, 95–103.

NICHOLS, S. (2004) 'Imagining and Believing: The Promise of a Single Code', *Journal of Aesthetics and Art Criticism*, 62, 129–39.

_____ (forthcoming) 'Just the Imagination: Why Imagining Doesn't Behave Like Believing', *Mind & Language*.

_____ and STICH, S. (2003) *Mindreading: An Integrated Account of Pretence, Self-awareness, and Understanding Other Minds* (Oxford: Oxford University Press).

ROLLS, E. (1999) *The Brain and Emotion* (Oxford: Oxford University Press).

SCHROEDER, T. (2004) *Three Faces of Desire* (Oxford: Oxford University Press).

SRIPADA, C., and STICH, S. (2006) 'A Framework for the Psychology of Norms', in P. Carruthers, S. Laurence, and S. Stich (eds.), *The Innate Mind: Culture and Cognition* (Oxford: Oxford University Press).

7

Why Irony is Pretence

Gregory Currie

Children thrive on pretence. So, in less obvious ways, do grown-ups. Take irony: our speech and other actions pass in and out of ironic mode, as we pretend to congratulate, approve, admire, and, occasionally, criticize and deplore.[1] Some deny that irony is a form of pretence, and I aim to show that they are wrong. In the process I separate the pretence theory from some restrictive assumptions: that irony is essentially communicative, that it is essentially linguistic, that it is essentially critical. I show how the pretence theory is extendable in natural ways to cover dramatic, situational, and what I will call 'suppressed' irony—a category so far lacking the publicity it deserves. I conclude with some thoughts on what a sensibly modest theory of irony, like mine, should try to be.

1. THREE THEORIES

Irony is traditionally thought to involve saying one thing and meaning its opposite. Cicero says that, with irony, 'what you say is quite other than what you understand', and Quintilian calls it that 'in which something contrary to what is said is to be understood'—a view preserved in the dictionaries of Johnson and Webster and present even in recent commentary.[2] The idea has, says Gregory Vlastos, 'stood the test of time' (1991: 21).

Versions of this paper have been read at the Universities of Maryland, Nottingham, and Barcelona. Thanks to Stephen Barker, Peter Carruthers, Manuel Garcia-Carpintero, Peter Lamarque, Jerry Levinson, Genoveva Marti, Shaun Nichols, Georges Rey, and Kendall Walton for their comments. Special thanks to Deirdre Wilson who, in her paper at the conference 'The Imaginative Uses of Pictures and Language' (University of Nottingham, July 2005) identified a serious error in an earlier version.

[1] For versions of the pretence theory of irony see e.g. Clark and Gerrig 1984; Walton 1990: 222–3; Kumon-Nakamura et al. 1995 (for whom pretence is 'pragmatic insincerity'; this would make the echoic theory of Sperber and Wilson a pretence theory); Clark 1996: 369–74. Kendall Walton has suggested that pretence plays an important role in many aspects of linguistic and other behaviour. Steve Barker (2004) may be the most extreme advocate of pretence theory for linguistic phenomena; he holds that sentence meanings are not propositions but speech-act types, and that compositionality requires us to invoke pretence in order to explain how we get complex speech-act types from simple ones.

[2] Quintilian, *Institutio Oratorica*, quoted in Vlastos 1991: 21. Cicero, *De Oratore*, quoted in Vlastos 1991: 28 n. 24.

For a theory that has lasted so long, this one explains astonishingly little (Sperber and Wilson 1981). Questions can be ironic, as with 'Have you won the Nobel Prize yet?' This irony is not accounted for by specifying some word that is contrary to the intended sense of the question, since no question is seriously intended. Or take 'You sure know a lot', said to someone who does indeed know a lot but who is too keen to impart what he knows; it would be a very feeble comment on his practices to be asserting that, really, he does not know much. And Vlastos's own example of Socratic irony:

(1) teach me more gently admirable man, so that I won't run away from your school (Gorgias 489d),

makes no sense if we understand Socrates really to be exhorting Callicles *not* to teach him more gently.[3]

People aware of these problems and sensitive to developments in linguistic theory have tended to adopt one of two approaches. The first is Sperber and Wilson's 'echoic' account according to which irony is a kind of free indirect quotation involving the expression of a negative attitude towards a thought attributed to some other person or type of person.[4] The second, long campaigned against by Sperber and Wilson themselves, is the pretence theory. According to this view, Socrates is pretending, in (1), to plead with Callicles not to be so harsh with him: pretending to say something which is a—no doubt exaggerated version of—something Callicles would like Socrates really to say, or so Socrates' performance suggests. Here, as elsewhere, the irony is not a matter of replacing words by their contraries, but of pretending to do something rather than really doing it. These two approaches have much in common: rejection of the contrary-saying view of Cicero; insistence that the ironic utterance serves to express a negative attitude rather than constituting a non-literal statement of such an attitude. Sometimes it is suggested that these two views are the same, or that they do not differ in essential ways. I believe that the views are different, and that the echoic theory fails to account for something that distinguishes irony from other forms of so-called echoic utterance. Yet there is merit in the echoic theory, and the pretence theory has not always been presented in the strongest way. Some rethinking is required.

Someone might worry that we are leaving the traditional view behind too quickly. Can this ancient, resilient view be wholly wrong? We need not say it is wholly wrong: it can be read as a version of the pretence theory, according to which the ironist pretends to say one thing but really says the opposite.[5] The

---

[3] For criticism of Vlastos's treatment of Socratic irony, see Nehamas 1998.

[4] See Sperber and Wilson 1981; Sperber 1984; Wilson and Sperber 1992; Sperber and Wilson 1995, 1998; Wilson 2000.

[5] It is notable how quickly advocates of the traditional theory appeal to pretence, games, and role-play in describing particular instances of irony. Cicero remarks that Socrates was always 'pretending to need information and professing admiration for the wisdom of his companion'

mistake is in the latter part. While ironists pretend to say things, the idea of really saying the opposite of what one pretends to say plays no role in explaining the effects or attractions of irony. The ironist pretends to assert, or to question, or to endorse, and in doing so expresses an attitude towards those who do or would say or question or endorse in this way, or towards people and actions and attitudes which the pretence otherwise brings to mind. This expressing need not be a case of saying.[6] Indeed, irony does not need language; I may stagger back in a parody of horrified distaste when confronted by an austerely elegant Sung vase, ironically expressing my rejection of your ludicrously demanding aesthetic standards.[7]

But if the traditional view is not wholly wrong, it is badly wrong, so its longevity remains a puzzle. I am grateful to Genoveva Marti for suggesting a solution: advocates of the traditional view locate irony in a contrast between (as we would now put it) semantic meaning and speaker's meaning. This is wrong, but there certainly is a contrast between the kinds of *effects* one intends by one's ironic utterance and the effects one would probably intend if one were speaking seriously. With (1), someone speaking in a serious, non-pretending way would be taken as intending to avoid humiliation at the other's hands by flattering him. In fact, we take Socrates to be intending something like the opposite effect: humiliating Callicles by giving voice, in pretend mode, to a perspective on Callicles' intellectual and rhetorical powers which is absurdly inflated.

That said, I think we may move directly to the pretence theory.

2. IRONY AS PRETENCE

I start with a formulation due to Herb Clark and Richard Gerrig, partly because it is a detailed and systematic attempt to flesh out the intuition behind the pretence theory, and partly because it was the focus of Sperber's attack on pretence theories in general. According to Clark and Gerrig (1984: 122), a speaker, S, speaks ironically when:

(Cicero 1913: Book I. xxx). Quintilian says that Socrates 'assumed the role of an ignorant man lost in wonder at the wisdom of others' (1920: ix. 2. 44–53). And Vlastos describes Socrates as 'casting himself as a pupil' of Callicles (see Vlastos 1991: 26). There are hints of the pretence theory in other ancient formulations, such as this from the *Rhetoric to Alexander*, once attributed to Aristotle: '*Eironeia* is [a] saying something while pretending not to say it or [b] calling things by contrary names' (quoted in Vlastos 1991: 26). [a] seems promising: better, anyway, than [b]. But it is not quite right: the ironist pretends to say something while *not* saying it. Grice, who abandoned the traditional view in favour of the pretence theory, does not seem to have understood the former as a version of the pretence theory (see Grice 1989: 54).

6 Since ironic utterances embed—'If Albert is going to give us one of his delightful sermons I am leaving'—this raises problems familiar from the debate over expressivism. I cannot deal with these problems here; a good place to start is Blackburn 1984: ch. 6, sect. 2, and moving on to Gibbard 1990: ch. 5.

7 But cases of verbal irony are the commonest and easiest to characterize, so I stick with them for the purposes of this chapter.

(i) S speaks to an audience A;

(ii) in so doing S pretends to be S′, saying something patently uninformed or injudicious to an audience A′ which is taken in by the utterance; they should, as part of the pretence, be seen as assenting to what is said, or at least as giving it a degree of consideration it does not deserve;

(iii) where A is intended to understand the pretence in (ii).[8]

On this view, irony involves a pretence that one seriously gives voice to an absurd or at least defective thought, and, in doing so, is taken seriously by an audience. This audience—the A′ of (ii)—may be, but need not be, real. We have irony when the speaker addresses two audiences, one comprehending and the other not. But we also have irony, according to Clark and Gerrig, when it is merely understood as part of the pretence that there is this uncomprehending audience (A′) present.

In so far as it goes beyond the basic idea that irony is a form of pretence, this proposal has many defects. Seeing them will get us to a better formulation.

3. AUDIENCE, COMMUNICATION, EXPRESSION

Why should an ironic utterance involve the pretence that the speaker speaks seriously to the gullible audience of Clark and Gerrig's definition? Sometimes the pretence in irony involves the idea that the speaker assumes there is an audience that will take her seriously; on other occasions, the effect of ironic utterance is heightened by the pretence that, while the speaker utters what is in fact an absurdity confident in the belief it will be taken seriously, no one will take it seriously. If A is an inveterate exaggerator whom no one believes, and you say, in the style of A, 'I was there to save the situation', I understand that I am to imagine A saying this to his usual, sceptical audience—at least, I don't see why I should be forbidden, by the very nature of irony itself, from imagining this. The gullible audience might be there at one further intentional remove: We are to pretend that {A believes that [the audience takes him seriously]}. But even that need not be so; A may be the sort of person who doubts whether he has a sympathetic audience, but who feels strangely compelled to boast anyway.

So much for the insistence on the pretence of a credulous audience. But Clark and Gerrig also say that there must really *be* an audience, or at least that the speaker must believe that there is one; the ironist's intention must include the intention to communicate with an audience, and to make it clear to that audience

---

[8] Clark says that irony is pretence in his 1996: 369–74, without offering any explicit definition. My (ii) alters Clark and Gerrig's formulation; they say that A′ is supposed to be an audience which 'misses' the pretence. Clark and Gerrig's overall exposition makes it clear that the real point is that this audience should not merely take the utterance for a seriously meant assertion, for that would leave open the possibility that they regard it as serious but absurd. The idea is, rather, that this audience should assign the utterance a greater degree of credence than it warrants.

that the utterance is a case of pretence.[9] That irony is an essentially communicative activity, and one that requires transparency from the speaker, is a view
widely shared. Vlastos, advocating the contrary-saying view, tells us that irony
must be 'altogether innocent of intentional deceit' (1991: 27). This accounts
very badly for much ironic utterance.[10] Irony often involves a detour down the
garden path.[11] It can be a short one; we may not get the irony in 'I'm mad about
good books—can't get my fill' right away, but the next line helps: 'And James
Durante's looks give me a thrill'.[12] Sometimes people get through the whole performance and don't catch on. Tories were very irritated by the irony of Defoe's
'Shortest Way with Dissenters' and its argument for the extermination of Meth-
odists. For 'it would not, on first reading, seem impossible that an extreme Tory
could argue in this manner' (Booth 1983: 319). The communicative view might
be reformulated so as to insist merely that the audience have to be given a fighting
chance of getting it. This would not help. We can have irony which the audience is intended not to get; a defeated prisoner may have to keep the irony in his
confession to himself. And there can be irony without any audience in fact or in
the speaker's mind. When I go out without my umbrella only to encounter heavy
rain, my utterance of 'Great' is an ironic comment on failure meant for me alone.

So irony is a form of expression. In speaking ironically, one expresses an attitude. This may be intended as a form of communication as well, as when a
disgusted facial expression is intended to communicate one's disgust to others.
But what is essential is the expression, not the communication. This is not a point
of dispute with Sperber and Wilson, who say that 'the attitude expressed by an
ironical utterance is invariably of the rejecting or disapproving kind' (1995: 239).
As we shall see, I disagree with Sperber and Wilson about what sorts of attitudes
need to be expressed in irony.

4. TARGETS

Even with these requirements concerning the audience removed, Clark and Gerrig's proposal will not do. As Dan Sperber points out, merely pretending to assert

---

[9] As their clauses (i) and (iii) make plain.

[10] And contributes to some misidentifications of Socratic irony on Vlastos's part. Vlastos contrasts
the genuinely ironic passage from *Gorgias* quoted above with what he takes to be a different sense
of *eironeia* in *Republic* 337a, where Thrasymachus, exasperated, complains about Socrates' 'habitual
shamming (*eironeia*)', saying that Socrates would 'sham and would do anything but answer if the
question were put to you'. According to Vlastos, this passage involves an imputation of lying and
cannot, therefore, represent a case of irony proper (1991: 25). But Vlastos is not entitled to this
final conclusion.

[11] Sperber and Wilson say that many of the best examples of irony are garden-path utterances
(1995: 242). The fact that irony often leads to 'garden-path' effects is a further reason for classing it
apart from metaphor; metaphors can be difficult to understand, but they do not typically function
to persuade us, temporarily, that the speaker really means what he literally says.

[12] This is Frank Sinatra's version. The original lyric by Ralph Freed has the puzzling 'And
Franklin Roosevelt's looks give me a thrill'.

that $2 + 2 = 5$, that the moon is made of cheese, or a host of other 'patently uninformed or injudicious' things, would not count as saying anything ironical. We need in addition the idea that the pretence draws attention to something we might call a *target* (see Sperber 1984: 131). Suppose A is known for his relentless uttering of wildly false assertions; seeing A coming towards us, I say, '$2 + 2 = 5$, the moon is made of cheese . . .', carrying on in this manner for some while. This is irony, because its target is A's profligate unreliability.

Clark and Gerrig recognize, in some measure, this requirement, since they say that the content of the pretence should be worthy of hostility, indignation, or contempt (1984: 122) Presumably, they mean that thinking or asserting that content would be worthy of such a reaction; I for one have no hostility to the *proposition* that $2 + 2 = 5$. But then it is true that anyone who pretend-asserts '$2 + 2 = 5$' is drawing attention to something which, were it asserted, would provoke a negative reaction, so the clause concerning hostility does not help to distinguish irony from the wider class of pretend assertions. The idea of a target seems to add what is missing here: it is not irony merely to pretend to say something that would be ridiculous if seriously asserted, but it is irony to pretend to say something, intending thereby to draw attention to something ridiculous.

Should we say, then, that the target of the pretence—in this case A's relentless spreading of falsehood—should be worthy of a hostile, or at least in some way negatively evaluative, reaction, and that the pretence should be intended to provoke this reaction? Sperber and Wilson, who disagree with Clark and Gerrig about much, agree with them that irony is essentially disapproving; they require an 'associated attitude of mockery or disapproval' (Wilson and Sperber 1992). This is too strong; when I say, of my daughter, 'She is very excited. Father Christmas is coming tonight', I am pretending, in the service of irony, to assert that Father Christmas is coming tonight. But I am not expressing hostility to, indignation at, contempt, mockery, or disapproval of my daughter for believing this. What makes the remark ironic (and perhaps a little questionable) is the invitation in my pretended assertion to attend to her epistemically limited perspective.[13]

This suggests a general point about the nature of ironic pretence. The pretence one engages in with irony is partly one of behaviour; one pretends to be doing something which one is not doing: speaking seriously and assertively, seriously asking a question, seriously expressing distaste. But the pretence that is fundamental to irony is not a pretence of doing; it's a pretence of being. In pretending to assert or whatever, one pretends to be a certain kind of person—a person with a restricted or otherwise defective view of the world or some part of it. Socrates pretends to be a person who is overawed by the (actually very modest) intellect and rhetorical power of Callicles; I pretend to be someone with a small child's view of the world; and Emma Woodhouse pretends to be someone with

---

[13] Muecke says that '[s]imple ignorance is safe from irony' (1969: 30). I think the example shows that this is not quite true.

Mr Knightly's unreasonably critical view of Emma herself, when she says, 'Especially when one of those two is such a fanciful, troublesome creature!' adding for Mr Knightly's benefit, 'That is what you have in your head I know.'

What is the connection between the idea of a target of irony and the defective outlook that the ironist pretends to have? Often they are the same thing; they are the same in the three examples I gave just now. In each of those cases, the speaker pretends to adopt a limited perspective, and in so doing expresses something about some person's occupancy of that perspective: Socrates expresses a relatively strong form of rejection of the perspective he imputes to Calicles; Emma, a somewhat more affectionate condemnation of Mr Knightly's view of her (a view which, in some moods, she is inclined to share); myself, a wholly affectionate depiction of my daughter's naive belief in Father Christmas. This last case is somewhat of an exception, but that is easily explained: those who pretend to adopt a perspective which seems to them limited or defective in some way are more likely than not to be intending some criticism of it.

In other cases, the relationship between the perspective adopted in pretence and the target is more complicated. We may have something to learn from Sperber and Wilson here, and this is a convenient moment to introduce their theory.

Sperber and Wilson (1981) originally formulated a theory of what they called 'echoic mention', according to which irony is indirect quotation which can, in turn, be accounted for as a case of mentioning the proposition expressed by the utterance. Later, they generalized the theory somewhat: an utterance may count as an ironic comment on the assertion of a proposition P without counting as mentioning P, as in the case of irony which exaggerates or, as with the following, understates:

(2) *Mother*: Anyone would think I was an ogress, and the companion a martyr.
   Son: I think that might be a possible view of the position, Mother.[14]

Here the son draws attention to the deficiencies of the mother's perspective by pretending to adopt a perspective which is slightly less unreasonable than hers, a perspective which at least acknowledges as a possibility that which from her own perspective is utterly absurd. According to Sperber and Wilson, all that is required for the ironic targeting of the tendency to believe P is that the ironic utterance have a content which resembles the content of P and which, because of that resemblance, serves, in the context of utterance, to draw attention to P (see Wilson and Sperber 1992; Sperber and Wilson 1994: 229). Resemblance is a matter of 'a sharing of logical and contextual implications' (Wilson and Sperber 1992: 65).

Appeal to resemblance is central to Sperber and Wilson's account of the function of echoic utterances, and is a recurrent feature of expositions of relevance theory, of which they are the founders. The appeal is sometimes objected to on

---

[14] Ivy Compton-Burnett, *Mother and Son* (New York: Messner, 1955).

the grounds that everything resembles everything (see e.g. Stanley 2005). But there is surely something in the idea that in a given context certain pairs of things strike us as resembling each other while other pairs do not, and this may allow one of the pair to put us in mind of the other. If the idea of resemblance as Sperber and Wilson use it turns out to be seriously and irremediably flawed, we shall need to think again about this aspect of their programme. But I am willing to accept it for the moment. My aim is to show that they need pretence as well. However, while resemblance is a useful notion here, I don't wish to be confined to resemblance with respect to implications. When, in Compton-Burnett's exchange (2), the son pretends to have a certain perspective on his mother's behaviour—seeing it as possibly open to certain criticism—he pretends to a way of looking at the world which dimly recognizes certain obligations to others that most of us see very clearly and the mother, apparently, not at all. His pretended perspective resembles hers much as the optical perspective of a very poorly sighted person resembles that of one who is wholly blind, and I doubt whether this is entirely accounted for in terms of implication.[15] So I prefer to speak of perspectives, or points of view, one of which puts us in mind of the other by virtue of having certain limitations that resemble the limitations of the other, and I treat identity between points of view as a limiting case of this. I leave it for another occasion to say more about the kinds of resemblance we may encounter in irony: in particular cases, such a resemblance is not difficult to recognize.

So what matters is that the ironist's utterance be an indication that he or she is pretending to have a limited or otherwise defective perspective, point of view, or stance, F, and in doing so puts us in mind of some perspective, point of view, or stance, G (which may be identical to F or merely resemble it) which is the target of the ironic comment.[16] Perspectives can be of many kinds, and on just about anything. But irony is, I think, limited by the requirement that it target perspectives only of a certain kind: those to which we can apply a standard of reasonableness. It would not be irony to pretend to the most literal of limitations of point of view, blindness, even if in doing so I seek to draw attention to the blindness of another. Tendencies to believe or desire in certain ways, or to have certain emotional reactions, are fair game, even in cases where no personal blame attaches to the person whose perspective is being singled out. If Martians are less subject to emotional outbursts than we are, they may comment ironically on our failings by pretending to be as emotionally irrational as we are. Perhaps they are wrong, and our style of emotional responding is the more sensible, or is as sensible as theirs, given our differing circumstances. In that case their ironic commentary would

---

[15] As this example shows, such resemblance is highly context-dependent; in the country of the blind a very poorly sighted person might put us in mind of someone with very good eyesight.

[16] Perhaps it would be more strictly true to say that the target is some person's really having that perspective, or some tendency on the part of a group of persons, or persons in general, to have or be attracted to having that perspective. These are refinements that do not, in themselves, divide me from the echoic theorists, so I do not emphasize them.

lack justification; the important point is that irony represents—and hence may misrepresent—its target as unreasonable in some way, or at least as falling short of some salient standard of reasonableness.

We can now answer another criticism of the pretence theory offered by Sperber. Imagine that Bill is prone to say of himself:

(3) I am a very patient person.

In response to a display of temper from Bill, Judy says, ironically:

(4) Bill is such a patient person.

Here, Bill, or rather Bill's tendency to say or think things like (3), is the target of the irony. As Sperber points out, Judy cannot be pretending to *be* Bill, since Bill would not say (4). This is no criticism of the view that Judy pretends to be adopting a perspective in the service of expressing something about a suitably related perspective actually occupied by Bill. In pretending to assert (4), Judy makes it plain that she is pretending to occupy a perspective according to which Bill is a patient person, and thereby draws attention to Bill's tendency to think exactly this about himself, though he would express it in other words. Perhaps Bill never actually says things like (3), though we all suspect that he thinks them. No matter—it is the perspective that is the target of Judy's ironic comment, not any particular utterance or formulation. Judy engages in a performance which makes it pretence that she does something—asserting that Bill is a patient person—and which we are thereby encouraged to imagine her doing. But the target of her performance is not any doing of that exact thing by Bill.

5. PRETENCE OF MANNER

The idea that irony involves some sort of match by resemblance between points of view explains why ironic utterances can take such a variety of forms: there are ironic assertions, questions, orders, and insults, as well as ironic gestures and facial expressions. Anything that serves to indicate that one is pretending to a point of view will do. There are even ironic pretendings. Suppose Albert is an enthusiastic player of war games. Welcoming guests for lunch, I say:

(5) You must excuse Albert for the moment. He is outside fighting for his life.

I am not expressing reservations of any kind towards Albert's or anyone's belief that Albert is fighting for his life; no one, including Albert, believes that he is. Rather, my pretend assertion of (5) picks out for consideration Albert's wholeheartedly engrossed—and hence rather ridiculous—pretending that he is fighting for his life. With (5), I really am pretending to assert that Albert is fighting for his life. But I am also pretending to pretend to assert this *in a very engaged way*; I am pretending that my pretence is an enthusiastic, wholehearted joining in with Albert's own pretence.

Authors of fiction, whose utterances are pretended assertions made in the service of getting us to imagine various things, sometimes involve a similarly complex pretence. In *Persuasion*, Jane Austen introduces Anne Elliot to us by saying:

(6) [Sir Walter Elliot's] two other children were of very inferior value.

It is immediately apparent that this description does not correspond at all to how Austen expects us to imagine Anne, but rather to how, in the story, she and her sister are thought of by Sir Walter Elliot. Austen is pretending to assert things about someone called 'Anne Elliot', but her pretence is not straightforward; we are not to take the words she uses to correspond to how we should imagine Anne. Rather, Austen pretends to be pretending in a straightforward way, when in fact her pretence is ironical, targeted at Sir Walter's certainly defective perspective. So Austen's pretence is complex. She is pretending, as fiction writers do, to tell us something. But in addition, she is pretending that her pretence is straightforward, when in fact it is not.

In these two cases ((5) and (6)) we have a *pretence of manner*. The speaker pretends to be pretending in a certain way, when in fact he or she is not pretending in that way, though he or she certainly is pretending. That pretence of manner can make for irony opens up the possibility that one can utter an assertoric sentence ironically, and at the same time really be asserting it.[17] Take this example, put to me by Stephen Barker: You and I have just landed on a flight that touches down both in Melbourne and in Anchorage. Stepping off the plane there are evident signs that we are in Melbourne. Failing to notice them, you ask where we are. I say, in an ironic tone:

(7) Well, we are either in Melbourne or in Anchorage.

Does the pretence theory have to deny that I am asserting (7)? If it did, it might be in trouble. After all, (7) is true, I believe it, and I want to get you to believe it, because your believing it will help you to see that, given the temperature, we have to be in Melbourne. But a pretence-based account of the irony in (7) can live with the assumption that I really am asserting (7). All that needs to be observed is that I am doing something *more* than asserting (7). My pretence in uttering (7) need not be the pretence that I am asserting it. I might be genuinely asserting it, yet pretending to have the kind of interest in it we normally have in disjunctions: namely, its providing us with the basis for an inference, should further information come in, of the form A or B, not A, so B, and so getting us to a definite conclusion about where we are. I am pretending, in Frank Jackson's terms, that

---

[17] That is, asserting *P* for the same audience as that for which the utterance is intended to count as ironic. Irony and lies may, unproblematically, coexist in the same performance, where one audience is supposed to see the point and another to be deceived. That is how it is with Frank Churchill, whose remark about the dangers of opening windows are meant to be taken seriously by Mr Woodhouse and ironically by Emma.

the disjunction is robust with respect to the falsity of each of its disjuncts.[18] My target is your being uncertain about the truth of the first disjunct, when a glance around would tell you that it is true.[19]

These two examples help to resolve a general problem. Let's understand the phrase 'pretends to ϕ-in-manner-Σ' to refer to acts of pretending in which one really does ϕ, but in which one pretends to do it in manner Σ. Thus pretending to ϕ-in-manner-Σ is quite distinct from pretending-to-ϕ. We might initially think of the class of pretendings with the capacity to generate irony as the class of pretendings-to-ϕ, and therefore be skeptical of the idea that pretending is itself a potential value of the variable ϕ. For what would it be to pretend to pretend? Is that logically possible? If so, is it something that we are psychologically capable of? Answering 'No' to either of these last two questions suggests that pretence cannot be the target of irony. But we should not conclude this, whatever difficulty we may see in the notion of pretending to pretend. For irony can also be generated by the class of pretendings to ϕ-in-manner-Σ, which does allow pretending to be a potential value of ϕ without our having to countenance pretending to pretend.

6. POSITIVE IRONY

I said that irony need not always be critical, as with my ironic remark about Julia's belief in Father Christmas. But why should it be that irony is always the pretended adoption of a *defective* outlook? One answer is that this is simply analytic of the concept *irony*, and you might as well ask why bachelors are unmarried. But we can put the question another way: If, necessarily, irony is a practice of pretending to adopt a defective outlook, why isn't there a symmetrical practice, whatever we might choose to call it, of pretending to adopt a superior outlook? Pretty obviously, the answer is this: people are good at identifying ways of seeing, or thinking about, or reacting to the world which they consider inferior to their own; they are not very good at identifying ways of seeing, or thinking about, or reacting to the world which they would consider superior to their own, and when they do, they usually go on to adopt them. In fact, there seems to be something close to a pragmatic paradox involved in the idea of pretending to see things more clearly, more rationally, more dispassionately, than you actually do see them.[20]

---

[18] See Jackson 1987: 22–3. I prefer Jackson's account to the Gricean explanation in terms of violation of conversational rules.

[19] Many thanks to Stephen Barker, who persuaded me that an example I started with would not do.

[20] As long as the pretence involves some pretended adoption of a specific standpoint; there is nothing approaching paradox in my merely pretending *that* I am more rational or dispassionate than I actually am.

In another sense, irony is sometimes positive, as with Grice's (1989: 54) 'What an egotist you are, always giving yourself the satisfaction of doing things for other people.'[21] Here the speaker pretends to adopt the (certainly defective) standpoint of one who, come what may, insists on explaining actions as the result of selfishness. But this is done so as to compliment the speaker's conversation partner on his generous motivation. Why is positive irony, in this sense, rare? For this reason: to achieve this positive effect, the ironist has to go one step further than is required for irony itself: he or she has to perform an action in which the pretend adoption of a defective standpoint serves to highlight the defects of that standpoint, or of one suitably related to it; he or she has also to find a way to use the pretence so as to highlight some positive trait or action. So positive irony is *not* like positive commentary; commenting positively on something is not doing more than commenting, it is just making a certain kind of comment, and we would expect to see plenty of positive and negative commentary. Positive irony, on the other hand, is irony plus something else, and the something else is not easy to bring off.

7. THE SCOPE OF PRETENDING

I have one final point to make about how the pretence theory is to be understood. Someone whose utterance is ironic engages in pretence, and engaging in pretence means performing an act of some kind. But we need to distinguish between what the utterer does and what we might call the *pretence content* of the doing—the part of the act which lies within the scope of the pretence. The pretence content often corresponds closely to the performance itself. When I say, ironically, 'It's a lovely day', as we are lashed by rain, you are likely to imagine me seriously (and ludicrously) asserting exactly that, though you know that in fact I am not doing any such thing. But sometimes, the pretence content is related in more complex and subtle ways to the nature of the performance itself. A ballet dancer pretends to be a swan. Does she pretend to be a dancing swan? A swan in a tutu? No. We are to imagine that she is a swan, but not that she is a dancing swan in a tutu, even though her dancing in a tutu is integral to the actions which constitute pretending to be a swan. Aspects of staging and make-up in theatre are often highly stylized, and we are not always intended to imagine that the character has a facial expression or is clothed in the garments corresponding to the facial expression or the clothing of the actor on stage.[22] Acts of pretence sometimes require from us a sophisticated imaginative response: one which picks and chooses between

---

[21] Sperber and Wilson discuss the asymmetry between positive and negative irony in various places (e.g. 1998), and I am indebted to them for having identified a problem. Our treatments are somewhat different.

[22] Artists have sometimes advocated a minimalist approach to stageing precisely because this encourages the use of imagination in creative ways; see e.g. comments on Jarry in Carroll 1993.

elements of the performance, and which sometimes adds further elements which are merely implied by the performance, rather than being explicit in it.

This point has important consequences for another criticism of the pretence theory. Sperber claims that the pretence theory is inconsistent with there being an ironic tone, because an utterance made using an ironic tone is an utterance which 'makes any pretence impossible. There is no audience, real or imaginary, that would fail to perceive the derogatory attitude and hence the ironic intent it conveys' (1984: 135). Sperber might as well say that plays can never effectively take place on sets that are manifestly artificial: after all, no audience would fail to realize the artifice of the situation. But the case of staged performance makes it plain that we easily bracket out elements of what we are given in a pretence. Just as a dancer in a tutu can pretend to be a swan without pretending to be a swan in a tutu, so an ironic utterance of P, using an ironic tone of voice, need not constitute a pretence of [seriously asserting P in an ironic tone of voice]. Instead, the ironist pretends, using an ironic tone of voice, [seriously to assert P].[23]

This is relevant to yet another criticism of the pretence theory offered by Sperber. Consider the ironic:

(8) Jones, this murderer, this thief, this crook, is indeed an honourable fellow.

Sperber says that there is no speaker who could seriously utter such a blatant contradiction, nor an audience which could assent to it (1984: 133). One point to make is that Sperber is encouraging us to consider the wrong question. It is not relevant to ask whether there is such a speaker and such an audience. The relevant question is whether we can *pretend* that there is such a speaker and such an audience. We are able to pretend all sorts of absurd things, and often take delight in doing so; why can't we pretend this? Note also that imagining someone saying or thinking an absurdity is not always as difficult as imagining the absurdity being the case.

However, another way to deal with this and like cases would be to argue that the pretence content has to be carved out from the whole utterance. We might hear irony in (8) by splitting it into an ironic part:

(8a) Jones is indeed an honourable fellow

and a part which provides information in the light of which the serious assertion of (8) would be ludicrous, namely:

---

[23] We may signal our irony with a tone of voice, but that tone is not always needed, even when we want our irony understood. Why is there such an irregular relationship between irony and ironic tone? The ironist pretends to a limited perspective: pretends to be saying or doing something that only someone who failed to see certain facts or values in a lively and sympathetic way would say or do. However, we cannot count on universal agreement about what is a limited perspective, and quite often we do come across people whose perspective really does seem to us to be limited in this way. So the mere fact that your utterance derives from (what seems to me to be) such a perspective is no guarantee that you are speaking ironically. That's why we dispense with ironic tone most often when in the company of people who share, in some detail, our own perspectives and whom we think of as sensitive to even subtle shifts of perspective. See Pexman and Zvaigzne 2004.

(8b) Jones is a murderer, a thief, and a crook.[24]

Which account of (8) is right? Do we imagine the serious utterance of an absurdity, namely (8) itself, or do we imagine the utterance of the not intrinsically absurd (8a), made incongruous by the assumption of (8b) as background knowledge? I don't need to answer this question. The answer may depend on precise details of the context or the tone of the utterance, or it might be up to auditors to respond in their own different ways. All we need say is that any theory of irony based on pretence should acknowledge the possibility of very complex and hard-to-regiment relations between the totality of the performance and what constitutes the content of the pretence.

I have arrived at the view that irony is a matter of pretending to a limited perspective in a way which is expressive of a view you have about the limitations of some suitably related perspective, where those limitations compromise, to some degree, the reasonableness of the perspective. All this ignores a certain fragility in irony itself; there are conditions that can make it difficult or even impossible to achieve an ironic effect, even assuming one fulfills the conditions stated. A full analysis of these conditions would be a distraction from those aspects of irony where we find the pretence and echoic theories in competition, but I will note one example: the pretence nature of the performance ought not to be strongly signalled by the context of the performance. Theatrical performances, particularly comic ones, are sometimes undertaken by people who wish, through their pretence of being a certain sort of person, to express their thoughts or feelings about some point of view which they take to be limited in some way. While such performances may contain moments of irony embedded within the fictional contexts they create, it does not seem right to describe the whole performance as ironic simply because of the nature of the project.[25] The kind of pretence we naturally label ironic generally requires a context that contains no explicit or conventional signals that what is said or done is pretence, and should rely instead on aspects of the ironist's own performance to hint at the ironic intent.

8. THE ELABORATION OF PRETENCE

My approach so far has been defensive. I've been concerned to provide a formulation of the pretence theory, plausible on independent grounds, which avoids

---

[24] This account of the distinction between what is within the scope of the pretence and what is outside corresponds to the distinction made by Clark and Gerrig between depictive and other aspects of what they call 'demonstration'; they further separate these other aspects into Supportive, Annotative, and Incidental Aspects (1990: 768). Precedent for this approach can be found in treatments of other linguistic phenomena. One plausible theory of epithets has it that they serve to create a duality of propositions associated with the utterance. Thus, one who says 'The Dean said he would come to the meeting, but the idiot forgot' can be said to have communicated both that (i) the Dean said he would come to the meeting but he forgot, and (ii) the Dean is an idiot. See Corazza 2005.

[25] I am grateful to Manuel Garcia-Carpintero here.

criticisms that have been, or might be, levelled against it. I now turn to what seems to me the distinctive advantage of the pretence theory over its echoic rival. The point is best brought out by considering a pair of cases given by Sperber and Wilson which illustrate, they say, the fact that irony is but one echoic form. They make the point that one can echo a remark in the process of endorsing it, as with:

(I) *Peter*: It's a lovely day for a picnic.
     [They go on a picnic and the sun shines.]
     Mary: It's a lovely day for a picnic, indeed.

just as one can echo in a dissociative, ironic way:

(II) *Peter*: It's a lovely day for a picnic.
     [They go on a picnic, and it rains.]
     Mary: It's a lovely day for a picnic, indeed.

Sperber and Wilson say that 'these utterances are interpreted on exactly similar patterns; the only difference is in the attitudes they express' (1995: 239). But there is in fact another great difference between these two cases. In the second case, if Peter responds with 'Yes, I'm so glad we decided to come', this would naturally be seen as an imaginative elaboration of Mary's pretence. If Peter said exactly that in the case where everything went well (as with (I)), there would be no tendency to see his effort as an imaginative elaboration of a game.[26] It could be understood only as serious agreement with Mary's remark. In (II), but not in (I), Mary effectively opens the door to pretending, whether or not Peter decides to go through.[27]

Friends of Sperber and Wilson might say that this argument assumes what it seeks to establish. When rain spoils the picnic and Mary says, 'It's a lovely day for a picnic, indeed', she is not, on Sperber and Wilson's account, engaging in any pretence; why should they grant that any further extension of the comment-ary—perhaps Peter joins in by saying, 'Yes, I'm so glad we chose today of all days for it'—is pretence either? The answer is that, intuitively, such an exchange seems awfully like pretence; Peter and Mary seem to be making up a playful

---

[26] It is not important for this point that Peter and Mary be together, or that the elaboration be conversational. A piece of literary irony invites elaboration from the reader, who may imagine certain propositions which extend the ironic line of thought, without her saying anything at all. A striking example of elaboration of another kind of literary pretence occurred in response to Wofgang Hildesheimer's (very unobviously) fictional biography, *Marbot*. Hildesheimer took J. P. Stern's straight-faced review as evidence that Stern had misunderstood, when in fact he was simply continuing the pretence (see Cohn 1999: ch. 5).

[27] In this respect, irony is like parody, which Sperber and Wilson regard as a close relative of irony. When in conversation I parody someone's poetic style, I make way for others to join in, elaborating in further imaginative ways. What distinguishes parody and irony? Sperber and Wilson say that parody has form as its target, while irony aims at content. But they acknowledge that there is no sharp distinction between these kinds; the important point is that they are both echoic tropes used to express critical attitudes. I agree that irony and parody are alike, and that little is to be gained by seeking a sharp distinction between them, but I say that their likeness consists in their being species of pretence.

dialogue full of sayings to which they are manifestly not committed. Calling this pretence is very natural, and would hardly be objected to by anyone untouched by this debate. At the very least, we are owed an account of why this is not, contrary to appearances, pretence. It might be argued that Peter's additional remark takes the conversation into pretend mode, but that Mary's ironic 'It's a lovely day for a picnic, indeed' is not, or need not be, pretence without that continuation. If the basis of this claim is that pretence is essentially shared, I reject it; there is plenty of reason to think that children and adults engage in solitary pretence. Or the argument might be that Mary's remark is distinctive in that it makes way for pretence, but that remarks which do this need not be pretence themselves. It is certainly possible to do things which provoke or set the stage for pretence but which are not themselves part of the pretence. But Mary's remark does not seem to be of this kind. If I say to you, 'Let's play a game of cops and robbers', there is no inclination, as the game proceeds, for us to look back and see this remark as part of the game itself; that is why it is a good example of something which provokes pretence without being pretence. But if Peter and Mary continue their ironic exchange about how sensible it was to go for a picnic, there is every reason to look back on Mary's 'It's a lovely day for a picnic, indeed' as being the first step in the pretence itself. Could it be said that Mary's 'It's a lovely day for a picnic, indeed' is ironic, but not pretence, unless her remark is taken up and elaborated on by Peter, in which case it becomes pretence retrospectively? Claiming that much would allow Sperber and Wilson to say that irony sometimes is, but does not have to be, pretence. I see no advantage in this implausible position apart from the defence it offers to the non-pretence view of irony. And to admit even this much would be a significant concession; it would be to say that an ironic statement, like Mary's in (II), is essentially a conduit to pretence, while the same type of utterance in (I) isn't. That would mean that pretence plays a part in a specification of the essential properties of irony, which is more than Sperber and Wilson seem willing to grant.[28]

9. EMPIRICAL EVIDENCE

Accounts of irony such as the echoic theory say something about the cognitive resources we bring to bear in understanding ironic utterances, and some of these

[28] I've argued that Mary's 'It's a lovely day for a picnic, indeed' is pretence in (II) but not in (I). As Wilson notes, some writers seek a very wide domain for the pretence theory, a domain that would include free indirect as well as direct quotation, and in some versions contexts such as (I) (see Wilson 2000: 425; the view goes back to Quine's remarks on indirect discourse as an 'essentially dramatic mode' (1960: 219)). We need to distinguish kinds of pretence. If there is a sense in which (I) and (II) both involve pretence, it is a thin, atrophied sense, distinct from the thicker, active sense that distinguishes (I) and (II). Mary's 'It's a lovely day for a picnic, indeed' is pretence in (II) in an active sense that naturally invites imaginative elaboration by Mary's conversation partners or by Mary herself (she could have said it quietly to herself while struggling home through the rain). If there is any pretence in (I) it is not of that substantial kind.

claims are open to test. Francesca Happé (1993) claimed support for the echoic theory from a study that examined comprehension of metaphor and irony by people with autism. She distinguished three groups of subjects: those who failed first-order false belief tests (non-ToM), those who passed first-order but failed second-order false belief tests (first-ToM), and those who passed both (second-ToM). The non-ToM group were able to comprehend similes ('He was like a tree'), but were generally incompetent with metaphor ('He was a tree'). The first-ToM group were competent with metaphor, but had difficulty with irony, while the second-ToM group were competent with both. Also, normally developing children of about five years old were distinguished according to whether they passed or failed second-order false belief tests. Those who passed were competent with irony, while those who failed were not; both were competent with metaphor.

Any account which makes irony simply another form of verbal trope, on all fours with metaphor, will not be able to explain this. Sperber and Wilson can explain it: irony, but not metaphor, requires the hearer to understand that the speaker speaks with the intention of directing our attention to another's thought, the one he or she is echoing. So with irony, but not with metaphor, one has to be able to think about thoughts about thoughts; one must be capable of what is called second-order metarepresentation.

Doubt has been expressed about the validity of Happé's results.[29] But there are other sources of evidence for the general claim that comprehension of irony requires understanding of thoughts about thoughts. Winner et al. (1998) found that poor performance on second-order theory of mind tests was highly predictive, for both right-hemisphere brain-damaged patients and normal controls, of poor discrimination between ironic joke-telling and lying. Shamay-Tsoory et al. (2005) found that comprehension of sarcasm correlated 'moderately but significantly' with performance on a rather sophisticated test of second-order theory of mind. Accepting Happé's results at face value, how does the pretence theory fare in explaining them? It is important to see exactly what capacity was probed in Happé's tests. Here is one of her scenarios:

Cake story
David is helping his mother make a cake. She leaves him to add the eggs to the flour and sugar. But silly David doesn't break the eggs first—he just puts them in the bowl, shells and all! What a silly thing to do! When mother comes back and sees what David has done, she says:
'Your head is made out of wood!'

---

[29] Courtney Norbury (2005) examined Happé's results concerning metaphor, drawing attention to small sample size and large within-group variation in language ability; these problems carry over to the study of irony. Using a larger sample, Norbury found that the first-ToM group was not significantly better at metaphor than the non-ToM group. Norbury was not able to obtain reliable results concerning irony (personal communication). See also Martin and McDonald 2005, which claims that impairments in general inferential reasoning, rather than in ToM, are associated with poor understanding of irony.

Q: *What does David's mother mean ? Does she mean David is clever or silly?*
Just then father comes in. He sees what David has done and he says: 'What a clever boy you are, David!'
Q: *What does David's father mean? Does he mean David is clever or silly?*

The pretence theorist ought to say that, in being ironic, David's father is pretending to assert that David is a clever boy. What is required in order to understand this? You might say that understanding pretence does not generally require second-order mind-reading skills, since pretending that *P* is logically on a par with believing that *P*, and understanding that someone believes that *P* requires only first-order theory of mind. This is a controversial issue, but we need not settle it here. For the question ought really to be this: what is required in order to understand that someone is pretending, in the specific case where the pretence is one of making an assertion? It would not be easy to provide an uncontroversial account of assertions and what is involved in their production, but fortunately we do not need one. The question asked is 'What does David's father mean?' And the children can be expected to get the right answer if they understand that, while David's father may have seemed to think that David is clever, he is really only pretending to think this. They are required to grasp the thought that:

(9) David's father pretends that [he thinks that {David is clever}].

This would require second-order mind-reading skills. If Happé's results support the echoic theory, they support the pretence theory also.

10. OTHER KINDS OF IRONY

We call many things ironic, and not all of them are covered by the account of irony I have given so far. This need not worry us; these other things are not, intuitively, of exactly the same nature as the cases of irony I have focused on so far: cases of irony proper, as I shall say. But an account like my own will gain in strength if it can be shown that it sheds some light on these other kinds. Here I focus on three phenomena, two of which are well known, while the third has not, I think, been clearly delineated. The first two, closely related, are *dramatic* and *situational* irony.[30] Electra mourns over the ashes she thinks are those of Orestes; Malvolio's hope is based on a letter we know is a fake. Through credulousness, wishful thinking, or merely because they don't know the facts, characters in fiction often have a limited perspective, highlighted by the more inclusive view granted to the audience. So 'dramatic irony' turns out to be simply the fictional representation of the kind of contrast between perspectives that one pretends to be the victim of when one speaks ironically. 'Situational irony' is a bloated

---

[30] Meanings assigned to these terms vary, but the meanings I assign to them here are common ones.

category that threatens to engulf anything we find surprising, incongruous, or unfair.[31] Sensibly restricted, it covers real circumstances that mirror those of dramatic irony, except that there need be no onlooker aware of the disparity at the time. It was ironic that they fled to the Falkland Islands just before the invasion, that she resigned the day before her promotion was to be announced, that we robbed the bank the day after its vaults had been emptied. If we had known differently we would have acted differently, and the representation of any of this in performance or literature would count as dramatic irony.

I call my third category '*suppressed* irony'. Suppressed irony, as I define it, isn't really irony in my sense, though it is an exploitation, usually for comic purposes, of the mechanisms by which irony operates. It will help explain the concept if I start with the idea of things being this way or that way in or according to a fiction. In a fiction, a character may speak in a genuinely ironical way, as with Emma's reply to Mr Knightly: 'To be sure—our discordancies must always arise from my being in the wrong.'[32] In *Emma*, it is fiction that Emma speaks ironically when she says this. But speaking ironically is speaking in pretend mode, and pretence creates fiction, so irony itself induces a further fiction. If Emma and Knightly had been real people, Emma's utterance would make it fictional that [she asserts that her disputes with Mr Knightly always arise from her being in the wrong]. Since Emma and Knightly are creatures of Austen's fiction-making, we have the embedding of a fiction within a fiction:

It is fictional (in *Emma*) that {Emma's utterance makes it fictional (in her game of pretence) that [she, Emma, seriously asserts that her disputes with Mr Knightly always arise from her being in the wrong]}.

This gives us nested fiction. We sometimes get what I am calling suppressed irony when we remove the second, small-scope *fiction* operator. In the passage from *Emma* which I've used to illustrate this process, the result would be odd, rather than humorous; the novel would be telling us that Emma seriously thinks that she is always in the wrong when she disputes with Mr Knightly, and this would be a very puzzling thing for us to be told. There are therefore no attractions in the idea of removing the small-scope operator in this case, and Austen wisely did not do it. But a certain kind of staged or filmed humour does this very often. Here are Nydia Westman and Bob Hope in *The Cat and the Canary* (1940):

'Don't these big empty houses scare you?'
'Not me, I was in vaudeville.'

---

[31] Thus Barbe (1993), in a study of situational irony, includes this as an example: 'Bill Davis, a member of the Vietnam Veterans Against War, stated: "War-profiteering is a sick business." Davis also referred to an advertisement for T-shirts, which promoted the war. Ironically, this ad was very prominently displayed in the exact same issue of the *Star* in which Mr. Davis is quoted.' This is ironic only in the bloated sense, since there does not seem to be any limited perspective implicated in this incongruity. See also her example (11).

[32] Quoted in Wilson and Sperber 1992: 64.

And here are Diane Keaton and Woody Allen in the Hope-inspired *Love and Death* (1975):

> 'And before Seretski, Aleksei, and before Aleksei, Alegorian, and before Alegorian, Asimov, and . . . '
> 'How many lovers do you have?'
> 'In the mid-town area?'

In these cases a character speaks seriously, so far as what is true in the fiction is concerned, seriously asserting that their vaudeville experience has prepared them for grim and ghostly buildings, seriously inquiring as to whether our interest in their lovers is confined to those in midtown. In doing so, they are represented as occupying absurdly defective perspectives, and that is part of what makes their remarks funny. To that extent the remarks are funny because they are *not* ironic. But they are funny also because the words are uttered by real actors (the technique does not work with literary fictions) with whom we share an awareness of the ironic possibilities in the remark.[33] The performance makes it common knowledge between actor and audience that the actor just said something which, if uttered in real life, could only be uttered ironically—that is, with the narrow-scope fiction operator restored.

11. LIMITED AMBITION

The cases just dealt with belong to kinds qualitatively different from the kind I have labelled irony proper, or so I say. On the other hand, there are cases which don't fall under my characterization of irony proper, but which it does not seem satisfactory to place in a distinct, though related, kind. For example, what I have said here would not serve to distinguish in a fully satisfactory way between irony and similar devices such as sarcasm. Perhaps there are attitudes expressed in sarcasm which are distinct from those expressed in irony; perhaps our practice of categorizing performances as ironic or as sarcastic are ad hoc, or unsystematizably complex, or responsive to contextual features that have nothing to do with speakers' intentions, or exceed in some other way the resources of the theory outlined here. This is not terribly worrying: Sperber and Wilson (1995) say that irony is 'not a natural kind', that we should not expect 'irony' to map neatly on to some independently identifiable subset of echoic utterances, that fine distinctions within the class of echoic utterances pale into insignificance beside the big distinction—that between echoic and non-echoic utterances. I agree, except to say that the real big distinction is between pretend and non-pretend utterances. All that any of us are doing is seeking a centre of gravity for irony: a place from

---

[33] This sense is reinforced by continual references within Hope's films to their fictional status and even to Hope's own real-life career as a comic, as when he (in *My Favourite Blond*) hears himself on the radio and says 'I hate this guy.'

which a range of irony-related cases spread out, with no clear point at which the label ceases to be applicable. The proper way to deal with cases within the region of this point is not to ask whether they really are or are not cases of irony, but rather to ask in what ways they are like or not like cases at the centre. As a case of particularized conversational implicatures Grice gave:

(10) In a letter of recommendation for one of his students B writes: 'Mr Smith is always neatly dressed and has beautiful handwriting.'

B can be thought of as pretending to occupy an absurdly limited perspective, pretending to think that something is a relevant contribution to the topic of Smith's suitability for a career when in fact it is obviously not a relevant contribution. But I cannot see any target here; B's pretending to occupy this perspective does not serve to draw attention to someone who does occupy this perspective or some relevantly similar one. The point of the remark is to draw attention to *Smith's* deficiencies, but this does not make Smith a target in the relevant sense. This is not centrally a case of irony, but it has clear affinities with irony as I have characterized it and might be cited as evidence of B's tendency to adopt an ironic tone.[34] If we can give an account of the relations between cases like these and more central cases, we need have no special interest in which ones we label 'ironic'. What a theory of irony must do is show that it has the resources to characterize, in intuitively acceptable ways, the place where irony's centre of gravity is, and to measure, again in intuitively acceptable ways, the distances from there to other places on the map, such as the location of (10). It is against this standard that the pretence theory should be judged.

REFERENCES

BARBE, K. (1993) 'Isn't It Ironic That . . . : Explicit Irony Markers', *Journal of Pragmatics*, 20, 579–90.

BARKER, S. (2004) *Renewing Meaning: A Speech-act Theoretic Approach* (Oxford: Oxford University Press).

BLACKBURN, S. (1984) *Spreading the Word* (Oxford: Clarendon Press).

BOOTH, W. (1974) *The Rhetoric of Irony* (Chicago: University of Chicago Press).

_____ (1983) *The Rhetoric of Fiction*, 2nd edn. (Chicago: University of Chicago Press).

CARROLL, N (1993) 'Historical Narratives and the Philosophy of Art', *Journal of Aesthetics and Art Criticism*, 51, 313–26.

CICERO, MARCUS TULLIUS (1913) *De Officiis*, trans. Walter Miller, Loeb Classical Library (Cambridge, Mass.: Harvard University Press).

CLARK, H. H. (1996) *Using Language* (Cambridge: Cambridge University Press).

_____ and GERRIG, R. J. (1984) 'On the Pretense Theory of Irony', *Journal of Experimental Psychology: General*, 113, 121–6.

---

[34] One might hear (10) as fully ironic: commenting on the tendency to avoid saying anything negative in a reference. But that would not be obligatory for all possible instances of (10).

CLARK, H. H. and GERRIG, R. J. (1990) 'Quotations as Demonstrations', *Language*, 66, 764–805.

COHN, D. (1999) *The Distinction of Fiction* (Baltimore: Johns Hopkins University Press).

CORAZZA, E. (2005) 'On Epithets qua Attributive Anaphors', *Journal of Linguistics*, 41 (1), 1–34.

GIBBARD, A. (1990) *Wise Choices, Apt Feelings* (Oxford: Clarendon Press).

GIBBS, R. (2000) 'Metarepresentations as Staged Communicative Acts', in D. Sperber (ed.), *Metarepresentation* (Oxford: Oxford University Press).

GRICE, H. P. (1989) 'Logic and Conversation', in his *Studies in the Ways of Words* (Cambridge, Mass.: Harvard University Press).

HAPPÉ, F. (1993) 'Communicative Competence and the Theory of Mind in Autism: A Test of Relevance Theory', *Cognition*, 48, 101–19.

JACKSON, F. (1987) *Conditionals* (Oxford: Blackwell).

JORGENSEN, JOHN, MILLER, GEORGE A., and SPERBER, DAN (1984) 'Test of the Mention Theory of Irony', *Journal of Experimental Psychology: General*, 113, 112–20.

KUMON-NAKAMURA, S., GLUCKSBERG, S., and BROWN, M. (1995) 'How about Another Piece of Pie: The Allusional Pretense Theory of Discourse Irony', *Journal of Experimental Psychology*, 124, 3–21.

MARTIN, I., and MCDONALD, S. (2005) 'Evaluating the Causes of Impaired Irony Comprehension Following Traumatic Brain Injury', *Aphasiology*, 19, 712–30.

MUECKE, D. C. (1969) *The Compass of Irony* (London: Methuen).

NEHAMAS, A. (1998) *The Art of Living* (Berkeley: University of California Press).

NORBURY, C. F. (2005) 'The Relationship between Theory of Mind and Metaphor: Evidence from Children with Language Impairment and Autistic Spectrum Disorder', *British Journal of Developmental Psychology*, 23, 383–99.

PEXMAN, P., and ZVAIGZNE, M. (2004) 'Does Irony Go Better With Friends?', *Metaphor and Symbol*, 19, 143–63.

QUINE, W. V. O. (1960) *Word and Object* (Cambridge, Mass.: MIT Press).

QUINTILIAN (1920) *Institutio Oratoria*, trans. H. E. Butler, Loeb Classical Library (Cambridge, Mass.: Harvard University Press).

SHAMAY-TSOORY, S. G., TOMER, R., and AHARON-PERETZ, J. (2005) 'The Neuroanatomical Basis of Understanding Sarcasm and its Relationship to Social Cognition', *Neuropsychology*, 19, 288–300.

SPERBER, DAN (1984) 'Verbal Irony: Pretense or Echoic Mention?', *Journal of Experimental Psychology: General*, 113, 130–6.

—— and WILSON, D. (1981) 'Irony and the Use–Mention Distinction', in P. Cole (ed.), *Radical Pragmatics* (New York: Academic Press).

—— and —— (1995) *Relevance: Communication and Cognition*, 2nd edn. (Oxford: Blackwell).

—— and —— (1998) 'Irony and Relevance: A Reply to Drs Seto, Hamamoto and Yamanashi', in Robyn Carston and Seiji Uchida (eds.), *Relevance Theory: Applications and Implications* (Amsterdam: John Benjamins).

STANLEY, J. (2005) 'Review of Robyn Carston, *Thoughts and Utterances*', *Mind & Language*, 20, 364–8.

VLASTOS, G. (1991) *Socrates: Ironist and Moral Philosopher* (Cambridge: Cambridge University Press).

WALTON, K. (1990) *Mimesis as Make-believe: On the Foundations of the Representational Arts* (Cambridge, Mass.: Harvard University Press).

WILSON, D. (2000) 'Metarepresentation in Linguistic Communication', in D. Sperber (ed.), *Metarepresentations* (Oxford: Oxford University Press).

—— and SPERBER, D. (1992) 'On Verbal Irony', *Lingua*, 87, 53–76.

WINNER, E., BROWNELL, H., HAPPÉ, F., BLUM, A., and PINCUS, D. (1998) 'Distinguishing Lies from Jokes: Theory of Mind Deficit and Discourse Interpretation in Right Hemisphere Brain Damage Patients', *Brain and Language*, 62, 89–106.

PART III
IMAGINATIVE RESISTANCE

8

On the (So-called) Puzzle of Imaginative Resistance

Kendall Walton

In *Mimesis as Make-Believe*, I happened upon a surprising peculiarity in interpretive practice: a curious reluctance to allow fictional worlds to differ in fundamental moral respects from the real world as we understand it (Walton 1990: 154–5).[1] It seemed to me that this might have been what David Hume was getting at in the final five paragraphs of 'On the Standard of Taste', although this attribution now strikes me as highly questionable. Revisiting the topic in a later essay, 'Morals in Fiction and Fictional Morality' (1994), I emphasized that there is actually a tangled nest of importantly distinct, but easily confused, puzzles in the vicinity, several of which can be traced uncertainly to Hume's observations.[2] My strategy in addressing them was *disentangle-and-conquer*. I do not claim to have successfully completed the conquest in my previous forays, nor will I do so now. But I did do some untangling, and without that there is no hope of conquest. I now see that there are even more strands to separate than I recognized previously. So more untangling is in order.

Several of the puzzles, and amalgamations of them, travel together in the recent literature under the name *the puzzle of imaginative resistance*.[3] This unfortunate appellation ignores their multiplicity, and is misleading in other respects as well. There are perceptive and illuminating discussions in the literature, nonetheless, with some promising suggestions about solutions. One contributor who is careful to distinguish the main strands of the tangle is Brian Weatherson. Weatherson

This essay began as a postscript to Walton 1994, but got out of hand. Thanks to Tamar Gendler and Shaun Nichols for very helpful comments.

[1] In the terms of my discussion in *Mimesis*, the peculiarity consisted in a strange insistence on the Reality Principle of implication, for deciding whether moral propositions of certain sorts are fictional.

[2] Tamar Gendler examines Hume's comments in some detail (Ch. 9).

[3] Of those who use this name, Gregory Currie (2002), Currie and Ravenscroft (2002), and Shaun Nichols (forthcoming) address only the imaginative puzzle; Stephen Yablo (2001) focuses on the fictionality one; Tamar Gendler (2000), Derek Matravers (2003), and Richard Moran (1994) have some of both in mind. In his response to Walton 1994, Michael Tanner (1994) touches only on the aesthetic puzzle and only touches as it.

(2004) recognizes four related puzzles, and examines three of them. The differences between the three are small, he says—I disagree about that—but he separates them clearly and gives them useful labels. I will look at two of these three—the *imaginative* puzzle and what he calls the alethic one, which I will rename the *fictionality* puzzle. But I will begin with the one he doesn't examine, the *aesthetic* puzzle.

1. THE AESTHETIC PUZZLE

The first several sections of 'Morals in Fiction' survey, briefly, the neighborhood of the *aesthetic* puzzle.[4] If a work of art is objectionable on moral grounds, does this diminish or destroy its aesthetic value?

I did not say nearly enough about the various kinds of moral objections one might have to a work (or a joke, or a cartoon, or a metaphor), and much of the literature on this topic is lacking in this respect as well. Two broad categories are obvious: Some works are vehicles by virtue of which the artist expresses sentiments or advocates a moral point of view that we may find objectionable. People sometimes 'make reprehensible claims or demands by writing poems, by telling stories, by creating fictions', I observed (Walton 1994: 28). We may condemn the sentiments or point of view and their expression, whether or not we think the artist has any chance of making converts or persuading anyone. Alternatively, we may worry, as Plato did, that a work will have morally deleterious effects, whether or not they were intended or envisaged by the artist. We may criticize a work for encouraging immoral attitudes or behavior or unwanted feelings in audiences; one might even fear succumbing oneself. And we may complain about a work's likely indirect consequences; its sales might line the pockets of a distributor who will bankroll evil causes, for instance.

Other moral objections are of neither of the above kinds. One who objects to the Egyptian pyramids because of their construction by slave labor, or to European high art on the grounds that it was made possible by an obscene concentration of wealth among the royalty or the clergy, needn't presume either that their creators were advocating morally obnoxious views or that the works might have unfortunate consequences. According to H. L. Mencken, the last movement of Beethoven's *Eroica* is 'not only voluptuous to the last degree; it is also Bolshevistic. Try to play it with your eyes on a portrait of Dr. Coolidge. You will find the thing as impossible as eating ice-cream on roast beef' (1926: 295). Mencken need not have supposed that Beethoven was endorsing Bolshevism, or that the *Eroica* Finale stands any chance of promoting it.

My own intuitions about these sketchily characterized examples, as to whether their (presumed) moral faults affect their aesthetic merit, are fuzzy, but insofar

---

[4] This issue has enjoyed a flurry of discussion recently, although it is certainly not new. Cf. Carroll 1996; Devereaux 1998; Gaut 1998; Jacobson 1997; John 2005; Kieran 1996.

as I do have inclinations, they go in different directions. I am less inclined to think that morally undesirable consequences, especially relatively indirect ones, detract from a work's aesthetic value than that serving as a vehicle whereby the artist advances morally obnoxious claims (at least if this is evident in the work) does. And—supposing that the Bolshevism that Mencken hears in the *Eroica* is really there, and is morally objectionable—I am more inclined to accept that it lessens the work's aesthetic value than that the construction of the pyramids by slave labor does. A single answer to the question of what, if any, bearing moral failings have on aesthetic value is not in the offing.

I did not mean to propose any such answer in 'Morals in Fiction', or even to decide at all definitely about any particular case. My main purpose in discussing the aesthetic puzzle, beyond providing an overview of the issues involved, was to clarify its relation to, and distinctness from, the others. What I called an 'aesthetic defect', in connection with *Triumph of the Will* (1994: 30), is simply a circumstance that is unfortunate from an aesthetic point of view: namely, the fact that the film's moral reprehensibility is likely to prevent people from appreciating it aesthetically. It remains an open question whether or not the film *possesses* aesthetic merit, whether its moral faults destroy or lessen its aesthetic value, or merely render its aesthetic value unavailable or inaccessible.[5] This question is not itself, I think, a very interesting or important one. Likewise the question of whether a racist joke which, let's suppose, ought not to be laughed at, is in fact funny, or whether the complaint 'That isn't funny!' should be taken as the literal truth.

What *is* important and interesting is the fact that moral failings in works of art *do* sometimes (not always) impede aesthetic appreciation, and the various ways in which they do. All of the varieties of moral defects I mentioned may do this, although the interference takes different forms in different cases. We may be unwilling to appreciate a work, or even experience it, because we think that doing so would itself be morally objectionable. In appreciating it, we would be profiting from slave labor, or letting ourselves in for temptation, or (in effect) declaring allegiance to or openness to an obnoxious moral perspective, or con-tributing to the work's undesirable indirect consequences. Sometimes a work's negative moral qualities may be so overwhelming or painful or guilt-inducing or distracting that we are simply unable to appreciate it even if we are willing. It is also important to recognize that—as Plato famously observed—immoral works of many varieties are often exceedingly powerful, despite—maybe even because of—their immorality; they may mesmerize or move us, even against our will. Of course, if authorities censor them, or if we refuse even to experience them, their moral flaws will have prevented their being appreciated.

How and why and when moral failings have inhibiting effects, as well as when, why, and how they are effective nevertheless, are rich areas for empirical

---

[5] Thanks to Daniel Jacobson for insisting that I clarify this point. Cf. his 1997. He also makes a good case for the idea that moral flaws are sometimes aesthetic merits.

investigation. I barely touched on them in 'Morals in Fiction'. And I didn't even touch on the important normative questions as to whether, in various instances, one ought to avoid enjoying a work—whether, for instance, it is wrong to laugh at a racist joke or to marvel at the pyramids. None of these questions requires that we decide whether moral defects lessen a work's actual aesthetic merit.

When moral considerations prevent us from appreciating a work of fiction, this is often, though not always, because we are unable or unwilling to *imagine* in the way the work calls for. This is the link between the aesthetic puzzle and the imaginative one. But insufficient attention to the distinction between them may make it seem that the imaginative puzzle concerns only matters having to do with morality. It doesn't. And neither does the fictionality puzzle. [6]

It is worth pointing out, also, that the aesthetic puzzle itself has non-moral analogues. I borrow an example from Frank Sibley. An apparently abstract photograph which strikes us as beautiful may be impossible to appreciate once we learn that it is a photograph of lesions on a human body, or gangrene, or ulcers. Or we may not *want* to enjoy it then, even if we can. It is less likely that we will think we *ought* not let ourselves appreciate it, that doing so would be morally objectionable. Sibley (2001) suggests that it may nevertheless be true to say that such a photograph is beautiful, that it possesses one kind of beauty anyway ('predicative beauty', as opposed to beauty *as a photograph of gangrene*, e.g., i.e. 'attributive gangrene-beauty').

2. THE IMAGINATIVE AND FICTIONALITY PUZZLES ENTANGLED

The most easily confused of the several tangled strands are the *fictionality* and the *imaginative* puzzles. The fictionality one, the focus of my observations in *Mimesis*, is the most perplexing of the bunch. We easily accept that princes become frogs, or that people travel in time, in the world of a story, even, sometimes, that blatant contradictions are fictional. But we balk—I do anyway, in some instances, and it is evident from the literature that I am not alone—at interpretations of stories or other fictions according to which it is fictional that (absent extraordinary circumstances) female infanticide is right and proper, or that nutmeg is the *summum bonum*, or that a dumb *knock-knock* joke is actually hilarious. Why the difference? This is the fictionality puzzle. The imaginative puzzle concerns not what is or isn't *fictional*, but what we do or do not *imagine*. These are different; I may recognize that something is fictional, true in the world of a story, without actually imagining it, or imagine something that I take not to be fictional

---

[6] §VIII of Walton 1994 aims to establish that the fictionality puzzle extends to non-moral propositions. My concentration on moral matters earlier in the essay may, misleadingly, have suggested the contrary, however. Weatherson 2004 and Yablo 2001 have much more to say about the scope of the fictionality puzzle.

(Walton 1994: 42–3).[7] People are sometimes unwilling or unable to engage in certain imaginings. Why? This is the imaginative puzzle.

Tamar Gendler has contributed a rich and interesting essay treating the fictionality and imaginative puzzles. She slides back and forth between them, however, characterizing what needs explanation sometimes as a failure to imagine, sometimes as resistance to taking something to be fictional. In several places she writes of resistance to 'making-believe', which might be construed either way.[8] She acknowledges the ambiguity, but contends that conflating the two readings is legitimate (at least in some contexts) on the grounds that 'what is true in a story is what the author gets the (appropriate) reader to imagine, if (appropriate) readers are unable or unwilling to [imagine that *p*], they will be unwilling or unable to [accept that *p* is fictional]' (2000: 58 n. 6). This will be so if an 'appropriate' reader is simply one who imagines what is fictional. But then a reader may resist reading appropriately, while acknowledging that that is what he is resisting; he may refuse to or fail to imagine what he recognizes to be fictional. Alternatively, a reader may deny that the proposition in question is fictional, resist the notion that to read appropriately is to imagine it. These resistances or failures are different, and demand different explanations.

Shaun Nichols has pointed out to me that there may be an epistemological link between imaginings and judgments of fictionality; a person who is unable or unwilling to imagine something may be a poor judge of whether it is to be imagined, whether it is fictional. It is largely because a work induces us to imagine something, in many instances, that we judge it to be fictional. (What I find myself imagining seeing when I look at a picture, for example, what I see 'in' it, is likely to be what it depicts—assuming that I am a 'normal' or properly qualified observer.) If I am incapable of imagining a particular proposition, or don't allow myself to imagine it, this test for fictionality will not be available to me.

3. THE IMAGINATIVE PUZZLE

To avoid begging questions, let's formulate the imaginative puzzle as neutrally as possible. Sometimes people do not engage in imaginings that one might expect them to. These may be imaginings of propositions that are fictional in a given work, or were clearly meant to be fictional, or imaginings a work seems apt for inducing, or ones that appear to be appropriate or called for or likely in situations not involving a work of fiction.

---

[7] Imagining a proposition is more than merely recognizing or entertaining or understanding or formulating it or supposing it to be so. Cf. Walton 1990: 19–21; also Gendler, Ch. 9.

[8] Gendler 2000: 62–3, 66, 75, 79. But see her more recent reflections in 'Imaginative Resistance Revisited' (Ch. 9). I avoid using 'make-believe' as a verb in my own writings because of its ambiguity. Other expressions in the literature which are susceptible to a similar ambiguity include: 'what we accept and imagine as fictionally true', 'fictionally assenting to', and 'imagining a fictional world'.

When people fail to imagine as expected, is this because they are unable to do so, or because they are unwilling to or refuse? Both answers have been proposed in the literature on 'imaginative resistance', and there are instances of both kinds. Sometimes we refuse, for any of a variety of reasons. And some imaginings are difficult or impossible to bring off, the difficulty or impossibility having different explanations in different cases. The imaginative puzzle—itself only part of the tangled nest we are addressing—divides into many.

I mentioned some reasons people may have for declining to engage in an imagining; there are others as well, not all of them moral reasons. Imagining can sometimes lead to belief or acceptance, so one may avoid imagining subscribing to a moral perspective that one considers pernicious or reprehensible (or to a false factual claim), for fear of succumbing to it (Walton 1994: 32).[9] The danger, I should add, may be merely that the person will take it more seriously than she thinks she should, or regard it as less than utterly absurd, as an alternative to be considered; even that, she may think, would be bad enough. My orientation example suggests that imaginings can encourage behavior in accordance with a point of view one rejects, even if one continues to reject it (Walton 1994: 33–5). It is likely that the more confident a person is of her convictions, the more she will want not to be 'oriented' differently, not to be induced by imagining to act contrary to them. But the less confident she is, the more susceptible she might feel, the more danger she might think there is of her being corrupted.

Some of the other reasons one may have for eschewing imaginings are related to these, but some are rather different. Imaginings not connected at all with a point of view or an attitude one is intent on rejecting—reliving a terrifying experience, for instance, or imaginatively anticipating one that one greatly fears—may be just too painful to endure. Many of us find imaginative experiences elicited by some violent movies or tragic literature unpleasant or intolerable. What makes the experience painful may be not so much *what* is imagined as the manner in which it is, the vividness of one's imaginative experience, induced by a vividly realistic portrayal. But there may be certain horrendous scenarios that one simply cannot imagine in a tolerably detached manner.

Bernard Williams presents the possibility of a person who regards certain courses of action as *unthinkable*, or who thinks it *insane* to consider what one ought to do in some hypothetical bizarre and monstrous situation:

It could be a feature of a man's moral outlook that he regarded certain courses of action as unthinkable. ... Entertaining certain alternatives, regarding them indeed as *alternatives*, is itself something that he regards as dishonourable or morally absurd. But, further, he might equally find it unacceptable to consider what to do in certain conceivable situations. Logically, or indeed empirically conceivable they may be, but they are not

---

[9] A number of empirical studies bear this out. See Cialdini 2001 and the studies he refers to: Tversky and Kahneman 1973; Bacon 1979. Currie 1995 and Gendler 2000 both cite relevant empirical work.

to him morally conceivable .... For him, there are certain situations so monstrous that the idea that the processes of moral rationality could yield an answer in them is insane: they are situations which so transcend in enormity the human business of moral deliberation that from a moral point of view it cannot matter any more what happens. Equally, for him, to spend time thinking what one would decide if one were in such a situation is also insane, if not merely frivolous. (Williams 1973: 92)

If a work of fiction encourages readers to imagine performing actions of certain kinds (by encouraging them to empathize with a character who performs them, for instance), the person Williams has in mind may put it down. And one may refuse to read a novel if it demands simply having to choose, in imagination, between monstrous alternatives in a bizarre situation. It need not be part of Williams's suggestion that, in either instance, the person fears being lured to adopt, in real life, a point of view or to take on an attitude she wants to avoid, or to behave as though she did. Faced, in imagination, with a dreadful choice, one can and probably will imagine deciding, as best one can, in accordance with one's actual moral principles. If, as might happen, all of the alternatives would be wrong on one's actual moral principles, there may be pressure to revise one's principles, though not necessarily to adopt principles contrary to one's better judgment.

Gendler 'wants to trace the source of [our unwillingness to imagine morally deviant situations] to a general desire not to be manipulated into taking on points of view that we would not reflectively endorse as authentically our own' (2000: 56; see also p. 79). The impression of being manipulated may increase one's aversion, no doubt. But a susceptible person might worry that the imagining itself, regardless of how it is induced, will tempt him to adopt a point of view he wishes to avoid, or to give it more credence than he thinks it deserves. My aversion to sticking pins into a portrait of a loved one and so, inevitably, imagining harming her does not depend on an impression that someone is directing my imagining. And my aversion need not (though it might) involve a worry that imagining thus will encourage or nourish a desire actually to harm the person.

These armchair observations about instances in which one might refuse to imagine in certain ways are, of course, subject to empirical confirmation or disconfirmation, although I don't think they are likely to be very controversial. They are claims only about what *sometimes* happens, and they are not very specific. In any case, it seems to me obvious and unsurprising that people do, in various kinds of situations and for a variety of understandable reasons, resist engaging in certain imaginings, however much there is to learn about the details of when and how and why this is so. This branch of the imaginative puzzle is not very puzzling.

There is considerably more mystery, not to mention confusion, about what might be difficult or impossible to imagine, and why. Much has been written about whether logical or metaphysical impossibilities can be imagined, whether imaginability is a good test for possibility, and also about the prospects for imaginings that go beyond one's prior experiences—imagining something blue or the taste of vegemite, if one hasn't seen anything blue or tasted vegemite, or imagining what it is like to be a bat.[10] I am not prepared to deny that impossibilities can be imagined. (Cf. Walton 1990: 32–4, 64). And I take no stand on whether, or how far, a person's imaginings might transcend her prior experience. Gregory Currie (2002) offered the intriguing suggestion that what he calls *desire-like* imaginings, in contrast to *belief-like* ones, are especially difficult to bring off when they do not accord with one's actual desires.[11] I am not yet convinced that these are fundamentally different kinds of imaginings. We need to understand how this difference sorts with the difference, which I and others recognize (though I don't understand it as well as I would like to), between imagining *that* . . . (including imagining that I desire such-and-such) and imagining *X-ing* (e.g. imagining desiring . . . , imagining feeling . . . , and also imagining believing . . .). Also, we need an explanation of why desire-like imaginings should be difficult.

If asked to imagine experiencing a series of tones descending in pitch while remaining at the same pitch, we are likely to be stumped. We cannot imagine such an experience, one might suppose, because the experience itself is impossible. But it is not impossible. 'Shepard tones' are series of tones that seem to descend in pitch while remaining at the same pitch (Shepard 1964). And once one has heard Shepard tones, one is likely to be able to imagine the experience, to call up an auditory image of the Shepard tones from memory. (What seems impossible initially is an instance of imagining *X-ing*, in a sense that doesn't reduce to propositional imagining. There is no difficulty at all in imagining *that* one enjoys an experience as of a tone descending in pitch while remaining at the same pitch.)

4. THE FICTIONALITY PUZZLE

It would be surprising if the fictionality and imaginative puzzles were not linked in some important way, since fictionality is defined in terms of imagining. That they are is claimed or assumed in much of the literature on 'imaginative resistance', even (or especially) when the two puzzles are not clearly differentiated. But it is not easy to say what the link is, and there is disagreement about which branch of the imaginative puzzle connects with the fictionality one.

A proposition is fictional if it is *to be* imagined, if a story or other work of fiction prescribes imagining it. We might think of what is fictional as what appreciators, qua appreciators of the work in question, *ought* to imagine. But this encourages a misconception about how the puzzles are related: Since *ought* implies *can*, one might suppose, we ought to imagine something only if it is possible to do so; so we will rightly refuse to judge a proposition to be fictional if we are

---

[10] Cf., e.g., the essays collected in Gendler and Hawthorne 2001.
[11] Peter Carruthers (2003) raises objections to Currie. Currie considers a different suggestion in his 2003.

unable to imagine it. But this *ought* is a conditional one, which does not imply *can*. One ought to imagine *p if* one is to appreciate fully the work in question, i.e. full appreciation requires imagining *p*. But imagining *p* and full appreciation might not be possible. Those who think we cannot imagine metaphysical impossibilities or blatant contradictions needn't deny that they can be fictional, that some works enjoin imagining them.[12] It is generally agreed that (at least some) blatant contradictions and metaphysical impossibilities *can* be fictional. In arguing against what she calls the impossibility hypothesis—the hypothesis that 'imaginative resistance' is explained by the fact that the relevant scenarios are conceptually impossible, and hence unimaginable—Gendler claims that impossibilities can be imagined. She may well be right. But if by 'imaginative resistance' here she means resistance to accepting the scenarios in question as fictional, as she seems to, this claim is unnecessary.

'Imaginative resistance', Gendler thinks, is due primarily to our *unwillingness* to imagine certain propositions, not an inability to do so (2000: 56, 74 79; but see also p. 73 n. 25). Assuming, again, that it is the fictionality puzzle that she has in mind here, this is unsatisfactory; unwillingness to imagine something does not account for resistance to judging it to be fictional. A person who refuses to imagine that Mother Teresa is a drug-dealer, or that the Holocaust is a hoax, may accept with no hesitation whatever that this is true in the world of a story; she might condemn the story or refuse to read it just because it does make this fictional. To use one of Gendler's examples, I may be unwilling to imagine that my beloved Aunt Ruth looks like a walrus; 'I may simply not want to notice the way in which her forehead juts forward . . . or the way that her eyes bug out, or the fact that . . . lines beneath her nose . . . look a bit like tusks' (2000: 80). Yet I may recognize all too well that an unflattering portrait depicts her as looking thus, or that someone might or did write a story in which, fictionally, she was locked up in a zoo because she was virtually indistinguishable from an escaped walrus. I may refuse to look at the picture or read the story, given that it does make this fictional, so as to escape the invitation or inducement to engage in the uncomfortable imaginings.

'My best suspicion' as to why we resist allowing fictional worlds to differ from the real world when we do, I said, is that it 'has something to do with an inability to imagine [certain kinds of dependence relations] being different from how we think they are, perhaps an inability to understand fully what it would be like for them to be different' (Walton 1994: 46). This is not an endorsement of the impossibility hypothesis that Gendler objects to, since I hold neither that conceptual impossibilities in general are unimaginable, nor that what is unimaginable cannot in general be fictional. What seems to me to be important is a very particular kind of imaginative inability, one that attaches to propositions expressing

---

[12] Kathleen Stock concurs that what is fictional need not be imaginable (2003: 108).

certain sorts of supervenience relations, which the imaginer rejects. This is barely a beginning. But both Brian Weatherson (2004) and Steven Yablo (2001) suggest plausible ways of developing similar lines of thought.[13]

5. WHY 'THE PUZZLE OF IMAGINATIVE RESISTANCE' IS UNFORTUNATELY SO CALLED

The untangling I have undertaken above and in 'Morals in Fiction' should make evident how misleading it is to apply this label to the nest of issues treated in that essay. Pluralization—'the *puzzles* of imaginative resistance'—would bring out the multiplicity of the strands, but its mischaracterization of most of them would be glaring. The aesthetic puzzle, which concerns the relation between aesthetic and moral values, involves resistance to imagining only very indirectly. The resistance constituting the fictionality puzzle is not *imaginative* resistance, resistance to imagining, but resistance to accepting that something is fictional. Among the imaginative puzzles, those concerning what we *cannot* imagine are not puzzles of imaginative *resistance*; inability is not resistance. This leaves only our *unwillingness* to engage in certain imaginings in certain circumstances, which *is* aptly described as 'imaginative resistance'. But although this unwillingness is important, and is surrounded by important unanswered questions, it is not itself particularly puzzling.

The fictionality puzzle, especially, certainly is puzzling; indeed it is much more than a puzzle. Calling it that (as I have done) suggests that it is relatively superficial, subject perhaps to a quick and definitive solution, if not an easy one. This is far from the case. As anyone immersed in it can testify, to wrestle with the fictionality puzzle is to enter, by a side door, absolutely fundamental mysteries about the nature of concepts, supervenience relations, response dependence, normative judgments, and the imagination.

I have no complaints about the word 'of' in 'the puzzle of imaginative resistance'.

REFERENCES

Bacon, F. T. (1979) 'Credibility of Repeated Statements: Memory for Trivia', *Journal of Experimental Psychology: Human Learning and Memory*, 5, 241–52.
Carroll, N. (1996) 'Moderate Moralism', *British Journal of Aesthetics*, 36, 223–37.
Carruthers, P. (2003) 'Review of Currie and Ravenscroft, *Recreative Minds*', *Notre Dame Philosophical Reviews*, 11 (12).

---

[13] Weatherson 2004: 16–18, 21–4. Yablo (2001) proposes that the fictionality puzzle applies to propositions involving *response-enabled*, or 'grokking' predicates (e.g. 'oval').

CIALDINI, R. B. (2001) 'Systematic Opportunism: An Approach to the Study of Tactical Social Influence', in J. P. Forgas and K. D. Williams (eds.), *Social Influence: Direct and Indirect Processes* (Philadelphia: Psychology Press), 25–39.

CURRIE, G. (1995) 'The Moral Psychology of Fiction', *Australian Journal of Philosophy*, 73 (2), 250–9.

——(2002) 'Desire in Imagination', in Gendler and Hawthorne (2002), 201–22.

——(2003) 'The Capacities that Enable Us to Produce and Consume Art', in M. Kieran and D. Lopes (eds.), *Imagination, Philosophy, and the Arts* (London: Routledge), 293–304.

——and RAVENSCROFT, I. (2002) *Recreative Minds: Imagination in Philosophy and Psychology* (Oxford: Oxford University Press).

DEVEREAUX, M. (1998) 'Beauty and Evil: The Case of Leni Riefenstahl's *Triumph of the Will*', in J. Levinson (ed.), *Aesthetics and Ethics* (Cambridge: Cambridge University Press), 227–56.

GAUT, B. (1998) 'The Ethical Criticism of Art', in J. Levinson (ed.), *Aesthetics and Ethics* (Cambridge: Cambridge University Press), 182–203.

GENDLER, T. S. (2000) 'The Puzzle of Imaginative Resistance', *Journal of Philosophy*, 2, 55–81.

——and HAWTHORNE, J. (eds.) (2002) *Conceivability and Possibility* (Oxford: Oxford University Press).

HUME, D. (1965) 'Of the Standard of Taste', in his *Of the Standard of Taste and Other Essays* (Indianapolis: Bobbs-Merrill), 3–24.

JACOBSON, D. (1997) 'In Praise of Immoral Art', *Philosophical Topics*, 25 (1), 155–99.

JOHN, E. (2005) 'Artistic Value and Opportunistic Moralism', in M. Kieran (ed.), *Contemporary Debates in Aesthetics and the Philosophy of Art* (Oxford: Blackwell), 331–41.

KIERAN, M. (1996) 'Art, Imagination, and the Cultivation of Morals', *Journal of Aesthetics and Art Criticism*, 54 (4), 337–51.

MATRAVERS, D. (2003) 'Fictional Assent and the (So-called) "Puzzle of Imaginative Resistance" ', in M. Kieran and D. Lopes (eds.), *Imagination, Philosophy, and the Arts* (London: Routledge), 91–106.

MENCKEN, H. L. (1926) 'Music and Sin', in *Prejudices, 5th ser.* (New York: Alfred A. Knopf), 293–6.

MORAN, R. (1994) 'The Expression of Feeling in Imagination', *Philosophical Review*, 103 (1), 75–106.

NICHOLS, S. (forthcoming) 'Just the Imagination: Why Imagining Doesn't Behave Like Believing', *Mind & Language*.

SHEPARD, R. N. (1964) 'Circularity in Judgments of Relative Pitch', *Journal of the Acoustical Society of America*, 36 (12), 2346–53.

SIBLEY, F. (2001) 'Aesthetic Judgements: Pebbles, Faces, and Fields of Litter', in J. Benson, B. Redfern, and J. R. Cox (eds.), *Approach to Aesthetics* (Oxford: Oxford University Press), 176–90.

STOCK, K. (2003) 'The Tower of Goldbach and Other Impossible Tales', in M. Kieran and D. Lopes (eds.), *Imagination, Philosophy and the Arts* (London: Routledge), 107–24.

TANNER, M. (1994) 'Morals in Fiction and Fictional Morality', *Proceedings of the Aristotelian Society*, suppl. vol. 68, 51–66.

TVERSKY, A., and KAHNEMAN, D. (1973) 'Availability: A Heuristic for Judging Frequency and Probability', *Cognitive Psychology*, 5, 207–32.

WALTON, K. L. (1990) *Mimesis as Make-Believe: On the Foundations of the Representational Arts* (Cambridge, Mass.: Harvard University Press).

—— (1994) 'Morals in Fiction and Fictional Morality', *Proceedings of the Aristotelian Society*, suppl. vol. 68, 27–50.

WEATHERSON, B. (2004) 'Morality, Fiction and Possibility', *Philosophers' Imprint*, 4 (3).

WILLIAMS, B. (1973) 'A Critique of Utilitarianism', in J. J. C. Smart and B. Williams, *Utilitarianism, For and Against* (Cambridge: Cambridge University Press), 75–150.

YABLO, S. (2001) 'Coulda, Woulda, Shoulda', in Gendler and Hawthorne (2001), 441–92.

9

Imaginative Resistance Revisited

Tamar Szabó Gendler

1. INTRODUCTION

Several hundred years ago, Hume offered some brief remarks on a striking feature of our imaginative repertoire. While we are generally both ready and able to entertain even the most fantastic and improbable scenarios, there appear to be systematic exceptions: in certain circumstances, it is unexpectedly difficult to (bring ourselves to) imagine what an author describes. Half a decade ago, drawing on an insight of Kendall Walton's and borrowing a term from Dick Moran, I dubbed a special instance of this phenomenon *The Puzzle of Imaginative Resistance*.[1] 'The Puzzle of Imaginative Resistance', I suggested, is 'the puzzle of explaining our comparative difficulty in imagining fictional worlds that we take to be morally deviant' (Gendler 2000: 56).[2]

Recently, a number of authors have suggested that both the attributed genealogy and the choice of term were unfortunate. Hume's concerns are

I am grateful to Jeff Dean for organizing a session at the November 2004 American Society for Aesthetics Meetings where this chapter was originally presented, to my commentator Dustin Stokes for his excellent commentary on that early draft, and to the audience at that session for their questions and comments. A very early draft of Sections 4 and 5 was presented at the Technical University in Budapest in May 2004, and I am grateful to audience members there for helpful questions and discussion. For help with subsequent drafts, warm thanks are due to John Holbo, David Jehle, Shaun Nichols, Kendall Walton, and Brian Weatherson, and especially to Tyler Doggett, Andy Egan, Emily Esch, Jonathan Ichikawa, Zoltán Gendler Szabó, and Kelly Trogdon

[1] Cf. Walton 1994; Moran 1994; Gendler 2000. Though I hope the discussion below will be comprehensible even to those unfamiliar with earlier works, readers wishing to gain an overview of the issues might fruitfully consult the three essays just listed, along with Weatherson 2004.

[2] The basic problem is this: 'When an author invites us to contemplate a fictional scenario, she seems to have a great deal of freedom in how she directs our imagination. Among the things she can make fictionally true are . . . that animals marry, that time travel occurs, that alchemy is good science, and so on. But she seems to have much *less* freedom in what she makes fictionally true as far as matters of moral assessment are concerned. The trick that allows an author complete freedom in dictating whether or not character A murders character B is much less effective if what the author wants to dictate is that the murder is, for instance, praiseworthy, or noble, or charming, or admirable. So the puzzle is this: what explains why a trick so effective in so many realms is relatively ineffective here?' (Gendler 2000: 58).

primarily with non-fiction rather than fiction. And there are a number of related puzzles that I failed to identify or address: whereas my original account conflated problems of truth in fiction with problems of imaginability, there are important differences between them;[3] and whereas my original discussion was limited to morally deviant fictional scenarios, there are related cases that should be accommodated in a fully comprehensive account.

Because I focused only on certain features of the landscape, the solution I proposed in 'The Puzzle of Imaginative Resistance' (2000)—roughly, that we don't imagine morally deviant worlds because we don't want to—is incomplete.[4] I will offer appropriate concessions in the pages that follow, and I present my new positive view at the end of Section 3. That said, I remain committed to four of 'Puzzle's' main claims,[5] and I will devote the bulk of this essay to defending them.

First, I remain convinced that the engagement which distinguishes imagination from mere supposition plays a crucial role in the phenomena we are concerned with explaining. Insofar as our relation to the text is one of detached supposition, the perplexing responses that give rise to the puzzles are mitigated; it is only when we engage imaginatively—an engagement that is, in some difficult-to-pin-down way, self-involving—that forceful resistance of the relevant kind begins to emerge.

Relatedly, I continue to believe that cases that invoke interesting resistance arise where the reader takes the author to be making simultaneous claims about the fictional and the non-fictional world. In the earlier paper I described these as cases where 'export' is mandated; below I will describe them as involving 'pop-out' sentences.[6] The basic claim here—as before—is that resistance phenomena arise because imaginative engagement is also a form of actual engagement. When we imagine, we draw on our ordinary conceptual repertoire and habits

---

[3] For careful sorting out of four puzzles that earlier discussions tended to conflate, see Weatherson 2004. My focus here will be primarily on what Weatherson calls the *imaginative* puzzle.

[4] For important—and in many cases, decisive—criticisms, see Currie 2002; Currie and Ravenscroft 2002; Doggett 2004; Holbo 2003*a*, 2003*b*; Matravers 2003; Mothersill 2002; Stock 2003, 2005; Stokes forthcoming; Trogdon 2004; Walton, Ch. 8; Weatherson 2003, 2004; Weinberg and Meskin forthcoming and Ch. 10; Yablo 2002. I have learned an enormous amount from these essays and from discussions with their authors; my debts should be apparent to anyone familiar with them.

[5] Though Matravers (2003) and Walton (Ch. 8) rightly consider it imprudent, I will sometimes use the expression 'imaginative resistance' for the family of phenomena which surround the puzzle that I discussed in the earlier paper. Where it is important to distinguish among members of the puzzle family, I will do so explicitly.

[6] It will turn out that these cases overlap in significant ways—and for non-accidental reasons—with certain of the cases that violate the principle that Brian Weatherson has called *Virtue*. Roughly speaking, the relevant *Virtue*-violating cases are cases where the lower-level facts in a story determine that p, but where (the author of) the story nonetheless asserts that not-p. (Cf. Weatherson 2004: 18.)

of appraisal, and as the result of imagining, we may find ourselves with novel insights about, and changed perspectives on, the actual world.

Third, I remained convinced that there *is* something special about the moral (or at least the appraisal-involving) cases, in contrast to the wider range of cases on which other authors have focused. Our failure to imagine them can be traced to a certain sort of unwillingness that amplifies—in subtle and complicated ways—what other authors have rightly identified as a certain sort of inability.

Finally, I remain convinced that a successful characterization of the resistance family needs to explain not only our specific resistance to accepting as fictional the contents of certain stories, but also our more general reluctance to adopt metaphoric perspectives that emphasize similarities we prefer to overlook.[7] These cases provide an important foil neglected by many other accounts. In the next section, I will provide an example of the sort of case I have in mind.

2. INTERLUDE: NURSERY SCHOOL NOMENCLATURE

At nursery schools throughout the United States, classes have names like Kangaroos, Ladybugs, Koalas, and Teddy Bears. It would be acceptable—though barely—for a school to have classes named Monkeys, Dogs, Cows, and Mice. But it would, presumably, be very odd indeed for classes at a nursery school to be called Cockroaches, Vultures, Maggots, and Mosquitoes. Now, whatever the explanation, it cannot be that three-year-olds are more like ladybugs than they are like cockroaches—or more like kangaroos than they are like vultures. Three-year-olds may jump around excitedly, but they also descend voraciously on the snack table; they may not have beaks and wings, but they also don't have tails and pouches. This gives rise to the *Problem of Nursery School Nomenclature*: the problem of explaining why so many nursery schools have a Bumblebee room, but no nursery schools have a Dung Beetle room, given that (in some reasonable sense of *harder*), it's no harder to imagine your child as a dung beetle than as a bumblebee.

Most of us have a reasonable folk theory about the Problem of Nursery School Nomenclature. We (tacitly) realize that framing things in certain ways activates certain behavioral dispositions and affective propensities, and we (tacitly) realize that the dispositions and propensities associated with notions like maggothood and vultureness are ones which we wish to avoid when thinking of our children. Moreover, an enormous body of empirical psychological research backs up these folk intuitions. One of the most striking and well-confirmed results of social-psychological research over the last two decades is that mental representations can

---

[7] Cf. Moran 1989; Walton 1993; to which I am here indebted.

be activated in a multitude of ways, and that awakening the associative patterns linked with a particular stereotype, mental image, protocol, or motor routine tends to awaken the perception and action dispositions associated with it.[8] So our tacit sense that there is something distasteful about thinking of our child as a cockroach or a mosquito is based in a genuine sensitivity to a feature of our psychology. The Problem of Nursery School Nomenclature arises from our implicit awareness of the psychological costs associated with allowing ourselves to frame things in certain ways.

Notice, however, that I said '*allowing* ourselves to frame things in certain ways'. Nursery school nomenclature is puzzling because it involves a case where we *can* do something, but we *don't*. And the reason we don't do it is because we don't want to—that is, because we *won't*. My suggestion in 'Puzzle' was that imaginative resistance is the result of similar mechanisms. I wrote: 'the primary source of imaginative resistance is not our *inability* to imagine morally deviant situations, but our *unwillingness* to do so' (Gendler 2000: 57).

For reasons that I will explain at the end of the next section, I now think that solution is incomplete.[9] But it will be helpful nonetheless to classify solutions along the spectrum that this distinction suggests. Some solutions—like Walton's tentatively endorsed impossibility solution[10]—are *can't* solutions: they say that in cases of imaginative resistance we don't follow along with the author because, for example, we can't figure out what it would *mean* for something to be both an instance of something that is morally good and an instance of something that is gratuitous torture. Other solutions—like the solution I proposed in 'Puzzle'—are *won't* solutions: I said that in cases of imaginative resistance we don't follow along with the author because we don't want to think about these things, even though we could.

Putting things this way oversimplifies somewhat, but it provides a useful initial framework for thinking about the range of positions in reacting to our puzzle. I will return to this distinction in my discussion below. But now I want to go back to Hume's original text, which I think will help us get a clearer handle on the phenomena we are worried about.

3. HUMEAN RESISTANCE

Although the connection between Hume's original remarks and contemporary discussions of imaginative resistance has sometimes been overstated, there is

---

[8] For detailed discussion of these issues, see Gendler 2006.

[9] Again, see papers cited in n. 4.

[10] Walton seeks 'an explanation of why we should resist allowing fictional worlds to differ from the real world with respect to the relevant kind of dependence relations'. Though he considers a number of explanations, he writes that his 'best suspicion . . . is that it has something to do with . . . an inability to understand fully what it would be like for them to be different' (Walton 1994: 46).

much to be learned by revisiting the text itself. For Hume notices features—or his text encourages the reader to notice features—that have received inadequate attention in many recent discussions. The now familiar passage appears near the end of 'Of the Standard of Taste':

Where *speculative* errors may be found in the polite writings of any age or country, they detract but little from the value of those compositions. There needs to be but a certain turn of thought or imagination to make us enter into all the opinions which then prevailed and relish the sentiments or conclusions derived from them. But a very violent effort is requisite to change our judgment of manners, and excite sentiments of approbation or blame, love or hatred, different from those to which the mind from long custom has been familiarized . . . I cannot, nor is it proper that I should, enter into such [vicious] sentiments. (Hume 1985/1757: 247)

Hume is pointing out an apparent topical asymmetry in our responses to various forms of writing. Texts that misrepresent certain things strike us as inadequate in ways that texts that misrepresent other sorts of things do not. Whereas texts involving *detached factual* inaccuracies ('speculative errors' from which 'sentiments or conclusions' might be 'derived') are relatively unproblematic, texts that produce *involved evaluative* inaccuracies (implicating us in a 'judgment of manners' or exciting 'sentiments of approbation or blame, love or hatred' that are 'different from those to which the mind from long custom has been familiarized') face a cluster of related problems. What distinguishes the class of problematic cases from those that are unproblematic, and what sorts of problems do they confront?

Hume's text identifies two features as characteristic of the troublesome class. First, they are cases involving *valenced normative appraisals*: we are asked to assess something as mannerly or unmannerly, praiseworthy or blameworthy, lovable or hateable, where each of the pairs identifies two points along a normative spectrum where one end is desirable and the other is not. Second, they are cases that require the reader's *imaginative involvement*: it is *we* who are making the 'judgment of manners', *we* in whom the relevant sentiments are being 'excited', and *we* who are receiving the risky and improper invitation to 'enter into' some vicious frame of mind.

On Hume's picture, these characteristic features are non-accidentally related. At base, normative judgments of praiseworthiness and blameworthiness are summary assessments of our tendencies towards attraction and repulsion—tendencies that are themselves the result of 'long custom' and habituation. As a result, altering our judgments—even playfully—will be both difficult and dangerous: difficult because it will require the overcoming of long-entrenched patterns of response which are likely to be evoked even in the contemplation of explicitly imaginary scenarios, and dangerous because such overcoming may render these undesirable patterns of response available even in the contemplation of actual ones.

In light of this, Hume identifies three sorts of problems that typically confront such texts (those that call upon us to make deviant, imaginatively involved, valenced normative appraisals).The first is that the presence of such demands may 'detract ... from the value of these compositions'. We might tentatively call this the *Problem of Aesthetic Value*, though it's not completely clear that it is specifically *aesthetic* value that Hume has in mind.[11] (Because I have nothing particularly interesting to say about it, I will set aside this issue in the ensuing discussion.[12]) The second is that we find it difficult to 'enter into' their world-view by our usual 'turn of thought or imagination'—if we succeed in doing so, it is only by means of a 'very violent effort'. Let's call this the *Problem of Imaginative Barriers*. The third is that entering into such worldviews strikes us as being in some way 'improper'—the sentiments in question are 'vicious' ones, and even if we somehow succeed in adopting them, we will have violated a norm that we hold ourselves to. Let's call this the *Problem of Imaginative Impropriety*.[13] Finally, let's call cases where both of the latter two obtain—that is, cases where we both confront imaginative barriers and experience a feeling of imaginative impropriety—cases that evoke *Humean Resistance*.

Hume doesn't give a specific example, but I take it that the sort of case he has in mind is this. Reading a text from ancient Greece—something like the *Euthyphro*, let's say—I find it a relatively straightforward matter to enter imaginatively into a mindset where I 'relish the sentiments or conclusions' drawn from the assumption that the Greek gods are in control of certain matters of daily life; I can put myself into a mood where I imagine that it really matters that one keep one's hearth burning lest Hephaestus be offended, or that if one faces an important practical decision, one should check in with the Oracle at Delphi. I may not fully work out all the implications of my imaginative commitments, but I'm genuinely involved and engaged in them, and when I'm asked to make inferences that require me to treat those assumptions as (imaginatively) true, I'm ready and willing to do so. By contrast, something very different happens when the author of the historical text seems to be assuming that I share his normative valenced appraisals of certain situations that I am engaged with quasi-observationally: on the question of whether it is morally acceptable to beat one's slave to death, for instance—indeed, on the question of whether it is morally acceptable to own a slave in the first place—I experience two things when I respond to the implied invitation to enter into such a mindset: I find that doing so requires, as Hume remarks, 'a very violent effort' (this is the Problem of Imaginative Barriers), and I find myself reluctant to try to make that effort—it feels that doing so would be 'improper' or 'vicious' (this is the Problem of Imaginative Impropriety).[14]

[11] Indeed, the detraction may simply consist in the difficulties enumerated in the remainder of the passage.

[12] For further discussion of this question, see Walton (Ch. 8).

[13] Weinberg and Meskin offer a related distinction between what they call *the puzzle of imaginative refusal* and *the puzzle of imaginative blockage*. See Weinberg and Meskin forthcoming and Ch. 10.

[14] For an alternative use of the *Euthyphro* in discussing imaginative resistance, see Holbo 2003a.

So it looks as if Humean Resistance arises when we feel ourselves to have been asked by an author to make valenced normative appraisals in an involved way which differ from those that we are accustomed to making; in such cases, we find that doing so requires significant effort, and that undertaking such an effort would be distasteful. By contrast, when we are making appraisals that are neither normative nor valenced, and when we are doing so in a detached way, Humean resistance does not arise. Moreover—though this does not rest directly on anything that Hume himself says—intermediate cases provide an interesting foil.

Consider, first, cases where we are asked to contemplate deviant valenced normative appraisals in a detached way—as when we are asked to suppose just for the sake of argument that child slavery is morally acceptable. Such cases seem, at least to me, to evoke a palpable feeling of something akin to imaginative impropriety. Even though I am not engaged in a full-fledged act of *imagining*, there seems to be something unseemly about supposing for the sake of argument that the Rwandan genocide was not such a bad thing because the victims were poor, or that the policy of deliberately infecting Native Americans with smallpox was acceptable because a great country was built as a result. In such cases, the distancing introduced by the demand that I merely *suppose* is sufficient to eliminate at least some of the relevant imaginative barriers. I do have *some* grasp on the content I am supposed to be entertaining[15] (even if, on reflection, I realize that content to be incoherent[16]). But the Problem of Imaginative Impropriety remains: even if I *can* suppose these sorts of things, I find myself not *wanting* to.[17] In related fashion, cases where I am invited to adopt a metaphoric perspective that I find repugnant—like the nursery school

---

[15] Remember: all we're looking for is the sort of grasp that one has in ordinary cases of fiction-induced imagining—cases where one may well be explicitly committed to the incoherence of the content one is contemplating.

[16] As Jonathan Ichikawa and Emily Esch have pointed out to me, such feelings of impropriety may arise even when the content in question is not explicitly evaluative: as, for example, when I am asked to suppose that blacks are genetically inferior to whites, or that the Holocaust never happened. In both cases, I think, the resistance can be explained by the framework presented above: the association between accepting the purported fact and accepting a problematic norm is sufficiently strong that the normative claim colors the descriptive one. (One would thus expect similar feelings of impropriety to arise for a religious fundamentalist asked to suppose for the sake of argument that fetuses lack souls.)

[17] Interestingly, we don't seem to face the same problem when the story's moral standards are *higher* than those we accept in ordinary cases: I don't sense imaginative impropriety when I suppose for the sake of argument that, for instance, 'In throwing away the Oxfam envelope, Giselda did something morally culpable: after all, there were starving children in Africa.' It may be that in such cases I am not imagining the proposed content with the requisite vividness, and that if I were to do so, I would find myself facing imaginative barriers. Indeed, as Kelly Trogdon points out (personal correspondence), if we modify the example slightly, we do seem to confront such barriers—along with feelings of impropriety: 'In throwing away the Oxfam envelope, Giselda did something morally on a par with deliberately murdering innocent children.' I don't yet have a good account of what is going on here.

nomenclature cases from Section 2—evoke impropriety without barriers.[18] It's not that I *can't* recognize the relevant similarities; it's that I don't want to focus on them.

By contrast, cases which involve extreme disruptions of conceptual relations that are salient to us at the time of imagining may confront us with something akin to imaginative barriers without an associated sense of imaginative impropriety. Though there may be actual-world approximations[19], the cleanest examples of this kind involve the sorts of fictional cases that authors like Yablo (2002) and Weatherson (2004) have presented—cases where we feel that we can't even begin to make sense of what it would be for something to be simultaneously five-pointed and oval-shaped, or to be indistinguishable from a fork yet be a television.[20] In such cases, though we presumably feel no impropriety about attempting to do so, even a 'violent effort' to imagine the indicated content leaves us feeling blank.

In short, there seem to be four sorts of cases that we need to consider[21]:

  (i) Cases that evoke feelings of imaginative impropriety without imaginative barriers: call these *pure won't* cases;

 (ii) Cases that evoke imaginative barriers without feelings of imaginative impropriety: call these *pure can't* cases;

(iii) Cases that evoke both feelings of imaginative impropriety and imaginative barriers, but where it is the imaginative impropriety that explains our failure to imagine the world (the felt imaginative impropriety eclipses the imaginative barriers, so the doomed imaginative project is not even attempted): call these *won't–couldn't cases*;

 (iv) Cases that evoke both feelings of imaginative impropriety and imaginative barriers, but where it is the imaginative barriers that explain our failure to imagine the world (the imaginative barrier eclipses the motivating force of the imaginative impropriety, so that the unappealingness of imagining such a world does not become apparent); call these *can't–wouldn't cases.*

---

[18] As I discuss in Section 8, these two classes of cases will turn out to be connected in interesting ways.

[19] It is difficult to come up with actual cases, since the disrupted conceptual connections must be sufficiently salient and sufficiently localized to render the internal tension graspable at a single moment. Cases of wildly delusional beliefs, such as those arising from Cotard or Capgras or Mirror-Man syndromes, may be examples. Or perhaps the mutual bafflement of theists and atheists at the other's interpretation of the common evidence concerning the (non-)existence of a supremely powerful deity. (Examples from history and anthropology—which appear to provide natural mining grounds for such cases—are generally parasitic on disagreements about 'detached factual' matters. Indeed, the phenomenon discussed in n. 16 seems to arise here as well: barriers to imagining some sort of conceptual disruption may 'infect' our ability to imagine the detached factual considerations that support it.)

[20] In the sense required by the generation rules governing anything but the most absurd stories: see Sections 6–8 below.

[21] Thanks to Kelly Trogdon for suggesting this way of looking at the problem.

I think that cases where we reject invitations to adopt metaphoric perspectives we find repugnant are pure won't cases—as are cases where we reject invitations merely to suppose. And I think that cases where we reject invitations to imagine things like Weathersonian fork-tables and Yablonian five-pointed ovals are pure can't cases. The interesting question is how to classify classic cases of Humean Resistance. Weatherson (2004) and Yablo (2002) and Walton (in his 1994 'best guess') seem to classify them as pure can't cases; Gendler (2000), Currie (2002), and Stokes (forthcoming) seem to classify them as pure won't cases. But I now think that classic cases of Humean Resistance are won't–couldn't cases. And I think their dual structure is what's interesting about them. Imaginative impropriety is present because the content in question strikes us as somehow repugnant; and imaginative barriers are present because the content in question strikes us as somehow incoherent. Moreover, the two are deeply intertwined: Imagining something that we take to be immoral makes salient the impropriety of categorizing it as moral, and thereby renders salient the incoherence of doing so. In short, *cantians* and *wontians* offered complementary insights while making complementary errors. Neither recognized that in cases of classic imaginative resistance, each had captured part of the truth.

4. EXTENDING THE CASE TO FICTION

Humean Resistance, as it has been characterized so far, applies to the contemplation of historical or culturally alien texts, rather than texts that are explicitly fictional. In this section I want to extend the discussion I have been offering by considering a problem that I will call *Authoritative Breakdown*.[22] Explaining what I mean by this term will require a brief excursion through some earlier writings on the topic of imaginative resistance.[23].

In the original 'Puzzle' (2000) paper, I contrasted cases where 'I am asked to make-believe that: p holds (where p is some non-moral proposition that I do not believe holds)' with cases where 'I am asked to make-believe that: m holds, where m is some moral proposition that I do not believe holds'. Our default response to the first sort of case, I suggested, is acceptance, whereas our default response to the second sort of case is non-acceptance. I went on to suggest that the second of these should perplex us, since while believing at will is, in general, precluded by the aims of belief, *make-believing* at will is not merely permitted by

[22] For an interesting related proposal, see Matravers 2003; for criticism of some of the details of that proposal, see Weatherson 2004. My discussion in this section is indebted to the writings of both of these authors.

[23] Most of these writings—including 'Puzzle'—conflate issues about fictional truth with issues about imagination. In the discussion below, I will be primarily concerned with the issue of mandated imaginings, rather than the (importantly related and (as we will see in Section 6) intertwined) issue of truth in fiction.

the aims of make-belief, it is what the practice is about in the first place. So the existence of cases where our default reaction to an invitation to make-believe is resistance rather than acquiescence demands explanation.[24] In short, the puzzle is why there's an asymmetry (to the extent that there is one) between one class of cases and another, and whether there's anything systematic to be said about which sorts of prompted imaginings fall into which class.

It is useful in this regard to consider the following widely quoted passage from Dick Moran's 'Expression of Feeling in Imagination':

> If the story tells us that Duncan was *not* in fact murdered on Macbeth's orders, then *that* is what we accept and imagine as fictionally true. If we start doubting what the story tells us about its characters, then we may as well doubt whether it's giving us their right names. However, suppose the facts of the murder remain as they are in fact presented in the play, but it is prescribed in this alternate fiction that this was unfortunate only for having interfered with Macbeth's sleep, or that we in the audience are relieved at these events. These seem to be imaginative tasks of an entirely different order. (1994: 95)

Moran's remark nicely brings out a crucial feature of cooperative reading: that, as a default principle, if an author does whatever is normally required for prompting the reader to imagine that p is true in the story—which in simple cases amounts to asserting, in the story context, that p—then the reader will imagine that p is true in the story.[25] Without something like this default in place, the practice of storytelling would be impossible. As Moran remarks (read this as a claim about mandated imagining rather than about truth in fiction): 'If we start doubting what the story tells us about its characters, then we may as well doubt whether it's giving us their right names.'[26]

---

[24] An important clarification: When some readers encounter the family of puzzles that concern us here, they are inclined to take the problem as one of absolute imaginability, and so they respond by identifying complicated cases where it is true in a story that, for instance, torturing baby seals is the *summum bonum*, and where readers like themselves are prepared to imagine this. But it is crucial to remember that the Problem of Imaginative Barriers is a problem about relative difficulty, *not* a problem about absolute impossibility. In producing a work of fiction, an author has tremendous cultural resources at her disposal: the entire stock of literal language, an enormous battery of common metaphors, a copious set of conventions governing genre, and an abundant inheritance of previous fictional works to which she can make subtle and not-so-subtle reference. With enough ingenuity, these resources can, I suspect, be used to make any local bit of content not only true in a story, but also straightforwardly imaginable. So the issue is *not* whether there are stories in which, for example, counter-moral propositions are true, or imaginable; the issue is why making some sorts of propositions imaginable takes a different *kind* of effort than making other sorts of propositions imaginable. For related discussion, see Currie 1990; Priest 1999; Sorensen 2002; Stock 2003, 2005; Weatherson 2004; Yablo 2002.

[25] Matters become more complicated if we consider certain sophisticated forms of postmodern fiction; in the discussion above, I am implicitly restricting myself to simple cases of traditional narrative. I am also assuming (contrary to the advice of Tyler Doggett and John Holbo, who have convinced me that the problem merits careful attention) that the text in question does not contain unintentional mistakes. (For a few brief remarks on this, see n. 29.)

[26] This is not to deny that names themselves immediately generate associations in the mind of the reader. In this sense, the author's choice might be 'mistaken' (if it prompts the 'wrong'

We are now in a position to articulate the more general puzzle that I think underlies the phenomenon I earlier called imaginative resistance. It is a puzzle about the limits of authorial authority and the nature of reader responsiveness. The puzzle, as I now understand it, is this. In order for the practice of fiction-telling to be possible, the following principle must hold as a default:

Authorial authority with respect to imaginative guidance: If the author of a fictional work follows standard conventions for fictionally asserting p, then the engaged reader will be disposed to imagine p'.[27]

But for certain claims where the author appears to have followed the requisite conventions, the engaged reader nonetheless fails to imagine p. The puzzle is this:

The Puzzle of Authoritative Breakdown: the puzzle of identifying those features that systematically co-occur with, and explain, breakdowns of authorial authority.

The Puzzle of Authoritative Breakdown is, I think, an appropriately generalized version of the puzzle that I earlier called the Puzzle of Imaginative Resistance.

5. POP-OUT

One very interesting thing about cases of authoritative breakdown is that they typically exhibit a feature that I call 'pop-out'. Pop-out passages are passages where, instead of taking the author to be asking her to *imagine* some proposition p that concerns the fictional world, the reader takes the author to be asking her to *believe* a corresponding proposition p' that concerns the actual world. Consider, for example, the following two story excerpts (following with variation Walton 1994):

Good Giselda
The next morning, Giselda killed her baby on the grounds of its gender. In killing her baby, Giselda did the right thing; after all, it was a girl.
Bad Giselda
The next morning, Giselda killed her baby on the grounds of its gender. In killing her baby, Giselda did not do the right thing; after all, it was a human being.

---

imaginings). (Thanks to Brian Weatherson for discussion of this issue.) As the rather sobering social psychology literature reminds us, we are inclined to very different evaluations of otherwise identical *Curriculum Vitae* depending on the gender and race associated with the name that appears at the top of the document; it is difficult to see why a similar chain of associations should not be set into play when we are imaginarily engaged with a work of fiction.

[27] We might consider the parallel principle of *Authorial authority with respect to fictional truth* by replacing 'then the engaged reader will be disposed to imagine p' with 'then it will be true in the story that p'. I think the issues of mandated imagining and truth in fiction are importantly intertwined, in the sense that what is true in a story is roughly what the cooperative and informed reader will be disposed to imagine (modulo worries about imaginative limitations; see e.g. Weatherson 2004). I return to this issue in n. 29 and 31.

In both of these cases, the first sentence of the story follows the default principles articulated above: the author has followed the standard conventions for fictionally asserting *p* (that Giselda killed her baby on gender grounds), and this has resulted both in *p* being true in the fiction, and in a disposition on the part of the engaged reader to accept this and imagine *p*.[28]

Note, however, that the sentence stays firmly within the story. Nothing inclines me to think that in prompting me to *imagine* something about what Giselda did in the Giselda fiction, the author is simultaneously asking me to *believe* some corresponding thing about the world outside the Giselda fiction (except in the uninteresting sense that the Giselda fiction is something we are talking about here in the actual world).

By contrast, the second sentence of each of the stories pops out. Both strike us as not merely asking us to *imagine* that it is true in the Giselda fiction that Giselda did the right (or wrong) thing in killing her baby on the grounds of its gender, but also as asking us to *believe* that it is true in *this world* that someone exactly like Giselda would be doing the right (or wrong) thing in killing her baby on such grounds. In the case of the Bad Giselda story, this causes no difficulties. Since we (presumably) do believe that killing a baby on the grounds of its gender is wrong, we face no imaginative barriers to imagining it to be true in the Giselda fiction as well; nor do we encounter any feelings of imaginative impropriety. But in the case of the Good Giselda story, difficulties emerge. We take the final sentence to be a simultaneous invitation to imagine and to believe—and we reject the invitation to believe. And I suggest that it is at least in part because we are unable to disentangle the invitations that we reject the invitation to imagine.[29] In the rest of the chapter, I will offer some thoughts about why and how this phenomenon arises.

I begin by noting that pop-out seems to happen in virtually all of the examples presented in the literature on imaginative resistance (though in other ways I think there are important differences among the various examples).

---

[28] Of course, it may be *unpleasant* to imagine Giselda killing her baby, and it may be especially unpleasant to imagine her killing her baby on gender grounds, but it does not, I take it, strike us as *improper* in the Humean sense to imagine it being a fact in the Giselda fiction that Giselda killed her baby for this particular reason.

[29] Again, a parallel explanation goes for the corresponding issue of truth. Faced with a pop-out assertion which we are inclined to deny in the actual case, we respond with what in 'Puzzle' I called a 'doubling of the narrator': we accept the first sentence of the first story as true in the story, but we accept the second sentence of the first story as being nothing more than what the narrator *thinks*. Because we see no obvious way of allowing the second sentence to be true *merely* in the story, and because we take the analogue of the second sentence to be false in the actual world, we likewise take the second sentence to be false in the story as well, and resist imagining its truth.

This captures one of the distinctive ways in which cases of imaginative resistance differ from cases of what we take to be authors' errors (see n. 25). In the case of errors, we remain within the grip of the story; we think 'that's simply not true (in the story)'. But in the case of resistance, we 'jump out' of the story; we think 'that's simply not true (in the actual world)'. (Further discussion of this phenomenological difference can be found in Sect. 6.)

Consider Weatherson's (2004) opening story, which ends with the following passage:

Craig saw that the cause of the bankup had been Jack and Jill, he took his gun out of the glovebox and shot them. People then started driving over their bodies, and while the new speed hump caused some people to slow down a bit, mostly traffic returned to its normal speed. So Craig did the right thing, because Jack and Jill should have taken their argument somewhere else where they wouldn't get in anyone's way.

The final sentence pops out in the sense just described. And it pops out not merely because of the 'So' or the content. We encounter the same pop-out phenomenology even if we offer the appraisal in a more integrated way, or if we alter the story so that it is akin to the second Giselda story rather than the first:

... when Craig saw that the cause of the bankup had been Jack and Jill, he did the right thing: he took his gun out of the glovebox and shot them.

Or:

... when Craig saw that the cause of the bankup had been Jack and Jill, he did the wrong thing: he took his gun out of the glovebox and shot them.

In both cases, we take the moral assessment as a simultaneous invitation to imagine something in the context of the story—*and* to believe some corresponding claim about the actual world.

Moreover, we get a similar pop-out phenomenon with non-moral cases as well. Consider the final sentence of Kendall Walton's (1994) Knock-Knock story (which, by stipulation, is embedded in a context where we take the entire passage as literally intended):

He told the knock-knock joke for the forty-third time. Everyone laughed uproariously. It was the funniest joke in the history of the world.

Or the second-to-last sentence of Stephen Yablo's (2002) Maple Leaf story:

Hang on, Sally said. It's staring us in the face. This is a *maple* tree we're under. She grabbed a jagged five-fingered leaf. Here was the oval they needed! They ran off to claim their prize.

Or the final two sentences of Weatherson's (2004) Alien Robbery story:

So Sam decided that it wasn't Lee, but really a shape-shifting alien that looked like Lee, that robbed the bank. Although shape-shifting aliens didn't exist, and until that moment Sam had no evidence that they did, this was a rational belief. False, but rational.

In each of these cases, I want to suggest, authoritative breakdown arises because we take the invitation to imagine the relevant claim as true in the story as a simultaneous invitation to believe some corresponding claim about the actual world. And since we take the corresponding claim about the actual world to be false, we resist believing it, and hence resist imagining its fictional counterpart. This suggests that if, somehow, there were some sort of 'pop-out blocker' which could restrict our attention to the relevant passages insofar as they concern the fictional world, then authorial authority would return. But what would such a mechanism look like?

I've already suggested—both here and in the original paper—one type of pop-out blocker that is at least partially successful: namely, the technique of supposing rather than imagining.[30] I suggested above that this technique can—in the case of non-fiction and presumably in the case of fiction as well—bring us some way towards focusing only on the suppositional context (in this case, the fictional world), and not simultaneously in the actual world. Understanding how this could work requires getting clear on why pop-out occurs in the first place.

6. THE HYPOTHESIS

My tentative hypothesis is this: Passages exhibit pop-out effects whenever they express *appraisals* (some sort of decision about concept application) that are either *mandated by* (required by all of) or *prohibited by* (permitted by none of) the principles of generation that the reader has tacitly been taking to govern the generation of fictional truths, in conjunction with whatever else she takes to have been mandated as true in the story.[31] That is, pop-out occurs when an appraisal that the author offers is either *superfluous* (because it is implied by what has been

---

[30] Shaun Nichols helpfully suggests that the distancing that results from supposition is a special case of a more general distancing phenomenon that arises from iteration. For interesting discussion of these issues, see Nichols 2003.

[31] Clearly, this hypothesis bears important connections both to Weatherson's notion of *Virtue* and Yablo's notion of *grokking* (response-enabled) concepts. See Weatherson 2004 and Yablo 2002.

Following Walton 1990, we might provisionally distinguish between *primary* and *implied* fictional truths, where primary fictional truths are those generated (most) directly by whatever conventions govern our use of the fiction as a prop in a game of make-believe, while implied fictional truths are generated from these primary truths indirectly, by means of principles whose articulation has turned out to be enormously difficult. In parallel fashion, primary mandated imaginings would be those prompted (most) directly by whatever conventions govern our use of the fiction as a prop in a game of make-believe, while implied mandated imaginings would be those generated from those primary mandated imaginings indirectly, by means of principles whose articulation has not even been attempted. (For debate-shaping discussion of the topic of truth in fiction, see Lewis 1983; Currie 1990; Walton 1990. For recent work, see Hanley 2004 and papers cited therein. For a view that comes close to the one I am inclined to endorse (see n. 27), see Bonomi and Zucchi 2003).

In saying this, I am acting as if interpretation of fiction were a straightforward linear process, where we begin at the beginning of a text with the fictional acceptance of a bunch of low-level facts, and proceed through a narrative accepting or rejecting appraisals of them. Matters are obviously a good deal more complicated: the interpretative process is far more holistic than this picture suggests, complicating the distinction between lower-level and higher-level facts. Still, the idealization is a useful one. (For related discussion of why we are inclined to follow an author in her presentation of low-level facts but resist her higher-level appraisals, see Weatherson 2004.) (Thanks here to Jonathan Ichikawa and David Jehle.)

said already, in conjunction with the principles of generation governing truth-in-fiction in the context of the story), or *proscribed* (because it is precluded by what has been said already, in conjunction with the principles of generation governing truth-in-fiction in the context of the story).

Why do superfluous or proscribed appraisals result in a feeling of pop-out? This is a difficult question, and I don't have a full answer. But my best guess is that it results from two sources. The first is the superfluity or proscription of the assertion. The explanation here is quasi-Gricean: since the author *couldn't* be using the words to tell us something informative (merely) about the fictional world, we look for some other way that the phrase might be informative. But what way could that be? This brings us to the second source, which is the democratic nature of appraisal itself. While it is up to the author to set up the basic facts of the fictional world, she has only limited control over the principles of generation that govern what else is true in the story: the reader's associative repertoire and evaluative flexibility also play a role in determining which principles are at play. So negotiations about appraisals take place on disputed territory that falls under the jurisdiction of both reader and author. They concern whether certain concepts could be legitimately applied to certain sets of facts—and this is a concern that transcends the bounds of the fictional.

To see this hypothesis at play, suppose—very schematically—that the reader of a story has accepted some set of basic facts about the fictional world ($F_1 - F_n$), and that she considers a certain range of principles of generation ($P_1 - P_n$) to be viable ways of extending what is true in the story. And suppose that the story now continues with the author offering one of three appraisals. Appraisal A1 follows from $F_1 - F_n$ on *none* of $P_1 - P_n$; appraisal A2 follows from $F_1 - F_n$ on *all* of $P_1 - P_n$; and appraisal A3 follows from $F_1 - F_n$ on only *some* of $P_1 - P_n$. If what I have been saying is correct, then the following predictions should be borne out (at least in simple cases). First, both A1 and A2 should produce a phenomenon of pop-out, whereas A3 (which gives the reader new information about what is true *in the story*) should not. At the same time, since A2 and A3 are both permitted by at least some of $P_1 - P_n$, the reader should feel that the relevant appraisal is true in the context of the story; this means that the pop-out induced by A2 may go largely—even entirely—unnoticed.[32] And finally, since A1 is permitted by none of $P_1 - P_n$, the reader should see no way for it to be true in the story. But since A1 is an *appraisal* (and not merely a fact at the level of $F_1 - F_n$), and since appraisals are under the author's and reader's joint control, the resulting feeling should be not (merely) one of bafflement—that is, the sense that the author is asking us to imagine something as being true *in the story* that simply doesn't make sense—but (also) one of resistance—the sense it is because A1′ (the real-world analogue of A1) is not true that there is something amiss with A1.

---

[32] Though we may find ourselves thinking about the actual world in a novel way—a point well emphasized by Plato, Iris Murdoch, and Martha Nussbaum (among others).

The neatness of these results suggests that there are indeed two components—superfluity/prohibition, on the one hand, and appraisal, on the other—that together contribute to the phenomenon of pop-out. We can see this by considering cases where each occurs without the other. When appraisals are merely permitted (that is, neither mandated nor proscribed) by the facts-plus-principles that the reader is operating with, there is no sense of pop-out: the appraisals are treated roughly as if they were basic facts about the fictional world. And where the mandated or proscribed content involves low-level facts rather than appraisals, there is likewise no sense of pop-out: prohibited claims are treated as mistakes, superfluous ones as redundancies.[33]

Moreover, the account predicts that pop-out should disappear when we introduce a supposition clause. This is so for two related reasons. First, since the principles of generation governing supposition are maximally permissive (as with absurdist stories, nothing in particular is prohibited or mandated by the 'rules' governing the story), there are, *a fortiori*, no prohibited or mandated appraisals, and hence no pop-out. Second, when we engage in supposition, we deliberately suppress our familiar associative patterns. Because supposition requires this sort of distancing, normal patterns of appraisal are suspended, and tendencies to look for some actual-world analogue are correspondingly curtailed. (Moreover, the first may contribute to the second: the absurdness of the proposed content may play a role in preventing the sort of engagement that imagination requires.[34])

Finally, the account sits well with the distinction offered above between the Problem of Imaginative Barriers and the Problem of Imaginative Impropriety. Imaginative barriers arise when the generation principles that the reader has accepted leave no way for A to be true in the story. Imaginative impropriety arises when the reader considers adopting a set of generation principles that she finds problematic. Classic imaginative resistance arises when a reader can't imagine a certain moral claim being true in a story (Imaginative Barriers) because she won't bring herself to adopt the requisite set of generation principles governing the use of moral appraisals (Imaginative Impropriety). So classic imaginative resistance arises when we can't because we won't.

7. APPLICATIONS

The account is best tested through the consideration of particular cases. Consider again the passage from Weatherson's (2004) 'Freeway' case:

Craig saw that the cause of the bankup had been Jack and Jill, he took his gun out of the glovebox and shot them. People then started driving over their bodies, and while the

---

[33] My account here is indebted in obvious ways to that of Weatherson (2004). Consider also Lewis's discussion of Sherlock Holmes in Lewis 1978; cf. also Doggett 2004. (See also n. 25 and 29 above.)

[34] John Holbo nicely describes these as cases where our imagination 'bounces off' the text.

new speed hump caused some people to slow down a bit, mostly traffic returned to its normal speed. So Craig did the right thing, because Jack and Jill should have taken their argument somewhere else where they wouldn't get in anyone's way.

My suggestion is that the final sentence pops out because its truth is prohibited by the truth-in-fiction principles that the reader has tacitly been taking to govern the generation of fictional truths in the story, in conjunction with whatever else the reader takes to have been made true in the story. Presumably the latter includes that Craig shot Jack and Jill because they caused the traffic bankup, and that after he shot them, people started to drive over their bodies, allowing traffic to return to its normal speed. For the typical reader, the truth-in-fiction principles that she has been tacitly taking to govern the generation of fictional truths in the story prohibit it from following that, in so doing, Craig did the right thing. But since the passage involves an *appraisal*—a question about whether a particular higher-level concept can be understood as applying to some set of lower-level facts—the reader's attention turns to the actual world. Recognizing the falsity of what she takes to be the actual world analogue of *p*—that if someone had done something like what Craig did, he would have done the right thing—the reader experiences resistance.

Similar analysis might be offered for the other examples discussed in Section 5; in each case, the relevant segment pops out because its truth is prohibited by the truth-in-fiction principles that the reader has tacitly been taking to govern the generation of fictional truths in the story, in conjunction with whatever she takes to have been made true in the story so far.[35] But since the claims in question involve appraisals, the reader's attention turns to their actual-world analogues. Since she believes these to be false, resistance arises.[36]

Consider now the mandatory analogues of these cases, which I have suggested should produce pop-out without resistance:

He told the knock-knock joke for the forty-third time. Everyone laughed uproariously. *But* it was *not* the funniest joke in the history of the world. (Walton 1994, italicized words altered from original)

She grabbed a jagged five-fingered leaf. Here was the *five-pointed object* they needed! (Yablo 2002, italicized words altered from original)

Though I think these cases do produce pop-out, it is true that the effect is much less pronounced than in the prohibited cases, and that the effect is even less in the leaf example than in the knock-knock case. The first of these observations has already been explained: redundant pop-outs can easily pop back in, so unless we are alert to their potential appearance—as we are in cases like this one, where we have been thinking about prohibited pop-outs—we may well

---

[35] Again, modulo worries about the holistic nature of interpretation.
[36] I am thus acknowledging the force of important objections to my original account raised by Matravers 2003; Stock 2003, 2005; and Weatherson 2004.

miss them. (Remember also that the explanation of why redundancy results in pop-out is a pragmatic one—so if we have the sense that there is some reason for the phrase to be expressed in the context of the story, then we will not experience feelings of pop-out; as long as the reader can see a way of understanding the appraisal-involving sentence as articulating a non-obvious implication—as, for example, when the author tells us who committed the crime at the end of a mystery story—then pop-out is not forced.[37]) But the theory also explains the second observation—that the pop-out is less pronounced in the leaf case. Because there is a reading on which the underlined phrase is understood as information-providing (that they were in need of an object that was five-pointed) rather than appraisal-involving (that a particular concept—five-pointedness—applies to this particular circumstance), the conditions for pop-out may not be satisfied. If we replace the second sentence with something like 'In doing this she grabbed hold of a five-pointed object', pop-out returns; here, as in our other cases, the sentence is taken as making simultaneous claims about the world of the story and the world outside the story.[38]

In short, the hypothesis proposed in Section 6 has done a good job explaining the phenomenological profile identified in Section 5. It looks like passages do exhibit pop-out effects when they involve appraisals that are either mandated or prohibited by the principles of generation that the reader has tacitly been appealing to, and that imaginative barriers arise in the prohibited cases. So far, so good. But we still haven't got to the bottom of things. For the question remains: Why do we accept these principles of generation, and not others?

8. RESIDUAL ISSUES

I don't have a general answer to this question, but I do have a few thoughts to offer in closing. In order to present them, I will first need to step back a bit and say a bit more about what goes on when we engage in the practice of make-belief.

Imagination and pretense involve what I have elsewhere (2003) called *partial mapping*: it is key to the practice of fiction construction that things in stories may have some but not all of the properties of their actual-world analogues. The three little pigs share with their actual-world counterparts the properties of being pink and four-legged and Q-tailed, but unlike actual pigs, they can speak and scheme and build homes from straw or bricks. Winnie the Pooh shares with his actual-world counterparts the property of being brown and furry and stuffed with fluff,

---

[37] Indeed, one way for the author to cue the reader that standard import–export rules have been suspended is to issue a series of apparently obvious claims: 'New York is in New York, Paris is in France, London is in England.' Gricean rules tell you that the reason why the author is reporting these obvious matters is to flag other ways that the fictional world is not like the actual world. (Thanks to Tyler Doggett and Andy Egan for this point.)

[38] If you don't feel this, make sure that you're not still thinking of the sentence as information-providing.

but unlike actual stuffed bears, he can sing and recite poetry and give birthday gifts. Nor are these isolated examples: think of the Three Bears, Babar, the Cat in the Hat, Curious George, Stuart Little, the Owl and the Pussycat, Frog and Toad, the musicians of Bremen, the Cheshire Cat, Paddington, the Giving Tree, Thomas the Tank Engine, Tubby the Tuba, Humpty-Dumpty, Pinocchio, the Velveteen Rabbit, SpongeBob SquarePants, the Gingerbread Man—or any of the countless other talking, thinking animals and vegetables and minerals that fill children's literature. It would, I take it, be rather unreasonable to protest that Paddington couldn't *really* be a stuffed bear (in the story) since he walks and speaks and eats marmalade, or that Tubby isn't *really* a tuba, since tubas don't have arms or legs or feelings.

But if we can do this so easily for owls and trains and sponges and cookies, why are we so reluctant to engage in this sort of partial mapping for rightness and goodness and justice?[39] I don't have a complete story to tell—but in examining the answer that I will ultimately propose, it will be helpful to consider a particular example in a bit of detail.

In chapter 8 of *Alice's Adventures in Wonderland* (Carroll 1865), Alice finds herself in a lovely garden where she observes a colorful parade of playing cards:

First came ten soldiers carrying clubs; these were all shaped like the three gardeners, oblong and flat, with their hands and feet at the corners: next the ten courtiers; these were ornamented all over with diamonds, and walked two and two, as the soldiers did. After these came the royal children; there were ten of them, and the little dears came jumping merrily along hand in hand, in couples: they were all ornamented with hearts. Next came the guests, mostly Kings and Queens. . . . Then followed the Knave of Hearts, carrying the King's crown on a crimson velvet cushion; and, last of all this grand procession, came THE KING AND QUEEN OF HEARTS.

When the procession came opposite to Alice, they all stopped and looked at her, and the Queen said . . . 'What's your name, child?' 'My name is Alice, so please your Majesty,' said Alice very politely; but she added, to herself, 'Why, *they're only a pack of cards*, after all. I needn't be afraid of them!' (Italics added)

Now, even if we do not have a fully comprehensive mental image of the scenario[40], it is, I take it, true in the Alice-in-Wonderland fiction that the Queen of Hearts, who is a playing card, has ten heart-sporting children; that spade cards are gardeners, whereas club cards are soldiers; that cards ornamented with kings and queens are royalty—and so on. A reader who reported imaginative barriers in the face of such claims would, it seems fair to say, be considered a bit of a

---

[39] I suspect that some of our ease in the former cases stems from our ability—indeed, our tendency—to ascribe intentional attributes to almost any entity whose motions are consonant with the motions typical of agents. But I think this is only part of the story.

[40] For discussion of the relation between the content of the mental image and the content of what is imagined therewith, see Williams 1966; Peacocke 1985. See also Sorensen 2002.

bad sport. But note that, in order to understand the Alice story, we must simultaneously exploit a range of conflicting mapping principles each drawing on
a different feature of our associational repertoire: people have hands and feet in
a roughly diagonal configuration, so the hands and feet of the playing cards are
arranged likewise; spades are associated with gardening, so spade-sporting cards
are gardeners; children resemble their parents, so heart-sporting cards are the
children of the King and Queen of Hearts; kings and queens tend to be friends
with other kings and queens, so the King and Queen of Clubs are royal guests.
And so on.

Moreover, we do this despite the fact that it introduces all sorts of tensions:
If the five of spades is an adult, shouldn't the five of hearts be an adult too? If
the seven of spades is a gardener, shouldn't the King of Spades be a gardener
too? These inconsistencies do not result in imaginative barriers: we are easily able
to circumscribe our attention, focusing on one set of similarities in one context,
another in another.[41] Nor is there any sense of imaginative impropriety. One
may think that monarchy is a distasteful form of government, or object to parades
on aesthetic grounds. But none of this seems to get in the way of imaginatively
engaging with the *Alice in Wonderland* story.

Now (as I suggested in a similar context in 'Puzzle') one might object by saying
that this is a particularly nonsensical example: nothing that is what *we* mean by
a 'playing card' could do anything like what *we* mean by 'stealing some tarts'.
But then again, nothing that we mean by a 'memory' could turn into what we
mean by a 'silvery thread'; nothing that we mean by a 'purple crayon' could draw
a world in which the artist then 'walks'; and nothing that we mean by a 'rainbow'
could have a 'daughter' who dances and sings and eats dewdrops.[42] Fictional
'counting as' is cheap.[43] As long as the inconsistency does not stare us in the face
(and sometimes even when it does), we countenance all sorts of combinations
as being true in fiction, and credit ourselves with having imagined them, even
though we are in no position to make full sense of what that combination would

---

[41] Though it does mean that in ascertaining derived truths, we are not fully at liberty to follow
our own initiative.

[42] Cf. *Harry Potter and the Goblet of Fire* (Rowling 2000), *Harold and the Purple Crayon* (Johnson
1955), and *Ozma of Oz* (Baum 1907) respectively.

[43] At the same time, 'counting as' can be *too* cheap. Suppose I were to tell the following story—call
it 'Frege's Nightmare': 'Once upon a time there was a number—the number two—who was a
great Roman orator who conquered Gaul and died on the Ides of March.' One might object, quite
reasonably, that the sense in which I have thereby told a story in which the number two crossed
the Rubicon is attenuated at best. But what makes it true in something more than name only that
the knave of hearts stole some tarts in *Alice*, but not that the number two was stabbed by Brutus
in 'Frege's Nightmare'? I suspect that part of the answer has to do with subtle matters of literary
convention and mental imagery and the relation between them. But it is clear that the issue merits
further exploration. (Indeed, Weatherson worries that an 'in name only' story is all that I have told
in the 'Tower of Goldbach' (cf. Gendler 2000; Weatherson 2004; also Stock 2003, 2005); for a
very different issue, see Robertson 2003.) But, to reiterate a point made several times above, to the
extent that we are worried about asymmetries rather than absolute prohibitions (see n. 24), the issue
is rendered slightly less urgent.

amount to.[44] It is crucial to realize that if one refuses to grant this, one has basically opted out of the fiction game altogether.[45]

I have suggested that imaginative barriers arise when—given the truth-in-fiction principles that the reader has tacitly been taking to govern the generation of fictional truths in the story—the author makes a claim that is incompatible with whatever else the reader takes to have been made true in the story. This means that the wider the range of principles the reader is considering, the smaller the number of mandated and prohibited appraisals there will be, and the less potential for resistance will arise. But if the range of principles gets too wide, then nothing particular will be mandated or prohibited. And this—for the reasons discussed in Section 4 above—is tantamount to reader disengagement. I think that what happens in what I above called 'can't' cases is that—for some reason—the reader cannot see any non-arbitrary way of adopting some *limited* range of truth-in-fiction principles that could do the requisite work of rendering *p* (along with already accepted claims) true in the story—no way for *p* to be true that does not involve opening the floodgates to the sort of free-for-all that mere supposition involves. And while I suspect that this has to do with our grasp of the concepts at issue—see, for example, Yablo's (2002) discussion of *oval* or Weatherson's (2004) of *table*—I will for the time being take it as a brute fact.

What I want to suggest is that even if this is part of the explanation of what is going on in cases of classic Humean Resistance, it is not the full story. Consider a modified version of the previously quoted passage from *Alice in Wonderland*. The passage describes your child's nursery school graduation ceremony (or, if you prefer, the movements of a group of refugees, or historically underrepresented minorities):

First came the Cockroaches, their filthy wings folded at their sides: next the Vultures; eager for carrion, clawing at one another for the few remaining morsels. After these came the Maggots; there were ten of them, and the nauseating things inched sluggishly along the floor. Next came the Mosquitoes, whining shrilly in their aggravating and annoying way ... and last of all this grand procession, came THE KING AND QUEEN OF DUNG BEETLES.

When the procession came opposite to Alice, they all stopped and gawked at her, and the Queen of the Dung Beetles screeched ... 'What's your name?' 'My name is Alice, so please your Majesty,' said Alice, suppressing her revulsion; but she added, to herself, 'Why, *they're only a bunch of nursery school children* (*refugees/Hutus/Jews/homosexuals/Palestinians*), after all. I needn't be disgusted by them!'

Now, as far as barriers go, this passage should be no harder—indeed, presumably somewhat easier—to engage with imaginatively than the original passage from *Alice*. But—for now familiar reasons—I take it that it nonetheless evokes

---

[44] Remember the warnings in n. 15 and 20.

[45] For more detailed discussion and argumentation, see Gendler 2000: sect. 6.

a feeling of imaginative impropriety. I will take it as a datum that we find it distasteful to imagine our children—or members of the groups listed above—with our attention directed in these ways.[46]

I am naw in a position to state my conclusion which is that what goes on in the case of classic Humean Resistance is a complicated combination of what goes on in the five-fingered oval case, and what goes on in the refugee parade case. What happens is that—to some extent consciously, to some extent unconsciously—the imaginative impropriety associated with viewing something like slavery or torture in anything like a positive light ends up constraining the set of truth-in-fiction principles we are ready to entertain. If this were not part of the explanation, then we would much more readily do with terms like 'right' or 'beautiful' what we do with terms like 'cat' (in *The Cat in the Hat*) or 'carpet' (in *Aladdin*): engage in the sort of partial mapping where the term retains some but not all of its features, the sort of partial mapping that does not induce pop-out. We would allow that in such cases 'right' means most of what it does in ordinary cases, except that it also applies to the thing that Giselda did in killing her baby just because it was a girl.

Now, *cantians* are committed to saying that in doing this, we lose a handle on the concept of 'right'—in the way that to allow an oval to be five-fingered or a table to be a fork is to lose a handle on the concept of 'oval' or 'table'. *Wontians* allow that there are ways that it could be true—merely in the story—that Giselda did the right thing in killing her baby because it was a girl, or that Craig did the right thing in shooting Jack and Jill, or that Sam's belief in shape-shifting aliens was rational—where 'right' or 'rational' just means: enough of the things that right or rational means for you to call this a case of rightness or rationality.[47]

If cantianism is correct here, then we've learned something very interesting about a certain class of appraisal-involving terms: that you can't do with them what Lewis Carroll did with the playing cards in *Alice in Wonderland* (or what I did with $5 + 7 = 12$ in the Goldbach story (Gendler 2000)), thinning them down in ways that many of their most important associations are lost while nonetheless proceeding to tell a comprehensible story. But I'm left with the residual feeling that with cantians—as with their more famous namesakes—there's something a bit too rule-bound about this picture of morality and its kin. Couldn't I really—if I were more flexible in my

[46] Recall Arthur Danto's apt reminder that one fundamental function of artistic engagement is to adopt perspectives that lead us to focus selectively on certain features of our environment: it is 'one of the main offices of art less to represent the world than to represent it in such a way as to cause us to view it with a certain attitude and with a special vision' (Danto 1981: 167).

[47] It might seem that there is a third position here—*hardianism*—according to which it is merely hard to imagine the prescribed content. But (see n. 24) I think that hardians are just cantians or wontians who make a relative rather than an absolute claim. (For the record, I suspect that most wontians are deep-down hardians—and that many cantians are as well.) (Thanks to Tyler Doggett and Andy Egan for the term *hardian*.)

associational commitments—imagine a case where Craig or Giselda did the right thing *just in the story*? Isn't my reluctance to do so a bit like my reluctance to enroll my son in the Maggots room instead of the Pandas? Isn't it, deep down, in part that I am not prepared to have my nice pure cantian image of rightness distorted by letting it become associated with something ugly and nasty like murder or slavery—even in a story? And isn't it because I'm not willing to let myself imagine this that I can't see a way for it to be true?

My inclination is to think that, to some extent, in some cases at least, the answer is *yes*. If so, then the solution I proposed in 'Puzzle' was right in spirit, if not in detail. And so I'm inclined to think, for the reasons just offered.

REFERENCES

BAUM, L. FRANK (1907) *Ozma of Oz*. Available through Project Gutenberg at <http://www.gutenberg.org/etext/486>.

BERMÚDEZ, JOSÉ LUIS, and GARDINER, SEBASTIAN (eds.) (2002) *Art and Morality* (London: Routledge).

BONOMI, ANDREA, and ZUCCHI, SANDRO (2003) 'A Pragmatic Framework for Truth in Fiction', *Dialectica*, 57(2), 103–20.

CARROLL, LEWIS (1865) *Alice's Adventures in Wonderland*. Available through Project Gutenberg at <http://www.gutenberg.org/etext/11>.

CURRIE, GREGORY (1990) *The Nature of Fiction* (Cambridge: Cambridge University Press).

_____ (2002) 'Desire in Imagination', in Gendler and Hawthorne 2002, 201–21.

_____ and RAVENSCROFT, IAN (2002) *Recreative Minds: Imagination in Philosophy and Psychology* (Oxford: Oxford University Press).

DANTO, ARTHUR (1981) *The Transfiguration of the Commonplace* (Cambridge: Cambridge University Press).

DOGGETT, TYLER (2004) 'Moral Properties and Moral Imagination' (unpublished Ph.D. diss., MIT).

GENDLER, TAMAR SZABÓ (2000) 'The Puzzle of Imaginative Resistance', *Journal of Philosophy*, 97 (2), 55–81.

_____ (2003) 'On the Relation between Pretense and Belief', in Kieran and Lopes 2003, 125–41.

_____ (2006) 'Imaginary Contagion', *Metaphilosophy*, 37.

_____ and HAWTHORNE, JOHN (eds.) (2002) *Conceivability and Possibility* (Oxford: Oxford University Press).

HANLEY, RICHARD (2004) 'As Good As It Gets: Lewis on Truth in Fiction', *Australasian Journal of Philosophy*, 82 (1), 112–28.

HOLBO, JOHN (2003*a*) 'Imaginative Resistance'. At <http://homepage.mac.com/jholbo/homepage/pages/blog/giant%20thoughts/resistance.html>.

_____ (2003*b*) 'The Varieties of Imaginatively Resistant Experience'. At <http://homepage.mac.com/jholbo/homepage/pages/blog/giant%20thoughts/resistance2.html>.

HUME, DAVID (1985/1757) 'On the Standard of Taste', repr. in his *Essays: Moral, Political and Legal* (Indianapolis: Liberty Fund), 227–49.

JOHNSON, CROCKETT (1955) *Harold and the Purple Crayon* (New York: Harper).

KIERAN, MATTHEW, and LOPES, DOMINIC M. (eds.) (2003) *Imagination, Philosophy and the Arts* (London: Routledge).

LEWIS, DAVID (1978) 'Truth in Fiction', *American Philosophical Quarterly*, 15 (1), 37–46; repr. with Postscript in Lewis 1983, 261–80.

—— (1983) *Philosophical Papers*, i (New York: Oxford University Press).

MATRAVERS, DEREK (2003) 'Fictional Assent and the (So-Called) "Puzzle of Imaginative Resistance"', in Kieran and Lopes 2003, 91–106.

MORAN, RICHARD (1989) 'Seeing and Believing: Metaphor, Image and Force', *Critical Inquiry*, 16, 87–112.

—— (1994) 'The Expression of Feeling in Imagination', *Philosophical Review*, 103 (1), 75–106.

MOTHERSILL, MARY (2002) 'Make-Believe Morality and Fictional Worlds', in Bermúdez and Gardiner 2002, 74–94.

NICHOLS, SHAUN (2003) 'Imagination and the Puzzles of Iteration', *Analysis*, 63, 182–7.

PEACOCKE, CHRISTOPHER (1985) 'Imagination, Experience and Possibility: A Berkeleian View Defended', in John Foster and Howard Robinson (eds.), *Essays on Berkeley* (Oxford: Oxford University Press), 19–35.

PRIEST, GRAHAM (1999) 'Sylvan's Box: A Short Story and Ten Morals', *Notre Dame Journal of Formal Logic*, 38 (4), 573–82.

ROBERTSON, TERESA (2003) '(In the Fiction/Myth) the Number Seventeen Crosses the Rubicon', *Southwest Philosophy Review*, 19 (1), 125–34.

ROWLING, J. K. (2000) *Harry Potter and the Goblet of Fire* (New York: Scholastic).

SORENSEN, R. (2002) 'The Art of the Impossible', in Gendler and Hawthorne 2002, 337–68.

STOCK, KATHLEEN (2003) 'The Tower of Goldbach and Other Impossible Tales', in Kieran and Lopes 2003, 107–24.

—— (2005) 'Resisting Imaginative Resistance', *Philosophical Quarterly*, 55, 607–24.

STOKES, DUSTIN (forthcoming) 'Time Travel, Talking Pigs and Alien Values: On Imaginative Compliance and Imaginative Resistance'.

TANNER, MICHAEL (1994) 'Morals in Fiction and Fictional Morality/II', *Proceedings of the Aristotelian Society*, suppl. vol. 68, 51–66.

TROGDON, KELLY (2004) 'Moral Imaginative Resistance' (unpublished ms available at <www.nyu.edu/gsas/dept/philo/gradconf/papers/Trogdon.pdf>.

WALTON, KENDALL (1990) *Mimesis as Make Believe* (Cambridge, Mass.: Harvard University Press).

—— (1993) 'Metaphor and Prop-Oriented Make-Believe', *European Journal of Philosophy*, 1 (1), 39–57.

—— (1994) 'Morals in Fiction and Fictional Morality', *Proceedings of the Aristotelian Society*, suppl. vol. 68, 27–50.

WEATHERSON, BRIAN (2003) 'Furniture in Ficton and Fictional Furniture', at <http://brian.weatherson.net/mfp.htm>.

—— (2004) 'Morality, Fiction and Possibility', *Philosophers' Imprint*, 4 (3), <www.philosophersimprint.org/004003/>.

WEINBERG, JONATHAN, and MESKIN, AARON (forthcoming) 'The Cognitive Architecture of Imaginative Resistance'.

WILLIAMS, BERNARD (1966/1973) 'Imagination and the Self', repr. in *his Problems of the Self* (Cambridge: Cambridge University Press), 26–45.

YABLO, STEPHEN (2002) 'Coulda, Woulda, Shoulda', in Gendler and Hawthorne 2002, 441–92.

10

Puzzling over the Imagination: Philosophical Problems, Architectural Solutions

Jonathan M. Weinberg and Aaron Meskin

1. INTRODUCTION: METAPHILOSOPHICAL REFLECTIONS

To what must a philosophical account of the imagination be true, and upon what resources may such an account draw? Surveying philosophical engagement with the imagination in recent decades, we see that both these questions frequently receive the same answer: a combination of the precepts and posits of everyday psychology, and the intimations and intuitions of a full-fledged philosophy of mind. Indeed, many of the questions about the imagination that philosophers have wrangled with have come from a conflict between those two domains. For example, one common version of the so-called puzzle of emotions and fiction is generated by a conflict between two pieces of folk psychology, on the one hand—that we do not believe that fictional characters exist, and that we do feel real emotions directed at fictional characters—and a piece of philosophical psychology, on the other—that emotions require belief in the existence of their objects.[1] Typical responses to this puzzle have similarly drawn upon an admixture of ordinary psychological concepts and philosophical maneuvering. For example, Kendall Walton deploys the folk-psychological notion of make-believe to ground his approach to the puzzle, and to attempt to finesse our ordinary belief that we *really* feel emotions towards fictional characters, by arguing that it is only *make-believe* that we feel such emotions by, as it were, imagining ourselves into the fiction (Walton 1978, 1990). Walton does think that we feel what he terms 'quasi-emotions', by which he means to refer to whatever typically combines with belief, evaluation, or assessment to constitute emotion, and which is thus almost exactly like an emotion, except for the missing bit of cognition.

[1] For versions of the puzzle that can be interpreted along these lines, see Walton 1978; Carroll 1990; and Currie 1997.

Still, quasi-emotions are not emotions, and so the philosophical claim that emotion requires belief is saved.[2]

Our main purpose in this chapter is not to criticize Walton's account (though see below, and indeed see Meskin and Weinberg 2003), but we share with other theorists the sense that Walton's account cannot capture the phenomenological robustness of our affective responses to fiction (Carroll 1990; Gendler and Kovakovich 2005). For folk psychology offers no resources to adjudicate the status of affective responses to fiction, and the standard tools of philosophical analysis are all designed to draw sharp lines—and are thus ill-equipped to accommodate the sense in which there seems to be something right, yet something wrong, with saying that our fictionally directed affective responses really are emotions. And if we are restricted to folk psychology, philosophy of mind, and the tools of philosophical analysis, then it is hard to avoid the sense that our solution to the paradox of fiction must also include a definite declaration as to whether such responses are or are not emotions. Philosophers are left, then, needing to make the best of a bad situation. We must pick our solution, and then do enough philosophical tap-dancing to distract us from the discomfort that stems from having to stipulate one way or another on a claim that tugs us in both directions.

Our proposal, then, is to break out of the restriction to folk and philosophical resources, and look for some added help from science in solving such philosophical conundrums; or, at least, for those conundrums as they arise with regard to the imagination. Perhaps some quandaries are such that philosophical navigation of them will not be assisted by any significant appeal to science—it is hard to see what empirical discovery will aid us with the sorites paradox, for example—but it should hardly be surprising that many puzzles of the *imagination* might begin to dissolve with the appropriate application of cognitive science. The imagination, after all, is a faculty that creatures like us contingently possess and deploy in distinctive ways. Such contingencies are just the sorts of things that science—psychology in this particular case—can help us understand.

Although these claims about the imagination and science are likely to be uncontroversial, nonetheless it remains difficult to see *how* to harness science to help with philosophical puzzles about the imagination. It will not do for philosophers to make a neo-Quinean attempt to turn such puzzles over to science wholesale. One obvious problem is that such puzzles may not have yet struck the fancy of scientists, and it strikes us as perverse for philosophers to sit idly by, waiting for scientists to come along and do the work for them. Moreover, and more importantly, what counts as a scientific answer to a scientific question may not count as a philosophical answer to a philosophical problem. We hope that

---

[2] It is worth noting that although the belief condition plays a significant role in Walton 1978, his discussion in Walton 1990 does not seem to be underwritten by any such commitment.

philosophers will be able to learn from science, but in a way that allows for the survival of philosophy in a recognizable form.[3]

Our suggestion is that philosophers interested in the imagination shift their methodology from the traditional paradox-and-analysis model to a more empirically-oriented phenomena-and-explanation model. As we have just discussed, when philosophers confront a puzzling set of propositions, their traditional approach is to look for a way to reconfigure the concepts deployed in the propositions, casting about for formulations that look sufficiently natural and motivated from the perspectives of metaphysics and folk psychology, and which dissolve the apparent contradiction. We advocate instead that the puzzling propositions be treated merely as initial descriptions of a set of phenomena for which the philosopher must now seek a good explanation. Scientific considerations enter in at least two ways. First, they can provide further data against which competing explanations can be evaluated. Second, they can be an extremely important source of theoretical machinery to be deployed in candidate explanations.

The benefits of incorporating a bit of science into our practice go beyond just having more facts to bounce off and more theoretical machinery to play around with. By adopting a more empirical perspective, the evaluative measures for candidate explanations may be transformed. On the one hand, an empirically driven explanation of a phenomenon may look a bit messy from the perspective of the project of traditional conceptual analysis (see, for example, Griffiths's (1997) account of emotions, which fails to respect the tidiness of traditional analytic accounts of the topic), but it is also true that a bit of conceptual analysis that may initially appear clear and well-motivated may look unmotivated once an empirical perspective is brought to bear. (To stay in the domain of the emotions, consider how an empirical perspective can make the emotion/quasi-emotion distinction seem like an implausibly ad hoc maneuver.)

Our strategy in this chapter is to make the case for the phenomena-and-explanation model by instantiating it. We will first articulate an empirically informed cognitive architecture of the imagination, drawing significantly on work in this area by Shaun Nichols and Stephen Stich. We will thereupon apply that cognitive architecture to three standing philosophical problems concerning the imagination: the puzzle of fiction and emotions (which has already concerned us here briefly), the puzzle of imaginative resistance, and the challenge of demarcating the supposition/imagination distinction. We will show how an appeal to this cognitive architecture can shed new light on each of these issues, and make new solutions available that might not have been visible from the perspective of either folk psychology or traditional philosophy of mind.

---

[3] To be clear, then, we are not advocating for aesthetics anything like what Hilary Kornblith has called the 'replacement thesis' for epistemology: the view he locates in Quine 'that epistemological questions may be replaced by psychological questions' (Kornblith 1994*a*).

2. THE ARCHITECTURE OF THE IMAGINATION

While the imagination has been an important topic of philosophical interest for centuries, and our imaginative capacities, particularly in the context of pretend play, have long been of interest to the science of psychology (Harris 2000: 1–7), we are primarily inspired by the work on this subject that has been done by cognitive psychologists and empirically-oriented philosophers over the last two decades. Imagining and pretending have been investigated by these researchers in the context of their work on autism, childhood development, and the folk-psychological capacity of 'mindreading'. While there is still some dispute about the exact nature of the cognitive mechanisms which underwrite these capacities, we believe that two crucial insights have emerged from this research: that there are significant functional similarities between imaginative states and belief states, but that *distinct* cognitive systems underwrite our imaginative and doxastic capacities.

The functional similarity between beliefs and imaginings itself consists in two related phenomena. First, imaginative states and belief states (and the respective systems of which they are a part) are functionally similar insofar as they interact with (largely) the same mental mechanisms. That is, by and large, if the belief system takes input from or produces output to a cognitive mechanism, then the imagination system does as well (and vice versa). For example, the belief system drives various inferential mechanisms, and the imagination system does too—the same is true with respect to the affect systems. Second, the relevant cognitive mechanisms treat representations from both systems in roughly the same way.[4] In Shaun Nichols's terms, imaginative states (or 'pretense representations') and beliefs states are in a 'single code'. As he puts it, 'On the single code hypothesis, if a mechanism takes pretense representations as input, that mechanism will process the pretense representation much the same way it would process an isomorphic belief' (2004: 131).

But, importantly, the similarity is not perfect. There are some mechanisms with which the belief system interacts but the imaginative system does not. For example, while beliefs often interact with our action control system, it seems that imaginings do not typically do so. Likewise, perception almost always influences the contents of our belief box very directly, but the interaction between perception and imagination is typically much more tenuous and indirect (though see below on 'streaming' input).

What is the empirical evidence that supports the claim that imaginative states and belief states are functionally similar? One source of evidence comes from the work on childhood pretense by Alan Leslie (1994*a*). This work suggests that children as young as two years old engage in inferential processing in the context of pretending. Furthermore, the inferences they engage in while pretending mirror

---

[4] Again, the key is similarity, not identity.

the inferences they would make in ordinary life. For example, in the famous tea-party experiment performed by Leslie, children are seen to be capable of making ordinary inferences about the effects of upturning cups full of liquids within the context of pretense (1994*a*).

Another source of evidence that supports the claim of functional similarity between imagining and believing can be found in the research which shows that readings designed to prompt the imagining of emotionally laden scenarios can arouse autonomic responses that would be expected in non-imaginative contexts (Lang 1984). While this does not settle the questions outlined above about our emotional responses to fiction, it is relevant to the point at hand as an explanandum to be accommodated.

The second insight—that beliefs and imaginings are the products of two distinct cognitive systems—stems largely from the fruitful debate about simulative accounts of pretense and imagination that has taken place over the last ten years or so. Simulationists, such as Gordon and Barker (1994) and Currie and Ravenscroft (2002), have been impressed by the functional similarity between beliefs and imaginings, and inspired by this phenomenon to offer accounts of pretense and imagining that, in essence, involve the *redeployment* of our ordinary doxastic system. But in order to explain the workings of our imagination (especially in the context of its engagement with fiction), a separate system—distinct from belief—must be posited. Our engagement with fiction essentially involves *interaction* between belief and imagining; e.g. beliefs about genre may play a role in the direction of our imagination, as can beliefs about stars in the context of theatrical and/or cinematic works. While our experience of fiction may be entirely in the head, it is not entirely in the imagination. And for this reason, simulationist and metarepresentational approaches to the imagination which try to get by with just the belief system will not suffice (see Weinberg and Meskin 2005). We will thus speak freely of both a 'belief box' (BB) and an 'imagination box' (IB) throughout the remainder of this essay, although our talk of 'boxes' is meant only to refer to functionally distinct pieces of the cognitive architecture, and should not be assumed to have any neurophysiological implications.[5]

As we have just pointed out, many of the mechanisms that interact with the imagination are ones that also interact with the belief system. A few such dual-purpose mechanisms are worth discussing briefly: (1) the affect systems, (2) the monitoring systems, (3) the inference mechanisms, (4) the Updater, and (5) various domain-specific processes.

(1) *Affect systems*:   As noted above, our affective responses to fictional characters and events have long puzzled philosophers, especially since it can seem an

---

[5] While we have borrowed the basic idea of the IB from Nichols and Stich (2000, 2003*b*), we have not borrowed their terminology. Nichols and Stich refer to the IB as the *PWB*, or *possible worlds box*. But since it seems as if we are capable of imagining the impossible (see Section 4 below), this terminology is a bit misleading.

intuitive piece of folk psychology that only beliefs can properly be the causes of such emotions as pity and fear. But recent scientific accounts of the emotions have not observed this intuition, and the philosophical literature on emotions has reflected this shift away from a strict cognitivism about the emotions. From Griffiths's (1997) Ekman-inspired affect programs to Prinz's (2004) embodied perceptions to Robinson's (2005) affective appraisals, naturalistically minded philosophers have followed the lead of such psychologists as Zajonc (1984) and LeDoux (1996) in positing non-doxastic triggers for our emotions. Once the presence of such accounts loosens the tie between belief and affect, we can more easily accept the idea that representations in the imagination can produce emotions as well. And indeed, we argue in Meskin and Weinberg 2003 that it is plausible that the IB can drive the affect systems in much the same way that they are driven by the BB, and that thereby the puzzle of emotions and fiction is dissolved. And as we shall argue here, that dissolution is just the beginning of the philosophical pay-offs.

(2) *Monitoring systems*: One noticeable feature of our interaction with fiction is our ability to export, in metarepresentational form, the contents of the fiction. That is, we are able to form (by and large) automatically beliefs about what is true in the fictions with which we engage. How is this done? We suggest that monitoring systems—posited by Nichols and Stich (2003*a*) to explain some forms of self-awareness—will be crucial to doing so. As Nichols and Stich point out, a person who believes that *p* is (under normal circumstances) typically capable of easily, accurately, and unselfconsciously forming a belief with the content *I believe that p*. The same is true for many of the other propositional attitudes. For example, if you occurrently desire that *p*, you are typically able—with just a little reflection—quickly and easily to form the belief that *you desire that p*. So too with imaginative states. This capacity is easily explained by assuming that we are endowed with monitoring systems, which function by copying representations from the belief box (or desire box, or imagination box), prefixing 'I believe that' (or 'I desire that' or 'I imagine that') to them, and inserting the resulting representation back into the belief system. Of course, this much will provide a reader of fiction only with beliefs about the contents of their imagination; but since there is an intimate connection between the contents of what one imagines when one reads a fiction and what is true in that fiction, use of the monitoring systems will be crucial.

(3) *Inference mechanisms*: As was mentioned above, research by psychologists such as Leslie (1994*a*) and Harris (2000) provides ample evidence that the imagination interacts with our ordinary inferential systems in much the same way as does the belief system. The patterns of reasoning in which children engage, while in the context of pretense, mirrors their reasoning in ordinary (i.e. non-imaginative) contexts. And this point can be supported by careful observation of the workings of ordinary fictions, which rely heavily on the capacity of consumers

to make inferences within the context of their fiction-guided imaginings. It is not just the hero in the horror movie who hypothesizes about the origins, nature, and motivations of the monster—viewers of such fictions engage in such ratiocination too (Carroll 1990).

(4) *Updater*: A particularly important piece of the cognitive architecture for our purposes is the mechanism (or set of mechanisms) that Nichols and Stich (2000) have termed the 'Updater'. This mechanism—perhaps a part of the inference mechanisms—handles the crucial task of updating (i.e. altering, adding, and deleting) beliefs in the face of new information, in order to render the BB and IB each internally consistent. But this mechanism is clearly required to make sense of our imaginative engagement with fiction, for we regularly update the contents of the IB in light of new input from a fiction.

(5) *Domain-specific processes*: The systems mentioned above are just a few of the many largely automatic systems that we suspect will interact with both the IB and the BB. Folk biology, folk physics, and folk psychology[6] all get deployed in our interaction with fiction, so it is reasonable to suppose that the systems that underwrite those capacities are able to interact with the IB in much the same way that they interact with the BB.[7] And in the context of our discussion of imaginative resistance, we are particularly interested in mechanisms that underwrite our moral capacities—that is, the moral judgment system(s). While we are not prepared to argue at this point that the IB interacts with *all* the mechanisms that underwrite ordinary moral judgments, it is worth noting that it is crucial to our engagement with ordinary narrative fiction that *some* moral mechanisms be engaged by the imagination. We would not be able to make sense of the punishments and rewards that befall the characters in fictions—or the moral emotions of those characters—were we not able to make moral judgments about the fictional (and hence imagined) events which befall them (Carroll 1998). Following the narrative connections in much standard fiction simply requires moral judgment, because those connections can often be understood only in moral terms.

---

[6] For evidence for the existence of such systems, see e.g. McCloskey 1983; Premack 1990; Leslie 1994*b*; Baron-Cohen 1995; Atran 1998; Nichols and Stich (2003*b*). All we require for our purposes is that these systems exist independently of any particular set of representations in the BB, and thus that they do not operate in the imagination as a set of representations in the IB. There are active, ongoing debates as to whether such systems should be construed as either *modular* or *innate*, and this chapter is neutral with regard to such debates. Also, we should note that one of the standard methodologies for investigating such mechanisms is by having subjects make judgments about hypothetical cases; we are therefore confident that these systems are used not just on the BB, but on the IB as well.

[7] 'The kinds of details that authors rely on audiences to supply come in all different shapes and sizes, ranging from facts about human biology to facts about geography, history, politics, religion, and so on. In many cases, the author relies upon what we know or believe about human psychology in order for her narrative to be intelligible' (Carroll 1998: 321). Our point is that it is not simply factual knowledge that is required—the work of various domain-specific systems that underwrite our ordinary capacities to judge in these domains is also required.

While the aforementioned mechanisms interact with both beliefs and imaginings, there are also special-purpose mechanisms that must be posited to make sense of the workings of the imagination and pretense. We mention two of particular importance:

(6) *Inputter*:   While we take it that we are not free to believe what we want—i.e. doxastic voluntarism is generally false—by and large we *are* free to imagine just about whatever we want.[8] Some mechanism or set of mechanisms must allow us to insert contents, just about any content whatsoever, into the IB, on the basis of a decision to do so. We will call whatever mechanisms subserve our capacity to imagine what we want the 'Inputter'. It is worth noting that there are at least two ways in which the Inputter may work to add contents to the IB—it may function by adding one proposition at a time on the basis of distinct decisions to do so (as in some conscious daydreaming), or it may involve one overarching decision to open the gates, as it were, to a stream of incoming information (as in the case of standard film spectatorship). Perhaps this suggests that there really are two distinct mechanisms here. We are currently agnostic about the matter, although it will be useful below to distinguish between the two modes of Inputting (however they are implemented).

(7) *Script Elaborator*:   Nichols and Stich (2000) point to the need to posit some mechanism that 'fills in' pretend or imaginary scenarios beyond what we are explicitly directed to imagine or infer in the context of imagining. They call this mechanism the 'Script Elaborator', and we follow their usage below. In fact, Nichols and Stich consider the possibility that the Script Elaborator also serves the function that we have assigned to the Inputter—that of providing the initial contents for imagining or pretending. And considerations of parsimony, as well as the apparently similar functional roles of the Inputter and Script Elaborator, might seem to make this an attractive suggestion. After all, both the Inputter and the Script Elaborator seem to work by providing the IB with contents that are not produced by some inference mechanism or other (e.g. the Updater). That being said, it is our contention that the Inputter and the Script Elaborator can be usefully distinguished. Some of the argument for this is laid out below, but one observation in support of the point can be made now: there is a significant distinction to be made between the generative process of creating propositional content for insertion into the IB and the process of putting contents—from whatever source—into the IB. We take the Script Elaborator to subserve generation, while the Inputter handles insertion.

---

[8] Modulo cases of blockage, of course; see below for further discussion of cases where imaginative voluntarism fails.

With this rough sketch of the architecture of the imagination in place,[9] we can turn to our solution of the three aforementioned challenges: the paradox of emotions and fiction, the puzzle of imaginative resistance, and the distinction between imagination and supposition.

3. EMOTIONS AND FICTION

Recall the puzzle of emotions and fiction described above. Rather than taking the traditional analytic step of choosing a proposition to discard and then working to explain away its appeal, we suggest that a more fruitful place to start would be to canvas the relevant phenomena and then look for an empirically based framework with which to explain them. Thankfully, the wealth of work that has been done on the topic makes the first part of that strategy fairly straight-forward. There are, we take it, four important phenomena that any account of our emotional engagement with fiction needs to make sense of (cf. Meskin and Weinberg 2003; Weinberg and Meskin 2005): (1) our affective responses to fic-tions are phenomenologically and physically robust; (2) these affective responses are fictionally directed (i.e. their intentional objects are fictive); (3) our affect-ive responses do not result in the full range of behaviors that standard emo-tions produce (we may cry and shriek at the movies, but we do not—at least typically—engage in either flight or fight); and (4) such affective response have an ambiguous relationship to full-fledged emotional responses—we are pulled both towards categorizing these responses as emotions and away from such a classification.

Our suggestion is that the cognitive architecture outlined in Section 2 is par-ticularly well suited to explain these phenomena. For if the imagination system is capable of driving the affect systems, then we should expect that interacting with works of fiction—works which, by their very nature, are designed to engage the cognitive imagination—will often cause affective responses; hence, we have an explanation for (1) above. Moreover, that the representations in the ima-gination are of the same syntactic and semantic form as the representations in the belief box provides a natural explanation for the fact that our imagination-driven affective responses are fictionally directed (phenomenon (2) above). For it is plausible that affective states and processes typically inherit their intentional

[9] Let us emphasize briefly that this is, at best, a partial sketch, for surely other mechanisms will be required for a total theory of the imagination. For example, a fuller picture would require an account of imaginative attention, since not all representations in the IB are equally salient at all times. Also, as has been argued by Currie (2002), we might need to appeal to a system of imaginative desires as well. We are skeptical that this is so (Weinberg and Meskin 2005).

objects from the cognitive states that produce them—a belief of the form 'That snake is poisonous' quite often generates fear of the reptile in question. The same is plausibly true about imaginative states and the affective responses that they drive. The fact that our imaginatively-driven affective responses do not result in the full gamut of behavioral responses can be explained by appealing broadly to the functional dissimilarities between belief states and states of imagining and, more specifically, by pointing out the obvious fact that many behaviors require relevant *motivational* input (i.e. not simply cognitive input from the belief box or the imagination box). While a belief that one is being threatened by a tiger will typically interact with a (standing) desire not to be harmed and result in flight behavior, imagining that one is threatened by a tiger does not interact in the same way with that standing desire. So (3) is naturally explained. Finally, the functional similarity but non-identity between believing and imagining helps explain (4)—the ambiguous nature of fiction-driven affect. To the extent that we focus on the fact that many ordinary emotional responses are caused by beliefs, but affective responses to fiction are caused by distinct cognitive states (i.e. ima-ginings), and moreover, that belief-caused affect may interact with our motiv-ational and action-production systems in a way that imagination-caused affect may not[10]—to the extent that we focus on such differences, we will tend to resist characterizing the latter as full-fledged emotions. But to the extent that we focus on the functional similarity between belief and imagination, as well as the phenomenological and biological similarities between fictive and non-fictive affect, we will be pulled towards assimilating fictionally driven affect to the gen-eral category of the emotions. So, by taking each such inclination as a datum to be explained, and not an intuition to be refereed, the naturalistic approach can score as a success what the more traditional approach must count as an unsolved problem.

4. IMAGINATIVE RESISTANCE

One puzzle about the imagination that has been of particular interest to philo-sophers over the last two decades is the so-called puzzle of imaginative resistance ('so-called' since, as a number of commentators have pointed out and as we shall discuss below, there are in fact a range of distinct, related puzzles here).

We begin with Tamar Gendler's (2000) characterization of the puzzle which was first introduced by Moran (1994) and Walton (1994): how to make sense of 'our comparative difficulty in imagining fictional worlds that we take to be morally deviant' (Gendler 2000: 56). The imagination is largely unconstrained by our non-moral beliefs; i.e. we can, by and large, imagine things that are incon-sistent with our non-moral beliefs. Yet it seems significantly constrained by our

---

[10] Our thanks to Shaun Nichols for pointing out the relevance here of these downstream causal differences between belief-caused affect and imagination-caused affect.

moral attitudes. For example, it is fairly easy to imagine worlds in which cats can fly, or in which slavery is believed to be just, but it is comparatively diffi-cult to imagine worlds in which it is morally acceptable to torture flying cats for no reason, or in which slavery is just (and not simply believed to be so). Why is this so?

In fact, the puzzle of imaginative resistance does not appear to be simply, or perhaps even primarily, a moral puzzle. As Stephen Yablo (2002) and Brian Weatherson (2004) have pointed out, there are a range of non-moral cases that generate similar phenomena. The imagination is only *largely* unconstrained by non-moral beliefs; it can be difficult to imagine worlds that are inconsistent with our aesthetic, semantic, and metaphysical beliefs too. So it would be a mistake to assume that the moral phenomenon that Gendler describes deserves distinct-ive treatment (although it would be just as mistaken to assume without argument that all these phenomena call for the same explanation). Moreover, the puzzle of imaginative resistance is not simply a puzzle about *difficulty* in imagining. As Gendler herself argues, unwillingness, rather than difficulty, may play some sig-nificant role in explaining some of the relevant phenomena: when the reader is asked to imagine a morally reprehensible view, she may cease so to imagine out of a desire not 'to export [from imagination back to belief] ways of looking at the actual world which she does not wish to add to her conceptual repertoire' (Gendler 2000: 77).

So we suggest dividing the broad set of phenomena about our resistance to imagining certain contents that are inconsistent with our beliefs and attitudes into two distinct puzzles: the *puzzle of imaginative refusal* and *the puzzle of ima-ginative blockage*. The former has to do with our unwillingness (or even flat-out refusal) to imagine certain contents; the latter with the difficulty (which may rise to full-fledged incapacity) of imagining such contents, no matter how well-motivated we are to try.

In the remainder of this section, we shall focus on the puzzle of imaginative blockage, although we shall have a bit to say about imaginative refusal along the way. It is our contention that the architecture that we have laid out above has all that is required to explain the phenomena that Gendler and others have described so richly. But first, we should say a few words about alternative approaches to solving the puzzle. On our view, extant proposals to solve the puzzle of imaginat-ive resistance have been significantly hampered by an unwillingness to go beyond the limited resources that folk psychology and metaphysics can provide.

Folk psychology brings a mixed bag of explanatory resources to bear on the world, including appeals to propositional attitudes, the emotions, and such notions as agency and responsibility. Generally, folk psychology focuses on and appeals to aspects of our psychology that have some sort of phenomenological presence. But we do not find folk psychology able to offer much to explain the unconscious or tacit aspects of our cognition, except insofar as it treats unconscious states as merely 'hidden' versions of their conscious brethren.

That's part of why it is appropriate to attribute to Freud the discovery of the unconscious, and also why that discovery first took the form of positing unconscious versions of the typically conscious beliefs and desires of ordinary folk psychology. So the workings of many of the various and sundry cognitive components we identified in Section 2 simply lie beyond folk psychology's reach. This includes the very mechanisms of folk psychology itself (which are, we suspect, domain-specific processes). We therefore predict that, while folk psychology might help explain imaginative refusal—since resistance and the desires that underwrite it tend to be phenomenologically salient—imaginative blockage will prove too experientially thin to fall within its explanatory ambit. The feeling of blockage is, after all, not much more than an experienced incapacity, perhaps combined with a sense of frustration with the author whose work might thus be asking the impossible of us. It offers to introspection no sense of *why* we face such an incapacity, and this is surely part of why it has remained an interesting philosophical problem.

For example, as noted above, Gendler argues that paradigmatic cases of moral imaginative resistance in the context of fiction are rooted in a reader's unwillingness to consider in the imagination that which she would not want to carry over into her belief system. This explanation may account for *some* imaginative refusal, in particular cases of fiction in which we might reasonably take ourselves to have been invited to engage in such export. But it does not even handle all cases of refusal, since it seems possible to generate refusal even in contexts in which export is not at issue. For example, even if we were explicitly to disclaim any intentions of exportation, we expect the average reader would exhibit some refusal at being invited to imagine various graphically horrible events befalling them or their loved ones. (Perhaps our account in Section 3 may help in such an explanation: because affect can be produced by representations in the IB, imagining such events would have unpleasant emotional effects.) And this exportation-refusal account does not even begin to explain imaginative blockage, and philosophers such as Weatherson and Yablo have documented several cases where it seems that we cannot imagine various things, no matter how much we may want to do so.

We turn now to the other machine in the philosopher's toolkit that is frequently deployed here, metaphysics. Such notions as supervenience and metaphysical necessity have been deployed in popular accounts of imaginative resistance, perhaps most famously by Walton, who argued (1994) that our resistance to imagining moral falsehoods stems in large part from the fact that the moral supervenes on the non-moral.[11] Yet it is clear that metaphysical notions *by themselves* can do little explanatory work. We would not expect our imaginations to be constrained by the very many metaphysical necessities of which human cognition is presumably ignorant, like water $= H_2O$ in pre-chemistry days; nor

---

[11] Though note that Walton's full account here is itself a 'metaphysics plus psychology' view; see below.

has it ever been constrained by the putative supervenience of the mental on the physical. And indeed, even now, fully cognizant of the chemical facts and the necessity of that identity, we suspect that we would feel no blockage when engaging, say, in a fantasy fiction in which water is a unitary element. To acknowledge that what we are imagining is that water is unitary, one need not take us thereby to have invalidated the kind of imagination–possibility link so favored by many metaphysicians. (See e.g. Hill, Chapter 11.) There are some standard maneuvers here. Proponents of scientific essentialism can reinterpret such imaginings as perhaps only epistemic possibilities of a sort; or perhaps for our purposes we need only a notion of fictional possibility that is weaker still than the epistemic modality. But our point is that metaphysicians would need to appeal to *some* such machinery to explain these imaginings *away*; and their having to do so is evidence for our claims here that the metaphysics by itself can't do much work in accounting for imaginative blockage.

The appeal to psychology, then, is inevitable. Metaphysics can thus enter into the game only by way of a bit of psychology, if one contends that perhaps it is the noticed or attended to impossibilities that prompt blockage. For example, in his 1990, Currie proposes a psychologized account of truth in fiction, and challenges the more purely metaphysical accounts found in Lewis (1978). One advantage he claims for his account is that Lewis's account has trouble making sense of fictions with any impossible contents whatsoever, whereas his account correctly predicts that we would have no difficulties engaging with a fiction in which Gödel's Incompleteness Theorem is shown to be false—at least in part because that theorem is so *complicated* that someone could well believe in its negation without ever noticing that it was, in fact, impossible.

Weatherson (2004) attempts a highly sophisticated version of a metaphysics-plus-folk-psychology account; roughly speaking, what prompts imaginative blockage is when we are instructed to imagine some claim which could be true only in virtue of some lower-level facts, but we are also forbidden to imagine any lower-level facts which would make the higher-level claim true. (One example involves a fiction that invites us to imagine that an object is a television set, also that it is perceptually indistinguishable from a knife and fork.) Yet, by his own lights, he cannot explain 'Tower of Goldbach'-type cases in which imagining a mathematical (or other conceptual) impossibility seems crucial to appreciation of the fiction, and instead argues that we (or at least many of us) cannot, in fact, imagine their contents. But we find this claim implausible. To read 'Tower of Goldbach' without imagining that $5 + 7 \neq 12$ is to fail fully to engage with the story; and to do so in a way that obscures the impossibility of what has been imagined is to fail to appreciate the story.[12] The robust way in which we can make sense of the events of the story, find a global coherence in its plot, and judge

---

[12] We are thus disagreeing with Gendler's own account of how her story works. So be it—we think the author's theory fails to account for some key aesthetic aspects of her own creation.

an overall rightness in the way its various pieces fit together—these aesthetic facts place a high burden of proof on anyone who would argue that we do not, in fact, imagine that $5 + 7$ does not equal 12 at the relevant parts of the story.

So neither metaphysical impossibility itself, nor appeal to unsatisfiable in-virtue-of relations, can explain the blockage phenomena. Our strategy is to take the insights of the metaphysical approach, but transpose them more fully into a psychological key. We claim that the conflict involved is not between fictional claims and metaphysical necessities, nor between supervenient and subvenient levels of the fictional world, but between different pieces of our cognitive architecture. We appeal to the account of the cognitive architecture of the imagination sketched in Section 2.[13] Of the large host of usually automatic systems that manipulate the IB, several of them can both add representations to, and remove representations from, the IB. Some of them are IB-specific mechanisms, like the Script Elaborator, but because this is a hybrid (or 'single code') architecture, many of them operate more typically on the BB, including various modular reasoning systems. Thus it is possible to get a conflict between these various systems—in particular, a situation may arise in which one system (most typically the Inputter) will insert a representation and attempt to maintain its presence even while another (most typically the Updater) will try to remove it. And that, on our account, is exactly what happens in cases of imaginative blockage.[14]

Let us start with a simple case, and work up from there. How is it that we typically cannot imagine, for example, bald contradictions? To do so would be to find both a p and a $\sim p$ representation in the IB. But the Updater will notice the contradiction, and remove at least one of the offenders. That's what would happen with a similar conflict between two beliefs, and the single-code approach considers the IB and the BB both to be generally subject to the same sorts of coherence-driven revision processes. We can attempt to keep the contradiction in the imagination, by directing the Inputter to reinsert the representation; but again it (or the other) will automatically be taken away. A component of our automatic cognition will simply not permit the contradiction to remain. So long as the Updater is active, and we are not given some way of disguising the contradiction in question—say, by transforming it into a more unsurveyably

---

[13] Nichols (2004) offers a very brief sketch of how one might explain imaginative blockage in architectural terms; our theory here can be taken somewhat as providing a larger and systematic theoretical framework to ground the appeal he makes there to what he calls 'moral response mechanisms' in explaining cases of resistance to imagining moral falsehoods.

[14] While it might seem odd initially to think that the 'blocked' proposition is even briefly added to the IB, there is some evidence that this is how things work in the case of beliefs (i.e. even propositions that will almost immediately be rejected as false are initially added to the BB). See Gilbert, Krull, and Malone 1990.

complicated contradiction—then we just can't keep the representation in the IB. We just find it unimaginable.[15]

Now, let us consider the paradigm case of blockage from the literature on fiction: moral falsehood. Suppose that one is reading a piece of fiction, and that everything has been going smoothly—the automatic systems have had no problem enabling us to comply harmoniously with the instructions of the author—when we reach an invitation to imagine some morally abhorrent proposition A. Our analysis is that a set of different cognitive systems are now in conflict: we insert A into the IB via the Inputter; but a moral judgment system will respond to the morally salient features of the scenario and place $\sim$A in the IB; and at the same time, the Updater registers the resulting conflict.[16] This sets the stage for the blockage.

Under some circumstances, when we run into such a conflict in the imagination, we simply end up with either the A or $\sim$A removed by the Updater. But everything is not equally fungible: some contents have been inserted by specialized mechanisms, most typically the domain-specific systems discussed earlier, which will continue to insert them even should the Updater kick them out. And the Inputter itself is importantly unlike anything that creates beliefs, especially in that we can stipulatively undertake to treat some of its deliverances to the IB as sacrosanct. Most of the time while we're engaging in a fiction, once we've been instructed to imagine p, we will only allow p to be permanently removed from the IB should we come to believe that we are no longer so instructed (e.g. if we take ourselves to now be instructed to imagine that some character X was dreaming that p; cf. the 1985–6 season of *Dallas*). Our hypothesis is that typical cases of blockage in fiction will involve conflicts between a stipulated content, on the one hand, and on the other, a content produced by a modular system such as a moral judgment system (as in our current example) or an arithmetic system (in the 'Tower of Goldbach'). The conflict cannot be defused by simply rejecting either content, then, since for different reasons neither content can be easily removed from the IB—one of them is fixed as a part of compliance with the instruction to imagine, and the other is fixed by a mechanism whose functioning lies outside the range of the Updater. If we're not engaging in a fiction, then most likely we'll just cease attempting to Input the problematic representation. If we are engaging in a fiction, but the problematic proposition is not central to the fiction's

---

[15] Note: one might get around this by merely *supposing* the contradiction, thereby perhaps rendering the Updater inoperative; see below on the architectural commitments of supposition versus imagination.

[16] It is possible that the moral judgment systems attempts, rather, to remove the odious A more directly; in that case, the conflict is between the Inputter and the moral judgment systems. We know of no data at this time to motivate one hypothesis over the other, and for our purposes, the important thing is that the basic strategy of our blockage story is the same either way.

progress, we might simply choose to disregard this one invitation, and continue otherwise unhampered with our engagement with the fiction. But sometimes there's no way to imagine the rest of the work without imagining the problematic proposition, and we can only resolve the blockage by disengaging from the fiction altogether.

In the case of the morally abhorrent propositions, then, it is important that the relevant moral judgment systems act on the IB without themselves being representations in the IB, and thus when the Updater removes the $\sim$A representation, another system will immediately be putting it back in.[17] Its only way to resolve the conflict would be to remove A—but it would be doing so even while we, in trying to comply with the fiction, persist in attempting to Input that A. At that point, we can no longer proceed with our attempt to imagine A. Hence, with cases of blockage we typically (but only typically) have no option but to decline the invitation to imagine altogether: we have been asked to do something that we do not yet see how to do.

That 'yet' is important, though. For we may be shown some trick, some means of redirecting our attention, that can prevent the automatic systems from doing their usual job. We mentioned earlier the possibility of reformatting offensive representations so that their conflicts might fly beneath the radar of the Inputter. (Surely we do this not just in the IB but in the BB as well, as in cases of cognitive dissonance.) Other such tricks might include the morally and affectively disabling conditions of many cartoons, which keep us from attending to the prima facie moral demands of sentient creatures like Wile E. Coyote or Daffy Duck, enabling us to take pleasure in a world where their pains are morally nugatory, or perhaps even praiseworthy. Similarly, some science fictions squiddishly hide their time-travel paradoxes behind an ink cloud of uninterpreted techno-sounding gobbledygook, which allows us to imagine that there's *some* explanation, beyond our ken, for the prima facie paradoxical events, and thereby relax our impulse to seek out the impossible and allow ourselves, willing suckers, to be dragged along in the story's tentacles.

One rare but important trick for handling blockage does not circumvent it, but rather steers straight into it. As we emphasized earlier, appreciating Gendler's 'Tower of Goldbach' requires that we look at its impossibility head on. It is worth noting the sorts of devices Gendler deploys to allow us to do so: the appeal to the Almighty; the winking humor; and, above all, the way the story offers *something* to do with the usually unsustainable proposition that $5 + 7$ fails to equal 12. We normally cannot imagine such a thing, because we cannot see any way to do so. The representation slips away automatically as soon as we consider it. But Gendler's story doesn't just ask us to imagine it; it also tells us *how* to do so—for example, by considering that it entails the falsity of Goldbach's Conjecture, and

---

[17] See note 16.

that gathering five mathematicians and seven mathematicians in one place will not constitute a gathering of twelve mathematicians. We may not imagine it as effortlessly and automatically as we do contents that do not violate a modular system, but with the author's help we can sustain it in the imagination with some modicum of effort.[18]

But, without the aid of such devices, we are blocked. Attempting to imagine A, we can cast about for a way to consider the morally abhorrent proposition without getting entangled with the output of the moral judgment systems, but none will prove easily forthcoming. So, we are stuck: we are instructed to do something that we are simply unable to do.

Our account easily generalizes to other cases of blockage reported in the literature. Most typically, one of the systems involved in the conflict will be the Inputter itself, although we're not sure whether this is a necessary condition on blockage. Depending on the other system involved, we might generate different sorts of blockages. Often the conflict is not between the initially imagined proposition, but some other proposition that we automatically derive from it. For example, we Input A to the IB; some inference system notices that A entails B, and so adds B to the IB; some other modular system places ∼B in the IB; and the Updater notices the conflict. In such a case, ∼B cannot be removed, because it is automatically produced by a modular system. At this point, our imagination is stymied, and we have no choice but to opt out of imagining both A and B.

Although we think that modular systems are typically implicated in the more interesting cases of blockage, it is also possible to generate cases where the conflict arises from two separate products of the Inputter. The explicit contradiction case we started with would be of this sort, but of course the conflict can arise more indirectly, between an Inputted proposition and a proposition inferred from another Inputted proposition. In Weatherson's cases of unfulfillable 'in virtue of' relations, the inference in question is from some realizable state of affairs to its being realized in *some* way or other; but a further imagined content blocks any such realization.[19]

5. IMAGINATION AND SUPPOSITION

Our ordinary language terms 'imagine' and 'suppose' seem to pick out two closely related but distinct mental activities. On the one hand, they look as if they have much in common, since they both seem to be distinct from belief (e.g. neither is governed by norms of truth, and both exhibit a voluntarism that is decidedly

---

[18] This non-monotonic aspect of blockage—that a longer, more adorned version of a story will allow us to imagine something that a strictly shorter story will not—is something else that a purely metaphysical theory would not be able to accommodate, and merits a full-length treatment of its own in a separate paper.

[19] We would also suggest that this strategy can accommodate Yablo's 'grokking' cases as well (see Yablo 2002), but for reasons of space we will not pursue that strategy in detail here.

non-belief-like) but are nevertheless both belief-like to a significant extent. On the other hand, it has seemed to many that there must be a difference between the two states, since we find it easy to suppose things that we cannot (or cannot easily) imagine (Gendler 2000; Weatherson 2004). In particular, we generally have no trouble supposing anything at all for the sake of *reductio* in a logic class, but the imagination (as we have discussed above) is not so free. Philosophers have wondered what explains this difference. But, just as with the puzzles of fictive affect and imaginative resistance, the tools of traditional philosophy are simply unable to carve imaginative nature at the right joints.

For example, Weatherson has proposed that imagination, but not supposition, must always be fine-grained, i.e. filled in with significant detail (Weatherson 2004). But in the course of many imaginings, we do not notice that myriad aspects of what we imagine are only imagined in coarse-grained detail. To take two widely-performed imaginings, we doubt that either the itsy-bitsy spider's waterspout ascent or London Bridge's dilapidation are typically imagined with much specificity. For our purposes, that his proposed account of the distinction fails is less interesting than what we suspect is the explanation for its apparent attraction in the first place: namely, when one considers paradigm cases of supposition and imagination, something like a difference in grain can indeed be observed. And if one approaches the issue of the supposition/imagination distinction too traditionally, it can be hard to see what further resources could be brought to bear on the issue—and so an inessential difference between some cases gets reified into an attempted analysis of all cases. Similar problems face Gendler's account of the distinction. She claims that 'imagination requires a sort of participation that mere hypothetical reasoning does not' (Gendler 2000: 80), and that this suggests 'that imagination is distinct from belief, on the one hand, and from mere supposition on the other' (2000: 81). Insofar as Gendler understands participation as involving self-directed judgments, as is suggested-by her claim that we 'take ourselves', when imagining that M holds, to be 'implicated in the way of thinking that M presupposes' (2000: 80), we see no reason to think that this carves imagination and supposition off neatly from one another. For there is no reason to think that imagining is *essentially* participatory (in this sense) rather than merely *typically* participatory. For similar reasons, Peacocke's (1985) distinction between supposition and 'the phenomenologically distinctive state' of imagining is equally problematic, since imaginative states need not involve phenomenology (e.g. in the context of very long novels it is unlikely that each proposition that you imagine has associated phenomenology), and there is no reason to think that suppositions cannot be phenomenologically rich (e.g. 'suppose that there was a house that looked exactly like yours except it was left-right mirror-inverted').[20]

Better, then, to enumerate a broader set of phenomena, no one of which may be sufficient to establish a sharp distinction, but which collectively can provide

---

[20] Sean Landis (2005) makes similar criticisms of Gendler and Peacocke.

the explananda for a richer architectural account. We will just suggest five here, as enough to begin to motivate our account—but remember that, in principle, our method supports recruiting as large a data set as may prove relevant.

Here are some basic aspects of what we mark off in ordinary practice as 'imagining' or 'supposing'.

(i) When supposing that *p*, one typically only follows out *p*'s consequences (broadly construed); in imagining, one frequently embellishes *p* in arbitrary ways. This difference seems to be underwritten by different norms that govern the practices in which supposition and imagination usually take place. For example, while it is perfectly appropriate to embellish in the context of engaging imaginatively with fiction, the norms that govern the practice of using supposition in indirect proof seem to prohibit embellishment.

(ii) As described above, many things can be easily supposed. Indeed, it seems that *anything* can be easily supposed, even patent contradictions and ethically repulsive propositions. But as was also discussed above, imagining has some (albeit unusual) sticking points. That is, there is some degree of both imaginative blockage and imaginative refusal, but little suppositional refusal and still less (perhaps no) suppositional blockage.

(iii) Supposition's typical epistemic roles are establishing conditionals via hypothetical argument, and as the basis for arguments by *reductio*. Imagining's typical epistemic role is in demonstrations of possibility, not infrequently to be then deployed as counterexamples to arguments.

(iv) Supposition is almost always used for epistemic purposes, though it can be used for fairly specialized recreational purposes, such as playing with logic puzzles. Imagining, on the other hand, can be used epistemically, but is deployed in a much larger range of activities, including the construction of and engagement with fictions, role-playing games, and daydreaming.

(v) It is rare to confuse either supposing or imagining with believing,[21] but it seems fairly likely that we commonly confuse supposing and imagining with one another. A supposition may slide into a daydream via free association if one is not paying close attention, for example, and it may be impossible to say where the one activity leaves off and the other commences.

Now, none of these explananda provide us with the means of constructing a condition that applies to all instances of imagining and none of supposing (or vice versa). But, when considered in light of the single-code architecture, they suggest an entirely different *kind* of way of distinguishing supposing from

---

[21] There is a usage of 'I suppose' that is typically used to express belief, usually in a concessive way: 'Oh, I suppose you're right—we really do need to accept the Johnsons' invitation to their daughter's ballet recital.' But we take it that this usage is robustly different from the usages that typically express suppositions, and that no one gets confused between these different usages. (There is also a similar usage for 'I imagine' as a weakened expression of belief.)

imagining: *they are mental activities which involve different characteristic sets of cognitive processes engaging with the IB*. Moreover, for both supposing and imagining, and for each process in the architecture, one can specify whether its engagement is typical, atypical, or variable.[22]

Engagement with the monitoring systems seems to be typical of both, in that we have no trouble whatsoever forming beliefs about what we are imagining or supposing. Similarly, both imaginings and supposings are often initiated by our decisions to consider particular propositions, and thus use of the Inputter is typical for both (although there appear to be differences with respect to how the Inputter functions in the two cases; see below). Inference systems are almost always deployed in the imagination—perhaps free daydreams do not use them, but these are a relatively infrequent form of imagining—and are part and parcel of supposition.

It is rare for us to engage in imagination without deploying many of our content-specific systems. As noted earlier, for example, moral evaluation is a necessary component of a great deal of our engagement in fiction. And even if we sometimes engage in stories with fantastic creatures or wondrous technologies, nonetheless such stories typically exploit, rather than contravene, the basic tenets of folk biology or folk physics. With supposition, however, we find that some, but not all, instances recruit these systems. When a philosopher teases out the sparsest of implications from a set of premises, she may well suspend the use of the content-specific systems. But when a detective engages in supposition to determine the consequences of a hypothesis as to how the murder might have been committed, she will make use of a wider range of cognitive resources. Such activity may typically be categorized as supposition, and not imagining; the phrase 'I suppose' or 'suppose that' is often used to introduce such activities.[23] We suspect that the norm for such ratiocinative activity is to reason coldly and dispassionately, and thus without bringing the affect systems on-line, and that this norm of affectlessness largely explains why such activities are labeled 'supposition' more often than 'imagination'.

---

[22] We borrow this framework (although not the terminology) from Walton 1970.

[23] 'Could you scale that wall, Doctor?'

I looked out of the open window. The moon still shone brightly on that angle of the house. We were a good sixty feet from the ground, and, look where I would, I could see no foothold, nor as much as a crevice in the brickwork.

'It is absolutely impossible,' I answered.

'Without aid it is so. But *suppose* you had a friend up here who lowered you this good stout rope which I see in the corner, securing one end of it to this great hook in the wall. Then, I think, if you were an active man, you might swarm up, wooden leg and all. You would depart, of course, in the same fashion, and your ally would draw up the rope, untie it from the hook, shut the window, snib it on the inside, and get away in the way that he originally came.' (Arthur Conan Doyle, *The Sign of Four*; emphasis added).

With the Updater, however, we begin to see differences between the two kinds of mental activity. Our imaginings usually have a self-consistency enforced by the Updater (again, except perhaps in free daydreaming). But we are rarely called upon to enforce consistency in a supposition; in cases of indirect proof, we actually derive the contradiction, and then emerge from the supposition and draw the desired conclusion: i.e. the negation of the proposition introduced by the Inputter to commence the supposition.

The two systems that most clearly distinguish imagination and supposition are the affect systems and the Script Elaborator. Affect, indeed, is perhaps *the* paradigm distinguishing system. Our emotions are very often engaged in the imagination, but only very rarely in supposition.[24] This is a matter not merely of statistics, but of norms that govern the practices in which the two activities are typically used: the arousal of emotion is often an integral part of certain uses of the imagination, especially with the proper appreciation of works of fiction. Of course, some other works of fiction may fail to spark affect, and other deployments of imagination may simply be neutral on the question of affect, as is typically the case with many philosophical thought-experiments.[25] But while affect is often required in acts of imagining, and may be an unintended side-effect of some supposition, it is almost never a proper part of a supposing. (The only exceptions might be cases in which you are asked to suppose something for the sake of determining how you might feel. It is an open question whether such an exercise would require use of the affect systems rather than the deployment of a bit of folk psychology.) Indeed, it can get in the way of the pure inquiry for which supposition is usually deployed.

Elaboration similarly produces a stark asymmetry between imagining and supposing. We fairly often do embellish in the imagination, and even when we happen not to do so — for example, when we are too caught up in the action of a film to take the time to elaborate — nothing about imagination restricts us from doing so. But supposition would be worthless as an epistemic tool if we allowed propositions not properly inferable from the supposition to mingle with those that are. Full-fledged script elaboration, though commonplace in imagining, is quite rare in the context of supposition.[26]

---

[24] We have been convinced by informal conversations with Shaun Nichols that supposition can, under certain circumstances, involve the affect systems.

[25] But see Greene et al. 2001 for a consideration of the variable way in which affect sometimes does and sometimes does not enter into such classic thought-experiments as the 'trolley cases' of the ethics literature.

[26] Note also that the distinctions we have laid out between supposition and imagination have lent support to the view that the Script Elaborator and the Inputter are distinct mechanisms. For the phenomena we have canvassed have suggested that those two mechanisms also have distinct functional roles.

One other difference between supposition and imagination, hinted at above, has to do with the way in which the Inputter introduces contents into the IB. In imagining, we may put contents in one by one (either through deliberate decisions to do so, or because we recognize that they are required by other imaginative commitments; e.g. few fictions actually bother to state that shooting a human being can lead to their death, but it can be clear that we are meant to infer from a character's having been shot to her likely demise), or we may simply open ourselves to a stream of content (as in the case of our ordinary experience). So we distinguish between the 'punctate' mode of the Inputter, as opposed to its 'streaming' mode. Both modes are typical of imagining. But only the former way of inserting contents is typical of supposition. We do not form suppositions on the basis of overarching decisions to suppose whatever a film puts in front of us; nor is it acceptable to do so in the contexts in which we engage in supposition.

Our theory of the cognitive architectural differences between supposition and imagination (and between both of them and belief), can be summarized in Table 10.1.

Our five starter explananda are accounted for by these different profiles of the two activities. With explanandum (i), supposing involves less freedom because it does not involve the Script Elaborator. But since imagining *can* use that process—though it does not have to do so—it allows for all sorts of ways of extending and filling in the contents of the IB. This difference also goes a long way toward explaining (iii). By allowing elaboration, imagination is better at filling in details so as better to envision possibilities, whereas hypothetical reasoning requires precisely that we not so elaborate. (In that dimension, then, supposition is more belief-like than the imagination is; moreover, that it is constrained in this belief-like way goes some distance in explaining its distinctive epistemic value.) It is thus quite useful to us from an epistemic perspective that we can deploy the Script Elaborator when stocking our IB with contents, but that we need not do so. We also account for explanandum (iv) in terms of the larger set of processes that are typical of the imagination, which thereby enable a larger range of

Table 10.1. Architectural differences between imagination, supposition, and belief

	Imagination	Supposition	Belief
Affect	Variable	Atypical	Typical
Monitoring	Typical	Typical	Typical
Inference	Typical	Typical	Typical
Updater	Typical	Atypical	Typical
Domain-specific systems	Typical	Variable	Typical
Script Elaborator	Variable	Atypical	Atypical*
Inputter (punctate)	Typical	Typical	Atypical*
Inputter (streaming)	Typical	Atypical	Atypical*

* = but see below.

activities. As noted already, there are many fictions that it would not make sense to consume with the affect systems disengaged: our enjoyment of games of make-believe would be rather limited without appeal to the Script Elaborator, and the consumption of cinematic fictions would be seriously hampered if we could not use the Inputter in its streaming mode.

Explanandum (ii) is explained in terms of both activities' use of the Inputter, whereas only imagining typically involves the broader range of processes that are implicated in imaginative refusal and blockage (if our account in Section 4 is correct). Affect plays a large role in any account of refusal, and affect is atypical for supposition. Blockage typically involves a domain-specific system, and we have suggested that at least some supposition of the more formal, abstract variety need not engage that class of systems. For example, if the moral judgment systems are not engaged during a supposition, then they will not be inserting the troublesome ~A when we try to suppose a morally abhorrent proposition A. Without the ~A, there's none of the conflict that leads to blockage in typical imagination cases. Similarly, our explanation of blockage calls on the Updater, which is typical in imagination but atypical in supposition. So supposition has none of the architectural entanglements that can lead to blockage in the case of imagination.

Now, does it matter that we get no strict distinction between supposing and imagining? For example, cases in which we engage in hypothetical reasoning to determine what sorts of outcomes are possible (i.e. to determine not what *will happen*, but what the *range* of things that *might happen* is) may be cases where we allow the Script Elaborator to do some constrained embellishing on the relevant propositions. And such cases seem to fall in a gray area between supposition and imagination. With this framework in place, we can see that, in fact, those activities are best viewed not as altogether distinct, but rather as just variations within the more general type of IB-involving cognitions. Perhaps we might stipulate a term such as 'considering' to serve as a technical term neutral between all these different ways of engaging with a proposition in the IB. We could then see 'supposing' and 'imagining' as simply picking out different varieties of considering, in a rough way and without any strict difference between them. And thus explanandum (v) is accommodated: not only will there be intermediate cases that do not fit squarely within either activity's characteristic set of processes (as in the sort of case mentioned above), but also one might easily cross into or out of such a case simply by some processes coming on- or off-line.[27] Yet neither will likely be confused with belief, since belief takes place in a different representational system altogether (though one in the same representational code), and it seems that the monitoring systems are sensitive to this fact.

---

[27] As can happen when one is asked to suppose something (for the sake of argument) that generates significant affect. This can often lead to embellishment and, arguably, full-fledged imagining.

But what is the basis for our continued insistence that belief involves a distinct representational system, while imagination and supposition are simply different ways in which one representational system may be used? Why does the distinction between belief and generic consideration push us towards positing two boxes, while the difference between supposition and imagination is explained by the redeployment of one box (the IB)? There is, after all, a whiff of simulationism about our approach to the Supposition/Imagination distinction, since we see those states as stemming from different ways of deploying the same system (with various other mechanisms on- or off-line). Why do we resist the redeployment move in the belief/consideration case?

A number of factors are relevant here. First, whereas the differences between supposition and imagination are generally differences of degree (i.e. they are, at most, the difference between typicality and atypicality), the differences between belief and consideration are far more stark. For example, although we have characterized interaction between belief and the Inputter as atypical, it would be closer to the truth to say that they do not interact at all. There simply is no non-pathological process whereby contents are inserted into the belief box merely on the basis of a decision to do so.[28] And something similar is true with respect to the BB and the Script Elaborator. It is plausible that, insofar as the mental mechanisms are working properly, the Script Elaborator simply cannot interact with the BB. Second, there are a number of important processes left out of the table that distinguish belief from both imagination and supposition. For example, and most centrally, beliefs typically interact with desires and the practical reasoning system, and, in so doing, play a central role in driving the action guidance system. But while imaginings may interact with our desires, neither imaginings nor suppositions typically play any significant role in decision-making or action guidance. And even when the imagination (in the context of pretense) does function in action guidance, its role in generating action may be quite different from the role of ordinary belief in ordinary decision and action contexts. Children do not, after all, typically eat pretend pies made of mud. Finally, we may note that (as was mentioned above) there are good reasons to think that the imagination and belief often run synchronically. We have argued elsewhere (Weinberg and Meskin 2005) that it is simply impossible to make sense of our engagement with fictions without appealing to two distinct representational systems that continuously interact throughout the experience. But nothing like this is the case with respect to supposition and imagination: we note no phenomena that call for the synchronic workings of these two forms of consideration. Given these two

---

[28] That being said, the streaming mode of the Inputter is mirrored, to a large extent, by the interaction of the belief system and the perceptual systems in ordinary contexts. Nonetheless, we think that the conscious control one typically has over the streaming function of the Inputter (as evidenced in our ability to shut it off without turning off the perceptual input) does distinguish it from the BB's responsiveness to perceptual experiences.

points, it seems legitimate to posit a two-box architecture rather than the one-box architecture that some early simulationist accounts seem to posit, or some three-box architecture that might seem suggested by the supposition/imagination distinction.

We conclude this section by suggesting that this framework for a theory of supposition and imagination might also be useful in developing a theory of conceivability, in particular with an eye towards providing guidance to philosophers as to when an act of the imagination can provide evidence for a modal claim. Just as a scientific theory of vision should help us to distinguish successful from unsuccessful instances of visual perception, so too a theory of the cognitive architecture of the imagination should help us to distinguish accurate from inaccurate judgments of possibility and impossibility. Shaun Nichols (Ch. 12) has suggested some ways in which general architectural concerns might enable a skeptical critique of certain appeals to intuition: namely, those concerning 'absolute modalities'. But our account also suggests that looking at the particular mechanisms that might (or might not) be involved in a given act of the imagination might also have more specific payoffs for an epistemology of modal intuition.

By way of illustration, consider that some mechanisms may only be able to act properly on representations that are properly formatted. Gerd Gigerenzer (1998), for example, has suggested that our mechanisms for probabilistic inference cannot function well with percentage-format information, but perform admirably with frequency-format information. Likewise, we conjecture that some domain-specific mechanisms might have format requirements. Suppose, for example, that our folk-psychological systems for detecting the presence of other minds depends on receiving appropriate input from perceptual or imagery systems. This is a very plausible hypothesis, with evidence going back over half a century (Heider and Simmel 1944; see Scholl and Tremoulet 2000 for a more recent summary of evidence for systems dedicated to the perception of animacy). It would follow that some classic thought-experiments in the philosophy of mind might show less than their authors had thought. For example, Block's 'nation of China' argument (1978) and Searle's 'Chinese room' argument (1980) both require the judgment that particular possible sets of circumstances are not ones in which mentation is instantiated. But it is part of the very design of those arguments that we are discouraged from imagining anything that looks like the sort of being that can trigger our mind-detection systems. So—unless one is prepared to argue that a necessary condition on mindedness itself is happening to look like whatever humans are evolved to detect as mindedness—a thought-experiment designed to provide evidence that one can have a particular functional organization without thereby having a mind may, in fact, rely on a mere trick of our cognitive architecture that has been accidentally exploited by those philosophers. Attending to the particulars of cognitive architecture, then, may make available critiques (and, surely, validations) of modal intuitions and thought-experiments that would not be available without such attention.

6. CONCLUSION

We have considered three distinct philosophical issues concerning the imagination: the puzzle of emotions and fiction, imaginative resistance, and the supposition/imagination distinction. For each, we have argued that taking the underlying cognitive architecture of the imagination seriously puts positions in view that are not visible from a perspective that includes only folk-psychological and metaphysical machinery. The puzzle is transformed into a set of explananda, which are then amenable to scientific explication. The particular contours of imaginative resistance, initially resistant to being mapped, turn out to match the contours of our cognition. And where more traditional analytic approaches to the supposition/imagination distinction will be stymied by a range of intermediate cases, the architectural approach shows that the cases are appropriately seen as indeed *legitimately* intermediate, for they correspond to the range of mechanisms that can be brought to bear (or not) in the imagination. This chapter thus serves as an advertisement for a particular kind of naturalistic approach to philosophical problems involving the imagination: attending to the cognitive architecture can enrich philosophy, without thereby replacing it.

REFERENCES

ATRAN, SCOTT (1998) 'Folk Biology and the Anthropology of Science: Cognitive Universals and Cultural Particulars', *Behavioral and Brain Sciences*, 21, 547–609.

BARON-COHEN, SIMON (1995) *Mindblindness: An Essay on Autism and Theory of Mind* (Cambridge, Mass.: MIT Press).

BLOCK, NED (1978) 'Troubles with Functionalism', in C. W. Savage (ed.), *Perception and Cognition: Issues in the Foundations of Psychology*, Minnesota Studies in the Philosophy of Science 9 (Minneapolis: University of Minnesota Press), 261–325.

CARROLL, NOËL (1990) *The Philosophy of Horror, or; Paradoxes of the Heart* (New York: Routledge).

—— (1998) *A Philosophy of Mass Art* (New York: Oxford University Press).

CURRIE, GREGORY (1990) *The Nature of Fiction* (New York: Cambridge University Press).

—— (1997) 'The Paradox of Caring: Fiction and the Philosophy of Mind', in Hjort and Laver 1997, 63–77.

—— (2002) 'Desire in the Imagination', in Gendler and Hawthorne 2002, 201–21.

—— and RAVENSCROFT, IAN (2002) *Recreative Minds: Imagination in Philosophy and Psychology* (Oxford: Oxford University Press).

GENDLER, TAMAR SZABÓ (2000) 'The Puzzle of Imaginative Resistance', *Journal of Philosophy*, 97 (2), 55–81.

—— and HAWTHORNE, JOHN (eds.) (2002) *Conceivability and Possibility* (Oxford: Oxford University Press).

—— and KOVAKOVICH, KARSON (2005) 'Genuine Rational Fictional Emotions', in Kieran 2005, 241–53.

GIGERENZER, GERD (1998) 'Ecological Intelligence: An Adaptation for Frequencies', in D. D. Cummins and C. Allen (eds.), *The Evolution of Mind* (New York: Oxford University Press), 9–29.

GILBERT, DANIEL T., KRULL, DOUGLAS S., and MALONE, PATRICK S. (1990) 'Unbelieving the Unbelievable: Some Problems in the Rejection of False Information', *Journal of Personality and Social Psychology*, 59 (4), 601–13.

GORDON, ROBERT, and BARKER, JOHN (1994) 'Autism and the "Theory of Mind" Debate', in George Graham and G. Lynn Stephens (eds.), *Philosophical Psychopathology: A Book of Readings* (Cambridge, Mass.: MIT Press), 163–81.

GREENE, J. D., SOMMERVILLE, R. B., NYSTROM, L. E., DARLEY, J. M., and COHEN, J. D. (2001) 'An fMRI Investigation of Emotional Engagement in Moral Judgment', *Science*, 293 (Sept. 14), 2105–8.

GRIFFITHS, PAUL (1997) *What Emotions Really Are: The Problem of Psychological Categories* (Chicago: University of Chicago Press).

HARRIS, PAUL (2000) *The Work of the Imagination* (Oxford: Blackwell).

HEIDER, F., and SIMMEL, M. (1944) 'An Experimental Study of Apparent Behavior', *American Journal of Psychology*, 57, 243–9.

HJORT, METTE, and LAVER, SUE (eds.) (1997) *Emotion and the Arts* (New York: Oxford University Press).

HUME, DAVID (1987) 'Of the Standard of Taste', in E. F. Miller (ed.), *David Hume: Essays Moral, Political, and Literary* (Indianapolis: Liberty Classics), 226–49.

KIERAN, MATTHEW (ed.) (2005) *Contemporary Debates in Aesthetics and the Philosophy of Art* (Malden, Mass.: Blackwell).

——— and LOPES, DOMINIC (eds.) (2003) *Imagination, Philosophy and the Arts* (London: Routledge).

KORNBLITH, HILARY (1994a) 'Introduction: What is Naturalistic Epistemology?', in Kornblith 1994b, 1–14.

——— (ed.) (1994b) *Naturalizing Epistemology*, 2nd edn. (Cambridge, Mass.: MIT Press).

LANDIS, SEAN (2005) 'Imagination and Supposition' (unpublished ms, Texas Tech University, Lubbock).

LANG, P. J. (1984) 'Cognition in Emotion: Concept and Action', in C. Izard, J. Kagan, and R. Zajonc (eds.), *Emotions, Cognition and Behavior* (New York: Cambridge University Press), 192–226.

LEDOUX, JOSEPH (1996) *The Emotional Brain: The Mysterious Underpinnings of Emotional Life* (New York: Simon and Schuster).

LESLIE, ALAN M. (1994a) 'Pretending and Believing: Issues in the Theory of ToMM', *Cognition*, 50, 211–38.

——— (1994b) 'ToMM, ToBy, and Agency: Core Architecture and Domain Specificity', in L. Hirschfeld and S. Gelman (eds.), *Mapping the Mind: Domain Specificity in Cognition and Culture* (New York: Cambridge University Press), 119–48.

LEWIS, DAVID. (1978) 'Truth in fiction', *American Philosophical Quarterly*, 15, 37–46.

MATRAVERS, DEREK (2003) 'Fictional Assent and the (So-Called) "Puzzle of Imaginative Resistance"', in Kieran and Lopes 2003, 91–106.

MCCLOSKEY, MICHAEL (1983) 'Intuitive Physics', *Scientific American*, 248 (4), 122–30.

MESKIN, AARON, and WEINBERG, JONATHAN (2003) 'Emotions, Fiction, and Cognitive Architecture', *British Journal of Aesthetics*, 43 (1), 18–34.

MORAN, RICHARD (1994) 'The Expression of Feeling in Imagination', *Philosophical Review*, 103, 75–106.

NICHOLS, SHAUN (2004) 'Imagining and Believing: The Promise of a Single Code', *Journal of Aesthetics and Art Criticism*, 62, 129–39.

____ and STICH, STEPHEN (2000) 'A Cognitive Theory of Pretense', *Cognition*, 74, 115–47.

____ and ____ (2003*a*) 'How to Read Your Own Mind: A Cognitive Theory of Self-Consciousness', in Q. Smith and A. Jokic (eds.), *Consciousness: New Philosophical Essays* (Oxford: Oxford University Press), 157–200.

____ and ____ (2003*b*) *Mindreading: An Integrated Account of Pretense, Self-awareness and Understanding Other Minds* (Oxford: Oxford University Press).

PEACOCKE, CHRISTOPHER (1985) 'Imagination, Possibility and Experience', in J. Foster and H. Robinson (eds.), *Essays on Berkeley* (Oxford: Oxford University Press), 19–35.

PREMACK, DAVID (1990) 'The Infant's Theory of Self-propelled Objects', *Cognition*, 36, 1–16.

PRINZ, JESSE (2004) *Gut Reactions: A Perceptual Theory of Emotions* (New York: Oxford University Press).

ROBINSON, JENEFER (2005) *Deeper than Reason: Emotion and its Role in Literature, Music, and Art* (New York: Oxford University Press).

SCHOLL, BRIAN, and TREMOULET, PATRICE (2000) 'Perceptual Causality and Animacy', *Trends in Cognitive Science*, 4 (8), 299–309.

SEARLE, JOHN (1980) 'Minds, Brains, and Programs', *Behavioral and Brain Sciences*, 3, 417–24.

WALTON, KENDALL (1970) 'Categories of Art', *Philosophical Review*, 79, 334–67.

____ (1978) 'Fearing Fictions', *Journal of Philosophy*, 75, 5–27.

____ (1990) *Mimesis as Make-Believe: On the Foundations of the Representational Arts* (Cambridge, Mass.: Harvard University Press).

____ (1994) 'Morals in Fiction and Fictional Morality', *Proceedings of the Aristotelian Society,* suppl. vol. 68, 27–50.

WEATHERSON, BRIAN (2004) 'Morality, Fiction, and Possibility', *Philosophers' Imprint*, 4 (3).

WEINBERG, JONATHAN, and MESKIN, AARON (2005) 'Imagine That', in Kieran 2005, 222–35.

YABLO, STEPHEN (2002) 'Coulda, Woulda, Shoulda', in Gendler and Hawthorne 2002, 441–92.

ZAJONC, ROBERT (1984) 'On the Primacy of Affect', *American Psychologist*, 39, 117–23.

PART IV
IMAGINATION AND POSSIBILITY

11

Modality, Modal Epistemology, and the Metaphysics of Consciousness

Christopher S. Hill

I will be concerned in this chapter with three interrelated topics. First, I will examine modal arguments for property dualism, and will try to show that they are seriously and irremediably flawed. The criticisms I will offer are rooted in ones that I have presented before (Hill 1981; 1991: 90–5, 98–101; 1997), but they will, I believe, clarify and deepen those earlier lines of thought. Second, I will try to explain the two dimensions of modality that have come to be known as *metaphysical possibility* and *metaphysical necessity*. It is widely held that these two modalities are of fundamental importance for philosophy of mind, and for other branches of philosophy as well, but there is little agreement as to how they are to be defined. I will propose reductive accounts of these modalities, and will also try to describe the reasons for their philosophical significance. Third, I will attempt to identify the sources and forms of our knowledge of metaphysical possibility and metaphysical necessity. It is often held that conceivability is somehow the foundation of our epistemic access to these metaphysical modalities. I will maintain that this conception of our epistemic access is mistaken, and will seek to replace it with a more adequate view.

I believe that the first of these topics is closely related to the second and third—so much so that it is inadvisable to pursue it in isolation from the others. I also think that consideration of the first topic clarifies what is at stake when we consider the others, and more generally, that consideration of the first topic plays a useful role in setting the stage for a broader discussion. Of course, if one chooses to pursue all of the topics simultaneously, as I will do here, one will inevitably fall short of achieving any sort of finality. What is worse, in treating all of them simultaneously, one incurs a significant risk of superficiality. I believe, however,

I thank John Greco, Anil Gupta, Ernest Sosa, and Timothy Williamson for their illuminating comments on earlier versions of this chapter, and Gupta and Williamson for additional discussions. I have also been helped by the comments of an anonymous referee for Oxford University Press. (Among other things, the referee made me aware of a paper by Williamson (2004) that proposes a theory of the metaphysical modalities that is essentially the same as the one I develop in the present chapter.) Finally, I gratefully acknowledge the advice of my colleague Joshua Schechter concerning the problem I discuss in n. 5

that the advantages of honoring the interconnections of the topics outweigh the associated costs and risks.

I

Modal arguments for property dualism constitute a large and variegated family, but there is a common underlying idea that is captured by the following rather simple line of thought:

First premise: We are able to conceive coherently of ghosts and zombies. Hence, we are able to conceive coherently of situations in which pain exists without being accompanied by φ-activity, and we are able to conceive coherently of situations in which φ-activity exists without being accompanied by pain. (I here use the expression 'φ-activity' to stand for a certain neurobiological property—the neurobiological property that will in fact turn out to be correlated most intimately with pain.)

Second premise: If it is within our power to conceive coherently of its being the case that P, then it is genuinely possible that P.

Lemma: By the first and second premises, it is genuinely possible for pain to exist without being accompanied by φ-activity, and genuinely possible for φ-activity to exist without being accompanied by pain.

Third premise: If it is genuinely possible for X to exist without being accompanied by Y, then X is not identical with Y.

Conclusion: Pain is not identical with φ-activity.

The defining features of modal arguments for property dualism are all here: the claim that it is possible to conceive of pain independently of conceiving of the neurobiological process that normally accompanies it, and to conceive of the given neurobiological process without conceiving of pain; the claim that conceivability is a reliable test for possibility; and the claim that if it is possible for entities to exist separately, then they actually are distinct. As is widely acknowledged, each of these elements has a strong intuitive appeal.

II

With a view to fixing ideas, I will begin by making a claim about the nature of conceiving, and two claims about what is involved when we *coherently* conceive of its being the case that P. I will not defend these claims, because it seems to me that they enjoy a tremendous amount of intuitive plausibility. The burden of proof is on the person who denies them.

The claim about the nature of conceiving is just that conceiving is a propositional attitude, and that it is therefore a relation between agents and propositions. To be a bit more specific, to conceive of something is to fit concepts together in such a way as to form a Fregean thought, and actively to entertain that thought. (Thus, here as elsewhere in the present chapter, propositions are assumed to be

Fregean thoughts—that is, truth-assessable representations that have concepts as their constituents.) So much for the nature of conceiving. The first claim about coherent conceiving is the following: if it is true that we can coherently conceive of its being the case that P, then it must also be true (a) that we are able to entertain the proposition that P, (b) that the proposition that P is compatible with the laws of logic, (c) that the proposition that P is compatible with the laws of mathematics, and (d) that the proposition that P is compatible with all of the a priori principles that are constitutive of the relevant concepts, and in particular, with all of the a priori principles that govern the concepts that the proposition that P contains. Finally, I wish to claim that in addition to being necessary conditions of our being able to conceive coherently of its being the case that P, (a)–(d) are also sufficient for us to have this ability. In short, (a)–(d) capture the essence of coherent conceiving.

It will be convenient in the future to have a common label for the propositions that are invoked in conditions (b)–(d)—that is, for the laws of logic, the laws of mathematics, and the propositions that are constitutive of their constituent concepts. Propositions of these three kinds are a priori, but also, unlike such a priori propositions as *I am here now* and *I exist*, they are cognitively robust, playing essential roles in the edifice of human knowledge. Because they are both a priori and robust, it is natural call them *AR-propositions*, and that is how I will refer to them in the future.[1]

---

[1] It may be useful to say something about the nature of propositions that are constitutive of concepts. Of course, we still lack a fully adequate account of this matter, and as a result, we are still unable to answer Quine's skepticism about constitutivity in a fully satisfactory way. But we are far from being completely in the dark about what it is for a proposition to be constitutive. Thus, in the first place, we can all recognize examples of constitutivity when we encounter them—or at least, we can do this in a large range of cases. Here are two examples:

Bachelors are unmarried.
If S knows that P, then it is true that P.

Anyone who possesses the relevant concepts can appreciate that they are partially constituted by these propositions. Second, it is possible to say quite a bit about constitutive propositions in a theoretical vein. Suppose that the proposition that P is partially constitutive of the concept C. It appears that all of the following are true. (i) We regard P as available for use in justifications of other propositions that contain C, and for use in explanations of the truth of other such propositions, but we do not regard it as desirable or even possible to provide a justification for P, or an explanation of the truth of P. (ii) We are committed to honoring P as valid when we are writing fictions or engaging in pretenses. (iii) We are committed to giving P highly preferential treatment in contexts in which we are obliged to make revisions in our belief systems. (iv) We are committed to betting on P even when the stakes are very high. (v) We are committed to treating P as valid in contexts in which we are engaged in counterfactual and other forms of modal reasoning. (vi) We are committed to treating P as operative in characterizing the belief systems of other agents, provided only that those agents are assumed to possess C. In view of these considerations, it seems fair to say that the concept of a constitutive proposition is capable of playing a fruitful role in cognitive science, and to expect that, like all empirically fruitful concepts, it will become more precise and acquire a better experiential grounding as science progresses.

A few words of explanation: (i) I have claimed that if the proposition that P is partially constitutive of a concept C, then we are committed to viewing P as valid in contexts in which we are engaged in modal reasoning. An example may help to clarify this assertion. Suppose we

Assuming that the present picture of coherent conceiving is correct, we can conceive coherently of the truth of any entertainable proposition that is not precluded by AR-propositions. In particular, then, it is possible to conceive coherently of the truth all of the following:

(1) Hesperus is not identical with Phosphorus.

(2) Water does not consist of H_2O molecules. Rather, it consists of XYZ molecules.

(3) Contrary to popular belief, the Washington Monument is not made of granite, but rather of limestone.

(4) George W. Bush is an android, not a human being.

(5) The mother of James I of England was not Mary Queen of Scots, but rather one of her ladies in waiting.

More generally, it is possible to conceive coherently of the truth of any a posteriori proposition.

The foregoing account of coherent conceiving has another important consequence. It implies that our knowledge of coherent conceiving is a priori knowledge. It implies this because it implies that the question of whether it is within our power to conceive coherently of its being the case that P turns on questions about consistency or compatibility with propositions that are a priori. Compatibility is a logical property, and knowledge of logical properties is a priori knowledge.

This is not to say that the account implies that we are generally able to tell whether it is in our power to conceive coherently of its being the case that P. As is well known, there is no mechanical procedure for answering questions about compatibility. Rather, to show that a proposition is compatible with other propositions, one must use imagination and ingenuity. In particular, in order to show that a proposition is compatible with other propositions, it is necessary to visualize a situation in detail, to construct an interpretation of the propositions with respect to the objects and properties that figure in the situation, and to establish that the propositions come out true under this interpretation. In short,

---

are concerned to establish that a counterfactual conditional $A > B$ is true. Suppose also that our strategy is to consider a nearby possible world W in which A is true and to try to show that B is true in W as well. If P seems relevant to this task, we will feel entitled to assume that P is true in W in addition to A. We will then rely on both A and P in attempting to establish the truth of B. (ii) I have also claimed that if P is partially constitutive of C, then we are committed to viewing P as operative in characterizing the belief systems of others. What I mean by this is that if we believe that another agent A possesses the concept C, then we will think it prima facie appropriate to assume that A believes that P. Further, if we should find that A does not believe that P, we will withdraw the attribution of C unless we find that A is prepared to defer to our judgment about the correct use of C, and therefore, to revise his belief system by adding the belief that P.

one must construct a *model* of the relevant propositions. It is generally possible to construct appropriate models in simple cases, but the task of constructing a model for a complex case can call for cognitive resources that we do not possess.

In view of these considerations, no theory of conceivability should claim that it is in general possible to settle questions about coherent conceiving by a priori techniques. All that can be claimed, and all that the foregoing account of conceivability does claim, is that it is possible to know a priori whether a given conceiving is coherent if it is possible to know this at all.

Assuming that the foregoing theory of conceivability is correct, what can we infer about the relationship between coherent conceiving and possibility? Is the former a sufficient condition for the latter, as the second premise of the foregoing modal argument claims? It turns out that the answer is either yes or no—depending on what form of possibility one has in mind.

When philosophers speak of possibility, they sometimes mean *conceptual possibility*. It is conceptually possible that P if the proposition that P is compatible with all of the propositions that count as AR-propositions—that is, if the proposition that P is compatible with the laws of logic, the laws of mathematics, and the a priori principles that are constitutive of the concepts that they contain. Possibility of this sort is virtually the same thing as coherent conceivability. Inevitably, then, if it is within our power to conceive coherently of its being the case that P, then it is conceptually possible that P. It follows that this conception of possibility sustains the second premise of the foregoing modal argument.

We encounter a quite different situation when we turn to consider the form of possibility that is generally known as *metaphysical possibility*. As characterized by Saul Kripke and Hilary Putnam in seminal writings of the early seventies (Kripke 1971, 1972; Putnam 1975), the scope of metaphysical possibility is much more tightly constrained than the scope of conceptual possibility, and knowledge of metaphysical possibility is at least partly a posteriori in nature.

According to the picture that was developed by Kripke and Putnam, if it is metaphysically possible that P, then it must be the case that the proposition that P is compatible with all AR-propositions; but in addition, it must be the case that the proposition is compatible with a large and heterogeneous class of propositions that includes the following:

(6) All true propositions consisting of rigid designators and the identity predicate. (Example: the proposition that Hesperus is identical with Phosphorus.)

(7) All true propositions about chemical kinds that specify the molecular structures of the kinds. (Example: the proposition that water is composed of H_2O molecules.)

(8) All true propositions that specify the 'deep explanatory structures' of natural kinds. (Example: the proposition that an atom of gold has seventy-nine protons.)

(9) All true propositions about artifacts that describe the material compositions of the artifacts at the times when they first came into existence. (Example: the proposition that granite was the material used in the construction of the Washington Monument.)

(10) All true propositions that specify the artifactual categories to which artifacts belong. (Example: the proposition that this object [to which I am now pointing] is a lectern.)

(11) All true propositions about biological substances that specify the biological kinds to which the substances belong. (Example: the proposition that George W. Bush is a human being.)

(12) All true propositions about biological substances that specify the immediate progenitors of the substances. (Example: the proposition that Mary Queen of Scots was the mother of James I of England.)

Kripke and Putnam proposed a couple of ways of thinking of propositions that belong to these categories. They can be regarded as enumerating the essential properties of substances and kinds—the properties that substances and kinds have in all metaphysically possible worlds. Thus, for example, since the proposition that Hesperus is identical with Phosphorus is true, (6) tells us that *being identical with Phosphorus* is an essential property of Hesperus. Alternatively, we can think of (6)–(12) as placing constraints on relationships of trans-world identity. Suppose that x is a substance or kind existing in the actual world, and suppose also that y is a substance or kind existing in another possible world W. Suppose that P is a proposition about x that belongs to one of the foregoing categories. (Thus, it might be that x is George W. Bush, and the proposition that P is the proposition that George W. Bush is a human being.) Then, if y is to count as identical with x, the corresponding proposition about y must be true in W. On both of the conceptions of the role of (6)–(12), they endow the set of metaphysically possible worlds with a structure that significantly extends the structure that is imposed by the constraint that metaphysical possibility shares with conceptual possibility—the requirement that propositions describing metaphysical possibilities must be compatible with AR-propositions. Moreover, as reflection shows, it is in general impossible to know a priori whether a proposition belongs to one of the foregoing categories. Since a proposition cannot count as describing a metaphysical possibility unless it is compatible with the propositions that belong to the categories, it is in general impossible to know a priori whether a proposition describes a metaphysical possibility.

As is easily seen, when it is combined with the foregoing account of coherent conceiving, this account of metaphysical possibility implies that the following principle is false:

> If it is within our power to conceive coherently of its being the case that p, then it is *metaphysically* possible that p.

Coherent conceiving is not sufficient for metaphysical possibility, because the conditions that define coherent conceiving are much less restrictive than the conditions that define metaphysical possibility. It is possible for a proposition to satisfy the first set of conditions without satisfying the second set. But more: the principle is wildly and egregiously false. It is not even an approximation to the truth. This is because the conditions that define coherent conceiving are *vastly* less restrictive than the conditions that define metaphysical possibility. Moreover, the former conditions are to a large extent different in kind than the latter, for the latter include many requirements that derive from the realm of empirical fact.

We must conclude, then, that coherent conceiving does not by itself provide a satisfactory entrée to the realm of metaphysical possibility. But we should also take note of a positive fact. Although it is incapable of serving as a self-sufficient test for metaphysical possibility, it is quite well suited to serve as a component of a larger test, a test that is in fact capable of answering questions about metaphysical possibility in a reliable way. Suppose that we wish to know whether it is metaphysically possible that P. We may be able to answer this question by making use of the following four-step procedure:

(i) Applying the usual method of constructing models, determine whether the proposition that P is compatible with all of the propositions that count as AR-propositions.

(ii) Assuming that step (i) yields the result that it is possible to conceive coherently of its being the case that P, determine whether the proposition that P is compatible with the propositions that belong to categories (6)–(12).

(iii) Assuming that the outcome of step (ii) is positive, determine whether the proposition that P is compatible with any propositions that are not included among the propositions in (6)–(12), but that play similar roles in structuring the space of metaphysically possible worlds.

(iv) If the outcome of step (iii) is positive, conclude that it is metaphysically possible that P.

In this procedure, the initial test for coherent conceivability (step (i)) will deliver many positive results that do not correspond to genuine metaphysical possibilities. Accordingly, it is appropriate to think of steps (ii) and (iii) as filters. Their role is to eliminate the false positives that emerge from step (i), and to stamp the remaining outputs of step (i) with an imprimatur. The task of applying the procedure will be quite complex in a range of cases, and it will in fact often happen that our use of it is inconclusive. On the other hand, there will be many cases in which it quickly and smoothly produces an answer. Moreover, there are various shortcuts that can be used without substantially decreasing the procedure's reliability. Thus, for example, it seems that we can often tell that a set of propositions is logically consistent just by scanning the members of the set.

We have now arrived at the following result: if the foregoing theory of conceiving and coherent conceiving is correct, then the first of the following conditionals is true and the second one is false:

> If it is within our power to conceive coherently of its being the case that P, then it is *conceptually* possible that P.
> If it is within our power to conceive coherently of its being the case that P, then it is *metaphysically* possible that P.

We must now consider the implications of this result for our modal argument for property dualism. This means, of course, that we must consider which of the two forms of possibility we have been considering is most relevant to the argument. Should the argument be understood as concerned with conceptual possibility, or is it best understood as presupposing the framework of metaphysical possibility?

Reflection shows that the argument collapses when it is understood in the first of these ways. Consider what happens when we reformulate the argument so that it makes explicit reference to conceptual possibility:

First premise: We are able to conceive coherently of ghosts and zombies. Hence, we are able to conceive coherently of situations in which pain exists without being accompanied by φ-activity, and we are able to conceive coherently of situations in which φ-activity exists without being accompanied by pain.

Second premise: If it is within our power to conceive coherently of its being the case that P, then it is conceptually possible that P.

Lemma: By the first and second premises, it is conceptually possible for pain to exist without being accompanied by φ-activity, and conceptually possible for φ-activity to exist without being accompanied by pain.

Third premise: If it is conceptually possible for X to exist without being accompanied by Y, then X is not identical with Y.

Conclusion: Pain is not identical with φ-activity.

Here everything goes well until the third premise, but at that point the argument collapses. The third premise is straightforwardly false. Here are two counter-examples:

(13) It is conceptually possible for Hesperus to exist without being accompanied by Phosphorus, but Hesperus is in fact identical with Phosphorus.

(14) It is conceptually possible for heat to exist without being accompanied by molecular motion, but heat is in fact identical with molecular motion.

To appreciate the plausibility of (13), observe that people believed that Hesperus was distinct from Phosphorus for thousands of years. Moreover, they had good reason for believing this. Surely this makes it plausible that it is possible to conceive coherently of Hesperus existing independently of Phosphorus. The plausibility of (14) can be appreciated by noticing that there are no a priori grounds for rejecting the claim that heat is in fact identical with rapid vibratory motion in an aether-like field. It follows that there are no a priori obstacles to conceiving of a situation in which there is heat but no molecular motion.

There is also a theoretical rationale for rejecting the third premise. A claim of the form 'It is conceptually possible for X to exist without being accompanied by Y' is a claim about the relationship between the concept of X and the concept of Y. It is equivalent to the claim that there are no a priori ties between the concepts that require us to treat them as interchangeable in descriptions. On the other hand, the claim that X is not identical with Y is a claim about the relationship between the referent of the concept of X and the referent of the concept of Y. Clearly, it is not in general possible to infer conclusions about relationships between the referents of concepts from premises about relationships between concepts. If we were to treat such inferences as generally acceptable, we would be projecting facts about concepts out onto the world.

It turns out, then, that defenders of the modal argument are faced with a dilemma: if we interpret the modal argument as concerned with conceptual possibility, then its second premise is true, but its third premise is false. On the other hand, if we interpret it as concerned with metaphysical possibility, then the third premise is defensible, but the second premise is manifestly false. This is a dilemma because the only other possible interpretations lead to even more disastrous results. (The other two forms of possibility are epistemic possibility and nomological possibility. Reflection shows that neither of these forms of possibility can sustain both the second premise of the argument and the third premise.)

Before concluding this discussion of our sample modal argument, we should take note of a reply that might be offered on behalf of the argument by an advocate of property dualism. It must be acknowledged, the reply begins, that when the third premise of the argument is interpreted as a claim about conceptual possibility, it fails to hold. That is, it must be acknowledged that it fails to hold for the general run of concepts. But it might still hold when it is interpreted narrowly as a claim about the concept of pain and the concept of φ-activity. Thus, it might be that the concept of pain and the concept of φ-activity have special features that enable them to encode information about the essential natures of their referents, and that the attendant special informational relationships make it possible to pass from premises about the concepts to conclusions about their referents. Suppose, to elaborate a bit, that the a priori structure of the concept of pain fully (or at least adequately) captures the nature of pain itself, and that the same is true, *mutatis mutandis*, of the a priori structure of the concept of φ-activity. Under these assumptions, it might well be true that if the a priori structures of these concepts permit us to describe a situation as one that contains a pain without describing it as a situation that contains a case of φ-activity, or permit us to describe a situation as one that contains a case of φ-activity but that does not contain a pain, then the referents of the concepts are actually distinct.

Perhaps it will be useful to reformulate this reply as an explicit argument. The argument has three premises: (a) The essential nature of pain is captured by the concept of pain in such a way that it is possible to grasp that nature simply by reflecting on the content of the concept. (b) The same is true, *mutatis mutandis*, of the essential nature of φ-activity. (c) For any two natural kinds X and Y, if it is possible to grasp the essential natures of X and Y simply by reflecting on the contents of the concepts of X and Y, then it is possible to determine a priori whether X and Y are modally separable and, accordingly, possible to tell a priori whether X and Y are identical. The conclusion of the argument is of course the claim that it is possible to determine a priori whether pain and φ-activity are identical.

This argument seems to be enjoying a certain vogue, but when we consider it carefully, we find that there are substantial objections to premise (a) and premise (b). I will focus here on the objection to premise (a), deferring discussion of (b) to another occasion.

Why does it seem to be possible to grasp the essential nature of pain by reflecting on the concept of pain? I believe that the answer to this question has two parts. First, it is clear to us that the concept of pain is linked constitutively to the experience of pain: it is impossible to possess the concept fully and autonomously unless one is familiar with the experience of pain, and one is disposed to be guided by that experience in one's future use of the concept. Second, there is a powerful intuition to the effect that the experience of pain puts one directly in touch with pain itself, and therefore with the essential nature of pain. Starting from these two facts, it is easy to construct an explanation of our intuitive conviction that the essence of pain is fully captured by the concept of pain.

But why do we suppose that the experience of pain puts us in touch with pain as it is in itself? It is initially tempting to try to answer this question by appealing to the fact that when one has an experience of pain, one's awareness of the pain is *direct*: it is not the case that there is some other property π such that we are aware of pain in virtue of being aware of π. When we take a closer look, however, it becomes clear that this answer is inadequate. Thus, it is fully evident to us that it is possible to be directly aware of a property, in the relevant sense of 'directly aware', without having a grasp of its essential nature. Consider, for example, perceptual awareness of color. It is fully evident to us that such awareness is direct—that we are not aware of colors in virtue of being aware of other properties. But we do not suppose that perception puts us in touch with colors as they are in themselves. We are quite prepared to allow that our perceptual representations of colors may prescind from, and perhaps even significantly distort, the underlying physical realities.

What, then, is the correct answer? Why does it seem to us that the experience of pain puts us in touch with the essence of pain? I believe that the main source of this intuition is the fact that we do not normally draw a distinction between appearance and reality with respect to the experience of pain. We do not allow that it is possible for one to have an experience as of pain when one is not in pain, or that it is possible for one to be in pain without having an experience as of pain. In the case of the experience of pain, we are inclined to suppose, the appearance of pain *is* the reality. Because we are inclined to suppose this, we are also inclined to suppose that when one has an experience of pain, one is *ipso facto* in touch with the reality of pain—that is, with the way that pain is in itself.

My claim, then, is that at the deepest level, our intuition that the concept of pain gives us access to the essential nature of pain is due to our seeing no reason, and no enabling foundation, for drawing an appearance/reality distinction with respect to the experience of pain. Now if this claim is right, it is possible to undercut the intuition by showing that it is, after all, possible to draw a distinction of the sort in question. I believe that this can in fact be shown. Thus, there are a number of considerations, provided by introspection, philosophical reflection, and neuroscientific investigation, that support the view that the experience of pain is perceptual in character. To be more precise, they support the view that experiences of pain constitutively involve perceptual representations of bodily disturbances. Now when a form of awareness is perceptual in character, it is in principle possible to show that there is an associated appearance/reality distinction. This is because perceptual representations are naturally seen as appearances of the phenomena that they represent. Accordingly, the considerations that favor the view that the experience of pain is a form of perceptual awareness also favor the further view that it is possible to draw an appearance/reality distinction with respect to the experience of pain.

I have discussed the considerations favoring a perceptualist model of pain at some length in earlier work (Hill 2005). Here I will note just three of them. (a) One is generally unable to frame a conceptually based description that fully captures what one is aware of when one is aware of a pain. That is to say, what one is aware of when one is aware of a pain generally transcends, in complexity and in qualitative determinacy, the expressive resources of one's conceptual lexicon. But this is also true of such paradigmatic forms of perceptual awareness as vision and hearing. Generally speaking, one is unable to construct a conceptually based description that does justice to the content of a perceptual experience. (b) The experience of pain can take the form of *attentive* awareness. Examination of such awareness shows that it is similar in representational and functional characteristics to the various forms of attentive awareness that are associated with paradigmatic perceptual faculties. (c) We always experience pains as located in specific regions of the body. The same is true, *mutatis mutandis*, of the paradigmatic forms of perceptual experience. Perceptual experiences always assign egocentric locations to their objects.

This completes my objection to the modal argument for property dualism that we first encountered in Section II. In recent paragraphs, we have been considering an ancillary argument that was intended to buttress the modal argument. One of the pillars of this ancillary argument is the idea that it is possible to grasp the essential nature of pain by a priori examination of the content of the concept of pain. Reflection shows that the main source of this idea is the perception that it is impossible to draw an appearance/reality distinction with respect to the experience of pain. This perception comes to the fore quite naturally when one adopts the perspective of folk psychology. It turns out, however, that there are powerful theoretical reasons for rejecting it. Thus, there are powerful theoretical reasons for holding that experiences of pain are perceptual experiences. In mandating this view about experiences of pain, these reasons provide motivation for the further claim that experiences of pain constitutively involve perceptual representations. Perceptual representations are naturally seen as appearances of the phenomena that they represent. So, in particular, the representations that are constitutively involved in experiences of pain are naturally seen as appearances.

We have thus far reached eleven conclusions:

(a) To conceive of something is to fit concepts together in such a way as to form a Fregean thought, and actively to entertain that thought.

(b) To conceive of something coherently is to entertain a Fregean thought that is compatible with all propositions that count as AR-propositions.

(c) It is not always possible to know whether one is conceiving something coherently, but when it is, the relevant piece of knowledge is a priori knowledge.

(d) There are two different types of possibility that might be thought relevant to modal arguments for property dualism—conceptual possibility and metaphysical possibility.

(e) A proposition may be said to describe a conceptual possibility if it is logically consistent and compatible with all propositions that count as AR-propositions.

(f) The conditions that define metaphysical possibility are much more demanding: to count as describing a metaphysical possibility, a proposition must be compatible with AR-propositions, but, in addition, it must be compatible with a large and variegated set of true empirical propositions—propositions that in effect specify the essential properties of the objects and kinds with which they are concerned.

(g) If it is within our power to conceive coherently of its being the case that P, then it is *conceptually* possible that P.

(h) The corresponding principle about *metaphysical* possibility fails.

(i) To determine whether a proposition describes a metaphysical possibility, one must follow a complex procedure that involves testing for coherent conceivability and also testing for compatibility with the relevant empirical propositions.

(j) There are two ways of interpreting the modal argument for property dualism—one for each of the two forms of possibility. It fails on both interpretations.

(k) A certain argument that is designed to protect the modal argument from this objection is badly flawed.

III

It seems fair to say that the foregoing line of thought has some quite important virtues. It is reasonably clear and straightforward, and it is also internally cohesive, providing accounts of modality and knowledge of modality that are mutually supportive. Moreover, most of its components are well motivated, some by vivid and stable intuitions, and others by philosophical arguments.

It must be acknowledged, however, that it raises more questions than it answers. Some of these new questions are conceptual or metaphysical in character: they have to do with the nature and value of the concepts of metaphysical possibility and metaphysical necessity. Others are epistemological: they are concerned with the sources and forms of our knowledge of the metaphysical modalities. I will turn now to consider these additional questions. As we will see, they emerge naturally, and even seamlessly, from our reflections in the previous section. Because of this, it is necessary to address them in order to complete those reflections. But also, they are independently interesting. There are compelling philosophical reasons for pursuing them quite apart from their connection with the task of evaluating modal arguments for property dualism.

To begin with the conceptual or metaphysical questions, the foregoing line of thought fails to provide us with a comprehensive and well-grounded understanding of metaphysical possibility and metaphysical necessity. It explains metaphysical possibility in terms of metaphysical necessity, saying, in effect, that a proposition counts as metaphysically possible if it is compatible with the propositions that are metaphysically necessary. But it does not provide an explanation of metaphysical necessity. In lieu of an explanation, it provides a list of propositions that qualify as metaphysically necessary: it just tells us that AR-propositions are metaphysically necessary, and that propositions that belong to categories (6)–(12) share this status. As we all know, lists make poor definitions: even when a list succeeds in exhausting the extension of a concept, it provides us with no real grasp of the internal organization of the concept, and no real grasp of the rules that govern its use. But anyway, the present list falls short of exhausting the extension of the concept of metaphysical necessity. Its function is purely illustrative.

It may be that this account of the metaphysical modalities is sufficient to fix ideas, but it can hardly be regarded as satisfactory from a theoretical point of view. It leaves us with questions like the following: Can the concept of metaphysical necessity be defined by stating necessary and sufficient conditions? If not, is there a set of propositions that count as an implicit definition of the concept? Further, is there a property that is shared by all of the members of the extension of the concept? If so, what is it? If there is no common property, is the concept a family resemblance concept, or is it purely disjunctive in character? It is clear that these questions are of fundamental importance. It is therefore odd that they have received so little attention in the literature. For the most part, contributions to the contemporary discussion have characterized the concept in the way that I have above, by giving a partial list of the propositions to which it applies.

There is an intuition about metaphysical necessity that I have not yet mentioned. It is often said that the propositions that count as metaphysically necessary appear to be *unqualifiedly* necessary—that they are necessary in an absolute or unconditional sense. Writers sometimes express this intuition in quasi-technical parlance by saying that the metaphysically possible worlds are all the possible worlds there are. It is claimed that they are all of the possible worlds that have any sort of objective being, all of the possible worlds that might have been actual.[2] It is helpful to keep this intuition in mind, for it gives us reason to think that the concepts of metaphysical necessity and metaphysical possibility may have some sort of internal unity. But, taken by itself, it provides no motivation for specific answers to the foregoing questions. By itself, the idea of an unqualified form of necessity is too thin, too abstract and formal, to support a detailed theory of metaphysical necessity. The same is true of the idea of the totality of all objectively possible worlds.

This brings us to the basic epistemological questions about metaphysical necessity. Can we acquire knowledge of it? And if so, how? There has been a certain amount of discussion of these questions in recent years, but it is widely acknowledged that we have yet to achieve satisfactory answers. As I see it, progress has been impeded by a lack of clarity concerning what it is that knowledge of metaphysical necessity would be knowledge *of.* It seems that we must have a reasonably adequate account of the concept of metaphysical necessity in order to explain how a subject might come to know propositions involving that concept.

Inevitably, we also lack an adequate account of knowledge of metaphysical possibility. In Section II I described a procedure for acquiring knowledge of metaphysical possibility, but that procedure presupposes an ability to recognize metaphysical necessity. Thus, according to the proposal in Section II, it is possible to determine whether a proposition is metaphysically possible by determining whether it is compatible with a group of propositions that includes all AR-propositions and all propositions that belong to categories (6)–(12). This

---

[2] As against this view, it is sometimes maintained that there is a set of *conceptually possible* worlds, and that the metaphysically possible worlds are a proper subset of this set. Of course, if this second view were correct, it would not be true that the metaphysically possible worlds are all the possible worlds there are. But there is reason to reject the second view. Anything is conceptually possible that is compatible with our a priori knowledge. Thus, it is conceptually possible that the Statue of Liberty is made of plastic, that George W. Bush is a complicated puppet, and that Hesperus is not identical with Phosphorus. It seems that we are strongly inclined to doubt that these are *real* possibilities, that they are states of affairs that could actually have obtained. Since conceptual possibilities include bizarre possibilities of this sort, it seems that conceptual possibilities are different in kind than genuine metaphysical possibilities. Evidently, it is a distortion to think of metaphysical possibilities as conceptual possibilities that belong to a particular category.

claim clearly presupposes that the propositions in question are metaphysically necessary, and also that they are known to have that status. It must be, then, that we have some sort of independent access to metaphysical necessity. The proposal in Section II leaves that access unexplained.

Of course, until these epistemological issues are clarified, any evaluation of an argument that is concerned with either of the metaphysical modalities must be regarded as partial and provisional. This is true, in particular, of the foregoing assessment of modal arguments for property dualism. That assessment stands or falls with the claim that conceivability does not provide us with satisfactory access to metaphysical possibility. This claim is reasonably well motivated, as we observed earlier, but as long as the present questions about the nature of our access to the metaphysical modalities are unanswered, it cannot be said to possess any sort of final authority.

I will explore these metaphysical and epistemological questions in subsequent sections, developing them in greater detail and proposing tentative answers. My answers are partially inspired by ideas in the classic discussions of the metaphysical modalities, but they are quite different from most of the proposals in the contemporary literature. In particular, they diverge sharply from the proposals that have been put forward by David Chalmers (1996) and other philosophers whose theories of the modalities and modal knowledge have been thought to provide support for property dualism. As will be seen, my answers sustain the critique of modal arguments for property dualism that is offered in Section II.

IV

In his various writings about the metaphysical modalities, Kripke often uses the expression 'counterfactual situation' as an equivalent of the expression 'metaphysically possible world that is not actual'. This suggests the view that there is an intimate relationship between claims about metaphysical possibility and counterfactual conditionals. I will develop this view in the present section. To be more specific, I will maintain that it is possible to explain the metaphysical modalities reductively in terms of the subjunctive conditional *If it were the case that . . . then it would be the case that*_____. (Roughly speaking, counterfactual conditionals are subjunctive conditionals that presuppose the falsity of their antecedents.) There is much to recommend this theory. Thus, it predicts the intuitive resonance of claims about metaphysical necessity. Subjunctive conditionals play a large role in everyday thought. Because of this, if the theory were true, then we would have intuitions concerning claims about metaphysical necessity that were reasonably stable and robust. It seems that we do in fact have such intuitions. Further, as we will see, the theory predicts a number of specific intuitions about metaphysical necessity, among them the intuitions that favor the idea that the origins of artifacts and biological substances are metaphysically necessary. It also provides a basis for generating an independently plausible account of knowledge of the metaphysical modalities.

In order to develop the theory, it is necessary to assume an account of subjunctive conditionals. Partly because it is well known, and partly because I believe that it is largely correct, I will here adopt the account that is presented in David Lewis's *Counterfactuals* and related writings (Lewis 1973, 1986*a*, 1986*b*). But my proposal about metaphysical necessity is not linked indissolubly to Lewis's theory. There are other theories of subjunctives that would serve my purposes almost as well.

The main component of Lewis's theory is the following thesis about the truth conditions of subjunctives:

(15) A subjunctive conditional $A > C$ is true at a possible world W just in case either (a) A is not true at any of the possible worlds that are accessible from W, or (b) there is an accessible world at which both A and C are true that is more similar to W than any accessible world at which both A and $\sim C$ are true.

Here clause (a) is concerned with subjunctives whose antecedents are contradictory or impossible for some other reason, and (b) is concerned with subjunctives that have contingent or necessary antecedents. A world is said to be accessible from W if it is relevant to the semantic evaluation of subjunctive conditionals with respect to W—that is, if it has to be taken into account by anyone who is concerned to determine whether subjunctive conditionals are true at W. Lewis views accessibility as depending on similarity. (See Lewis 1973: 14; 1986*a*: 6.) Are all possible worlds accessible from W, or only some of them? That is to say, are all possible worlds similar to W in the ways that are relevant to the semantic evaluation of subjunctives? Or are only some of them similar to W in the relevant ways? Lewis considers these questions but in the end decides to leave them open (Lewis 1973: 15–16; 1986*a*: 6).

Now, as Lewis points out, it is possible to define an operator in terms of the subjunctive conditional that counts intuitively as expressing a form of necessity (Lewis 1973: 22). Here is the definition that he provides:

(16) $\Box A =_{df} \sim A > A$.

In combination with the foregoing account of the truth conditions of subjunctives, this definition entails that propositions containing $\Box$ have truth conditions that look like this:

(17) $\Box A$ is true at a possible world W just in case A is true at every possible world that is accessible from W.

(17) is sufficient to show that Lewis's operator really does express a form of necessity. In general, we have a necessity operator whenever we have an operator

that expresses truth with respect to all members of a unified range of possible worlds.[3]

It is possible, then, to use the subjunctive conditional to define an operator that expresses necessity. Is there any reason to think that this form of necessity is genuine metaphysical necessity? I will now maintain that the answer is 'yes': subjunctive necessity and metaphysical necessity are one and the same.

According to the standard picture of it, metaphysical necessity is absolute or unconditional necessity. That is, if a proposition counts as metaphysically necessary, then it holds in *all* possible worlds, and not just in a restricted subset of the set of possible worlds. Hence, as Lewis points out, subjunctive necessity comes to the same thing as metaphysical necessity just in case the following proposition holds (Lewis 1973: 23):

(18) *All* possible worlds are included in the possible worlds that are accessible from W (that is, in the possible worlds that are relevant to the semantic evaluation of subjunctive conditionals with respect to W).

If (18) is true, then Lewis's truth condition (17) comes to the same thing as (19):

(19) $\Box A$ is true at W just in case A is true at all possible worlds,

and Lewis's operator $\Box$ expresses genuine metaphysical necessity.

The question, then, is whether it is possible to prove proposition (18). I will begin by showing that it holds when we understand the variable 'W' to refer to the actual world. I will then generalize the argument to all values of 'W'.

Suppose for *reductio* that there is a respect R of comparison such that worlds that are similar to the actual world in respect R (to an appropriate degree) are relevant to the semantic evaluation of subjunctives with respect to the actual world, and worlds that are not similar to the actual world in respect R (to the given degree) are not relevant to the semantic evaluation of subjunctives. This assumption leads immediately to a problem, for whatever R may be, it seems that there are subjunctive conditionals that are concerned with worlds that lie well outside the sphere of worlds that is determined by R (and the appropriate degree). Moreover, we are prepared to regard many of these conditionals as having non-vacuous truth values—as being either false or non-vacuously true. (A subjunctive is vacuously true if it owes its truth to the impossibility of its antecedent.) If this is so, then the *reductio* assumption must be wrong.

There are various specific forms that our *reductio* hypothesis might take, and in each case, it is possible to show that we are prepared to entertain subjunctive conditionals that call the hypothesis into question. Suppose it is suggested, for example, that if a world W is relevant to the semantic evaluation of subjunctives,

---

[3] As far as I have been able to determine, Stalnaker was the first philosopher to point out that a concept of necessity can be defined in terms of the subjunctive conditional. He explicitly cites (16) as an appropriate definition. See Stalnaker 1968.

then it must be true that the laws of nature that hold in *W* coincide on the whole with the laws of nature that hold in the actual world. This suggestion is refuted by the fact that there are non-vacuous counterfactual conditionals that begin as follows:

If the laws of physics were different than they are in the actual world, ...

(If we regarded conditionals of this sort as vacuous, we would not argue for their truth or falsity by lines of thought that presuppose the possibility or their antecedent. But we do argue in this way.) Or suppose it is suggested that if a world *W* is relevant to the semantic evaluation of subjunctives, then the building blocks of *W* must be elementary particles and fields of the sort that are found in the actual world. This suggestion is refuted by the fact that there exist non-vacuous counterfactuals that begin like this:

If the building blocks were different than the actual building blocks, ...

It is possible, of course, to formulate hypotheses concerning the relevant respects of comparison that allow much greater departures from actuality than the foregoing hypothesis about laws of nature and the present hypotheses about building blocks. But all such hypotheses can be refuted. Thus, let *S* be any suggestion to the effect that the only worlds that are relevant to the semantic evaluation of subjunctives are similar to the actual world in respect *R* to degree *D*. It is possible to refute S by appealing to counterfactuals of the following form:

If the world were different in respect *R* to a degree that is greater than *D*, ...

We regard such counterfactuals as having truth values. Moreover, we do not see them as vacuously true, as is shown by the fact that we are prepared to give substantive reasons for accepting or rejecting them. In general, it seems, we do not regard a counterfactual as vacuously true unless we have an independent intuition to the effect that its antecedent is impossible. Implicit in our practice is a distinction between counterfactuals with genuinely impossible antecedents and counterfactuals with antecedents that merely countenance worlds that are radically different from our own world. We are prepared to entertain subjunctive suppositions that are concerned with worlds that are *arbitrarily* different than the actual world.

In view of these considerations, it appears that all possible worlds are accessible from the actual world. But more: where *W* is any possible world, it appears that all possible worlds are accessible from *W*. For suppose that this is not the case—that is, suppose that there is some respect *R* of comparison, and some degree *D* of similarity with respect to *R*, such that worlds must be similar to *W* in respect *R* to degree *D* in order to count as accessible from *W*. Now there must be some explanation of why it is that *R* and *D* serve as the criterion of accessibility. That is to say, there must be some features of our practice of evaluating subjunctive conditionals that establish *R* as the relevant form of similarity and *D* as the appropriate degree. But if our practice has the resources to specify *R* and *D*, then it must also provide the means, at least implicitly, for specifying worlds that lie outside the sphere of similarity that is determined by R and D. That is to say, it will provide the means to formulate a proposition that holds only in worlds that lie outside this sphere. Now any proposition can be used as the antecedent of a subjunctive conditional, so it will be possible, at least in principle, to frame meaningful conditionals that are concerned with worlds that lie outside the sphere in question. It follows that worlds that lie outside the sphere must be relevant to the evaluation of conditionals with respect to W. That is, worlds outside the sphere must be accessible from W.

We may conclude, then, that Lewisian subjunctive necessity is identical with genuine metaphysical necessity. That is to say, metaphysical necessity is *reductively explained* by Lewis's explicit definition of $\square$.

It may be worth noting that there is another, possibly more intuitive way of defining metaphysical necessity. This alternative definition is suggested by Lewis's reading for his necessity operator—viz. *It would be the case, no matter what, that* .... This reading is appropriate because, as Lewis shows, if $\square A$ is true at a possible world W, then, where B is any proposition whatsoever, the subjunctive conditional $B > A$ is true at W as well.

Using substitutional quantification, we can recast Lewis's reading for the necessity operator as a definition:

$$\square A =_{\text{df}} (\Pi Q)(Q > A).$$

Here the quantifier (ΠQ) is the universal substitutional quantifier. The *definiens* explicitly states that A would be true no matter what else was true. (A proposition of the form $(\Pi Q)(\dots Q \dots)$ is true just in case every proposition that results from substituting a proposition for the variable Q in the matrix $(\dots Q \dots)$ is true. For a general discussion of substitutional quantification, see Hill 2002: ch. 2.)

As is well known, given any necessity operator N, it is possible to define a corresponding possibility operator in terms of N and negation. Applying this familiar principle to the case at hand, we arrive at the following definition:

$$\Diamond A =_{\text{df}} \sim \square \sim A.$$

Just as Lewis's necessity operator expresses genuine metaphysical necessity, so this possibility operator expresses genuine metaphysical possibility.[4]

---

[4] The account of metaphysical necessity that I give in this section is closely related to the account that is presented in Williamson 2004. Indeed, from a formal perspective, the two accounts are exactly the same—Williamson even employs a propositional quantifier in giving his definition of metaphysical necessity. (As I understand him, however, he prefers not to view the quantifier as substitutional.)

Still, there are significant differences between his overall approach and mine. The most important of these has to do with the arguments we use in justifying the claim that metaphysical necessity is definable in terms of the subjunctive conditional. Williamson tends to rely on arguments that make use of premises that are relatively weak. That is to say, his arguments make little use of

V

My thesis, then, is that metaphysical necessity and metaphysical possibility can be reductively explained in terms of the subjunctive conditional. I have already given an argument for this view. In the present section I will sketch an additional argument.

This second argument has two premises. (a) When we reflectively consider the familiar examples of metaphysical necessity, we find that they are always propositions that we are prepared to presuppose as valid in our subjunctive reasoning. (b) When we consider the propositions that we presuppose as valid across subjunctive reasoning, we find that we are always prepared to regard them as metaphysically necessary.

As we saw, the paradigmatic intuitions about metaphysical necessity are of two kinds: some represent AR-propositions as metaphysically necessary, and the others attribute this status to propositions that belong to categories (6)–(12). Reflection shows that we presuppose that propositions of these two kinds are valid when we engage in subjunctive reasoning. It may be useful to look at a couple of examples. Consider, first, the basic laws of arithmetic. It is clear that we allow ourselves to make free use of these principles in subjunctive contexts, applying them whenever it becomes necessary to deploy such operations as addition and multiplication in working out the consequences of a subjunctive assumption. Next, consider any proposition P that specifies the immediate biological antecedents of a given human being x. It is plausible that when a reasoner believes P, he or she will be disposed to presuppose P in subjunctive reasoning that is concerned with x. For example, we are disposed to presuppose the proposition that Mary Queen of Scots and Lord Darnley were the parents of James I in

substantive information about the features of metaphysical necessity that distinguish it from other forms of necessity, and little use of substantive information about the characteristic features of the subjunctive conditional. Thus, for example, he never invokes the fact that many metaphysically necessary propositions are a posteriori.

As I see it, if one is to justify the claim that metaphysical necessity is definable in terms of the subjunctive conditional, it is necessary to make broad contact in the justification with our intuitions about metaphysical necessity (or our intuitions about metaphysical possibility), and also with our intuitions about the truth values of subjunctives. There are various ways of fulfilling these requirements. In Sect. IV above, I rely on the claims (a) that the class of worlds that are relevant to the semantic evaluation of subjunctives includes worlds that are arbitrarily different from the actual world, and (b) that our intuitions about the possibility of antecedents are independent of our intuitions concerning similarity to the actual world. In other arguments (see Sect. V and n. 7), I try to show that specific intuitions about metaphysical possibility correspond to specific aspects of our practice of evaluating subjunctives.

If one tries to justify a reduction of metaphysical possibility to the subjunctive conditional without making broad contact with intuitive judgments, one runs the risk that at the end of the day, one will have shown only that it is possible to define *a* necessity operator in terms of the subjunctive conditional. It will remain open whether that operator expresses metaphysical necessity.

evaluating the counterfactual, *If Lord Darnley had not married Mary Queen of Scots, but rather one of her ladies in waiting, then James I would never have existed.*[5]

---

[5] There is an objection to the line of thought of this paragraph that should be discussed. It can be formulated as follows: 'You have maintained that when we regard a proposition as metaphysically necessary, we are disposed to presuppose the proposition as true whenever we engage in subjunctive reasoning. But it seems that there are counterexamples to this claim. Thus, while we regard the laws of mathematics as metaphysically necessary, we are prepared to entertain, and even to embrace, certain counterfactuals in which such laws are denied. For example, although we regard the axioms of Peano Arithmetic as necessary, we think that the following propositions are true:

(i) If Peano Arithmetic were false, the problem would lie with the induction schema.

(ii) If there were only a finite number of primes, then Peano Arithmetic would be false.

How can it be true that we presuppose necessary propositions as true throughout our reasoning if we are prepared to deny them in both the antecedents and the consequents of subjunctive conditionals?'

To meet this objection, I need to clarify the vague phrase 'presuppose that metaphysically necessary propositions are true whenever we engage in subjunctive reasoning.' When I claim that we presuppose the truth of a proposition A in subjunctive reasoning, I mean to claim only that we disposed to accept the proposition that (ΠQ) $(Q > A)$, and to make use of its instances freely in spinning out subjunctive scenarios. Thus, for example, to say that we presuppose the truth of Peano Arithmetic in our subjunctive reasoning is to say only that we are disposed to accept the claim that (ΠQ) $(Q >$ Peano Arithmetic is true), and to make use of its instances whenever they seem relevant to a subjunctive scenario. Accordingly, there is no tension between saying that we presuppose that Peano Arithmetic in subjunctive reasoning and recognizing that (i) and (ii) are true. The claim that (ΠQ) $(Q >$ Peano Arithmetic is true) is fully compatible with the truth of (i) and (ii).

To appreciate this last point, it is sufficient to recall the familiar doctrine that the semantical rules for subjunctives guarantee that a subjunctive conditional is true if its antecedent is impossible. Since both (i) and (ii) have impossible antecedents, their truth follows immediately from this semantical rule. In other words, the truth of (i) comes to the same thing as the truth of the proposition that it's impossible for Peano Arithmetic to be false, and the truth of (ii) comes to the same thing as the truth of the proposition that it's impossible for there to be a finite number of primes. It is easy to see that both of these propositions about impossibility are compatible with the claim that (ΠQ) $(Q >$ Peano Arithmetic is true). Thus, it is clear that the claim implies neither that it is possible for Peano Arithmetic to be false nor that it is possible for there to be a finite number of primes.

I believe that this is the right way to answer the foregoing objection. It must be acknowledged, however, that there is a problem with the doctrine that subjunctives with impossible antecedents are always true. Of course, there are plenty of cases that appear to conform to the claim. Thus, the following are highly assertable:

(i) If Peano Arithmetic were false, the problem would lie with the induction schema.

(iii) If James I had had different parents, he would have had different DNA.

But there are also many subjunctives with impossible antecedents that have extremely low degrees of assertability. Here are two examples:

(iv) If Peano Arithmetic were false, the problem would lie with the claim that zero is not the successor of any number.

(v) If James I had had different parents, he would have had gerbil DNA.

Since (iv) and (v) are not assertable, it can seem inappropriate to regard them as true. But if it is inappropriate to regard them as true, there are counterexamples to the claim that subjunctives with impossible antecedents are true. Moreover, since (iv) and (v) appear to show that it is possible for subjunctives with impossible antecedents to be false, it must be wrong to claim that (i) and (iii) are true *because* their antecedents are impossible.

Are there any propositions other than metaphysically necessary propositions that we presuppose as valid whenever we engage in subjunctive reasoning? There is no reason to think so. It might at first seem otherwise, for it is clear that we presuppose the laws of nature in most of our subjunctive reasoning. But we do not *always* presuppose the laws of nature. Thus, as we noticed a couple of paragraphs back, we are perfectly willing to entertain counterfactual suppositions that explicitly conflict with the laws. Suppositions of that sort show up quite frequently in philosophy of religion and in philosophically oriented cosmology. In view of this, it is clear the subjunctive theory does not imply that the laws of nature are metaphysically necessary. By the same token, it does not imply the view, which has recently been defended by Dorothy Edgington (2004), that metaphysical necessity comes to the same thing as natural necessity.

I have relied heavily in this argument on the idea of treating a proposition as valid in subjunctive reasoning. I will now add a few remarks about the assumptions that motivate my use of this idea.

As I see it, our subjunctive reasoning reflects commitments to a range of propositions that have the following form:

If P, then $(\Pi Q)\,(Q > P)$.

Here I am imagining that the values of 'P' are the propositions that we treat as valid in subjunctive reasoning, such as the proposition that George W. Bush is a human being, and the proposition that Mary Queen of Scots and Lord Darnley were the parents of James I. Further, I see these particular commitments as deriving from commitments to certain more general propositions such as (20)–(23):

It appears, then, that if I am to maintain that subjunctive conditionals with impossible antecedents are true, I must explain why (iv) and (v) have low degrees of assertability in a way that is compatible with the claim that they are true. I think this can be done. The reason for their low degree of assertability is that they are *trivially* true: their truth follows directly from a semantic rule that stipulatively assigns truth to all subjunctives with impossible antecedents. Because they owe their truth to an arbitrary stipulation, subjunctives with impossible antecedents can be true without providing any information about the world. Moreover, they can be true without exhibiting any interesting inferential relations; they can be true even if their antecedents are inferentially irrelevant to their consequents. But there would be no reason to assert a conditional that neither provides information about the world nor exhibits an interesting inferential relationship.

Why then are (i) and (iii) so highly assertable? After all, they too have impossible antecedents, so they too are trivially true. The answer, I think, is that there are chains of valid reasoning running from the antecedents of (i) and (iii) to their consequents. In general, when we assert a proposition of the form $(\sim A > Q)$, where A is necessary, we do so because we see its antecedent as potentially providing a reason, in the context of things that we currently believe, for believing its consequent. That is to say, we assert the proposition because we wish to implicate our belief in the following more complex subjunctive proposition: if there were a reason to believe that $\sim A$, then, partially in virtue of that reason and partially in virtue of other propositions that we believe, there would be a reason to believe that Q. In short, propositions of the sort in question are asserted because they are used to implicate claims about epistemic relations among propositions.

(20) ($\forall x$) ($\forall K$) (if x is an artifact and K is the artifactual kind to which x belongs, then (ΠQ) ($Q > x$ is an artifact that belongs to K)).

(21) ($\forall x$) ($\forall K$) (if x is a biological substance and K is the biological kind to which x belongs, then (ΠQ) ($Q > x$ is a biological substance that belongs to K)).

(22) ($\forall x$) ($\forall M$) (if x is an artifact and y is the set of material components of which x was composed at the time of its origin, then (ΠQ)($Q > x$ is an artifact and x was composed of the members of Q at the time of its origin)).

(23) ($\forall x$) ($\forall S$) (if x is a biological substance and S is the set of immediate progenitors of x, then (ΠQ) ($Q > x$ is a biological substance and S is the set of its immediate progenitors)).

Finally, I see propositions like (20)–(23) as a priori propositions that are partially constitutive of certain of the concepts that occur in them—and in particular, of the subjunctive conditional. (That is, they are components of an implicit definition of the subjunctive conditional. They may also help to define other concepts, such as the concept of an artifact, and the concept of a biological substance.) These views afford a natural explanation of what is going on when we presuppose the validity of a proposition in subjunctive reasoning. For example, we presuppose the validity of the proposition that George W. Bush is a human being because we believe that this proposition is true and we have a general commitment that is captured by principle (21). Equally, we presuppose the validity of the proposition that Mary Queen of Scots and Lord Darnley were the parents of James I because we believe that this proposition is true and we have a general commitment that is captured by principle (23).

The views that I am recommending here appear to be closely related to the ones that Kripke endorses in the following passage (Kripke 1971; in Kim and Sosa 1999: 81):

So we have to say that although we cannot know a priori whether this table was made of ice or not, given that it is not made of ice, it is *necessarily* not made of ice.

In other words, if P is the statement that the lectern is not made of ice, one knows by a priori philosophical analysis, some conditional of the form 'If P, then necessarily P.' If the table is not made of ice, it is necessarily not made of ice. On the other hand, then, we know by empirical investigation that P, the antecedent of the conditional, is true—that this table is not made of ice. We can conclude by *modus ponens*:

$$P \supset \Box P$$
$$P$$
$$- - - - - - -$$
$$\Box P$$

This passage is concerned with a specific proposition, the proposition that a certain lectern is not made of ice. It is natural to suppose, however, that Kripke wishes to draw a general moral. To be specific, he wishes to endorse the view that if *P* is *any* a posteriori proposition about a particular object that is metaphysically necessary, then the corresponding proposition of form (24):

(22) If *P*, then it is metaphysically necessary that *P*,

can be seen to be true by 'a priori philosophical analysis'. The corresponding view that I wish to recommend is that if *P* is any a posteriori proposition about a particular object that counts intuitively as metaphysically necessary, then the corresponding proposition of form (25):

(25) If *P*, then $(\Pi Q)\,(Q > P)$,

can be seen to be true a priori. To this I add that the relevant propositions of form (25) are definitional in character, following from more general principles that are partially constitutive of the subjunctive conditional (and perhaps of other concepts as well).[6] The advantage of this additional claim is of course that it provides a kind of explanation of the a priority of propositions of form (23).[7]

---

[6] In adopting the view that propositions of form (25) are definitional, I am taking a position that is very similar to one that is put forward in a brilliant book by Alan Sidelle (1989). Sidelle maintains that if *P* is an a posteriori proposition that is metaphysically necessary, then the corresponding proposition of form (24):

(24) If *P*, then it is metaphysically necessary that *P*,

is true by convention.

[7] In addition to the two arguments given in the text, there is also a third argument for the view that metaphysical necessity can be defined in terms of the subjunctive conditional. Roughly speaking, the main idea of the third argument is this: if we assume that the view is correct, we can *explain* the validity of some of the most characteristic laws of metaphysical necessity, including the principle that the origins of biological substances are metaphysically necessary, the principle that the origins of artifacts are metaphysically necessary, and the principle that the molecular composition of chemical kinds is metaphysically necessary.

It is possible to explain the validity of these principles because it is possible to show that, given the purposes that the subjunctive conditional is designed to serve, there is strong motivation for including principles like the following in an implicit definition of the subjunctive conditional:

(a) $(\forall x)\,(\forall S)$ (if *x* is a biological substance and *S* is the set of immediate progenitors of *x*, then $(\Pi Q)\,(Q > x$ is a biological substance and *S* is the set of its immediate progenitors)).

(b) $(\forall x)\,(\forall M)$ (if *x* is an artifact and *y* is the set of material components of which *x* was composed at the time of its origin, then $(\Pi Q)\,(Q > x$ is an artifact and *x* was composed of the members of *Y* at the time of its origin)).

(c) $(\forall K)\,(\forall T)$ (if *K* is a chemical kind and samples of *K* are composed of molecules of type *T*, then $(\Pi Q)\,(Q > K$ is a chemical kind and samples of *K* are composed of molecules of type *T*)).

That is to say, it is possible to explain the validity of the aforementioned principles of metaphysical necessity because, first, they are deducible from (a)–(c), given the definition of metaphysical necessity in terms of the subjunctive conditional, and second, it is possible to explain why we are committed to (a)–(c) in terms of the purposes or goals of subjunctive reasoning.

Here, for example, is a sketch of the grounds of our commitment to principle (a). (i) Since subjunctive reasoning is concerned with possible worlds other than the actual world, we need a principle that specifies the conditions under which substances existing in the actual world can be said to exist in other possible worlds. It follows that we need a principle like (a), for (a) in effect provides conditions of trans-world identity for the special case of biological substances. (ii) When we reason subjunctively about a particular substance *x*, we generally presuppose the actual origin

VI

It is time now to return to the epistemological issues concerning the metaphysical modalities.

When we considered these issues initially, back in Section II, we observed that there is good reason to accept the following propositions:

(26) To conceive coherently of something is to entertain a conceptual represent-
      ation that is compatible with the full range of AR-propositions (that is, with
      the full range of propositions that are a priori and epistemically foundation-
      al).

(27) Coherent conceiving is a reliable test for conceptual possibility, but not for
      metaphysical possibility.

(28) Coherent conceiving fails as a test for metaphysical possibility because
      compatibility with AR-propositions is not a sufficient condition of
      metaphysical possibility. To establish that a proposition is metaphysically
      possible by a compatibility test, it is necessary to show that the proposition

of x. (This is because, when we are engaged in subjunctive reasoning about x, we are generally concerned with possible worlds that share an initial segment with the actual world—an initial segment that includes the actual origin of x. That is to say, we are generally concerned with worlds that 'branch off' from the actual world at some point in time that comes after the actual origin of x. Our subjunctive reasoning about x is not always limited in this way. For example, we occasionally consider what might have happened to x if x had been born in a different place. But this is the norm.) Accordingly, in framing a principle of trans-world identity that governs x, we need to formulate a principle that respects x's actual origin. The principle need not require that all of the features of x's actual origin be preserved. And in fact, such a principle would not serve our purposes, given that we occasionally want to be able to consider scenarios in which x's origin is a bit different. But the principle should be based on *some* individuating features of x's actual origin. (iii) Where x is any biological substance, there are a number of features of the actual origin of x that are individuating, and that could therefore serve as the basis for a principle of trans-world identity that applies to x. Thus, for example, x's origin can be distinguished from the origins of all other substances by specifying its place and time and the sortal that x exemplifies. However, there is a strong reason for preferring principle (a) to a principle that is based on place of origin, time of origin, and sortal. Thus, when we reason subjunctively about x, we are generally concerned with certain of the causal powers of x—we want to know what would have happened if certain non-actual stimuli had activated certain of x's actual causal powers. It is clear that a principle of trans-world identity that is based on x's biological antecedents will respect more of x's causal powers than a principle that is based on the place and time of x's birth. (iv) Why not have a principle of trans-world identity that calls for preservation of x's biological antecedents *and* the place and time of x's birth? Wouldn't such a principle respect even more of x's causal powers than principle (a)? Yes, but at the cost of drastically reducing the scope of subjunctive reasoning about x. A principle of trans-world that applies to x must satisfy four constraints. First, the principle must be based on properties of x that are genuinely individuating, in the sense that for any possible world W, there is at most one object in W that has those properties. Second, the principle must in some way honor the actual origin of x. Third, the principle must respect the characteristic causal powers of x. And fourth, the principle must allow us to consider x in an extremely broad range of counterfactual circumstances. (When it comes to counterfactual reasoning about x, we are greedy. We want more of it rather than less.) Principle (a) does a better job of honoring all four of these constraints than any principle that requires both sameness of biological antecedents and sameness of place and time of origin.

is compatible with *all* of the propositions that are metaphysically necessary. AR-propositions are metaphysically necessary, but so are a number of a posteriori propositions, including the ones that belong to categories (6)–(12).

In addition to these findings from Section II, we also have the following observation from Section III:

(29) The compatibility test for metaphysical possibility at best offers us a secondary and derivative procedure for acquiring modal knowledge. This is because the test presupposes that we have an independent way of recognizing metaphysical necessity.

Insofar as they are concerned with knowledge of the metaphysical modalities, these observations are largely negative. We would like an account of a reliable, autonomous procedure for obtaining knowledge of metaphysical necessity or of metaphysical possibility. (26)–(29) fail to provide such an account. Instead, (27) tells us that a certain procedure is unreliable, and (29) tells us that another procedure is not autonomous.

Fortunately, our recent reflections about the metaphysical modalities make it possible to add some positive claims to (26)–(29). Thus, among other things, they suggest two tests for determining whether a proposition is metaphysically necessary.

The first test is based on the claim that the propositions that we presuppose as valid in subjunctive reasoning are the propositions that are metaphysically necessary. Suppose that we are concerned to determine whether the proposition that P is metaphysically necessary. The claim implies that we can proceed by reflecting on the role that P plays in subjunctive reasoning. Suppose that when we analyze that role, we find that we are prepared to use P in elaborating subjunctive suppositions whenever it is relevant to them, and that we never rely on propositions that are incompatible with P in elaborating subjunctive suppositions. In effect, we will have found that we presuppose that P is valid in subjunctive reasoning. Assuming that the foregoing claim about metaphysical necessity is correct, this result makes it reasonable to conclude that P is metaphysically necessary.

The second test is based on the following definition of metaphysical necessity:

$$\Box A =_{df} (\Pi Q)(Q > A).$$

Suppose we wish to determine whether the proposition that P is metaphysically necessary. The definition implies that we can proceed by considering a representative range of propositions that have the following form:

(30) $Q > P$.

We must evaluate these propositions semantically. There is no doubt that we can do this, for there is no doubt that we possess one or more cognitive mechanisms designed specifically to evaluate subjunctives. Suppose that when we deploy these mechanisms, we find that our representative propositions of form (30) are all true. This finding will give us good reason to suppose that $(\Pi Q)\,(Q > P)$ is true, and by the same token, good reason to suppose that P is metaphysically necessary.

To illustrate, suppose that we wish to determine whether the proposition that $2 \times 3 = 6$ is metaphysically necessary. According to the present proposal, we can proceed by considering questions like the following:

Would it still be true that $2 \times 3 = 6$ if the only existing objects were abstract entities?

Would it still be true that $2 \times 3 = 6$ if everything was in constant flux, with objects dissolving into new objects as soon as they were counted?

Would it still be true that $2 \times 3 = 6$ if it seemed to me, after careful counting, that I had obtained conflicting results when I counted pairs of shoes and counted individual shoes—if, for example, it seemed to me that I had counted three pairs of shoes but seven individuals?

We have cognitive mechanisms that enable us to work out answers to these questions, and also to all similar questions. Presumably all of the answers are the same—'yes'. Taken collectively, these answers provide us with a rationale for embracing the following generalization:

$$(\Pi Q)(Q > (2 \times 3 = 6)),$$

and this generalization in turn gives us a reason for concluding that the proposition that $2 \times 3 = 6$ is metaphysically necessary.

Thus far we have been focusing on the question of how metaphysically necessary propositions can be recognized as such. We have not considered whether our beliefs about metaphysical necessity amount to knowledge. We may believe that it is metaphysically necessary that $2 \times 3 = 6$, but is this something that we know? Can we be said to know that it is metaphysically necessary that Lord Darnley and Mary Queen of Scots were the parents of James I? As I see it, it is plausible that we do in fact know such things to be true. Thus, if the theory of the metaphysical modalities I have recommended is right, then claims of metaphysical necessity are equivalent to generalized subjunctive conditionals. It seems reasonable to suppose that it is possible to know such conditionals, for they are concerned principally with questions of large-scale similarity, and it seems reasonable to suppose that we can know the answers to such questions, at least in some cases. Moreover, as Judea Pearl has emphasized in recent work, subjunctive conditionals can be confirmed and disconfirmed by empirical evidence (Pearl 2000: ch. 7). For example, the counterfactual *If I hadn't given her the medicine, she wouldn't have recovered* gives rise to the (indicative) prediction that if I withhold medication in similar cases, the patients will not recover. Now it seems to be the case that the subjunctive conditionals that we accept tend to be confirmed by the evidence that is relevant to them. If this impression is correct, then it is reasonable to regard our procedures for evaluating subjunctive conditionals as reliable, and by the same token, it is reasonable to regard our subjunctive beliefs as knowledge.

We have taken note of two procedures for determining whether propositions are metaphysically necessary. We should now observe that each of these procedures gives rise to a method for determining whether propositions are metaphysically possible. Suppose we wish to know whether the proposition that P has the latter status. There are two ways to proceed. (a) We can try to determine whether $\sim P$ is metaphysically necessary by considering and analyzing the role that $\sim P$ plays in subjunctive reasoning. If we find that we presuppose $\sim P$ as valid in such reasoning, we should conclude that P is not metaphysically possible. On the other hand, if we find that we do not presuppose $\sim P$ as valid, we may conclude that P is metaphysically possible. Of course, whichever conclusion we draw, we will be relying on the following definition of metaphysical possibility:

$$\Diamond A =_{df} \sim \Box \sim A.$$

(b) Alternatively, we can try to determine whether $\sim P$ is metaphysically possible by considering whether this proposition:

$$(\Pi Q)(Q > \sim P)$$

is true. If it is true, we must conclude that P is not metaphysically possible. Otherwise we may draw the opposite conclusion. As in the first procedure, our conclusion will be based on the standard definition of metaphysical possibility.

There is also a third way of determining whether propositions are metaphysically possible. Thus, we can proceed by using either of the tests for metaphysical necessity to obtain a list of the metaphysically necessary propositions that are ostensibly relevant to P, and then running tests to determine whether P is compatible with the propositions on the list. Of course, this procedure is an extended version of the one that we first considered back in Section II. Unlike that earlier version, this one is autonomous, in that it incorporates a procedure for recognizing metaphysical necessity.

In addition, it seems that there is a fourth way of recognizing metaphysical possibility. Unlike the first three methods, this one is not based on a procedure for recognizing metaphysical necessity. Rather, it is based on a procedure for recognizing nomological possibility. In order to apply the method to the proposition that P, one begins by considering whether P is nomologically possible. If one finds that it is, one concludes that P is also metaphysically possible. Here one is exploiting the fact that nomological possibility entails metaphysical possibility. On the other hand, if one finds that P is not nomologically possible, one is unable to draw a negative conclusion about metaphysical possibility. A negative conclusion about nomological possibility does not support a negative conclusion about metaphysical possibility, because there is no entailment running from metaphysical possibility to nomological possibility.

To elaborate: It seems that we have the capacity to assess propositions like the following for truth and falsity:

(31) It is possible to park the car in that space.

(32) It is possible for me to walk on that roof without falling off.

(33) It is possible for Senator Kerry to win the debate.

(34) It is possible to make a decent omelet from this type of cheese.

(35) It is possible to divert the water from the road by putting a culvert right there.

It also seems that this capacity is extremely valuable—that it is necessary to assess propositions like (31)–(35) in order to make practical decisions and to work out plans for the future.

I will say that propositions like (31)–(35) are concerned with *thick* nomological possibility. The proposition that *P* is concerned with thick nomological possibility if it is compatible with the propositions that are metaphysically necessary, the propositions that count as laws of nature, and the propositions that describe the nomologically relevant properties of the objects that are mentioned in *P*. Thick nomological possibility thus contrasts with *thin* nomological possibility. The proposition that *P* is characterized by thin nomological possibility if it is compatible with the propositions that are metaphysically necessary and with the laws of nature. Philosophers have thus far tended to focus on thin nomological possibility in cataloguing forms of possibility and describing their relationships, but it seems that it is actually thick nomological possibility that commands our attention in everyday life.

The suggestion, then, is that we have cognitive mechanisms that enable us to recognize thick nomological possibility, and that it is possible to use these mechanisms to derive conclusions about metaphysical possibility. Unfortunately, while this procedure provides us with a positive test for metaphysical possibility, it does not give us a negative test. We cannot use it to establish negative claims about metaphysical possibility.[8]

---

[8] I feel that it is quite plausible that propositions (31)–(35) are concerned with the form of possibility that I have called thick nomological possibility, but there is an alternative way of interpreting them that should be mentioned. On this alternative construal, (31)–(35) are equivalent to the following 'might' conditionals:

(31) If I were to try to park the car in that space, I might succeed.

(32) If I were to try to walk on that roof, I might not fall off.

(33) If Senator Kerry were to participate in the debate, he might win.

(34) If I were to use cheese of that sort to make an omelet, the result might be decent.

(35) If I were to put a culvert right there, it might divert the water from the road.

On this alternative construal of (31)–(35), what I say in the text about our having a capacity to recognize thick nomological possibility should be revised. It should be described instead as a capacity for assessing 'might' conditionals for truth and falsity. However, it would not be necessary to revise my claim that there is a fourth way of recognizing metaphysical possibility. Thus, given the theory of metaphysical possibility that is presented in Sect. V, and given also the semantic principles that appear to govern 'might' conditionals, 'might' conditionals like (31′)–(35′) entail the corresponding claims about metaphysical possibility. (For discussion of the semantics of 'might' conditionals, see Bennett 2003: 189–93.)

VII

I have tried to show that the classic writings about the metaphysical modalities are sustained by a well-motivated theory. This theory explains the concepts of metaphysical necessity and metaphysical possibility in terms of the subjunctive conditional, thereby establishing that they are deeply grounded in commonsense metaphysics, and also that they are unified and coherent. Moreover, since subjunctive reasoning is of fundamental importance to human thought and conduct, playing a large role in such essential activities as planning, decision-making, and causal analysis, the theory sustains (and explains) our intuitive sense that the metaphysical modalities deserve to play a foundational role in philosophy.

The theory also supports an account of modal knowledge. If it is correct, then there are a couple of valid procedures for recognizing metaphysical necessity, and several valid procedures for recognizing metaphysical possibility. Moreover, reflection suggests that if the theory is correct, then our beliefs about metaphysical necessity and metaphysical possibility can count as knowledge. Subjunctive conditionals can be confirmed and disconfirmed by empirical evidence. When we consider our subjunctive beliefs in relation to the relevant evidence, we find that there is reason to suppose that the cognitive mechanisms that are responsible for the beliefs are reliable.

Our conclusions about the metaphysical modalities and modal knowledge provide support for the objections to the modal argument for property dualism that I stated in Section II. Moreover, they suggest an explanation for the prima facie plausibility of the argument. We have distinguished between two forms of possibility—conceptual possibility and metaphysical possibility. Moreover, we have found that this distinction is sustained by a well-motivated theory. It appears, however, that it requires philosophical reflection to appreciate the distinction. Indeed, it was not till the discussions of Kripke and Putnam in the 1970s that philosophers began to pry conceptual possibility and metaphysical possibility apart. What I wish to suggest now is that the plausibility of the modal argument is due, at least in part, to a tendency to confuse or conflate these two forms of possibility. As we saw earlier, some of the premises of the modal argument come out true when we construe them as concerned with conceptual possibility, and others come out true when we construe them as concerned with metaphysical possibility. But neither interpretation sustains all of the premises. Why, then, has it *seemed* to many philosophers that there is a single interpretation on which all of the premises are true? I suggest that this impression is due to the fact that we find it difficult to distinguish between the two forms of possibility. It seems that there is a single interpretation that sustains all of the premises because it seems that there is a single form of possibility.

REFERENCES

BENNETT, JONATHAN (2003) *A Philosophical Guide to Conditionals* (Oxford: Oxford University Press).

CHALMERS, DAVID J. (1996) *The Conscious Mind* (Oxford: Oxford University Press).

EDGINGTON, DOROTHY (2004) 'Two Kinds of Possibility', *Proceedings of the Aristotelian Society*, suppl. vol. 78, 1–22.

HILL, CHRISTOPHER S. (1981) 'Why Cartesian Intuitions are Compatible with the Identity Thesis', *Philosophy and Phenomenological Research*, 42, 255–65.

——— (1991) *Sensations: A Defense of Type Materialism* (Cambridge: Cambridge University Press).

——— (1997) 'Imaginability, Conceivability, Possibility, and the Mind–Body Problem', *Philosophical Studies*, 87, 61–85.

——— (2002) *Thought and World: An Austere Portrayal of Truth, Reference, and Semantic Correspondence* (Cambridge: Cambridge University Press).

——— (2005) 'Ow! The Paradox of Pain', in Murat Aydede (ed.), *Pain: New Essays on Its Nature and the Methodology of Its Study* (Cambridge, Mass.: MIT Press), 75–98.

KIM, JAEGWON, and SOSA, ERNEST (eds.) (1999) *Metaphysics: An Anthology* (Oxford: Blackwell).

KRIPKE, SAUL (1971) 'Identity and Necessity', in Milton K. Munitz (ed.), *Identity and Individuation* (New York: New York University Press), 135–64; repr. in Kim and Sosa 1999.

——— (1972) 'Naming and Necessity', in Donald Davidson and Gilbert Harman (eds.), *Semantics of Natural Languages* (Dordrecht: Reidel), 253–355.

LEWIS, DAVID K. (1973) *Counterfactuals* (Oxford: Blackwell).

——— (1986*a*) 'Counterfactuals and Comparative Possibility', in his *Philosophical Papers*, i (New York: Oxford University Press), 3–31.

——— (1986*b*) 'Counterfactual Dependence and Time's Arrow', in his *Philosophical Papers*, i (New York: Oxford University Press), 32–66.

PEARL, JUDEA (2000) *Causality: Models, Reasoning, and Inference* (Cambridge: Cambridge University Press).

PUTNAM, HILARY (1975) 'The Meaning of "Meaning"', in his *Mind, Language, and Reality* (Cambridge: Cambridge University Press), 215–71.

SIDELLE, ALAN (1989) *Necessity, Essence, and Individuation: A Defense of Conventionalism* (Ithaca, NY: Cornell University Press).

STALNAKER, ROBERT (1968) 'A Theory of Conditionals', *American Philosophical Quarterly Monographs*, 2, 98–112.

WILLIAMSON, TIMOTHY (2004) 'Armchair Philosophy, Metaphysical Modality, and Counterfactual Thinking', *Proceedings of the Aristotelian Society*, 105, 1–23.

12

Imaginative Blocks and Impossibility: An Essay in Modal Psychology

Shaun Nichols

1. THREE QUESTIONS

The big philosophical questions about modality are metaphysical and epistemic: What are the truth-makers for our modal judgments? What justifies our modal judgments? These two questions are notoriously problematic.[1] What fact could make it true that *blue swans are possible*? And, assuming there is such a fact, what justifies our belief in that fact? Few philosophers think that there are easy answers here (see e.g. Gendler and Hawthorne 2002). Indeed, one might regard modal realism—the view that there exist infinitely many possible worlds (Lewis 1986)—as revealing the depth of philosophical desperation over modality.

Here I want to pursue the issue from a different direction. In addition to metaphysical and epistemic questions about modality, there is another question, which is sometimes treated as a shameful relative of the others: What is involved, psychologically, in making modal judgments? That is, in addition to modal metaphysics and modal epistemology, one might study modal *psychology*. This seems a promising avenue. For if we can characterize the psychology underlying modal judgment, then we will have a fixed point from which to explore the harder questions concerning modality. Furthermore, determining the psychological source of modal intuitions might help us determine to what extent we should trust the intuitions (see e.g. Hill 1997).[2] Here, then, is the guiding question of this essay: What is the best account of the cognitive underpinnings of modal judgment?

This chapter has benefited from discussion and comments from Steve Downes, Joe Heser, Aaron Meskin, Lije Millgram, Lex Newman, Dustin Stokes, Barry Ward, Jonathan Weinberg, and an anonymous referee for Oxford University Press. I'm especially grateful to Stacie Friend for several helpful suggestions.

[1] It's even problematic to state them as I have. For it might turn out that our modal judgments are uniformly false and unjustified.

[2] Some philosophers take their modal intuitions to be very strong evidence indeed of the modal facts. Kripke writes: 'If someone thinks that the notion of a necessary or contingent property... is a philosopher's notion with no intuitive content, he is wrong. Of course, some philosophers think that something's having intuitive content is very inconclusive evidence in favor of it. I think it is very

The approach taken here will be unapologetically naturalistic. The project of naturalistic modal psychology is nicely set by Blackburn, who maintains that the naturalist's charge is 'to explain the way in which we make modal judgments—the ease with which we noncollusively agree upon them' (1993: 62).[3] I will draw on modal judgment in children and on recent work on the imagination to sketch an account of modal psychology. I won't try to give a complete account of our modal psychology; rather, the primary focus will be on the relation between imagination and modal judgment. Unlike other treatments of modal judgment, however, the project here will not take as a primary constraint the modal intuitions of philosophers (cf. Yablo 1993). For the goal is to get an account of normal modal judgment that emerges in the absence of the potentially indoctrinating effects of philosophical training. Since the naturalistic investigation of modal judgment is almost entirely unexplored, at many junctures, I'll just be making my best guess. But we can start on fairly common ground by looking to philosophical remarks on the role of imagination in modal judgment.

2. MODAL PSYCHOLOGY AND IMAGINATION

Contemporary work on modality boasts an impressive diversity of proposals. According to Lewisian realism, there exists a set of possible worlds that grounds the truth of (true) modal claims. 'It is impossible that p' is true iff p is true at none of the possible worlds (Lewis 1986). Modal fictionalism can be viewed as parasitic on this: 'It is impossible that p' is true iff, according to the fiction of possible worlds, p is true at no possible world (Rosen 1990). Modal primitivism maintains that modal truths reflect fundamental irreducible features of the world. For instance, on one version of this view, the intuition that kangaroos might have had no tails reflects an irreducible modal property of kangaroos (Shalkowski 1996). And expressivists (e.g. Blackburn 1993) maintain that to say that it is impossible that p is true is to express a certain attitude that arises from the fact that when we try to imagine that p, we fail.

Despite this diversity in views, there is wide agreement about one aspect of modal psychology—that modal judgment depends crucially on the imagination.[4] We find this view expressed by modal primitivists (Shalkowski

heavy evidence in favor of anything, myself. I really don't know, in a way, what more conclusive evidence one can have about anything, ultimately speaking' (Kripke 1980: 42).

[3] Ultimately, Blackburn doubts that we can meet the naturalistic charge he sets. I think his pessimism unfounded for reasons set out in Sect. 6.

[4] The term 'conceive' is often used instead of 'imagine' here. But in the recent literature, some philosophers try to explicate 'conceivability' in a way that will maximize the likelihood that conceivability will be a good guide to possibility (e.g. Chalmers 2002; Yablo 1993). I do not want to prejudge issues about the epistemic propriety of forming modal beliefs from imaginative activities, so I will avoid using the term 'conceive'. But in any case, on standard accounts (e.g. Yablo 1993), propositional imagining is at the core of conceiving.

1996: 382), modal realists (e.g. Lewis 1986: 113–14), modal fictionalists (e.g. Rosen 1990: 340), and modal expressivists (Blackburn 1993; Craig 1985). Thus Scott Shalkowski writes: 'Certainly, conceivability, broadly construed, plays an important role in forming modal judgements. It is hard to see how we could get started on the modal enterprise without it' (Shalkowski 1996: 282). And Gideon Rosen notes that the modal realist is committed to the following:

(i) the modal truths are truths about a domain of universes; (ii) the principles which guide our imagination are true of that domain; so (iii) by and large, when we imagine in accordance with these principles the states of affairs we imagine are realized somewhere among the universes. (Rosen 1990: 340)

Like the modal realist, the fictionalist also adverts to imaginative tendencies. It is not our business here to judge between expressivism, primitivism, Lewisian realism, and fictionalism. What matters is that all of these accounts agree that imagination is essential to the psychology of modal judgment.

Although imagination is crucial for modal judgment, few philosophers would maintain that we can reduce modal concepts to imaginative tendencies. It's implausible, for instance, that 'impossible' should be identified with 'unimaginable'. We can recognize past cases in which people could not imagine that *p* despite the fact that *p* was true. Quantum mechanics provides a vivid example. Some people still maintain that they can't imagine how quantum mechanics could be true, but few of these would claim that this means that it's impossible that quantum mechanics is true. Similarly, we sometimes imagine propositions that we regard as impossible—I can imagine that arithmetic is complete, though I don't believe it's possible.[5] Thus, despite the widespread agreement that imagination plays a vital role in generating modal judgments, there is also fairly widespread agreement that modal judgments aren't equivalent to imaginative tendencies. I embrace this orthodoxy as well, and the proposal I'll ultimately promote maintains that modal judgments are delivered by imaginative activities, but not that they *reduce* to imaginative activities.

There is a further, familiar worry about the connection between imagination and modal judgment: why should we trust the move from imagination to modal judgment *at all*? What is the justification for moving from imaginative dispositions to modal beliefs? Since we are aiming for a naturalistic modal psychology

---

[5] Among contemporary philosophers, modal expressivists come the closest to identifying modal judgments with imaginative tendencies (e.g. Blackburn 1993; Craig 1985). But even expressivists recognize cases in which imaginative tendencies do not (and should not) track modal commitments (Blackburn 1993: 69; Craig 1985: 106). A typical expressivist treatment of this difficulty posits two separable steps in modal judgment: (i) the imaginative tendency (e.g. the inability to imagine that *p*) and (ii) the subsequent modal projection (e.g. holding that it's impossible that *p*) (e.g. Craig 1985: 106–7). A variety of factors might interrupt the transition from imaginative tendency to modal projection. For instance, we might come to see our inability to imagine that *p* as a product of our ignorance. In that case, we might be reluctant to project an impossibility onto the world.

here, we will pursue a less intimidating question: regardless of whether it's rationally appropriate, why are we inclined to move from imaginative dispositions to
modal beliefs? To explore this, the best strategy is to consider modal judgment in
a more ecologically plausible setting than philosophy departments.

3. MODAL JUDGMENT IN THE WILD

The previous section provides philosophical credentials for the view that imagination plays a vital role in generating modal judgments. In order to discuss the role
of the imagination in modal judgment, it will be important to have some picture
of the nature of modal concepts. As a preliminary, I should stress that I am not
going to suggest anything like definitions for modal concepts. Rather, the goal is
to consider the function of incipient modal concepts. This might then help us
understand why there is a connection between imagination and modal judgment.

Why do we have modal concepts? Although this is an interesting and perfectly
sensible naturalistic question, there is surprisingly little discussion of it in either
philosophy or psychology. People obviously do have modal concepts, even if they
are not quite the modal concepts that philosophers deploy. Indeed, as we will
see shortly, even three-year-old children apparently have modal concepts. Why
would we have such things? What function could they possibly serve? I will maintain that they function to enhance our abilities to make good decisions. The trick
is to say how modal concepts enhance decision-making. For it's not obvious (to
say the least) that *might* and *must* correspond to properties of the world that affect
us directly. So how do such concepts help decision-making?

To get a purchase on this, I want to turn to the early uses of modals by children. There is some extant research on modal judgment in older children. Daniel
Osherson (1976) finds that high school students evaluate modal arguments in
ways that conform with a portion of standard modal logic. This result is significant insofar as it shows that at least part of modal logic is not merely an
invention of philosophers.[6] But for present purposes, a more ethologically sensitive approach is preferable. To get a handle on the function of modal concepts,
it's best to look at how they're actually deployed in the wild. All the examples I
use here are genuine examples of spontaneous language use by children or parents drawn from the CHILDES (Children's Language Data Exchange System)
database for child language research (MacWhinney and Snow 1990).[7]

---

[6] The portion of modal logic Osherson investigates includes the modal negation rules, the modal
distribution rules, and the existence rules (if *p* is necessary, it is so; if *p* is so, it is possible). Osherson
did not include the strict implication rules; nor were any of the iteration rules tested. For what it's
worth, my guess is that people untrained in modal logic (or possible worlds semantics) will not
make judgments that conform to the S5 rules 'From $\Diamond\Box\alpha$ derive $\Box\alpha$' or 'From $\Diamond\alpha$ derive $\Box\Diamond\alpha$'.

[7] The CHILDES database is a collection of transcripts from everyday verbal behavior of several
children and their families. The database was initially established to study children's language,

This will come as no surprise, but in the CHILDES database children and parents rarely express judgments of absolute possibility and impossibility.[8] Rather, the modal talk of children and parents tends to focus on *risks* and *opportunities*. Here are some examples in which modals are used to represent *risk*.

Ross (2;7): Marky [a younger sibling] might fall. (MacWhinney and Snow 1990)

Adam (3): Do you want me stand up slippery bathtub?
Mother: No.
Adam: Why not.
Mother: Because you might fall and hurt yourself. (Brown 1973)

Father: I want to look at your new hat.
Abe (3;8): It's made out of paper; it could rip easily. (Kuczaj and Maratsos 1975)

Father: . . . I guess you can't play football then.
Abe (3;9): I can too I can too I can too.
Father: Would it help you if we got a helmet?
Abe: Yeah.
Father: How would it help?
Abe: It would hit the helmet instead of me.
Father: And what would happen then?
Abe: I'd not be hurt except it could still land on my nose. (Kuczaj and Maratsos 1975)

Father: You could fall and get hurt Ross.
Ross (4;2): No. Not if I hold on to here and here I won't.
Father: You could . . ... It's dangerous. (MacWhinney and Snow 1990)

Adam (4;2): Paul [a younger sibling], you might cut yourself on this. (Brown 1973)

Here are some examples of children deploying modals to represent *opportunities*:

Alison (2;4): We could march around or we could run around. (Bloom 1973)

Ross (3;3): Hi Titus [a cat]. I got her tail.
Father: You did.
Ross: She's under there. I could get her.
Father: Okay but don't be too mean to her okay? (MacWhinney and Snow 1990)

---

but it has been an invaluable resource for studying a number of features of child psychology (see e.g. Bartsch and Wellman 1995).

[8] It's not that children are incapable of making judgments about absolute possibility and impossibility. If asked, children will say that it's not possible for something to be red but not take up any space. My seven-year-old daughter explained to me that only *things* can be red, and things have to take up space.

Father: I can't make that one work.

Abe (3;7): You could glue it. (Kuczaj and Maratsos 1975)

Adam (4;1): We could put the animals in here. (Brown 1973)

Children use modals in other ways too, of course. Here are a couple:

Mother: We'll have to teach you some card games.
Nathan (3;9): We have cards?
Mother: Mmhm.
Nathan: Where?
Mother: I don't know.
Nathan: [They] could've got lost. (Sachs 1983)

Father: Was I bossy to [mommy] today?
Ross (3;8): You couldn't be 'cause you were at work. (MacWhinney and Snow 1990)

It's noteworthy that the children's modal claims probably can't typically be given a deflationary kind of epistemic interpretation. For instance, it's unlikely that when two-year-old Ross says 'Marky might fall', what he really means is '*for all I know* Marky will fall'.[9] When we turn to the use of modals for opportunities and past events, it's even less plausible to interpret children as only deploying deflationary epistemic modal notions. Children often point out that some future opportunity is available (e.g. 'You could glue it'), and they say that something that didn't happen *could have happened* (e.g. 'We could have broken the lamp'). It seems clearly unworkable to reduce these judgments to judgments of epistemic possibility.

Thus, well before they begin kindergarten, children seem to deploy non-epistemic modal notions. Given the typical use of modals in children and parents to represent risk and opportunity, I make the bold conjecture that a primary function of modal concepts is to enable the representation of risk and opportunity. Obviously, accurately assessing risks and opportunities would be a big help to decision-making.[10] So this gives us some purchase on the function of incipient modal judgment. Perhaps there are no modal properties in the world. But modal concepts enable the representation of risks and opportunities, and obviously if those representations turn out to be good predictors of risk and opportunity, that would come in rather handy.

---

[9] In addition, it's implausible that fictionalism accurately describes the psychological character of such early modal judgment. Surely Ross is not thinking, 'According to the fiction of possible worlds, there is a world in which Marky falls.'

[10] For ease of exposition, I advert to risks and opportunities as non-epistemic possibilities that can be accurately or inaccurately represented. However, this can be reframed in a less metaphysically controversial fashion simply by casting it in terms of accurate representations of *epistemic* possibilities. Accurately assessing epistemic possibilities would still be a boon for decision-making, even if one (mistakenly) thinks of them as something other than epistemic possibilities.

4. IMAGINATION AND EARLY MODAL JUDGMENT

If this is the right story about the function of early modal concepts, does this give us any way to address issues about the relationship between imagination and modality? Does the imagination play a role in generating early modal judgments about risk and opportunity? Presumably. To begin with, it's plausible that one of the primary functions of the imagination is to carry out hypothetical reasoning (Nichols and Stich 2003). We know independently that young children are competent with simple hypothetical and even counterfactual reasoning (Harris et al. 1996; German and Nichols 2003). We use this facility to determine best which outcomes follow from which antecedents: if the branch breaks, I will fall. In addition, it's likely that, at least sometimes, it is because the child can't imagine that *p* (given her standing beliefs) that she comes to think that there is no risk that *p*. The child can use this imaginative capacity to determine which outcomes are consistent and which inconsistent with her standing beliefs. If she is utterly unable to imagine some outcome, given her standing beliefs, then she comes to think that that outcome is impossible. One reason to think that such a process occurs is that if you ask a child whether something is possible—say, whether a hornet can get into the car—he will often proceed to imagine several different ways this might happen. The child imagines a hornet getting in through an open door or an open window or a broken windshield or an open vent. As these options are closed off by stipulation ('the doors, windows, and vents are all closed and unbroken'), the child will often come to think that, with those stipulations in place, it is impossible for the hornet to get into the car. That is, when all the ways of the hornet getting in that the child can imagine are foreclosed, the child can't imagine the hornet getting in and, as a result, judges that the hornet can't get in.

So, although it's been underexplored, it seems plausible that children form modal judgments from their imaginative activities. I've kept quiet about one important element here, though. In typical cases of imagination-driven modal judgment, among our important standing beliefs are standing *modal* beliefs. It's independently clear that not all of an individual's modal beliefs come from his own imaginative exercises. Some will come simply from testimony. We tell our children that fish can't breathe when they're out of water. Most children acquire this belief through testimony without seeking confirmation by pulling a guppy out of the aquarium to watch it suffocate. Some modal beliefs might also have an innate basis. For instance, one interpretation of recent infancy work is that infants have tacit knowledge that an object *can't* pop in and out of existence, vanish, or move through another solid object (e.g. Spelke et al. 1995). These standing modal beliefs often figure in the imaginative exercises that lead to further modal beliefs. In particular, the standing nomological modal beliefs constrain what we can imagine. Given the things that I already believe—e.g. that fish can't breathe out of water—I can't imagine the shark getting to me on the beach. From this, I form the belief that it's impossible for the shark to bite me up here on the beach. By contrast, given the things I already believe, I can easily imagine the hornet stinging me on the beach. From this, I form the belief that it's possible that the hornet sting me. This might cast some light on why modal judgments get delivered by the imagination. We use the imagination to determine which outcomes are consistent and which inconsistent with our other beliefs (including our standing modal beliefs).

How does this transition from imaginative activities to modal judgment work? One possibility is that people consciously exploit an explicit rule of the form 'if I can't imagine that p, then p is impossible'. But this seems excessively intellectualized. A more plausible alternative is that there's a basic causal connection between certain kinds of imaginative failures (or successes) and modal judgment. Our minds are wired such that certain sorts of imaginative failures issue in judgments of impossibility. That is, the link between imagination and modal judgment is an implicit feature of the system, perhaps installed by evolutionary processes or perhaps acquired through some very early learning process.[11]

As we saw earlier, modal philosophers reject the identification of imaginative tendencies and modal judgment. The modal psychologist should follow suit. I've suggested that we are naturally inclined to move from imaginative activities to modal judgment, but the imagination does not force us into unrevisable modal beliefs. For example, even if Joe can't imagine a mosquito bite causing serious illness, he might believe that it's possible because a reliable source has assured him that it is.

Now, has this procedure of using the imagination to gauge risk and opportunity been successful? Although it's hard to find experimental evidence on the issue, it's plausible that the procedure has conferred significant benefits on decision-making. Typically, when a person finds it easy to imagine that he will be hit by a car if he stays where he is, it has served the person well to believe that he is at risk. And typically, when the person cannot imagine that he will be hit by a car in his present location, it has served him well not to worry about being hit by a car.[12]

---

[11] One important feature of the above account is that the postulated connection is causal, not constitutive. That is, I don't want to claim that modal judgments are constituted by imaginative activities, only that they are (sometimes) caused by imaginative activities. But there are numerous open questions about which kinds of imaginative failures generate modal judgments and about the nature of the connection between imaginative failures and modal belief. One possibility is that whenever an agent can't imagine that p, he immediately forms a belief that it is impossible that p; this belief can then be overthrown in light of further consideration. Another possibility is that when an agent can't imagine that p, this activates a higher credence level for the proposition that it is impossible that p, but countervailing activations might prevent the agent from actually forming the belief that it is impossible that p.

[12] Interestingly, when adults imagine how some bad outcome might have turned out differently, they typically focus on some feature of the situation over which *they* had control. For instance, when people injured in accidents imagine ways in which the accident might not have happened, they

Although the evidence is again thin, there is some reason to think that a systematic use of the imagination to assess risk has been a boon in industry. It is now common in industry to use a sequenced form of risk analysis (Failure Modes and Effects Analysis (FMEA)) that attempts first to determine the potential failures of the product and the potential effects of the failure. This involves imagining various scenarios given standing beliefs about the product and the regularities. A number of companies, most prominently General Electric, maintain that adopting FMEA (as part of an overall process known as Six Sigma) dramatically increased their bottom line (see e.g. Slater 1998). The apparent success of FMEA speaks to the effectiveness of using the imagination to assess risks.[13]

Thus, we have one viable explanation for why it would benefit us to be inclined to move from imaginative activities to modal beliefs. When we couldn't imagine that p (given our standing beliefs), typically p didn't happen, and so p wasn't worth worrying about. However, when we could easily imagine that p, then p often did happen, and it was worth worrying about it. Presumably the success of this way of assessing risks depends on having standing beliefs that roughly reflect the regularities of the world. If the future stops resembling the past, our imagination will be rather less helpful at assessing risks.[14]

5. IMAGINATIVE BLOCKS

In the wild, our modal judgments are typically nomological. And the imagination plausibly plays an important role in delivering these nomological modal judgments. When we are engaged in such imaginative exercises, we take standing nomological beliefs as a starting point. Philosophers of modality are typically concerned with judgments about *absolute*, or unqualified, modalities. Here, of course, the situation is very different. For when we use the imagination to reach absolute modal judgments, we set aside our standing nomological beliefs. But even with these beliefs set aside, we still find ourselves forming modal beliefs from imaginative activities.

In the previous section, I suggested that there is an implicit psychological connection between certain imaginative activities and modal judgment. It's most implausible that this connection exists primarily in order to enable transitions

show a pronounced tendency to imagine scenarios in which they acted differently. One plausible explanation of this is that counterfactual thinking enhances the ability to prevent bad outcomes in the future, and people sensibly focus on features that are under their control (see Byrne 2005: ch. 5).

[13] One salient feature of this kind of risk analysis is that the people conducting these imaginative exercises are very well informed about the domain. Their imaginative exercises are not merely flights of unconstrained speculation. Something similar is likely true when people engage in risk assessment of ecologically familiar domains.

[14] The same consideration applies to hypothetical reasoning, of course—hypothetical reasoning will be less successful if the future stops resembling the past. And hypothetical reasoning is plausibly one of the primary functions of the imagination (Nichols and Stich 2003).

from imaginative activities to *absolute* modal judgments. Rather, the connection between imagination and modal judgment presumably earned its keep by facilitating *nomological* modal judgments. Nonetheless, it is plausible that we exercise this same connection when we form judgments about absolute modality from imaginative activities.[15] When we use the imagination to reach judgments about nomological impossibility, our standing nomological beliefs put constraints on what we can imagine. But when we set aside these nomological beliefs, we still find limitations on what we can imagine. And those more basic limitations can still give rise to modal judgments.

Absolute modal judgments are generated by imaginative limitations that persist even when we set aside our standing nomological beliefs. But we're not interested in any such case of an imaginative failure. Sometimes I can't imagine some scenario because I'm too tired or too distracted. We are interested in something more fundamental. Sometimes our inability to imagine something reflects a basic imaginative limitation. The canonical example is our inability to imagine a counter-arithmetical claim like $1 + 1 = 3$ (e.g. Craig 1975, 1985; Blackburn 1993). Since we're taking a cognitive approach here, we can rely on the competence/performance distinction to characterize this. When a person cannot imagine a scenario because he is fatigued or distracted, this counts as a performance error for our purposes. There are deeper limitations, though, that reflect our imaginative competency. For example, even when we are alert, attentive, fully informed, etc., the claim that $1 + 1 = 3$ taxes our very imaginative competency. Those are the limitations that we will focus on. Following Blackburn, let's call these 'imaginative blocks'.[16]

The imaginative blocks lead to judgments of absolute impossibility. Just as the fact that I can't imagine a shark getting to me on the beach leads me to think that it's impossible for a shark to get me there, analogously the fact that I can't imagine that $1 + 1 = 3$ leads me to think that it's impossible that $1 + 1 = 3$. Further, as with nomological judgments, the connection between imaginative activities and absolute modal judgment is defeasible; for instance, testimony from a trusted source can lead me to believe that something is possible despite my inability to imagine it. However, there is a crucial difference between nomological and absolute modal judgments. In the case of nomological modal judgment, the judgment typically depends on standing beliefs about the laws and the world. For judgments of absolute impossibility, we deliberately set aside those beliefs, yet

---

[15] Presumably it's important to our capacity to form nomological judgments from imaginative activities that the capacity be sufficiently flexible that diverse nomological beliefs can guide our imaginative activities. Thus, it makes sense that the connection between imagination and modal judgment would not be tied to a particular set of nomological beliefs.

[16] In her work on imaginative resistance, Gendler makes a compelling case that sometimes we resist imagining certain things (e.g. that the members of some minority group are naturally lazy and stupid) because we don't *want* to imagine those things (2000 and Ch. 9). On the taxonomy urged above, this too would be a performance limitation.

we still arrive at modal judgments. What we don't find is that if we suspend all beliefs about laws and the world, our imagination is completely unconstrained and our modal intuitions disappear. On the contrary, our imagination is still regimented, and modal intuitions still flow from the regimentation. This presents the modal psychologist with an obvious task—to explain why we have the imaginative blocks we do. I think there is a perfectly good naturalistic explanation that emerges from recent work on the cognitive architecture of the imagination. But before giving the explanation, I want to address one source of pessimism about the naturalistic project.

6. ANTI-NATURALISM

To give a naturalistic account of modal psychology, we need to explain why we have the imaginative blocks that we do. Ultimately, Blackburn doubts that we can meet the naturalistic charge. And it is precisely in explaining how our imagination is constrained that Blackburn thinks we will fall short. He thinks we will never be able to explain the imaginative blocks we have (Blackburn 1993: 71–4). On Blackburn's view, the attempt to explain our imaginative blocks will reach a dead-end because if we see our inclination to rule out *p* as the 'outcome of a contingent limitation', then 'we are already making something of the thought that *p* might be true' (p. 71). What is it to 'make something of a thought'? Blackburn says that to make something of a thought includes 'being able to explain how such a way of thought might arise, knowing how it might be rectified, understanding the practices of those whose thought it is, and so on' (p. 66). Thus, Blackburn seems to think that if we were to explain how the imaginative block against the proposition $1 + 1 = 3$ arises, we would accordingly be 'making something of' the thought that $1 + 1 = 3$ might be true; but if we make something of the thought that $1 + 1 = 3$ might be true, then we can't regard it as impossible.

Blackburn surrenders too quickly here. *Pace* Blackburn, a naturalist might be able to explain why we have an imaginative block against the proposition $1 + 1 = 3$ without being able to make anything out of thought that $1 + 1 = 3$ might be true. To see this, consider cognitive boundedness in other species. Chimpanzees can't make anything out of the proposition that the set of real numbers is finite. But obviously a cognitive ethologist can perfectly well make this observation about chimpanzee cognition without having to 'make something of the thought' that the set of reals might be finite. Now our situation is, granted, rather different, because the psychological facts are interestingly different. The chimp lacks the cognitive equipment to make out whether there are finitely or infinitely many reals; in our case, we can't make anything out of $1 + 1 = 3$ because of an imaginative block. But there's a crucial methodological similarity. When we study the chimp, we just note the way his psychology works. We don't have to worry about other ways that it might have worked to track other things (we know not what). Well, when we do the parallel naturalistic project on humans, we're the apes under investigation, and we should try, as far as possible, to achieve a similar distance. In particular, in pursuing a naturalistic explanation of the imaginative blocks, we are not obligated to 'make sense' of propositions that are excluded by our imaginative blocks. We are merely obligated to explain how the blocks arise.

7. ARCHITECTURAL EXPLANATION OF IMAGINATIVE BLOCKS

Why do we have the imaginative blocks we do? To answer this question in a naturalistic way requires consulting naturalistic approaches to the imagination. In this section I'll argue that naturalistic accounts of the imagination do indeed explain why we have the imaginative blocks adverted to by Blackburn.

The core feature of the theory of the imagination that can be used to explain imaginative blocks, I'll maintain, is the 'single code hypothesis', according to which representations in imagination will be processed by inferential mechanisms in the same way as isomorphic beliefs. To explain the single code hypothesis, it's important to get clear about some background assumptions concerning the cognitive architecture of the imagination. First, I will adopt the representationalist approach that is common in this area and say that propositional imagining involves 'pretense representations'. To imagine that Hamlet is a prince is to have a pretense representation with the content *Hamlet is a prince*. Second, I will assume that a pretense representation can have exactly the same content as a belief. Indeed, on contemporary accounts of the imagination, one can simultaneously have a belief with the content p and a pretense representation with the content p. This is nicely illustrated in an experiment of Alan Leslie's. Leslie had young children watch as he pretended to pour tea into two (empty) cups. Then he picked up one of the cups, turned it over and shook it, turned it back right side up and placed it next to the other cup. The children were then asked to point at the 'full cup' and at the 'empty cup'. Both cups were really empty throughout the entire procedure, but two-year-olds reliably indicated that the 'empty cup' was the one that had been turned upside down and the 'full cup' was the other one (Leslie 1994). On the most natural interpretation of this, the child is *imagining that the cup is empty*. But the child also, of course, *believes that the cup is empty*. This suggests that the crucial difference between pretense representations and beliefs is not given by the *content* of the representation. Rather, contemporary accounts of the imagination maintain that pretense representations differ from belief representations by their *function*. Just as desires are distinguished from beliefs by their characteristic functional roles, so too pretenses are distinguished from beliefs (see also Currie 1995). In our account of pretense and imagination,

Stephen Stich and I exploit the familiar illustrative device of using boxes to represent functional groupings, and we propose that there is, in addition to a belief box and a desire box, a 'pretense box' (Nichols and Stich 2000). The final important background assumption is that pretense representations interact with some of the same psychological mechanisms that belief representations interact with. Consider again Leslie's experiment. Virtually all of the children in Leslie's experiment responded the same way when asked to point to the 'empty cup'. How are these orderly patterns to be explained? The prevailing cognitivist view is that the pretense representations are processed by the same inference mechanisms that operate over real beliefs.[17]

With the functional architecture in place, we can now articulate the core feature of cognitivist accounts that I want to exploit. Stich and I suggest that the representations in the pretense box and the representations in the belief box are in the 'same code', to adopt a computational locution from Leslie (1987: 417). Of course, no one knows what the code is for representations in the belief box, so it's not possible to be specific about the details or the nature of the putatively shared code. But the critical point can be made without giving further detail about what the code is. The key point is just that, if pretense representations and beliefs are in the same code, then mechanisms that take input from the pretense box and from the belief box will treat parallel representations much the same way.[18] For instance, if a mechanism takes pretense representations as input, the single code hypothesis maintains that if that mechanism is activated by the occurrent belief that p, it will also be activated by the occurrent pretense representation that p. More generally, for any mechanism that takes input from both the pretense box and the belief box, the pretense representation p will be processed in much the same way as the belief representation p. I will count any theory that makes this claim as a 'single code' theory. As a result, while off-line simulation theorists don't frame the issue quite this way, they are plausibly viewed as single code theorists. For they maintain that various mental mechanisms process 'pretend

---

[17] Of course, there are probably also mental mechanisms that take input from the belief box but not from the pretense box. For instance, at least on the story that Stich and I tell, the practical reasoning mechanism takes beliefs and desires as inputs, but it does not take pretense representations as input (Nichols and Stich 2003).

[18] This doesn't, of course, mean that the mental processing of pretense representations will be *exactly* parallel to the processing of isomorphic belief representations. After all, the pretense representations do not feed into all of the same mechanisms as beliefs. Another obvious difference is that when the inference mechanisms (for instance) receive input from the pretense box, the outputs are typically sent back to the pretense box rather than to the belief box. Introspection presents yet another kind of case. For when I introspect my pretense representations, the output is a belief about what I'm pretending, and when I introspect my beliefs, the output is a belief about what I believe. So, if a single introspection mechanism processes both pretense representations and beliefs, then this mechanism treats pretense representations and beliefs in importantly different ways. These qualifications do not, I think, compromise the single code hypothesis, insofar as the qualifications seem independently plausible and well motivated.

beliefs' much like real beliefs (e.g. Currie 1995; Goldman 1989; Gordon 1986; Harris 1992).[19]

Part of the reason people have converged on the single code hypothesis comes from our impressive facility at predicting how other people will draw inferences. Why is it that we are so successful at predicting inferences? Do we have a superb theory of inference that beautifully tracks how people actually make inferences? From the earliest days of the debate between simulation theory and theory theory, this option has seemed massively profligate, and the simulation-based explanation has seemed overwhelmingly preferable (see Harris 1992; Stich and Nichols 1995). We excel at inference prediction because when we predict another's inferences, we exploit the very same inference mechanisms that we use when we draw inferences from our own beliefs, and those inference mechanisms treat the pretense inputs much as they would treat belief inputs (for discussion, see Nichols and Stich 2003; for some options on how this is implemented, see Carruthers forthcoming).

One consequence of the single code hypothesis is that if the candidate belief that p would be immediately rejected by the inference mechanisms, then the candidate pretense representation that p will also be immediately rejected by the inference mechanisms. While it's possible to believe disguised contradictions, most philosophers (and psychologists for that matter) would agree that at least in the typical case, we cannot believe obvious contradictions like $p\&-p$. The natural psychological explanation for this is that the inference mechanisms rebel at glaring contradictions—they won't tolerate patently contradictory representations in the belief box.[20] As noted earlier, the inference mechanisms also receive pretense representations as input, and on the single code hypothesis, since our inference mechanisms would reject the candidate belief representation $p\&-p$, so too would the mechanisms reject the candidate pretense representation $p\&-p$. This now gives us the basis for an explanation of the imaginative blocks that underwrite modal judgment. If we try to imagine that $p\&-p$, we encounter an imaginative block. On the single code hypothesis, this block is explained by the fact that the pretense representation that $p\&-p$ would engage our normal inferential systems. And just as our inferential systems would expel the belief representation $p\&-p$, so too do they expel the pretense representation that $p\&-p$.[21]

---

[19] Off-line simulation theorists often have additional commitments of course. For instance, many prominent versions of off-line simulation theory explicitly invoke pretend desires in addition to pretend beliefs, and also maintain that the practical reasoning system takes as input pretend beliefs and pretend desires (e.g. Currie and Ravenscroft 2002; Gordon 1986). Those additional stipulations are consistent with, but not required by, the single code hypothesis (cf. Nichols and Stich 2000; Nichols 2004).

[20] There's a salient issue about what counts as a patently contradictory representation, of course. I'm not sure where or how to draw the line, but I rely on uncontroversial instances of patently contradictory representations.

[21] This account of imagining contradictions is of a piece with some recent treatments of imaginative resistance (Nichols 2004 and forthcoming; Weinberg and Meskin, Ch. 10). Although

In summary, then, here's the reason we can't imagine that $p\&-p$:

i. Our imagination system is hooked up to our sober inferential system.

ii. Our sober inferential system rejects representations like $p\&-p$.

I've gone to some length to argue for (i), and I take it that (ii) is independently plausible. So, we have these imaginative blocks because of the structure of the imagination in our cognitive architecture. If the imagination were entirely detached from our logic circuits and was an unconstrained fantasy generator, then we would certainly not have the imaginative blocks that we do. The architecture of the imagination ensures that there are directions in which the imagination won't stray.[22]

There's a further question, of course, about why we're built in such a way that these two conditions hold. For (ii), the answer is comparatively easy. You don't need to be much of an evolutionary psychologist to agree that it would be adaptive for animals to stop believing p when they come to believe $-p$. For (i), there are a number of possible explanations, one of which is simply that hooking the imagination up to the inferential system was an easy way to facilitate effective hypothetical reasoning (e.g. Nichols and Stich 2003).

8. IMPLICATIONS

We now have in place a naturalistic sketch of a portion of our modal psychology. Humans apparently have an early emerging (and perhaps innate) psychological tendency to form modal judgments from imaginative activities, and this serves, I've suggested, to facilitate reasoning about risks and opportunities. This connection between imagination and modal judgment is exploited when imaginative blocks lead us to form judgments concerning absolute modalities. And we have a naturalistic explanation for why we have these blocks. Now I want to turn briefly to some implications. It's not at all clear what lay people mean by their modal assertions, and I have avoided trying to give a semantics for modal terms. As a result, even if everything I've said above is right, we still can't resolve big questions like whether lay modal judgments are typically true or justified. But I would like to use the modal psychology I've sketched to make a couple of limited observations.

I maintain that there is a block against imagining patent contradictions, we can apparently engage with contradictions in reasoning. I can, for instance, use first-order logic to prove for any arbitrary proposition that it follows from a contradiction. However, it's plausible that we need to distinguish these learned logical skills from the blocks that naturally emerge from the architecture of the imagination. See Weinberg and Meskin (Ch. 10) for useful discussion of the psychological processes by which we can imagine contradictions.

[22] For simplicity, I've focused on how the single code hypothesis explains why we have a block against imagining contradictions. But the single code hypothesis can also be used to explain imaginative blocks for other 'impossibilities' (see Weinberg and Meskin, Ch. 10).

When we try to answer the big questions about the metaphysical ground of modality and our epistemic access to it, there are numerous factors to consider. The typical constraints on theory building—simplicity, explanatory power, productivity—will all come into play. My concern here has been restricted to another factor—the genesis of modal intuitions that flow from the imagination, and in particular the genesis of imagination-driven intuitions about absolute modalities. Most modal philosophers want to provide theories that render those modal intuitions true and justified.[23] The intuitions are, of course, taken as defeasible—we can make modal mistakes. Nonetheless, the typical assumption is that, barring performance errors, our imagination-driven modal intuitions are largely true and justified. The modal psychology described here lends no support to prominent accounts of the metaphysics of modality. At least prima facie, the account of modal psychology I've sketched invokes no fancy metaphysics. There is no appeal to causal relations or psychological associations to modal primitives or possible worlds. Indeed, there is no appeal to causal relations or psychological associations with fictionalist renderings of possible worlds or primitive modalities. Rather, imagination-driven modal judgment has been explained in virtue of processes that are metaphysically humdrum. Naturalistic considerations explain why imaginative exercises generate modal judgments; and cognitive-architectural constraints explain why we have the imaginative blocks that issue judgments of absolute modality. So if the modal psychology offered here is right, these intuitions about absolute modalities are causally adrift from the metaphysical and semantic machinery invoked by prominent modal philosophers. Thus, whatever explanatory virtues modal realism, modal primitivism, or modal fictionalism might have, they do not extend to explaining the intuitiveness of many common judgments of absolute modalities. Of course, I've only offered a naturalistic account of a part of our modal psychology. If on the full account of modal psychology, the genesis of our absolute modal intuitions makes no contact with possible worlds, modal primitives, or associated fictions, this raises difficult questions about the propriety of using such metaphysical and semantic machinery to establish that our common modal beliefs are true and justified.[24]

---

[23] Shalkowski (1996) begins his article thus: 'Modal locutions are common enough to give modality an air of legitimacy. Frequently, we talk of things being necessary, possible, inevitable, or avoidable' (p. 375). On the first page of Lewis's *On the Plurality of Worlds* (1986), we find him asserting that 'things might have been different, in ever so many ways. This book of mine might have been finished on schedule. Or, had I not been such a commonsensical chap, I might be defending not only a plurality of possible worlds, but also a plurality of impossible worlds . . . or I might not have existed at all . . . or there might never have been any people. Or the physical constants might have had somewhat different values, incompatible with the emergence of life.' And in *Counterfactuals*, Lewis begins his defense of modal realism by saying, 'It is uncontroversially true that things might be otherwise than they are. I believe, and so do you, that things could have been different in countless ways' (Lewis 1973: 84).

[24] For related arguments, see Benacerraf 1973 and Margolis and Laurence 2003.

The modal psychology offered here thus might underscore difficulties for theories like modal realism and modal primitivism. At the same time, the modal psychology also undercuts attempts to treat modal judgments as merely conventional. For the imaginative blocks that generate judgments of absolute modality cannot be reduced to linguistic conventions. Our imaginative blocks derive from the character of our inference mechanisms. And the inference mechanisms are presumably shaped partly by natural selection, not just by linguistic conventions.

Finally, if the modal psychology sketched here is right, it might contribute to a skeptical view about the epistemic status of imagination-driven intuitions of absolute modality. Given certain widely shared assumptions, like the assumption that the future will resemble the past, it's plausible that the imagination provides a good guide to risk and opportunity. That's in part what it's designed to do. However, when this imaginative capacity is appropriated in the service of judgments of *absolute* possibility and necessity, it's less clear that we can trust the verdicts. For here the psychological systems are being used outside their natural domain. Hence, there's less reason to think that they will be successful guides in this foreign terrain of absolute modality. But obviously such a skeptical position would require a lengthy defense before it would worry the enthusiastic advocate of absolute modalities.

Thus, while the modal psychology scarcely settles the big questions in modal metaphysics and modal epistemology, it does hold promise for partly constraining the theoretical space. And it provides a relatively firm ground from which to explore broader questions about the nature of modality and our access to it.

REFERENCES

BARTSCH, K., and WELLMAN, H. (1995) *Children Talk about the Mind* (Oxford: Oxford University Press).

BENACERRAF, P. (1973) 'Mathematical Truth', *Journal of Philosophy*, 70, 661–80.

BLACKBURN, S. (1993) 'Morals and Modals', in *Essays in Quasi-Realism* (Oxford: Oxford University Press), 52–74.

BLOOM, L. (1973) *One Word at a Time: The Use of Single Word Utterances before Syntax* (The Hague: Mouton).

BROWN, R. (1973) *A First Language: The Early Stages* (Cambridge, Mass.: Harvard University Press).

BYRNE, R. (2005) *The Rational Imagination* (Cambridge, Mass.: MIT Press).

CARRUTHERS, P. (forthcoming) *The Architecture of the Mind* (Oxford: Oxford University Press).

CHALMERS, D. (2002) 'Does Conceivability Entail Possibility?', in Gendler and Hawthorne 2002, 145–200.

CRAIG, E. (1975) 'The Problem of Necessary Truth', in S. Blackburn (ed.), *Meaning, Reference and Necessity* (Cambridge: Cambridge University Press), 1–31.

CURRIE, G. (1985) 'Arithmetic and Fact', in I. Hacking (ed.), *Exercises in Analysis* (Cambridge: Cambridge University Press), 89–112.

―――― (1995) 'Imagination and Simulation: Aesthetics Meets Cognitive Science', in A. Stone and M. Davies (eds.), *Mental Simulation: Evaluations and Applications* (Oxford: Basil Blackwell), 151–69.

CURRIE, G. and RAVENSCROFT, I. (2002) *Recreative Imagination* (Oxford: Oxford University Press).

GENDLER, T. (2000) 'The Puzzle of Imaginative Resistance', *Journal of Philosophy*, 97, 55–81.

―――― and HAWTHORNE, J. (eds.) (2002) *Conceivability and Possibility* (Oxford: Oxford University Press).

GERMAN, T., and NICHOLS, S. (2003) 'Children's Counterfactual Inferences about Long and Short Causal Chains', *Developmental Science*, 6, 514–23.

GOLDMAN, A. (1989) 'Interpretation Psychologized', *Mind & Language*, 4, 161–85.

GORDON, R. (1986) 'Folk Psychology as Simulation', *Mind & Language*, 1, 158–70.

HARRIS, P. (1992) 'From Simulation to Folk Psychology: The Case for Development', *Mind & Language*, 7, 120–44.

―――― (2000) *The Work of the Imagination* (Oxford: Blackwell).

―――― GERMAN, T. P., and MILLS, P. E. (1996) 'Children's Use of Counterfactual Thinking in Causal Reasoning', *Cognition*, 61, 233–59.

HILL, C. (1997) 'Imaginability, Conceivability, Possibility, and the Mind–Body Problem', *Philosophical Studies*, 84, 61–85.

KRIPKE, S. (1980) *Naming and Necessity* (Cambridge, Mass.: Harvard University Press).

KUCZAJ, S., and MARATSOS, M. (1975) 'What Children *Can* Say Before They *Will*', *Merrill-Palmer Quarterly*, 21, 87–111.

LESLIE, A. (1987) 'Pretense and Representation: The Origins of "Theory of Mind" ', *Psychological Review*, 94, 412–26.

―――― (1994) 'Pretending and Believing: Issues in the Theory of ToMM', *Cognition*, 50, 211–38.

LEWIS, D. (1973) *Counterfactuals* (Cambridge, Mass.: Harvard University Press).

―――― (1986) *On the Plurality of Worlds* (Oxford: Blackwell).

MACWHINNEY, B., and SNOW, C. (1990) 'The Child Language Data Exchange System: An Update', *Journal of Child Language*, 17, 457–72.

MARGOLIS, E., and LAURENCE, S. (2003) 'Should We Trust Our Intuitions? Deflationary Accounts of the Analytic Data', *Proceedings of the Aristotelian Society*, 103, 299–323.

NICHOLS, S. (2004) 'Imagining and Believing: The Promise of a Single Code', *Journal of Aesthetics and Art Criticism*, 62, 129–39.

―――― (forthcoming) 'Just the Imagination: Why Imagining Doesn't Behave Like Believing', *Mind & Language*.

―――― and STICH, S. (2000) 'A Cognitive Theory of Pretense', *Cognition*, 74, 115–47.

―――― (2003) *Mindreading* (Oxford: Oxford University Press).

OSHERSON, D. (1976) *Logical Abilities in Children* (Potomac, Md.: L. Erlbaum).

ROSEN, G. (1990) 'Modal Fictionalism', *Mind*, 99, 327–54.

SACHS, J. (1983) 'Talking about There and Then: The Emergence of Displaced Reference in Parent–Child Discourse', in K. Nelson (ed.), *Children's Language*, iv (Hillsdale, NJ: Erlbaum), 1–18.

SHALKOWSKI, S. A. (1996) 'Conventions, Cognitivism and Necessity', *American Philosophical Quarterly*, 33, 375–92.

SLATER, R. (1998) *Jack Welch and the GE Way* (New York: McGraw-Hill).

SPELKE, E., PHILLIPS, A., and WOODWARD, A. (1995) 'Infants' Knowledge about Object Motion and Human Action', in D. Sperber, D. Premack, and A. Premack (eds.), *Causal Cognition: A Multidisciplinary Debate* (Oxford: Clarendon Press), 44–78.

STICH, S., and NICHOLS, S. (1995) 'Second Thoughts on Simulation', in M. Davies and T. Stone (eds.), *Mental Simulation* (Oxford: Blackwell), 87–108.

YABLO, S. (1993) 'Is Conceivability a Guide to Possibility?', *Philosophy and Phenomenological Research*, 53, 1–42.

13

Meta-conceivability and Thought Experiments

Roy Sorensen

A meta-conception is a double act of imagination. The procedure is to answer a question by imagining someone answering that question via an act of imagination. Meta-conceptions are hypothetical hypotheticals. They stand to thought experiments as thought experiments stand to executed experiments.

As the unexpected term in the simile, the meta-conception provides a new point of comparison. Instead of picturing thought experiment as an extreme, we can picture it as an intermediate case.

Some of what passes for conceiving is meta-conceiving. Those who seem to be one degree removed from executed experiment are sometimes two degrees away; they conceive someone conceiving a possibility and infer the possibility on this second-hand basis.

Our powers of imagination are spottier than they appear. This is partly due to a sampling illusion; we cannot survey the possibilities we cannot imagine. The illusion is also sustained by our success at compensating. We make up for our limited horizon by imagining hypothetical imaginers who transcend our limits.

1. IMAGINARY THOUGHT EXPERIMENTS

'What would you build after everything could be done by pushing lots of buttons?' The engineer retorts that he would build a machine that can push buttons.

Thought experiments are labor-saving devices. Instead of actually executing the procedure, you answer by reflecting on the procedure. This is an extension of what normally happens when planning an experiment. Since experimenters are not dogmatic, they revise their opinion as details about the procedure emerge. So before carrying out the experiment, the experimenter has undergone some a priori self-improvement. What grows as a by-product can be deliberately cultivated.

A predecessor of this chapter was presented at the 'Thought Experiments Rethought' conference in Ghent, Belgium, on September 26, 2004. This chapter has been improved by remarks from Daniel Cohnitz, Erdinc Sayan, and a referee for this volume.

Opportunists accentuate the features of experimental procedures that promote a priori edification. The result is an experiment that is designed to support a hypothesis by reflection rather than by execution. Thought experimenters retrofit a posteriori tools to do a priori work.

A meta-conception is a further labor-saving device. Instead of actually executing a thought experiment, you imagine someone executing a thought experiment.

The added convenience comes at a price. Meta-conceptions tend to be less informative than thought experiments (except in the special case of meta-conceptions that are also thought experiments). And thought experiments tend to be less informative than executed experiments. A correct theory of thought experiments must reflect this ranking. Skeptics about thought experiments have trouble accounting for the fact that thought experiments are more informative than meta-conceptions. Those who believe that conceivability entails possibility share this problem. Their principle, I shall argue, implies that meta-conceptions are more informative than thought experiments.

Just as some thought experiments are aborted experiments, so some meta-conceptions are aborted thought experiments. Consider Professor Meta Conception who is trying to solve the postcard riddle: Is it possible to cut a hole in a postcard that is big enough for you to step through? The experimental approach is to equip oneself with scissors and postcards and try to produce such a hole. Professor Meta Conception, like most of her colleagues in the physics department, prefers to answer without violence. Some of her colleagues *depict* cuts on a blackboard. Other physicists visualize the cut lines in an imaginary rectangle. The hypothetical cuts of Professor Meta Conception activate the thought that length and area are not closely related. For instance, many meters of tape fit around a reel. Since Professor Meta Conception is given to mathematical abstraction, she conjectures that there is no limit to the lengths and areas that you can produce. Although she cannot conceive of a cut that would yield a hole big enough to walk through, she can conceive of someone conceiving such a cut. Professor Meta Conception's meta-conception justifies (to some degree) her affirmative answer to the postcard riddle.

Just as some promoters of experiment deny that thought experiments are evidence, some devotees of thought experiments deny that meta-conceptions are evidence. The devotees of thought experiment scold Professor Meta Conception and urge her to do the hard work of specifying a hypothetical cut that will yield a hole big enough to step through. They compare her free riding to the honest toil embodied in Professor Thut X. Periment's diagram (Fig. 13.1). Thut's uncle, X. E. Cutedexperiment, cuts the postcard, and walks through. This vividly corroborates the diagram. But most members of the physics department were so convinced by Thut's diagram that they denigrate his uncle's cutout as an educational stunt.

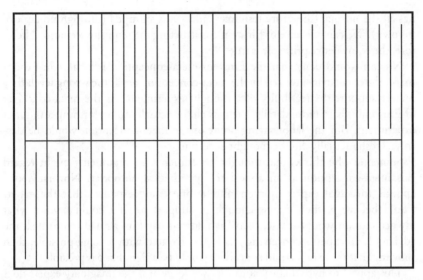

Figure 13.1 A solution to the postcard riddle.

2. DEFINITIONS OF 'THOUGHT EXPERIMENT'

If all meta-conceptions are thought experiments, then some meta-conceptions are counterexamples to definitions of 'thought experiment'. Including mine: 'A thought experiment is an experiment that purports to achieve its aim without the benefit of execution' (Sorensen 1992: 205). I say the aim of a thought experiment is to answer or raise a question by reflection on the experimental procedure. In a meta-conception there need only be reflection on someone reflecting on a design.

According to John Norton, 'Thought experiments are arguments which (i) posit hypothetical or counterfactual states of affairs, and (ii) invoke particulars irrelevant to the generality of the conclusion' (1991: 129). For instance, Albert Einstein argued for the equivalence between uniform acceleration and gravitation with a scenario involving a physicist who awakens in an elevator. The physicist cannot tell whether the elevator is at rest on a planet or is uniformly accelerating in space. The particulars invoked in the scenario are irrelevant in the sense of being eliminable; the thought experiment could be replaced with an abstract argument that never mentions the elevator.

Compare the elevator scenario with the following exercise. Imagine Einstein constructing a hypothetical scenario in which a physicist is charged with the task of determining whether he is in a uniformly accelerating frame or in a corresponding unaccelerated frame in a homogeneous gravitational field. The physicist has all the normal laboratory resources, and yet is stumped (through no fault of his own). We can conceive of Einstein constructing the requisite scenario. Therefore, the equivalence principle is true.

Norton would deny that the Einstein meta-conception is a thought experiment: the particulars invoked by the meta-conception are at the wrong level; they merely support the feasibility of a thought experiment. As the meta-conceiver of Einstein fills in more details, she gets closer actually to performing a thought experiment. But the labor-saving point of the meta-conception would be destroyed if she actually did the thought experiment.

Someone who thinks that thought experiments are arguments might regard this meta-conception as an appeal to hypothetical authority. Normally, one appeals to actual expert opinion. But if one could establish that the expert would believe *p*, then that is enough to support *p*. (If I could predict what my accountant would advise, then I would not pay him actually to furnish the advice.) If an expert's conceiving *p* is well correlated with *p* being possible, then showing that the expert could conceive *p* would be a sign that *p* is possible.

This appeal to hypothetical authority works even if the imaginary expert does not believe that his conceiving is correlated with possibility. Meta-conceptions make it clear that we are free to exploit the intuitions of those who have a low opinion of their intuitions. Consider a technician, Ira Robin, who does not believe that experiments provide evidence. (Perhaps Ira Robin has converted to skepticism about science and now goes to the laboratory simply to earn a living.) As long as Ira Robin has applied the appropriate methodology, his experiments provide information that his *colleagues* could exploit. Our ability to incorporate the results of unbelievers alleviates some anxiety about the circularity of experiments—and thought experiments.

Meta-conceptions do require the conceiving of a conceiver. It is not sufficient to conceive hypothetical behavior. The snowy tree cricket, *oecanthus fultoni*, is a natural thermometer. You can measure the temperature in Fahrenheit by counting the chirps over a thirteen-second period and adding forty. But the cricket is no more a conceiver of the temperature in Fahrenheit than a mercury thermometer is. Behavior carries modal information. But meta-conceptions are restricted to the imagination channel.

Let me release an earlier remark from its parentheses: Some meta-conceptions are thought experiments. For instance, thought experiments about thought experiments are meta-conceptions. Thomas Kuhn (1977: 255) imagines thought experimenters in a world in which objects move at uniform speed. He says that Galileo's thought experiments would then be too far out to refute Aristotle's definition of motion. Alasdair MacIntyre (1981: 2) argues that thought experiments can be blindsided by historical reversals. He asks what would happen if science were wiped out and then 'revived' on the basis of a miscellany of fragments. Thought experimenters would not be able to detect that there was anything awry. Skeptics enjoy debunking thought experiments with second-order thought experiments. Even if these skeptical meta-conceptions are self-defeating (Sidelle 2002: 311), they are genuine thought experiments.

3. THE LOGIC OF META-CONCEPTIONS

Those who wish to develop the epistemology of meta-conceptions will recycle the credentials offered for thought experiments. Certification efforts for thought experiments date back to the eighteenth century. David Hume appeals to the principle that conceivability implies possibility (and vice versa):

'Tis an establish'd maxim in metaphysics, *That whatever the mind clearly conceives includes the idea of possible existence, or in other words, that nothing we imagine is absolutely impossible.* We can form the idea of a golden mountain, and from thence conclude that such a mountain may actually exist, We can form no idea of a mountain without a valley, and therefore regard it as impossible. (1978 [1739–40]: 32)

Hume's justification of thought experiments has the side effect of also justifying meta-conceptions. For the entailment thesis 'Conceivability implies possibility' implies the meta-entailment thesis 'Conceivability of conceivability implies possibility'.

Here is a short proof. Assume the entailment thesis ('Conceivability entails possibility'). If it is conceivable that it is conceivable p, then two applications of the entailment thesis entitle us to infer that it is possibly possible that p. In other words, if CCp, then $\Diamond\Diamond p$. The reduction principle, 'What is possibly possible is possible', is derivable from the characteristic formula of the modal system S4: $\Box\Box p$ iff $\Box p$. So, given the entailment thesis, the conceivability of the conceivability of p implies the possibility of p. In other words, if CCp, then $\Diamond p$. Since the popular modal system S5 incorporates the theorems of S4, most philosophers will grant that the entailment implies the meta-entailment.

Hume also defends the converse of the entailment thesis: possibility implies conceivability. So he is further committed to the meta-converse: whatever is possible is conceivably conceivable.

Since the above reasoning is recursive, Hume is further committed to iterating the conceivability operator without limit:

1. If $C^n p$, then $\Diamond p$.

2. If $\Diamond p$, then $C^n p$.

Principle 1 seems mistaken, because meta-conceiving demands less specificity than conceiving. (A precise outline of a precise outline need not be a precise outline.) Principle 2 seems mistaken, because conceivers are limited beings. I can conceive of an equilateral pyramid. And I can conceive of conceiving it. But I can't conceive of it a hundredfold. Indeed, I just conceived the opposite: namely, my inability to conceive[100] an equilateral pyramid.

How did I do it? It would have been self-defeating to conceive the opposite by parsing a sentence containing 100 conception operators. Instead, I merely conceived of myself realistically, as a man without superhuman abilities. I can conceive a proposition by conceiving a proposition that implies it. Suppose a linguist gives you a disjunction that is too complicated for you to parse. The first disjunct of this complicated disjunction is 'Newborns lack kneecaps'. You can conceive of babies without kneecaps (because actual newborns lack kneecaps). So you can conceive the truth of the disjunction.

Meta-conceptions do demand greater conceptual maturity than thought experiments. A child who lacked the concept of conception could still do thought experiments (just as a child who lacks the concept of digestion can still digest). However, this child could not execute a meta-conception, because he must conceive of someone *conceiving* something.

4. WHY META-CONCEIVING DOES NOT COLLAPSE INTO CONCEIVING

There is an analogy between chains of perception and chains of conception; both are broken by interposing agents. David Sanford illustrates the principle in 'Some Puzzles about Prosthetic Perception' (unpublished, 2004). Imagine that Chris has amazing powers of imitation. She imitates sounds with the same fidelity as a mechanical hearing aid. Do you hear a distant lecturer by virtue of Chris whispering the lecture into your ear? Chris is as reliable as a mechanical hearing aid. So you gain as much knowledge of the lecture as you would through conventional prosthetic perception. However, Sanford denies that you hear by means of the human hearing aid. Sanford's explanation is that 'The presence of a mediating perceiver disqualifies the larger system as one of prosthetic perception.'

Perhaps the disqualification is connected with the contrast between testimony and perception. The audience following a live narration of a hockey game does not hear the hockey game; they are being told about it. Is the contrast based on the element of freewill introduced by the agent?

No. Suppose Chris is witnessing the lecture from within a soundproof booth. Chris cannot hear the lecture but can see the lecturer. Now suppose that Chris reads lips. She focuses on the lecturer's lips and begins to translate, mimicking the lecturer's voice. Does Chris now hear the lecture? No, she would have to open the door to hear the voice. There is no perceiver in the booth besides Chris. The problem is that there is a mediating perceptual system (vision). Perceiving in one modality cannot be by means of another modality. I cannot hear by seeing. Most perceptual prostheses are compatible with self-reliance because they are not themselves perceptual systems. However, a few do violate the requirement: The blind cannot be made to see by means tactile stimulation of their backs. The spoiler here is the use of another perceptual system (touch). The self-reliance requirement also explains why reliable synesthetes cannot see sounds or hear colors. In the case of synesthetes, information from one perceptual system trespasses into another system.

The self-reliance principle also seems to apply intra-modally. If I feel myself feeling for my wallet (say my left hand is gripping my right wrist), then that higher-order feeling is not a feeling for my wallet.

The popularity of perceptual models provides opportunities for a cognitive extension of the self-reliance requirement. Thomas Reid pictured memory as perception of the past. Inserting a human memory aid into the chain of recollection makes the process look like testimony rather than memory. His insistence on the immediacy of memory would also make him deny an otherwise attractive principle:

R: If you remember that you remembered that p, then you remember that p.

Note that the embedded past tense makes R less trivial than its present tense counterpart. 'If I remember that I remember that p, then I remember that p' is a tautology by virtue of the truth property of memory.

James Robert Brown (1991: ch. 2), and Kurt Gödel before him, regards conception as perception of a Platonic realm. Intermediate conceivers would then be intermediate perceivers. So if Brown accepts the self-reliance requirement, he will deny that meta-conceiving p implies conceiving p.

John Locke believed that introspection is perception of the mind. The 'mind's eye' provides an avenue for the self-reliance requirement to prevent the collapse of meta-conceiving into conceiving.

I deny that conceiving is a species of perception. However, I think that conceiving is analogous to perception, and this analogy helps me to recruit Sanford's principle for an explanation of why meta-conceiving does not imply conceiving.

5. THE HISTORY OF META-CONCEPTIONS

On close inspection some of Hume's appeals to conceivability are meta-conceptions. In *Dialogues Concerning Natural Religion*, Cleanthes generalizes:

Nothing is demonstrable, unless the contrary implies a contradiction. Nothing, that is distinctly conceivable, implies a contradiction. Whatever we conceive as existent, we can also conceive as non-existent. There is no being, therefore, whose non-existence implies a contradiction. Consequently there is no being, whose existence is demonstrable. (Hume 1947: 189)

Hume's conclusion is a universal generalization, not a particular statement such as 'Edinburgh exists contingently'. His premise is a sweeping claim about conceivability: 'Whatever we conceive as existent, we can also conceive as non-existent.' What is his evidence for the premise? He has not gone through the exercise of conceiving each thing to be non-existent. There are too many things.

Some things are inaccessible to us, but are accessible to others. I cannot conceive of something that is inconceivable to me. That would be contradictory. But I can conceive of *you* conceiving of something that is inconceivable to me. (I just did it!)

Hume searches for his self and takes his failure to be direct evidence that he has no self. Given his empiricist scruples, Hume cannot construe his failure to find his self to be direct evidence that others lack a self. He simply invites others to introspect and check whether they have a different result.

I cannot directly refer to a person who is yet to be born. I cannot conceive the *de re* proposition corresponding to the *de dicto* proposition 'The first person born in the twenty-second century is an hermaphrodite'. Direct reference requires causal contact. However, I can conceive of future people having that thought. For they will have the causal connection to ground the demonstrative. They can point to the first person born in the twenty-second century and utter the *de re* statement 'That baby is an hermaphrodite'. They can *name* the baby. The best we residents of the twenty-first century can do is to predict the name of the baby. (I am assuming a causal theory of names.)

Other individuals are inaccessible to me because they are confined to other possible worlds. In addition to alien individuals, there are uninstantiated kinds. Acquaintance with some kinds is a necessary condition for conceiving them.

David Lewis (1986: 159) can no more conceive of these aliens than anyone else. But he can conceive of others conceiving of them. This meta-conceivability allows him to frame an objection to linguistic ersatzism (the view that possible worlds are sets of sentences).

Anonymity can also arise by strength of numbers. There are $\aleph_0$ sentences of a natural language, but there are $\aleph_1$ real numbers. This higher order of infinity prevents us from directly referring to each number. Each real number is conceivable by an individual, but they are not co-conceivable by that individual.

The project of conceiving what I cannot conceive is self-defeating. But it is feasible to meta-conceive what I cannot conceive.

Premises of Hume's arguments are frequently generalizations about conceivability: *Any cause can be imagined without its associated effect. Each thing can be pictured as popping into existence without any cause whatsoever. Any history can be envisaged as continuing with a future that does not resemble the past.* These generalizations about conceivability might be supported inductively through laboratory investigation. But Hume seems to be proceeding a priori via deductive arguments. The meta-entailment, 'Conceivability of conceivability implies possibility', allows us to reconstruct his arguments so that they can be done from the armchair. As previously demonstrated, the meta-entailment follows the entailment principle, 'Conceivability entails possibility', and the entailment is universally ascribed to Hume.

I agree that it is somewhat anachronistic to recast Hume as trafficking in meta-conceptions. I just coined the term! But the anachronism is no more severe than interpreting Hume as a conductor of thought experiments. The term 'thought experiment' achieved currency after Hume's death, but thought experiments have been around since at least the pre-Socratics. So have meta-conceptions.

Contemporary proponents of 'Conceivability entails possibility' are more circumspect than Hume. The proof of the meta-entailment will give them pause. After accepting the meta-entailment, they will ask whether you have counterexamples to 'The conceivability of conceivability implies possibility'. You might snap back, 'I can conceive of someone conceiving of a counterexample. That should be sufficient refutation for someone who subscribes to "The conceivability of conceivability implies possibility".'

6. VERTICAL META-CONCEPTIONS

Meta-conceiving counterexamples is easier than conceiving them. For the conceiver must satisfy higher standards of precision than the meta-conceiver. I cannot form a clear idea of a chiliagon because it has 1,000 sides. But I can form a clear idea of a more gifted individual forming a clear idea of a chiliagon.

Derek Parfit is optimistic about what can be accomplished by thought experiment. However, he denies that utility monsters are conceivable (Parfit 1984: 389). He denies we can imagine someone being a million times happier than us. Yet Parfit says that we can imagine there being billions of people who are only marginally better off alive than dead. This asymmetry seems unprincipled. As an intermediate case, consider a man who lives for billions of years and, annually, is only marginally better off alive than dead. Possibly Parfit is correct about us not being able to conceive the utility monster. But our ability to conceive structurally analogous scenarios invites the conjecture that the inconceivability turns on some quirky fault of the human imagination. We can imagine more numerically gifted creatures who could imagine utility monsters. We can meta-conceive utility monsters.

Theologians frequently characterize our intellects as puny. William of Ockham granted that human beings cannot conceive of how free will could be compatible with God's foreknowledge. But he thought we could conceive of how a superior being could conceive it. St Augustine proposed a subjective theory of time to solve the problems of creation and foreknowledge. According to this theory, the present corresponds to what one perceives, the past to what one remembers, and the future to what one anticipates. Perceptual span varies with perceivers. Therefore, the duration of the present is relative to the perceiver. Since God has no perceptual limits, he can take in history in a single panoramic glimpse. So for God, there is no past or future. It is all one big Now. Hence God lacks *fore*knowledge even though he is all-knowing. There is no problem about what God was doing before he created the world because there is no *before* for God.

Human beings have trouble wrapping their minds around God's big Now. But they can conceive of thinkers with somewhat wider perceptual spans. These thinkers can in turn imagine thinkers with yet wider spans. We thus have a chain of conceivers leading up to the Supreme Conceiver.

Theologians admit that there are difficulties in characterizing God as perceiving anything. He does not have perceptual organs. God is an immaterial being. Proponents of negative theology, such as Maimonides and Thomas Aquinas, think God is so different from his material creation that positive descriptions of God are just disguised negative remarks. Truly positive truths about God are inconceivable to us. However, they are conceivable to angels. And since angels are intermediate between human beings and God, we can conceive of angels conceiving these truths.

Quantitative meta-conceptions allow us to transcend limits of attention, memory, and symbol manipulation. Linguists require speakers to be finite, but do not specify any further limit. This liberalizes linguistics. Syntacticians have taught me to compose contingent sentences that are too complex for me to understand. I cannot conceive of how my sentences could be true. But I can conceive of them being understood by speakers who have more working memory or swifter parsing.

Linguists generally assume that the speaker is finite. But even beings as limited as human beings can imagine infinite sentences being understood by super-thinkers who can perform super-tasks. These beings can solve many problems in number theory by inspection. For instance, if Goldbach's Conjecture is true, then an infinite being can verify its truth by checking an exhaustive list of the infinitely many potential counterexamples. I cannot conceive of this infinitely long proof, but I can conceive of the infinite being conceiving it. Upward meta-conceptions let us transcend our 'puny minds'.

Downward meta-conceptions allow us to shed some of the ill effects of our superiority. Mothers protect and comfort their children by seeing through the eyes of their children. Mom may be unable to conceive how a toddler could be sucked down the bathtub drain, but she can conceive of a toddler conceiving this catastrophe.

Some Christian theology involves downward meta-conceptions. How can God conceive pain? To understand pain, one must experience it firsthand. Furthermore, pain is always suffered contrary to your will. Since God is all-powerful, he cannot suffer pain, and so cannot understand a key feature of the human condition. One Christian response is to say that God solved this problem by imagining being a suffering man. Although God could not conceive pain, he could meta-conceive it. Indeed, Christians say that God actually feels pain by becoming incarnated as Jesus Christ.

7. CONCEPT EMPIRICISM

Qualitative meta-conceptions let the conceptually handicapped indirectly access possibilities that only healthy people can conceive. Those who cannot taste phenylthiocarbamide cannot conceive its bitter taste but can conceive others conceiving its bitter taste.

According to concept empiricism, the concept of F can be acquired only through the experience of F. This doctrine imposes severe limits on what can be conceived. For I can conceive of x being F only if I have the concept F. One objection to concept empiricism is that blind people have a fluent color vocabulary. They learn how to use color words grammatically and can even pass on color information. (A blind man will inform the luggage attendant that his bag is green with a red handle.) The concept empiricist can reply by characterizing the blind man as meta-conceiving color rather than conceiving colors.

The most famous objection to concept empiricism is Hume's missing shade of blue. Suppose that someone has experienced many shades of blue except for an intermediate shade. He can interpolate the shade. Hume breezily dismisses this counterexample as a singular case. Mystified Hume scholars object that one counterexample is enough to refute a generalization. Furthermore, the case is far from singular. We interpolate gaps in tone sequences, tactile experiences, tastes, and smells.

The concept empiricist might reply by characterizing interpolation as meta-conceiving. You cannot conceive the missing shade of blue. You are actually conceiving a more experienced person conceiving that shade. Your experiences with the neighboring shades give you sufficient basis to conceive of someone else conceiving the shade. This gives you an advantage over a color-blind man who is insensitive to blue. He cannot even conceive of someone conceiving that specific shade.

Normal people are trichromats who are sensitive to three basic hues. A small percentage of women are tetrachromats. They can see shades that no man can discern. The concept empiricist will say that no man conceives these shades. But men conceive women who can conceive.

No man or woman can conceive of a fourth spatial dimension in which a left shoe can be turned into a right shoe. However, Edwin A. Abbott has led millions of readers to conceive of creatures who can conceive of the fourth dimension. The first step of his method is to have us to conceive of conceptually impoverished beings. (As Heraclitus said, 'The way up is the way down.') In *Flatland* Abbott describes two-dimensional beings. They cannot conceive of the third dimension. Through mathematical adventures, these creatures come to conceive of beings that can conceive of the third dimension. After this downward meta-conceptioning, Abbott's three-dimensional readers are now poised to participate in mathematical adventures of their own, ones that allow them to envisage four-dimensional beings who can conceive of turning a left shoe into a right shoe by flipping it through the fourth dimension.

One may have doubts about the completeness of these exercises. Robert Heinlan's 'He Built a Crooked House' provides a stimulating inkling of the properties of a four-dimensional hypercube. But part of the allure of story lies in residual mystery.

Salvador Dali's 'Christus Hypercubus' depicts Christ being crucified on a tesseract (an unraveled hypercube). The religious interest of the painting peaks for those with *partial* understanding of tesseracts. If you were completely at home with tesseracts, the mystical aspect of the composition would be compromised.

Perceivers form chains that allow indirect perception of imperceptibles. I cannot see that a ship is approaching, but I can see that the lookout sees that a ship is approaching. In this sense, I can 'see' what is invisible to me. Through similar indirection, I can 'conceive' what is inconceivable to me.

8. THE APPEAL TO FUTURE THINKERS

The electric organs of weakly electric fish were an anomaly for Charles Darwin's theory of evolution. The organs of strongly electric fish could be explained as an adaptation for hunting or defense. Feeble currents produced by other fishes seemed useless:

The electric organs of fishes offer [a] case of special difficulty; for it is impossible to conceive by what steps these wondrous organs have been produced. But this is not surprising, for we do not even know of what use they are put. (Darwin 1897: 234)

Darwin can conceive of future biologists conceiving a function for weakly electric organs. Thus Darwin thinks it is possible that there is a function for the organs. He thinks that the scientific imagination will be expanded by greater knowledge of the habits and structure of weakly electric fish and their progenitors. Thus he optimistically concludes, 'serviceable transitions are possible by which these organs might have been gradually developed' (1897: 235).

Darwin was vindicated by the conjecture that the fish perceive their surroundings by means of disturbances to the electric field that they generate (Keeley 1999). Adaptationists tout many other success stories. New phenomena have expanded our conceptual scheme. We can predict further expansions that will enable future thinkers to conceive of functions for traits that currently seem pointless.

Darwin also faced conflicts with physics. The evolutionary interpretation of the fossil record implied that the Earth was at least several hundred millions of years old, perhaps billions of years old. William Thomson, later elevated to Lord Kelvin, used thermodynamic premises to calculate the Earth as between 20 million and 400 million years old (with just under 100 million being the most probable). Darwin was far more alarmed by Lord Kelvin than by the weakly electric fish. He could not conceive of any physical mechanism by which the sun could shine for the period demanded by his theory.

As with the weakly electric fish, Darwin could conceive of future physicists conceiving of such a mechanism. This appeal to meta-conceivability was not as persuasive, because physics, in the nineteenth century, appeared on the verge of becoming a completed science. Kelvin's estimate had also been corroborated by several separate lines of investigation. Despite this consilience, Darwin refused to infer the impossibility of the sun shining for billions of years from its inconceivability.

Darwin was once again vindicated, this time by the discovery of radioactivity. This undreamt-of phenomenon made it conceivable for the sun to shine for billions of years.

Appeals to meta-conceivability vary enormously in their plausibility. Parapsychologists react to conflicts with the laws of physics by appealing to the widening mental horizon of future physicists. We are less impressed by this appeal to meta-conceivability, because a record of fraud and wishful thinking dogs parapsychology.

Appeals to meta-conceivability are salient along the speculative frontier of knowledge. For instance, Rudolf Carnap (1950) noted that the sorites paradox depends on vague predicates. He believed that science was gradually replacing vague predicates with precise predicates. Carnap extrapolated: at the end of the process, language will be precise, so the sorites paradox cannot be formulated. Thus Carnap believed that waiting for the language to change would passively resolve the sorites paradox.

One objection to Carnap's strategy is that 'precise' is a vague term (since it is the complement of 'vague', which is itself vague). Hence Carnap has not conceived of a language (rich enough to express all important truths) that really is free of the sorites. Carnap could concede that he cannot imagine this future precise language. He could simply insist that he can imagine others imagining it. These future thinkers will have the language needed to frame the possibility.

Most meta-conceiving is of possibilities. But we also meta-conceive impossibilities. Eratosthenes suspected that it was impossible to double the cube. But, like the other mathematicians of ancient Greece, he could not conceive an impossibility proof. He could conceive of future mathematicians grasping the impossibility. Practices of proof construction improved piecemeal until the result was finally achieved in the nineteenth century.

Thomas Nagel (1998) defers to future philosophers who have a richer conceptual scheme. Nagel can conceive of the impossibility of the number 379 having parents. But he cannot conceive of the impossibility of zombies (physical duplicates of healthy, active human beings who have no mental states). When Nagel imagines his doorman from a third-person perspective, he feels free not to attribute qualitative conscious states. This is evidence that consciousness is a contingent feature of active human beings. But Nagel dismisses this evidence as misleading. Neuroscience suggests that consciousness supervenes on the brain.

Given this supervenience principle, it is impossible for the brain state to exist without consciousness. So Nagel thinks that there is a necessary truth about consciousness (akin to 'Salt is sodium chloride') that we have trouble grasping. Although Nagel cannot conceive the necessity, he can conceive of future philosophers conceiving it.

Illusions of contingency are caused by incomplete conceptual development. Failure of one's conceptual scheme to preclude a hypothesis is apt to be confused as proof that the hypothesis represents an objective possibility. A conceptual scheme is like a logical system. As one increases the stock of predicates, more propositions become theorems. These propositions narrow the range of possibilities. Thus we should predict that with each supplement to our conceptual scheme, more will be revealed to be necessary. The only way for a conceptual advance to introduce new possibilities is by exposing fallacious impossibility proofs or by giving us the vocabulary to express hypotheses that were previously ineffable.

The next step up from a future meta-conception is an extra-terrestrial meta-conception. The 'transcendental naturalist' Colin McGinn (1993) argues that human beings cannot conceive of how the brain could give rise to consciousness. But instead of inferring impossibility, he conceives of hypothetical Martians who can conceive of the mind–body relation as easily as we conceive the object–shadow relation.

9. CONCEIVING IDEAL CONCEIVABILITY

Since the meta-entailment ($CCp \rightarrow \Diamond p$) is less plausible than the entailment ($Cp \rightarrow \Diamond p$), we must either raise our opinion of the meta-entailment or lower our opinion of the entailment thesis. The downward revision seems more natural. In addition, there appear to be fresh opportunities to find counterexamples.

A temperate defender of the entailment thesis will concede that there is a sense of 'conceive' in which meta-conceiving is easier than conceiving. For instance, David Chalmers (2002) distinguishes between prima facie conceivability (where one relies on first appearances) and ideal conceivability (which is based on ideal rational reflection). Ordinary human imagination is fallible and limited. So it provides only a prima facie case for a proposition being possible or impossible. The strengths of that prima facie case vary with the imaginative task at hand. Psychologists might specify the conditions under which strengths or weaknesses should be expected. Since the appearance of an appearance is weaker evidence than an appearance, we should expect that meta-conceiving is easier than conceiving. Chalmers would agree that this would be a reason for concluding that the entailment thesis is false (when read in terms of prima facie conceivability).

Chalmers defends the entailment thesis only when construed in terms of ideal conceivability. Perhaps Hume also had this restriction in mind. Some Hume scholars interpret his ethics as an ideal observer theory. As Hume's friend Adam Smith emphasized in *The Theory of the Moral Sentiments*, the morally perplexed try to take the perspective of a judge who is well informed, rational, impartial, etc. Just as children learn to do what is right by predicting what their parents would advise, so an adult can guide his own behavior by predicting the advice of an impartial spectator.

If the ideal observer is *stipulated* to be correct, then the theory offers no guidance; one must already know what is correct to know the opinion of the ideal observer. Possibility is trivially implied by any propositional attitude that is idealized in this heavy-handed fashion.

Those with a lighter hand will draw an analogy with color. An object is red in virtue of the fact that standard observers judge it to be red. This analysis is not circular, because one can ascertain whether something is judged red independently of judging whether it is red. Similarly, one can judge whether an ideal observer can conceive of p without judging whether p is possible.

If Hume is right, 'possible' and 'conceivable' are co-intensional, even though they are not synonyms. They are like 'equilateral' and 'equiangular'. A triangle can be judged to be equilateral without judging that it is equiangular. Once you learn that 'equilateral' and 'equiangular' are co-intensional, you infer equilaterality from equiangularity, and vice versa. Similarly, news that 'possible' and 'conceivable' are co-intensional would allow us to jump from one to the other. The leap is impressively long between 'conceivable' and 'possible', because 'conceivable' is in the domain of psychology, while 'possible' is in the domain of metaphysics.

Ideal observer theories do not imply that ideal observers are actual. However, they do imply that ideal observers are possible. So those who base their atheism on the *impossibility* of omniscience may still have ontological reservations about the ideal observer theory. Maximal agents raise worries about impossibility results. A second concern is alienation. As the powers of the ideal observer grow, so he becomes increasingly unlike us. This undermines the analogy that makes the ideal observer knowable to us.

One compromise is to replace the ideal observer with an infinite progression of imperfect observers. Each is closer to perfection than his predecessor. None is perfect. If this sequence of hypothetical observers is denumerable, we can be democratic: p is ideally conceivable iff the majority of those in the sequence conceive p.

I am not sure whether the progression is an improvement over the traditional appeal to ideal observers. Either way, we should note that 'ideal conceivability' is a misnomer. If any human being ideally conceives p, then he is actually meta-conceiving p. He is conceiving of (specially credentialed) agents conceiving p.

He is drawing a conclusion from what he can conceive them conceiving, not from what he can conceive. The inference may be good or bad. But it is more likely to be good if he has clear understanding of how he is reasoning—via meta-conception rather than conception.

REFERENCES

Brown, James Robert (1991) *The Laboratory of the Mind* (London: Routledge).

Carnap, Rudolf (1950) *Logical Foundations of Probability* (Chicago: University of Chicago Press).

Chalmers, David (2002) 'Does Conceivability Imply Possibility?', in Tamar Szabo Gendler and John Hawthorne (eds.), *Conceivability and Possibility* (New York: Oxford University Press), 145–200.

Darwin, Charles (1897) *The Origin of Species* (New York: Modern Library, 1998).

Hume, David (1739–40) *A Treatise of Human Nature* (London); ed. L. A. Selby-Bigge (Oxford: Clarendon Press, 1888); 2nd edn. rev. P. H. Nidditch (Oxford: Clarendon Press, 1978).

——— (1947) *Dialogues Concerning Natural Religion*, ed. Norman Kemp Smith (Indianapolis: Bobbs-Merrill).

Keeley, Brian L. (1999) 'Fixing Content and Function in Neurobiological Systems: The Neuroethology of Electroreception', *Biology and Philosophy*, 14, 395–430.

Kuhn, Thomas (1977) *The Essential Tension* (Chicago: University of Chicago Press).

Lewis, David (1986) *On the Plurality of Worlds* (Oxford: Blackwell).

MacIntyre, Alasdair (1981) *After Virtue* (Notre Dame, Ind.: University of Notre Dame Press).

McGinn, Colin (1993) *Problems in Philosophy: The Limits of Inquiry* (Cambridge, Mass.: Blackwell).

Nagel, Thomas (1998) 'Conceiving the Impossible and the Mind–Body Problem', *Philosophy*, 73 (285), 337–52.

Norton, John (1991) 'Thought Experiments in Einstein's Work', in T. Horowitz and G. Massey (eds.), *Thought Experiments in Science and Philosophy* (Savage, Md.: Rowman and Littlefield), 129–48.

Parfit, Derek (1984) *Reasons and Persons* (New York: Oxford University Press).

Sanford, D. (unpublished) 'Some Puzzles about Prosthetic Perception'.

Sidelle, A. (2002) 'On the Metaphysical Contingency of Laws of Nature', in T. Gendler and J. Hawthorne (eds.), *Conceivability and Possibility* (Oxford: Oxford University Press), 309–36.

Sorensen, Roy (1992) *Thought Experiments* (New York: Oxford University Press).

Index